MW01035731

# THE
# PANZER LEGIONS

0  11557 03353  3

## Other titles in the Stackpole Military History Series

### THE AMERICAN CIVIL WAR
*Cavalry Raids of the Civil War*
*Pickett's Charge*
*Witness to Gettysburg*

### WORLD WAR II
*Armor Battles of the Waffen-SS, 1943–45*
*Australian Commandos*
*The B-24 in China*
*Backwater War*
*Beyond the Beachhead*
*The Brandenburger Commandos*
*Bringing the Thunder*
*Coast Watching in World War II*
*Colossal Cracks*
*D-Day to Berlin*
*Exit Rommel*
*Flying American Combat Aircraft of World War II*
*Forging the Thunderbolt*
*The German Defeat in the East, 1944-45*
*Germany's Panzer Arm in World War II*
*Grenadiers*
*Infantry Aces*
*Iron Arm*
*Luftwaffe Aces*
*Messerschmitts over Sicily*
*Michael Wittmann, Volume One*
*Michael Wittmann, Volume Two*
*The Nazi Rocketeers*
*On the Canal*
*Packs On!*
*Panzer Aces*
*Panzer Aces II*
*Retreat to the Reich*
*The Savage Sky*
*Surviving Bataan and Beyond*
*The 12th SS, Volume One*
*The 12th SS, Volume Two*
*Tigers in the Mud*

### THE COLD WAR / VIETNAM
*Flying American Combat Aircraft: The Cold War*
*Land with No Sun*
*Street without Joy*

### WARS OF THE MIDDLE EAST
*Never-Ending Conflict*

### OTHER
*Desert Battles*

# THE
# PANZER LEGIONS

## A Guide to the German Army Tank Divisions of World War II and Their Commanders

Samuel W. Mitcham, Jr.

STACKPOLE
BOOKS

Published in paperback in 2007 by
STACKPOLE BOOKS
5067 Ritter Road
Mechanicsburg, PA 17055
www.stackpolebooks.com

THE PANZER LEGIONS: A GUIDE TO THE GERMAN ARMY TANK DIVISIONS
OF WORLD WAR II AND THEIR COMMANDERS, by Samuel W. Mitcham, Jr., was
originally published in hard cover by Praeger, an imprint of Greenwood Publishing
Group, Inc., Westport, CT. Copyright © 2000 by Samuel W. Mitcham, Jr. Paperback
edition by arrangement with Greenwood Publishing Group, Inc. All rights reserved.

*Cover design by Tracy Patterson*

*Cover photo from* SS Armor on the Eastern Front, 1943–1945, *by Velimir Vuksic,
published by J. J. Fedorowicz Publishing Inc.*

Printed in the United States of America

10  9  8  7  6  5  4  3  2  1

FIRST EDITION

ISBN 0-8117-3353-X (Stackpole paperback)
ISBN 978-0-8117-3353-3 (Stackpole paperback)

**The Library of Congress has cataloged the hardcover edition as follows:**

Mitcham, Samuel W.
    The Panzer legions : a guide to the German Army tank divisions of World
War II and their commanders / Samuel W. Mitcham, Jr.
        p. cm.
    Includes bibliographical references and index.
    ISBN 0-313-31640-6 (alk. paper)
    1. German. Heer—Armored troops. 2. Germany. Heer—Officers. I. Title.
D757.54 .M58 2001
940.54'1343—dc21
                                                                00-034116

# Contents

Preface                                                                vii

**PART I:  THE PANZERWAFFE**
Chapter 1.  The History of the Panzer Forces                             3
Chapter 2.  The Wehrkreise                                              29

**PART II:  THE PANZER DIVISIONS**
1st Panzer                                                              37
2nd Panzer                                                              46
3rd Panzer                                                              53
4th Panzer                                                              59
5th Panzer                                                              65
6th Panzer                                                              71
7th Panzer                                                              79
8th Panzer                                                              87
9th Panzer                                                              93
10th Panzer                                                            101
11th Panzer                                                            104
12th Panzer                                                            109
13th Panzer                                                            112
14th Panzer                                                            119
15th Panzer                                                            124
16th Panzer                                                            129
17th Panzer                                                            137
18th Panzer                                                            143
19th Panzer                                                            149

20th Panzer                                                           153
21st Panzer                                                           157
22nd Panzer                                                           164
23rd Panzer                                                           168
24th Panzer                                                           174
25th Panzer                                                           179
26th Panzer                                                           185
27th Panzer                                                           190
116th Panzer (Formerly 16th Panzer Grenadier) Division               193
(130th) Panzer Lehr Division                                         201
155th Reserve Panzer (Formerly Replacement) Division                 206
178th Panzer Replacement Division                                    210
179th Reserve Panzer Division                                        212
232nd Panzer Division                                                214
233rd Reserve Panzer (Later Panzer) Division                         216
273rd Reserve Panzer Division                                        219
Panzer Division Clausewitz                                           221
Panzer Division Feldherrnhalle 1                                     223
Panzer Division Feldherrnhalle 2                                     226
Fuehrer Begleit Division                                             228
Fuehrer Grenadier Division                                           232
Panzer Division Holstein                                             235
Panzer Division Jueterbog                                            237
Panzer Division Kurmark                                              239
Panzer Division Muencheberg                                          242
Panzer Division Norway                                               244
Panzer Division Silesia                                              246
Panzer (Later Panzer Field Training) Division Tatra                  248
Panzer Grenadier Division Grossdeutschland                           250

Appendix I:  Table of Equivalent Ranks                               257
Appendix II:  The Higher Panzer Headquarters                         258
Appendix III:  Chronology of the Second World War                    270
Appendix IV:  Profiles of the Non-army Panzer Divisions              283
Appendix V:  German Staff Positions                                  286
Bibliography                                                         289
Index: Individuals                                                   295
Unit Index                                                           303

Photo essays follow pages 34 and 148.

# Preface

Created in the 1930s, the German *Panzerwaffe* (armored branch) revolutionized warfare for the rest of the 20th century, ending the era of the cavalry and non-motorized infantry formation and replacing it with something far faster and more lethal. This era of mobile warfare is with us still: the advent of the helicopter was just another step in its logical development. Operation Desert Storm was a blitzkrieg campaign, and there will be others.

This book provides a guide to the World War II German Army tank divisions from inception to destruction and surrender. The guide is divided into two parts. Part I provides a generalized history of the panzer force. This part also includes a section on the German military districts (*Wehrkreise*), which were largely responsible for creating the panzer divisions, generally along the lines specified by the Panzer Inspectorate. This information on the Wehrkreise is critical to an understanding of how the German military system worked in World War II. It functioned so smoothly and so unspectacularly that it has generally gone unnoticed by historians, but without it Hitler could never have won his victories. Also, without the Wehrkreise's replacement and training system, it would have been impossible for Germany to have kept its divisions in the field for six years.

Part II of the book provides entries, arranged chronologically, giving the history of each individual division and its commanders. Full entries are included on the German Army tank divisions. Although the focus of the book is on the Army tank divisions, the SS panzer divisions are covered briefly. These divisions were not created until 1943, when the German defeat was inevitable and Hitler's distrust of his generals and the General Staff was such that he began to replace them with a Nazi Party organization (the SS). They had no effect on the evolution of the blitzkrieg. The German theories on employment of tank and mobile divisions was already fully in place by the time the first SS panzer division was created. This comment is not meant to minimize their importance;

on the contrary, in the last two years of the war, the SS panzer divisions were exceedingly important, and they fought very well. Although the *Waffen-SS* (armed SS) fought side by side with the army, it was not part of it.

The histories of the motorized and panzer grenadier divisions are also not discussed in detail in this book. One exception is made: the elite Grossdeutschland Panzer Grenadier Divisions is covered as if it were a panzer division. This is because it *was* a panzer division—in everything but name. Many authors have cited it as a panzer division, but it was never officially designated as such, even when it had more panzers than almost any other German Army division. At a time when all the other army tank divisions had one or two panzer battalions, Grossdeutschland had three, and they were at nearly full strength. Also, the "G.D." Division is sometimes referred to as an SS unit. This is a myth—it never belonged to the SS.

The book also includes an index that should serve as a quick reference guide to individuals and panzer units.

I would like to thank all of the people who helped me in the preparation of this volume, especially my long-suffering wife, Donna. I would also like to thank the staffs of the U.S. Center for Military History at Carlisle Barracks, Pennsylvania; the U.S. National Archives; the Bundesarchiv; and the U.S. Air War College at Maxwell Air Force Base, Alabama. I would also like to thank Ms. Melinda Mathews and her interlibrary loan staff at the University of Louisiana at Monroe. Finally, thanks go to Dr. Heather Ruland Staines, military history editor at Greenwood, who is one of the best editors with whom I have had the privilege to work.

# PART ONE

# The Panzerwaffe

# CHAPTER 1

# The History of the Panzer Forces

Germany was defeated in World War I, largely by the tank. When the war ended in November, 1918, it had only 45 tanks at the front. The Allies had more than 3,500.

After the war, Germany was forced to sign the Treaty of Versailles. Under its terms, the German Armed Forces (*Reichswehr*) was limited to 115,000 men: 100,000 in the army (*Reichsheer*) and 15,000 in the navy (*Reichsmarine*). Conscious of why they won the war, the victors prohibited the Reichswehr from having an air force, a tank force (or Panzerwaffe), poisonous gas, or submarines. Despite this fact, General Hans von Seeckt, the commander in chief of the Reichsheer and the creator of the Reichswehr, was more liberal in what he allowed for his forces. Field Marshal Erich von Manstein later recalled that Seeckt had an "inner fire that inspired him and the iron will which made him a leader of men."[1] He envisioned a future favorable for the creation of a panzer arm (among other things) and was largely responsible for molding that future into his image of it.

The Treaty of Versailles was so unfair and repugnant that most Germans viewed its violation as the equivalent of a patriotic act. In 1922, the German foreign minister met with his counterpart from the Soviet Union—the other ostracized power in Europe—and signed the Treaty of Rapallo. Under its secret protocols, Seeckt's representatives (Major General Curt Hasse and Colonel Kurt von Schleicher) could now hold discussions with Russian diplomats about establishing secret military bases in the Soviet Union. Negotiations were protracted, but the Reichsheer was eventually able to establish three training centers in Russia: a gas school at Saratov, an aviation school near Lipetsk, and an armored training school near Kazan, on the Kama River. It was unofficially dubbed *Panzertruppenschule Kama*. Training lasted up to two years. Up to a dozen officers trained there at a time. Its directors of training included tank pioneer Major (later Lieutenant General) Ritter Ludwig von Radlmaier and Major (later Colonel General) Josef Harpe, who later commanded the 5th Panzer Army. Visiting observers included Major General (later Field Marshal and Minister of War) Werner von Blomberg, Major General Oswald Lutz, Lieutenant Colonel Heinz Guderian, and Lieutenant Colonel (later Field Marshal) Walter Model, among others. Ritter Wilhelm von Thoma, future commander of the Afrika Korps, was also associated with the school. By the late 1920s, the German firms of Krupp, Daimler, and Rheinmetall had all sent engineers and technicians to Kazan, where they worked on new tank designs—including what became the *Panzerkampfwagen I* and *II*—the Panzer Mark I (PzKw I) and Mark II (PzKw II), respectively.[2]

The Treaty of Versailles had allowed Germany one motor-drawn artillery battery and one motor transport battalion (*Kraftfahrabteilung*), controlled by the Inspectorate of Motor Transport Troops (*Inspektion der Kraftfahrtruppen*) in the Defense Ministry. This office, which was known as "In 6," was largely responsible for the development of the Panzerwaffe and was a major contributing factor to the philosophy of the blitzkrieg (literally "lightning warfare"), which began to evolve in the 1920s. Often this development took place in spite of the opposition of In 6's inspector general. The first inspector, Major General Erich von Tschischwitz, was in favor of the use of motorized and armored combat formations; however, neither of his immediate successors, Major General Oldwig von Natzmer and Colonel Alfred von Vollard-Bockelberg, believed in the use of tanks.[3] They looked upon In 6's mission as limited. In their view, motorized transport battalions were good for hauling supplies and very little else. Many of their young subordinates, however, disagreed. Chief among these was Heinz Guderian, the son of a Prussian general and himself a Prussian General Staff officer.

Guderian was born in East Prussia in 1888 and served on the Western Front in World War I, initially as a communications specialist and later as an infantry and General Staff officer. Later he served in the Baltic States, fighting with the quasi-legal *Freikorps* against the Bolsheviks. He was transferred to the Inspectorate of Motorized Troops in 1922 and was assigned to the 7th Kraftfahrabteilung, which was commanded by Major Oswald Lutz. By 1928, he was an enthusiastic proponent of armored and mobile warfare and was serving as an instructor of tank tactics at the Transport Division of the Defense Ministry.

Guderian has gone down in history as the "Father of the Blitzkrieg" and the creator of the German panzer force. Both titles are largely but not completely deserved, and his postwar memories, *Panzer Leader*, are self-serving and must be used cautiously. To accept Guderian's memoirs at face value would lead one to the conclusion that Guderian—almost alone—invented the blitzkrieg and was responsible for the evolution of the panzer branch. This would be an erroneous conclusion. The theories leading up to the blitzkrieg concept have their roots far back in Prussian military history—to 1807 and the era of Scharnhorst, Gneisenau, and Clausewitz.[4] This theoretical and doctrinal evolution continued with General Helmuth Karl Bernard von Moltke ("Moltke the elder") and General Count Alfred von Schlieffen, who emphasized rapid maneuver through the use of railroads and concentration of superior forces at the decisive point through the use of superior mobility.[5] As early as 1920, in fact, the General Staff devoted a considerable amount of space in its primary tactical and doctrinal manual, *Leadership and Battle*, to tanks and armored fighting vehicles. In this and other publications, the *Truppenamt*[6] spelled out in the 1920s that tanks were offensive weapons; they should be used at the decisive point (i.e., where the commander is seeking a decision); they should be used in masses; and they should be used to achieve and expand deep penetrations. The use of tanks in small numbers and on narrow frontages was discouraged.[7]

The most prolific German writer on armored tactics and theory in the 1920s and 1930s was Ernst Volckheim. Born in Prussia in 1898, he joined the army as a war volunteer, earned a commission in 1916, and was commander of a machine gun company in 1917. He was assigned to the 1st Heavy Panzer Company of the German tank corps in early 1918 and saw as much tank warfare as any Allied officer before he was seriously wounded on October 11, 1918, just a month before the armistice. Selected for retention in Seeckt's "Treaty Army," he was assigned to the Inspectorate of Motor Transport in the Defense Ministry in 1923. Two years later, he was an instructor of panzer and motorized tactics at the Infantry School at Doeberitz. In fact, for the rest of his career (which lasted until 1942), Volckheim was exclusively employed in the development of armored and motorized forces.

Volckheim's first book, *German Tanks in the World War* (*Die deutschen Kampfwagen im Weltkrieg*) (Berlin: 1923), was well received, both within and outside of the Reichsheer, and it began an incredibly prolific career for this talented tank officer, whose theories were backed by practical combat experience. From 1923 to 1927, Volckheim wrote no fewer than two dozen articles which were published in the *Militaer Wochenblatt*, the semi-official weekly journal of the Reichsheer.[8]

The *Militaer Wochenblatt* was edited by Konstantin von Altrock, a retired lieutenant general.[9] Described by Seeckt biographer James S. Corum as "a progressive military theorist," Altrock published a great many articles on armored warfare throughout the 1920s. Some of these were written by Germans; others were translations of the work of foreign authors. In 1924 and 1925, von Altrock even published a monthly supplement to the *Militaer Wochenblatt—Der Kampfwagen* (*The Tank*). Its featured writer was Ernest Volckheim.[10]

In 1924, Volckheim's *The Tank in Modern Warfare* was published. It was a basic text on armored warfare and tactics, and was endorsed by the Army Command (i.e., Seeckt) as the standard text on panzer warfare, even though Volckheim disagreed with the official Reichsheer doctrine, which favored light tanks. Volckheim held the opinion that the only advantage light tanks had over heavy tanks was their speed. Unlike the other prominent armored theorists of the 1920s, Volckheim believed that the battlefield of the future belonged to the slower but more heavily gunned tanks. World War II would prove him right.

Volckheim was a solid tactician and thinker but not a visionary. Unlike British armored theorist Major General J. F. C. Fuller, who went so far as to advocate all-tank armies, Volckheim viewed the tank force as basically an infantry support arm, like the artillery. He did not call for the establishment of full panzer divisions, although he did write in support of tank and armored car regiments. (The call for panzer divisions in an army which had no tanks and which was allowed only 10 divisions would have been Utopian in any case.) He was the first advocate of the use of tanks in an anti-tank role, called for the development of amphibious tanks, and was the first German to advocate placing a radio in every tank.[11]

Volckheim was not the only pre-Guderian panzer theorist and pioneer in the German Army. Lieutenant Wilhelm Brandt, an engineer by profession, wrote several major technical articles on armored warfare in the 1920s, and his productivity was exceeded by Fritz Heigl.[12] As early as January, 1927, Lieutenant Colonel Baron Werner von Fritsch, the chief of the Organizations Branch of the Truppenamt and the future commander in chief of the Army (1934–1938) wrote that "tanks most probably will become the operationally decisive weapon. From an operational perspective this weapon will be most effective, if concentrated in independent units like tank brigades."[13]

Werner von Blomberg, the chief of the Training Section of the Truppenamt, seemed to agree with Fritsch and was drafting training schedules for panzer regiments as early as October, 1927.[14] Six years later, Blomberg was Hitler's minister of defense.

Volckheim, von Altrock, von Fritsch, von Blomberg et al were not the only forward thinking officers in the Reichsheer in the 1920s. As early as 1921, Hans von Seeckt, the commander in chief of the army, was pushing for panzer training and development, even though it clearly violated the Treaty of Versailles. In 1924, he secretly ordered each *Wehrkreis* (military district) to make sure that every major unit have an Armored Officer, who would be responsible for training the troops in tank warfare. Major (later Lieutenant General) Ritter Ludwig von Radlmeier, who visited extensively in the United States, studying American armored tactics and doctrine, also wrote extensively about armored issues in German professional journals long before Guderian arrived on the scene. In fact, as early as 1926, Rheinmetall was producing illegal tanks. The first model weighed 20 tons and mounted a 75mm gun. This was followed shortly thereafter by a 9-ton model. Guderian did not even see a tank until 1929, when he was sent on a detached duty assignment to the II Battalion of the Swedish Guards. Here he saw a primitive German LK II tank from World War I and came back to the Fatherland enthusiastic about the idea of creating tank (panzer) divisions. Major General Otto von Stuelpnagel, the new inspector of motorized troops, rejected Guderian's ideas, stating that tanks should never be used in units larger than regiments.[15] Guderian, however, continued to advocate his concepts, both within military circles and to the general public.

Whether or not it is 100 percent correct to characterize Guderian as the father of the blitzkrieg and/or the panzer branch, he was most certainly their Apostle Paul. Opposition to his ideas only increased his fervor, which bordered on fanaticism. However, as author Roger Edwards noted, "[His] bluff approach was not always helpful in promoting the panzer cause."[16] Guderian was both supported and shielded by his mentor, Oswald Lutz, and the concept of the panzer division received a major boost in 1931, when Lutz was named chief of the Inspectorate of Motor Transport Troops. By this time, Lutz was a major general.[17] (See Appendix I for a table of equivalent ranks.) He promptly named Colonel Guderian his chief of staff. Other members of the staff included Major Werner Kempf, Major Walter Nehring, Captain Walter Chales de Beaulieu, and Captain Walter von Huenersdorff—an incredibly talented group of subordinates. Kempf later commanded a panzer division in Poland and an army on the Eastern Front during World War II; Nehring commanded the 18th Panzer Division, the Afrika Korps, and the 1st Panzer Army, among others; Chales de Beaulieu was chief of staff of the 4th Panzer Army in the East before running afoul of Hitler and being involuntarily transferred to the infantry; and Huenersdorff died commanding a panzer division on the Eastern Front. The result of the efforts of this outstanding team was a major speed-up in the technical development of armored, mechanized, and motorized forces. In 1931 and 1932, the firms of MAN, Krupp, Henschel, Daimler-Benz, and Rheinmetall-Borsig were given new contracts for the development of "agricultural tractors" (i.e., tanks).[18]

The idea of using panzers en masse received another major boost in 1933, when Adolf Hitler became chancellor of Germany. In the process, General Kurt von Schleicher was deposed both as chancellor and defense minister, and was replaced in the latter capacity by General of Infantry (later Field Marshal) Werner von Blomberg. Blomberg immediately promoted one of Schleicher's chief lieutenants, Kurt von Brelow, the head of the *Ministeramt* (Ministry Office) of the Defense Ministry, to the rank of major general—on the retired list. He was succeeded by Blomberg's own former chief of staff, the capable but ruthless Major General Walter von Reichenau.[19] Guderian later remarked that both Blomberg and Reichenau "favored modern ideas."[20] So did Hitler. He and the leaders of his Nazi Party considered themselves revolutionaries, so it is only logical that they would favor revolutionary ideas in the military realm as well. The notions of the blitzkrieg and of creating and employing large panzer formations were among the most revolutionary ideas of their time and, when Hitler first saw the new German tanks at an army equipment demonstration at Kummersdorf, he became very excited. "That is what I want!" he cried. "That is what I will have!" His support in the development of the Panzerwaffe would prove invaluable in the years ahead.

In 1929, Blomberg had been deposed as chief of the General Staff (then called the *Truppenamt* or Troop Office) by a Schleicher intrigue. In 1933 and 1934, he gradually froze out Schleicher's two principle military cronies, Colonel General Kurt von Hammerstein (the commander in chief of the army) and General of Mountain Troops Wilhelm Adams (the chief of the General Staff), and eventually compelled them to retire.[21] Hammerstein was replaced by General of Infantry Baron Werner von Fritsch, another forward-thinking officer who generally supported the panzer concept. The choice of Adams's successor, however, was less fortunate: General of Artillery Ludwig Beck.

Ludwig Beck was a well-educated and well-mannered philosopher in uniform. When he faced a problem in the military sphere, however, his first question was how it had been handled in the past. Beck saw tanks as infantry support vehicles—nothing more. When Guderian asserted that one day he would lead panzer divisions from the front and by radio, Beck replied: "Nonsense! A divisional commander sits back with maps and a telephone. Anything else is Utopian!"[22] There was little he could do to stop the growth of the panzer idea, however, despite the fact that there was considerable hostility, reaction, and prejudice against it within the armed forces—especially within the cavalry branch. On the other hand, Blomberg, Reichenau, and Fritsch all promoted greater and more intense testing and training of motorized units. In 1933, the army's seven motor vehicle battalions were redesignated motorized combat battalions—both changing and clarifying their major mission. In November 1933, the first panzer unit was created—*Kraftfahrlehrkommando* (Motor Vehicle Training Command) Zossen. It was named after its garrison town (the seat of the General Staff, about 30 miles south of Berlin) and was formed from the old 3rd Motor Vehicle Battalion, combined with some officers and technicians returning from Kama and some officers and men from the inspectorate of motorized troops. (Hitler had closed the panzer school at Kama because of his intense hatred of the Soviet Union.) Colonel Ernst Fessmann, the last commander of the training staff at Kama, became commander. Other officers in Motor Vehicle Training Command Zossen included Captain Wilhelm Conze, Captain Wolfgang Thomale and Major Hermann Breith. Breith and Conze later commanded panzer divisions and Thomale was chief of staff of the Panzer Inspectorate (1943–45).

Meanwhile, on April 1, 1934, Major Harpe, the future commander of the 5th Panzer Army, set up a gunnery training course, which soon evolved into the Panzer Gunnery School at Putlos. About the same time, the Army Motor Vehicle School opened in Berlin. By the summer of 1934, Krupp and Henschel (and later MAN) were secretly manufacturing Panzer Mark I (PzKw I) light tanks, and Motor Vehicle Training Command Zossen was already equipped with 55 of them. As a result, on July 1, 1934, a new Motor Vehicle Training Command Ohrdruf was activated. Its commander was armored pioneer Lieutenant Colonel Ritter Ludwig von Radlmaier. Its first battalion was commanded by Lieutenant Colonel Friedrich Kuehn; II Battalion was commanded by Major Ritter Wilhelm von Thoma.

In the meantime, the inspectorate of motorized troops had been upgraded to the inspectorate of mechanized troops. It became the Motorized Combat Troops Command on June 1, 1934. Lutz (now a lieutenant general) remained in charge, while Guderian remained his chief of staff. But even greater advances were on the way. On October 1, General von Fritsch secretly ordered the establishment of the 1st Panzer Brigade, which was to be subordinate to the commanding general, motorized cavalry corps. The 12th Cavalry Regiment, which was based at Dresden and Kammenz, was dismounted and became the first motorized infantry regiment in the army. Meanwhile, Motor Vehicle Training Commands Zossen and Ohrdruf were clandestinely recognized for what they were: the 1st and 2nd Panzer Regiments. That winter, the 12th Cavalry Regiment (Motorized) was reequipped with tanks and retrained, in order to form the 3rd Panzer Regiment. Meanwhile, Krupp began manufacturing the PzKw IIc (models a and b had already been discarded by the army) and began delivering them to the Reichsheer. Developed by Henschel, MAN, and Krupp, these tanks weighed 10 tons and were armed with a 20mm main battle gun.

Not only was the Panzerwaffe evolving and growing in 1935—the entire Reichswehr was expanding as well. By early 1935, it had grown too big, and Hitler learned that the Allies knew he was deliberately violating the Treaty of Versailles. On March 9, 1935, therefore, he announced to the world that Germany had created a *Luftwaffe* (air force). The Allies' reaction was so mild that, a week later, he renounced the Treaty of Versailles altogether. The defense ministry became the war ministry; the Reichswehr became the *Wehrmacht* (armed forces); and the Reichsheer became the *Heer* (army). Again the Allied reaction was mild. The shackles had been removed; the army was now free to expand to 36 divisions. Lutz, Guderian and the rest were determined that some of them would be panzer divisions. This occurred on October 15, 1935, the date celebrated thereafter as the "birthday" of the Panzerwaffe.

The first three panzer divisions were formed at Weimar, Wuerzburg, and Berlin, respectively. Each had two tank regiments, a motorized infantry regiment, a motorized artillery regiment, an engineer battalion, a reconnaissance battalion, an antitank battalion, and a signal company or battalion. Some had a military intelligence or cartographic unit as well, but they lacked service support, maintenance, and supply units of every description. The 1st Panzer Regiment at Zossen was moved to Wuenstorf and was renamed the 5th Panzer Regiment and the 2nd Tank Regiment at Ohrdruf was renamed the 1st Panzer Regiment. The 2nd, 3rd, 4th, and 6th Panzer Regiments were new formations, absorbing the former 4th, 7th, and 12th Cavalry Regiments. (The 4th and 12th Cavalry had already been equipped with tanks.) The 1st Panzer Division included the 1st Panzer Regiment at Ohrdruf (later Erfurt)and the 2nd at Eisenach; the 2nd Panzer Division controlled the 3rd Panzer Regiment at Kamenz and the 4th at Ohrdruf; and the 3rd Division included the 5th and 6th Panzer Regiments at Wuenstorf and Neuruppin, respectively. Shortly thereafter, the 3rd, 4th, and 6th Panzer Regiments were transferred to new garrisons at Bamberg, Schweinfurt, and Neuruppin.

All three panzer divisions were placed under a new organization—Panzer Troops Command (In 6), which replaced the Inspectorate of Mechanized Troops on September 27, 1935. Oswald Lutz remained the chief of In 6 and was promoted and became the first general of panzer troops. Panzer Troops Command was, however, as Werner Haupt wrote, "an impotent creature . . . being restricted to the supervision of purely tank-equipped units up to regimental strength only."[23] The structure was a result of the influence of General Beck, who did what he could to retard the development of the panzer forces. He also "kicked Guderian upstairs" and gave him command of the 2nd Panzer Division, even though he was only a colonel. (In 1938, the typical German division was commanded by a lieutenant general, only occasionally by a major general, and never by a colonel.) Beck thus ensured that the most dynamic and influential member of the panzer arm was posted away from Berlin. Guderian was succeeded as chief of staff of In 6 by Colonel Friedrich Paulus, a much more charming and conciliatory officer. He was, however, also weak-willed and indecisive—an officer who tried to get along with everybody, especially senior generals, even if it meant giving up on arguments when he knew he was right.[24] This move significantly slowed the development of the armored branch, because General Lutz also lacked Guderian's fire. No more panzer divisions would be established, for example, until late 1938.

Meanwhile, unit training for the panzer companies began as soon as the celebrations ended. The companies (which averaged only eight tanks per company in 1935) were drilled at their home bases and went through the gunnery school at Putlos on a rotating basis. To further facilitate training, the motor vehicle school was transferred to Wuensdorf, where it was renamed the Motorized Troop School. In 1936, most of the companies were expanded to 22 tanks—mainly the poor quality PzKw I. Despite this influx, by February 1936, companies were considered proficient enough to begin regimental-scale training, most of which took place at the Staumuehlen Maneuver Area on the Senne. The tank units did not participate in the reoccupation of the Rhineland, but they were in operational reserve.

In 1936, Friedrich Paulus was replaced as chief of staff of In 6 by Lieutenant Colonel Walther Nehring, who was arguably the most capable officer to come out of the Panzerwaffe in World War II (see 18th Panzer Division, Commanders, for a sketch of his brilliant career). Panzer Troops Command's performance immediately improved. In the fall of 1936, In 6 added two new tank regiments: the 7th Panzer at Vaihingen and the 8th Panzer at Boeblingen. As was standard procedure, they were formed around cadres supplied by older units. The cadres for the 7th, for example, came from the 3rd, 5th, and 6th Panzer Regiments. The older regiments sent the new units entire companies, which were replaced by men from the replacement units of the *Wehrkreise* (military districts—see below). In 6 also created the Staff, 4th Panzer Brigade, but it initially was a headquarters without combat units.

Also in 1936, In 6 created the 88th Panzer Battalion from volunteers from the 4th and 6th Panzer Regiments. The 88th (which initially consisted of only one company and a repair shop section) was sent to the Iberian peninsula, where it fought in the Spanish Civil War and was the first German tank unit in the Nazi era to see combat. It was equipped with PzKw I tanks and its commander was Major Ritter Wilhelm von Thoma. For three years, men were rotated to Spain and then back to Germany, assuring the Panzerwaffe of a sizable number of combat veterans even before World War II began. By 1939, the 88th Panzer's strength had been increased to three line companies and a repair company.

The expansion of the panzer units was paralleled by an increase in tank production. By the end of 1936, 3,000 light tanks had already been delivered to the units. In 1935, the first Panzer Mark III (PzKw III), manufactured by Daimler-Benz, came off the production lines. Early in 1936, the Army Weapons Office gave Krupp a contract to build another tank: the Panzer Mark IV (PzKw IV), which was supposed to be even better than the PzKw III. It was to be a medium support tank, but its initial models suffered for having a short-barreled gun (i.e., insufficient range). PzKw IVs began to arrive at the regiments before the end of 1936.

Unit training continued throughout 1937. That was the year that the Motorized Troop School at Wuensdorf became the Panzertruppenschule. It included five sections: tactical training, technical training, a regulations office, the Panzer Gunnery School at Putlos, and the Panzer Lehr Battalion at Wuensdorf, which was formed in October 1937 under the command of Major von Lewinski. Somewhat larger than the average battalion, its primary purpose was to test new tanks. Most of its men came from the 8th Panzer Regiment, which lost more than half its strength. It was, however, soon reconstituted at Boeblingen, Wuerttemberg, from recruits supplied by the military districts.

On October 12, after the Wehrmacht maneuvers of that year, several new tank units were formed, including the 11th Panzer Regiment at the Senne Maneuver Area, the 15th Panzer Regiment at Sagan, the I Battalion, 10th Panzer Regiment (I/10th Panzer Regiment) at the Stablack Maneuver Area, the 25th Panzer Battalion at Grafenwoehr Maneuver Area, and the 65th Panzer Battalion at the Senne Maneuver Area.

Incidentally, the panzer regiments at this time had one to three battalions, numbered I, II, and III, always using Roman numerals. On rare occasions, there was a IV Battalion as well. The abbreviation for the battalion was always followed by the regiment's number—i.e., III Battalion, 15th Panzer Regiment would be abbreviated III/15th Panzer or III/15th Panzer Regiment. Companies were always numbered using Arabic numbers. The 2nd Company, 10th Panzer Regiment would be abbreviated 2/10th Panzer Regiment. This system is used throughout this book.

As usual, the new units were formed around veterans from the older regiments. The 11th Panzer Regiment's cadres came from I/1st Panzer Regiment and II/4th Panzer Regiment (i.e., from the men of Wehrkreis VI, headquartered in Muenster). The 15th Panzer's cadres came from I/5th Panzer and I/2nd Panzer

Regiments (i.e., Silesians), and the I/10th Panzer received cadres from the 1st, 6th, and 7th Panzer Regiments. The 25th Panzer Battalion's cadres came from the 3rd Panzer Regiment and from Wehrkreis XII (Nuremberg), and the 65th Panzer Battalion's cadres were from the 7th Panzer Regiment. Later, the 11th Panzer moved to Paderborn, the I/10th Panzer was transferred to Zinten, East Prussia, the 25th Battalion was sent to Erlangen, and the 65th Panzer Battalion garrisoned at Iserlohn.

Once again, General Beck managed to exert a negative influence upon the expansion. He detached the 65th Panzer Battalion from In 6 and assigned it to the newly forming light divisions, which were being established to replace the cavalry. Lutz objected but was overruled. By now, however, all of Germany's panzer, motorized, and light divisions were under Army Group 4, which was commanded by General of Artillery Walter von Brauchitsch. It had, for the moment, supplanted In 6 as the main influence upon the development of the panzer arm.[25]

In late January 1938, it was discovered that the pro-Nazi minister of war, Field Marshal von Blomberg, had married a prostitute. Although he stepped out of character and treated the disgraced marshal with absolute and even astonishing kindness, Hitler had no choice but to send him into retirement.[26] The officer next in line for the post was General von Fritsch, who was somewhat hostile to the Nazis. Heinrich Himmler, the Reichsfuehrer-SS, and Reinhardt Heydrich, the head of the SD (*Sicherheitsdienst*, or Security Service), therefore, managed to force him into retirement on trumped-up charges of homosexuality. Hitler abolished the post of war minister, assumed the post of Supreme Commander himself, and established the command structure under which the Third Reich fought World War II. He created the High Command of the Armed Forces (*Oberkommando des Wehrmacht* or OKW) and named General of Artillery Wilhelm Keitel its commander in chief.[27] After making a deal with the Nazis, Brauchitsch was promoted to colonel general and named commander in chief of the High Command of the Army (*Oberkommando der Heeres* or OKH), which was theoretically subordinate to OKW, but which, in fact, was semi-independent and subordinate only to Hitler. As part of his deal with the Nazis, Brauchitsch had to consign several of his brother officers to the retired list. Among these was the non-Nazi chief of In 6, General Lutz. It has been suggested by certain authors that he was dismissed because he lacked a forceful personality. He was, in fact, removed because he questioned Hitler's war aims a little too forcefully. Lutz learned about his dismissal in a particularly tasteless manner: he read about it in a newspaper. He retired to Munich and, except for a brief period during which he headed a minor special staff (1941–42), he was never reemployed. He was replaced by the pro-Nazi General Guderian, who never lifted a finger to help his former mentor and never uttered a word of protest concerning his dismissal. Guderian was immediately promoted to lieutenant general and succeeded Lutz as In 6. He also succeeded General Lutz as commander of the recently formed XVI Corps, which controlled Germany's three tank divisions.[28]

Meanwhile, on the evening of March 10, 1938, XVI Corps was placed on full alert. Early on the morning of March 12, it marched into Austria, which was being annexed to the Third Reich. The invasion (which was peaceful) was spearheaded by the 2nd Panzer Division. It marched through Linz (Hitler's hometown) and St. Poelten and on to Vienna, arriving early on the morning of March 13. The entire division covered 420 miles in 48 hours, but it lost 30 percent of its tanks due to engine failure, tread failure, or sliding off icy roads. (The 2nd Panzer had no maintenance or supply units as yet.)

The 2nd Panzer Division remained in Vienna after the occupation and gradually became an Austrian unit. The only Austrian tank unit was redesignated 33rd Panzer Battalion and was incorporated into the newly formed 4th Light Division.

The fall of 1938 brought a new crisis. Hitler demanded Czechoslovakia cede the Sudetenland to the Third Reich. He pushed the world to the edge of war before London and Paris buckled and gave in to his demands. In the process, he horrified General Beck, who resigned in protest—the only German general to do so. He was replaced by the deputy chief of the General Staff, General of Artillery Franz Halder, who was also no friend of Guderian or the panzer branch.[29] This had no effect on Guderian's advancement, however. He was promoted to general of panzer troops effective November 1, 1938, and was named chief of mobile troops on November 20. In this new post, he had authority over the development and training of Germany's cavalry, antitank, motorized, and mechanized forces, as well as most of its panzer units—an authority denied the old Panzer Troops Command. Guderian was even granted direct access to Hitler.

Even before his new headquarters was activated, Guderian's panzer branch expanded again. On November 10, 1938, two new panzer divisions were formed: the 4th at Wuerzburg and the 5th at Oppeln. Four new panzer brigade staffs were also activated: the 4th at Stuttgart, the 5th at Bamberg, the 6th at Wuerzburg, and the 8th at Sagan. Several new units were also created, including the 23rd Panzer Regiment (at Mannheim-Schwetzingen), the 31st Panzer Regiment (Koenigsbrueck and Gross-Born), the 35th Panzer Regiment (Bamberg), the 36th Panzer Regiment (Schweinfurt) and the independent 65th, 66th, and 67th Panzer Battalions (at Sennelager, Eisenach, and Gross-Glienicke, respectively). The new independent forces, however, were assigned to the light divisions.

On March 12, 1939, the 3rd Panzer Division entered Prague, completing the peaceful conquest of Czechoslovakia. Less than a month later, on April 1, OKH formed the Staff, 10th Panzer Division. This unit initially had an occupation mission and, although the 8th Panzer Regiment was initially attached to it, the 10th was not yet ready to be listed among the combat tank divisions.

The most important assets Guderian's Mobile Troops Command received from the conquest of Czechoslovakia were tanks. They included 300 P-35 (t) medium tanks, built by the Skoda firm and armed with a 37mm main battle gun and two machine guns. Even more important were the P-38 (t)s, medium tanks built by the Praga Works. Similar to the P-35 (t), they were roughly equal to the PzKw III in strength and utility. The Czechs—under German supervision—continued to manufacture them until 1942. The P-35 (t)s were assigned to the 11th Panzer Regiment and the 65th Panzer Battalion. The P-38 (t)s formed the basis for what became the 7th and 8th Panzer Divisions.

With war rapidly approaching, the panzer units continued their development in the summer of 1939. The biggest step forward at that time was that they finally received their own supply units—up to 10 columns for fuel, ammunition, maintenance, etc. Also, there was another reorganization which at last brought some standardization to the tank divisions. As of August 1939, a full-strength tank division now theoretically included 394 officers, 115 officials, 1,962 non-commissioned officers (NCOs), and 9,321 enlisted men—a total of 11,792 men. It also had 1,402 trucks, 561 passenger vehicles, 421 armored vehicles (including panzers, scout cars, armored cars, etc.), and 1,280 motorcycles (711 of them with sidecars). The panzer brigade in each division had (or was to have) two tank regiments. Each panzer regiment had a staff, two panzer battalions, and engineer and intelligence sections. The standard panzer battalion had two light tank companies (PzKw Is and IIs), one medium tank company (PzKw IIIs and IVs), a tank supply column, a workshop company, and reconnaissance, intelligence, and light engineer sections.[30]

On the eve of the outbreak of war, the 2nd, 3rd, 4th, and 5th Panzer Divisions had 91 tanks: 69 PzKw Is and IIs (the latter with 20mm guns), 10 PzKw IIIs (37mm guns), and a dozen PzKw IVs (with 75mm guns). The 1st Panzer Division had 39 PzKw IIs, 56 PzKw IIIs, and 28 PzKw IVs—123 tanks in all. Table 1.1 shows the structure of the Panzerwaffe in August 1939.

Upon mobilization, In 6 became the Inspectorate of Panzer, Cavalry, and Motorized Troops under Lieutenant General Friedrich Kuehn. Guderian took command of the recently activated XIX Corps (an unofficial panzer corps), while General Erich Hoepner led the tank-heavy XVI Corps. The Replacement (or Home) Army was activated at the end of August and was responsible for mobilization, implementing the German draft, training and providing replacements for the various divisions of the field armies (see Chapter 2). Initially it formed seven panzer replacement battalions for the tank units.

On September 1, 1939, all 34 of Germany's panzer units (divisions and independent brigades and regiments) went to war against Poland.[31] They deployed a total of 2,820 tanks, of which 1,051 were obsolete PzKw Is and IIs and 301 were Czech tanks. Only 361 were really modern PzKw III and IV tanks. They nevertheless broke the back of the Polish Army within four days. On October 6, the last Polish unit surrendered.

The German experience in Poland indicated that the light tanks were not well suited for frontline action. On September 27, even before the campaign was over, the Army Weapons Office ordered an immediate expansion in the number of and manufacturing capacities for the PzKw IIIs and IVs. Only now did large-scale production of the PzKw III begin. The Altmark Chain Factory, Inc., of

**Table 1.1**
**Structure, German Panzer Force, August 1939**

| Division | Panzer Brigade | Panzer Regiment(s) | Panzer Battalion |
|---|---|---|---|
| 1st Panzer | 1st | 1st, 2nd | |
| 2nd Panzer | 2nd | 3rd, 4th | |
| 3rd Panzer | 3rd | 5th, 6th | |
| 4th Panzcr | 5th | 35th, 36th | |
| 5th Panzer | 8th | 15th, 31st | |
| 10th Panzer | | 8th | |
| Panzer Div. Kempf[1] | 4th | 7th | |
| | 6th | 11th, 25th | |
| 1st Light | | | 65th |
| 2nd Light | | | 66th |
| 3rd Light | | | 67th |
| 4th Light | | | 33rd |
| Panzer Troop School | | Panzer Lehr[2] | |

1. Panzer Division Kempf was a temporary, ad hoc formation, formed in East Prussia in August 1939. In addition to the units shown above, it controlled the SS Standarte (Regiment) Deutschland, an SS artillery regiment, an SS reconnaissance battalion, an antitank battalion, and an engineer company. It was dissolved after the Polish campaign.
2. The Panzer Lehr Battalion at Wuersdorf was upgraded and expanded to a three-battalion regiment in the summer of 1939.
Note: The independent 23rd Panzer Regiment was in OKH Reserve in August 1939. It was later redesignated 25th Panzer Regiment.

Berlin-Spandau, soon became the most important tank manufacturer in Germany, although Daimler-Benz, Henschel, MAN, and five other companies also produced PzKw IIIs. Large-scale series production of the PzKw IV, however, did not begin until 1942.

Several new armored units were created in the winter of 1939–40, including four new panzer divisions. They were formed from the old light divisions, which had proved unsatisfactory in Poland. All four received a regimental staff and at least one new tank battalion. The former 1st Light became the 6th Panzer Division and added the 11th Panzer Regiment; the 2nd Light became the 7th Panzer Division and gained the 25th Panzer Regiment; the 3rd Light Division was designated 8th Panzer Division and added the 10th Panzer Regiment; and the 4th Light became the 9th Panzer Division and added the 33rd Panzer Regiment. The Replacement Army also formed two replacement divisions for panzer units: the 178th at Liegnitz and the 179th at Weimar. In addition, the 40th Panzer Battalion was formed in Berlin in March 1940 under the command of Lieutenant Colonel Volckheim, from two cadre companies transferred from the 6th Panzer Regiment. With three companies of PzKw Is and IIs, it took part in the invasions of Denmark and Norway in April, 1940—the only tank unit to do so.

When Germany invaded France, Belgium, and the Netherlands on May 10, 1940, it had 3,105 tanks, of which 2,441 were at the front. Most of those not taking part in the invasion were PzKw Is and IIs. The main armored/motorized unit involved was Panzer Group von Kleist, which spearheaded the German attack. It included Guderian's XIX Corps (now dubbed a motorized corps), General of Infantry Hermann Hoth's XV Motorized Corps, and Lieutenant General Georg-Hans Reinhardt's XXXXI Motorized Corps.[32] Led by Ewald von Kleist, Panzer Group von Kleist controlled seven of Germany's ten panzer divisions, for a combined total of 1,250 tanks and armored cars.[33]

The next six weeks were arguably the greatest in the history of the Panzerwaffe. The panzer divisions broke through the French lines at Sedan and pushed all the way to the sea, establishing a "Panzer Corridor" and isolating the best French divisions, the British Expeditionary Force, and the Belgium Army in Belgium. These were then quickly destroyed or forced to evacuate to the United Kingdom, without any vehicles or heavy weapons. The French, meanwhile, established an emergency position, the Weygand Line, to the south of the Panzer Corridor. This the Germans—again spearheaded by their panzer divisions—attacked on June 5. Within a week the Weygand Line crumbled and shortly thereafter the vaunted French Army was in full retreat. Paris fell on June 14 and France surrendered on June 25.

Contrary to the expectations of many, the defeat of France did not end the war. England fought on, and Hitler's strategy changed. Ever since he wrote *Mein Kampf*, when he was in prison in 1923–24, his objective had not changed. He wanted *Lebensraum*—living space in the East—for the German people. This could only occur at the expense of Russia. In the summer of 1940, impatient as always, he decided to invade the Soviet Union, despite the fact that London had not been defeated—even if it meant accepting the risk of a two-front war. Hitler thought this risk was acceptable, because he felt he could conquer Russia in one campaign. (If he failed, the Third Reich would be in deep, deep trouble.) To accomplish the task of defeating the Soviet Union, he felt that he needed more panzer divisions. Since Germany lacked the required number of tanks and could not produce them in time, he simply ordered that the existing panzer units be reduced from two tank regiments to one; they would also be reinforced with an additional rifle (motorized infantry) regiment. Table 1.2 shows the formation of the 11th through the 20th Panzer Divisions.

To form the new divisions, OKH used the 2nd and 13th Motorized Divisions, as well as the 4th, 16th, 19th, 27th, and 33rd Infantry Divisions. Elements of the disbanded 209th, 228th, 231st, and 311th Infantry Divisions were also used. In addition, the 1st, 2nd, 3rd, 4th, 5th, and 10th Panzer Divisions lost their second tank regiment, and the independent 65th, 66th, and 67th Panzer Battalions were absorbed into the existing panzer regiments, becoming the III Battalions for the tank regiments of the 5th, 7th, and 8th Panzer Divisions, respectively.

Simultaneously, the 5th Light Division was formed. It included the former

**Table 1.2**
**The New Panzer Divisions, Mid-1940–Early 1941**

| Division | Wehrkreis | Formed | Ready for Service | Panzer Regiment |
|---|---|---|---|---|
| 11th | VIII | July 1940 | Oct. 15, 1940 | 15 |
| 12th | II | Oct. 1940 | Apr. 15, 1941 | 29 |
| 13th | XI | Aug. 1940 | Oct. 10, 1941 | 4 |
| 14th | IV | Aug. 1940 | Dec. 12, 1940 | 36 |
| 15th | VII | Oct. 1940 | Mar. 15, 1941 | 8 |
| 16th | VI | Aug. 1940 | Nov. 25, 1940 | 2 |
| 17th | VII | Oct. 1940 | Mar. 15, 1941 | 39 |
| 18th | IV | Oct. 1940 | May 1, 1941 | 18 |
| 19th | XI | Oct. 1940 | Mar. 15, 1941 | 27 |
| 20th | IX | Oct. 1940 | May 1, 1941 | 21 |

*Source*: Haupt, *Panzer*: 62.

staff of the 3rd Panzer Brigade and the 5th Panzer Regiment, both of the 3rd Panzer Division, as well as most of the former 33rd Infantry Division.

Meanwhile, Benito Mussolini suffered a series of defeats in North Africa and the Balkans. To prevent the Italian Empire in Africa from collapsing completely, Adolf Hitler ordered the creation of the Afrika Korps. He placed it under the command of Lieutenant General (later Field Marshal) Erwin Rommel and gave it control of the 15th Panzer Division and 5th Light (later 21st Panzer) Division. The first German troops arrived in Tripoli, Libya on February 11, 1941. The Afrika Korps continued to fight the British 8th Army in Libya, Egypt, and Tunisia until May 1943, when it was finally destroyed. In all the months he struggled against very heavy odds, Rommel only received one additional panzer division—the 10th—in late 1942/early 1943. His headquarters, however, was progressively upgraded to Panzer Group Afrika, Panzer Army Afrika, and Army Group Afrika.

Meanwhile, on October 28, 1940, Italy invaded Greece. Three weeks later, British air and naval forces entered the Balkan theater of operations. As a result, Hitler began to fear for the Ploesti oil fields of Rumania, the Achilles' heel of his war machine. In December 1940, after intensive diplomatic maneuvering, the 13th and 16th Panzer Divisions were transferred to Romania and Bulgaria.

Mussolini, meanwhile, failed to conquer Greece and even lost a quarter of the Italian colony of Albania. When an anti-German general deposed the Yugoslav government, with British ground forces already in Greece, Hitler decided to intervene. On April 6, he invaded Yugoslavia and Greece. The 2nd Army attacked Yugoslavia from Austria and Hungary, spearheaded by the 8th and 14th Panzer Divisions. The 12th Army invaded southern Yugoslavia and Greece with the 2nd, 5th, 9th, and 11th Panzer Divisions. The 4th, 12th, and 19th Panzer Divisions were also in the Balkans in reserve, but saw little or no action. Belgrade fell on the morning of April 12, with the 8th Panzer Division and the Das Reich SS Motorized Division entering the city at the same time. Meanwhile, the Panzerwaffe defeated the British Expeditionary Force and smashed most of the Greek Army. Only the 5th Panzer Division continued the advance to the south, along with the 6th Mountain Division. It boldly pushed through the pass at Thermopylae, advanced through Thebes, and captured Athens. The paratroopers, meanwhile, seized the Strait of Corinth and the 5th Panzer overran the Peloponnesus, pushing the British off the mainland of Europe for the second time in two years.

With hardly a pause, Hitler's panzer troops quickly redeployed for Operation Barbarossa, the invasion of the Soviet Union. Only the 5th and 2nd Panzer Divisions were unable to return north by June 22, 1941, when the invasion began.

The Panzerwaffe started its most fateful campaign without enough tanks in reserve. As early as December 1940, OKH had demanded tank production be increased from 230 tanks per month to 1,250. OKW rejected the request: the Luftwaffe and Navy had production priority.[34] Only nine of Germany's 21 tank divisions even had three battalions when the invasion began: the 3rd, 6th, 7th, 10th, 12th, 17th, 18th, 19th, and 20th. The panzers themselves were also not up to standards in terms of quality. Of the 3,208 tanks in the German panzer units, only 965 were PzKw IIIs and 439 were PzKw IVs: a total of 1,404 modern tanks.[35] They still had 878 Czech tanks in their battalions, as well as 180 completely obsolete PzKw Is and 106 PzKw IIs, which were still useful as reconnaissance vehicles, but certainly not in a tank battle. In short, the panzer branch was inadequately equipped for Barbarossa in every category. Its reserves can only be characterized as woefully inadequate numerically. It nevertheless won some truly remarkable victories. These are attributable to five factors: (1) the quality of the men; (2) the attitude of the men; (3) their training and experience; (4) the superior leadership qualities of the tank officers at all levels; and (5) teamwork. Due to the foresight of their leaders, the German tanks were equipped with radios.[36] The Soviet tanks generally were not. The Panzerwaffe also boasted a number of higher headquarters, specially designated to direct mobile operations. These included the 1st, 2nd, 3rd, and 4th Panzer Groups, which within six months became the first panzer armies (see Appendix II for a sketch of the higher-level panzer headquarters). For these reasons, in the summer of 1941, the panzer divisions managed to defeat and even humiliate an enemy whose tanks were by a wide margin numerically and qualitatively superior to their own.

There were fierce tank battles from the beginning. Red Army armored units counterattacked with reckless abandon from the first day of the campaign. On June 22, 1941, for example, the 25th Panzer Regiment of the 7th Panzer Division lost half of its vehicles at Olita, on the very first day of the invasion. The 14th Panzer Division alone destroyed 156 Soviet tanks west of Luzk in the first week. At the same time, the 11th and 16th Panzer Divisions were under heavy counterattacks from Soviet tank brigades around Dubno. The 16th Panzer especially suffered heavy losses, but destroyed 215 Soviet tanks. Although the enemy suffered much heavier losses than did the panzer divisions, they had an estimated 15,000 tanks, and, as we have seen, the German tank reserves were inadequate. It was not long before the tank strength of the average panzer division dropped below 100. It would drop even lower in the days ahead.

The greatest shock to the Wehrmacht, however, was not their losses. It was the fact that the Soviets had tanks which were better than theirs. On July 3, two Soviet tank corps attacked the 3rd Panzer Group west of Smolensk with 600 T-34 tanks. The T-34 weighed 28 tons and boasted a 76mm main battle gun. It completely outclassed the PzKw III and IV in every category except communications. And the Soviets classified the T-34 as a medium tank! Shortly thereafter, the KV-1 heavy tank made its appearance. It weighed 48 tons and carried a 76mm or 85mm high-velocity main battle gun, although some mounted a 152mm howitzer.[37]

The German reaction to the T-34 bordered on panic. Many officers wanted to simply copy the T-34, but this was impossible, because it had an aluminum diesel motor, and Germany lacked the aluminum. Instead, a commission of industrialists, manufacturers, and experts from the Army Weapons Office was immediately formed to study the problem. They acted quickly and, in November 1941, the Army Weapons Office made its decision, based on their findings. To combat the new Soviet tanks, it would build two tanks of its own: the PzKw V "Panther" (weighing up to 35 tons) and the PzKw VI "Tiger" (weighing up to 60 tons).

Despite their quantitative and qualitative inferiority, the panzer divisions fought the first great battles of encirclement on the Eastern Front and won them all. Massive Soviet forces were destroyed at Minsk, Smolensk, Uman, Vyasma, Bryansk, and Chernigovka on the Sea of Azov, just to mention a few. (See Appendix III for a chronology of this campaign, as well as of World War II.) In the Kiev pocket, the 2nd and 1st Panzer Groups (led by Guderian and von Kleist, respectively) encircled several Red armies. They were subsequently mopped up by the infantry. When the battle ended on September 20, Army Group South had captured 667,000 men, 3,718 guns, and 884 armored vehicles. It was, however, not enough. Due to the weather and the inadequate Soviet road system, the panzer spearheads sputtered in October and ground to a halt in early December. On December 6, Stalin launched his first winter offensive, and the Wehrmacht was soon in full retreat.

Instead of concentrating on reinforcing and sending replacements and new equipment to his veteran divisions, Hitler ordered the creation of new formations. As the war progressed, in fact, he became obsessed with numbers of divisions, even though casualties reduced his experienced units to the size of regiments. This short-sighted policy applied to the Panzerwaffe as well. As early as the beginning of October, Hitler (through OKH) ordered the creation of the 22nd, 23rd, and 24th Panzer Divisions. In February 1942, OKH ordered the

formation of the 25th Panzer Division in Norway as well. In the meantime, the
5th Light Division in North Africa was upgraded and renamed the 21st Panzer
Division.

Germany invaded Russia in 1941 by attacking on three sectors: northern,
central, and southern (as controlled by Army Groups North, Center, and South).
By the end of the spring thaw of 1942, it was only strong enough to assume the
offensive in one sector. Hitler chose the south. Consequently, OKH reduced the
tank strength of most of the panzer divisions on the other sectors to one battalion
per panzer regiment. Army Group South directed the offensive, which was less
successful, initially, than the Wehrmacht hoped. After launching an unsuccessful
offensive of their own against Kharkov, the Soviets, in general, retreated in
the direction of the Caucasus and Stalingrad, instead of fighting and allowing
themselves to be encircled. Hitler then made a decisive mistake: he divided
Army Group South into Army Groups B and A, and sent them toward Stalingrad
and the Caucasus, respectively. In doing so, he fatally divided his strength.
Army Group B was forced to defend its flanks with foreign allies (Hungarians,
Italians, and Romanians), while the 6th Army bled itself white in street fighting
in Stalingrad. Its three tank divisions, the 14th, 16th, and 24th, were among the
units which suffered needlessly high casualties. By the time Stalin launched his
counteroffensive on November 19, the 14th Panzer had only five tanks left, the
16th Panzer had 28, and the 24th Panzer had 55. All were destroyed by the time
Stalingrad surrendered on February 2, 1943.

Meanwhile, in North Africa, Army Group Afrika's supply lines collapsed. By
May 12, 1943, all German forces in Tunisia had been forced to surrender. Germany lost the 10th, 15th, and 21st Panzer Divisions, as well as several other
elite divisions. The German people called it "Tunisgrad."

Hitler's response was characteristic: he ordered all of the defunct divisions
from both the Stalingrad and Tunisia disasters rebuilt. The 10th Panzer was the
exception: it was never resurrected. The 15th Panzer Division was rebuilt as the
15th Panzer Grenadier Division. Another new unit, the 26th Panzer Division,
was created from the 23rd Panzer Division. The new 21st Panzer Division,
which was equipped with inferior foreign equipment, was sent to France, while
the 16th, 24th, and 26th went to Italy.

Hitler had relieved General Guderian of the command of the 2nd Panzer
Army on December 25, 1941, for retreating against orders. On February 20,
1943, he summoned him to Fuehrer Headquarters (now at Vinniza in Ukraine)
and recalled him to active duty. Guderian was appointed Inspector General of
Panzer Troops, effective February 28, 1943. In his memoirs, Guderian is critical
of General Kurt Zeitzler (the chief of the General Staff) and other generals for
not receiving the new inspectorate positively enough.[38] Their reaction, however,
is completely understandable. The Wehrmacht already suffered from a divided
command and this further fragmented it. The inspectorate (which included mobile or *Schnelle Truppen*—motorized, mechanized, and reconnaissance units
and antitank formations, but not assault gun units) was now placed under the

Panzer Inspectorate, which was independent of the Home Army (i.e., OKH) or OKW.[39] In addition, a Panzer Troops Command was established in each Wehrkreis. Although still part of the Replacement Army, it came primarily under the command and control of the Panzer Inspectorate.

The 155th and 233rd Motorized Reserve Divisions (at Ulm and Frankfurt/Oder respectively) also became part of the Panzer Inspectorate. They were converted into reserve panzer divisions shortly thereafter, and the 233rd was sent to Denmark.

In the fall of 1942, 11 new, independent battalions were created. Numbered 500 through 510, they were equipped with PzKw VI Tiger tanks.[40] The 501st and 504th Heavy Panzer Battalions were sent to North Africa and destroyed in "Tunisgrad." The rest were sent to the Eastern Front. Here they were attached to panzer divisions on an "as needed" basis, to add punch to attacks, offensives, and counteroffensives. As the war continued, they were often needed to make offensive action possible at all.

In Russia in 1941, Hitler launched offensives on all three major sectors simultaneously. In 1942, he could only attack on one. In 1943, he had to limit his offensive action to one part of one sector. He chose the Kursk area and attacked with the 9th Army and 4th Panzer Army, with Army Detachment Kempf covering the 4th Panzer's right flank.

During Operation Citadel, as the Germans code named their Kursk offensive, the army employed the new Panther and Tiger heavy tanks in large numbers for the first time. Unfortunately for the Third Reich, Hitler delayed launching the offensive from May (as originally proposed by Field Marshal Erich von Manstein, the commander in chief of Army Group South) to July 5. As a result, the Soviets were ready. On the first day of the battle, the Germans destroyed 400 Soviet tanks. But by now, they had more than 10,000 in the sector. The Germans had only 1,568 tanks and approximately 500 assault guns.

On the night of July 10, the Reds began their counteroffensives against the 4th Panzer Army. On July 12, they struck the 2nd Panzer Army (just north of the 9th Army) with 3,000 tanks. General Walter Model, commander of the 9th Army, was forced to pull three panzer divisions out of the attack to deal with the new threat, enabling the Soviets to concentrate their reserves against the 4th Panzer Army. On July 15, the offensive was halted. It had gained only 30 miles, at a cost of 1,500 tanks and assault guns. The Soviets lost twice that many, but they had four times as many.

From this point on, all roads led backward for the German Wehrmacht.

The years 1943 through 1945 are a chronicle of the efforts of the German armed forces to stave off total defeat, a strategy complicated by the irrational commands of the Fuehrer. Throughout this period, the Panzerwaffe acted as a "fire brigade" or as a rearguard for the retreating armies on all fronts.

By late 1943, the panzer force made up 10.7 percent of the German field army.[41] They now, however, made up a disproportionate percentage of the Wehrmacht's increasingly limited striking potential. When Germany invaded Russia in 1941, it had 120 frontline infantry divisions. Nearly all were first-class divisions—i.e., they possessed full offensive power. The losses in Russia, however, were massive, especially during the winter of 1941–42. More than 30 percent of those who crossed into Russia in 1941 were casualties. Naturally, the highest proportion of the losses were suffered in the infantry. By 1942, the average German infantry division in Russia had little or no offensive potential. Very few were first-rate units. To make matters worse, OKH had to reduce the combat effectiveness of the average infantry division in Army Groups North and Center to dangerously low levels to make it possible for Army Group South to launch its offensive that summer. The Stalingrad disaster, therefore, represented an even larger catastrophe than even its numbers indicated, because nearly all of the divisions lost there were first-class units. By mid-1943, the German Army only had about a dozen infantry divisions left which had more than minimal offensive potential. The burden of the counterattack and the offensive, therefore, fell almost solely to the panzer divisions.[42]

There were plenty of counterattacks to be launched. In early January 1944, for example, the city of Kovel was encircled. The 4th and 5th Panzer Divisions broke through Soviet lines and liberated the garrison.

In January 1944, the Russians broke the Siege of Leningrad. The 12th Panzer Division and the 502nd Heavy Panzer Battalion were hastily sent to the endangered sector, where they helped cover the withdrawal of Army Group North to the Panther Line.

In early 1944, eight German divisions (approximately 60,000 men) were encircled at Cherkassy. The 1st Panzer Army counterattacked, using the 1st, 3rd, 11th, 14th, 16th, and 17th Panzer Divisions. They managed to rescue about half of the encircled force.

In March 1944, the entire 1st Panzer Army was encircled near Kamenez-Podolsk. Brilliantly led by Hans Valentin Hube, the entire army, including the 1st, 3rd, 6th, 11th, 16th, 17th, and 19th Panzer Divisions, broke out and reached German lines in eastern Galicia on April 6.

The Soviet offensives were finally halted by mud, but there was nothing Germany could do to prevent Anglo-American aid from reaching the Russians. Between 1942 and 1945, Washington and London sent 13,000 tanks to the Red Army. The number of Soviet tanks built in the same period is not clear, but it was easily twice as great as that. Worse still, the Soviet tanks were qualitatively superior to the German tanks. German tank strength, meanwhile, peaked at 5,481 in early June 1944,[43] but about half of these were inoperative because of the failures of the German spare parts industry. The Third Reich managed to fight on in the East only because the quality of the German tank crews was never matched by Stalin's men.

Germany had lost its chance to win the war in December 1941, when it failed to take Moscow. In June 1944, it had its last chance to impose stalemate on the Allies, if it could repulse the D-Day invasion. The British and Americans landed on the shores of Normandy on June 6, 1944. Due to the interference of Allied fighter-bombers and the absence of several senior German commanders, including Field Marshal Rommel, the great panzer counterattack the Desert Fox envisioned was launched on June 9—48 hours later than Rommel had planned. It was too late. Rommel managed to tie down the Allies in hedgerow country, but was unable to throw them back into the sea. Because Hitler refused to send him infantry divisions from the 15th Army, Rommel was forced to commit his panzer divisions to hold the front in the *bocage* country—excellent terrain for infantry. When the Allies finally broke out into the interior of France—excellent tank country—Rommel's successors had virtually no tanks left. A good example was the Panzer Lehr Division. Formed in early 1944, it was the strongest army tank division in France on June 5, 1944, boasting almost 200 tanks. On June 6 and 7, during its approach march to Normandy, the division lost a third of its armored strength. By June 19, it had lost 123 tanks. By July 6, after a month of fighting in Normandy, it did not have a single operational panzer left.[44]

Hitler compounded the disaster in Normandy by refusing to allow a timely retreat. As a result, by the time the remnants of Army Group B escaped behind the Seine, it had 100 to 120 tanks and assault guns left. It had lost 2,300 tanks and assault guns in Normandy. And the retreat was not over.

Meanwhile, in the East, Stalin attacked Army Group Center with 22 armies, including several tank and guard armies—166 divisions in all. Army Group Center faced the onslaught with 36 divisions—34 of them infantry and two panzer grenadier. (There were no panzer divisions at the front and only one—the 20th Panzer—in reserve.) The army group was slaughtered; it was a disaster larger than Stalingrad. The 5th Panzer Division and 505th Heavy Panzer Battalion were sent to close the gap between the 3rd Panzer Army and the 4th Army on June 28, but it was too late. By the time the Russians outran their supply lines and the situation was stabilized, it was September and the front was in Poland.

In an effort to maximize the striking power of his tanks, Hitler ordered the creation of panzer brigades. Formed in the summer of 1944, they numbered 101 to 113. At full strength, they consisted of a staff company; a tank battalion of four companies (each company with 17 PzKw IVs or Panthers); a panzer grenadier battalion (with a staff company and four line companies); a panzer engineer company; a workshop section; and a transport section. The experiment was a terrible failure. The brigades were not strong enough and their formation violated the principle of unit integrity, for they were hastily formed and almost immediately committed to combat. The men who served in them were thrown into battle with strangers. At the same time, the veteran panzer units, which were famous throughout the world for their military teamwork, were denied the new equipment, which went to the inexperienced panzer brigades, where it was quickly lost. Several of the new brigades were committed to the Western Front in the fall of 1944 and were quickly destroyed. None achieved better than mediocre results and most did not accomplish even that.

The fact that Hitler had lost confidence in the General Staff and the army further complicated the situation for the panzer divisions. In 1943, the first SS panzer division was created. By 1944, the bulk of the best and newest equipment (including tanks) were going to the SS units, which had excellent human material (in the military sense), but whose officers often lacked the solid, professional leadership and General Staff training of the army units. Appendix IV gives a brief profile of the SS panzer units.

That same summer, the Panzer Division Type 44 and the Panzer Regiment Type 44 were established. Under this table of organization, a full-strength panzer division would have less than 12,000 men (as compared to more than 17,000 in 1939), and would have 86 PzKw IVs and 73 Panthers, as well as nine command vehicles. German tank strength was thus further diluted.

By the summer of 1944, Panther production reached its peak and a new tank was introduced: the Tiger II or King Tiger. Produced by Henschel, it was similar to the Panther but was much heavier, weighing in at 68 tons. It first saw action on the Eastern Front, when the 503rd Panzer Battalion "Feldherrnhalle" was thrown into action. Unfortunately for the Third Reich, the King Tiger brigades fared no better than the other panzer brigades. By early August, the brigade had already lost all of its heavy tanks.

As the German forces in the West pulled back into the Siegfried Line and the Soviet juggernaut temporarily ran out of steam on the Vistula, Guderian et al. again reorganized the Panzerwaffe. Panzer Division Tatra was formed in August, but it was a tank division in name only, since it only had one panzer company. The former independent panzer brigades were integrated into existing tank divisions, since it was clear to everyone that the panzer brigade experiment had failed. Several independent panzer battalions were upgraded to brigade status, the 109th Panzer Brigade was used to create Panzer Division Feldherrnhalle, and the 110th Panzer Brigade was used to rebuild the 13th Panzer Division. Several new panzer regiments were formed, including Panzer Regiment Fuehrer Begleit Division, Panzer Regiment Grossdeutschland, and Panzer Regiment Kurmark. Most importantly, the 6th Panzer Army was established in September. Along with the 5th Panzer and 7th Armies, its mission was to defeat the Allies in the Battle of the Bulge.

After Hitler's Ardennes Offensive failed in December, 1944, the days of the Third Reich were numbered. OKH prepared for the defense of the Fatherland by establishing Panzer Division 45. Under this table of organization, a panzer division had a tank regiment and a panzer grenadier regiment. The panzer regiment consisted of a staff and staff company, a panzer battalion, and a panzer grenadier battalion. The panzer battalion had 40 tanks (half of them Panthers, half of them PzKw IVs), 22 37mm and 20mm antiaircraft guns, and a workshop section. The panzer grenadier regiment had two battalions, each with three panzer grenadier companies (in SPW armored cars), three 20mm flak guns, a column of six PzKw IVs, and a supply company. The remaining panzer grenadier regiments lost their vehicles and became marching infantry, because Germany no longer had enough fuel to keep them motorized. Usually, these units were transferred to the infantry. All totalled, the 1945-type panzer division had 54 tanks—a far cry from the 200-plus tank divisions which so confidently overran Poland and France just a few years before. The panzer grenadier divisions already had a battalion of tanks and were now reorganized in exactly the same manner, so that the distinction between the tank and motorized infantry divisions disappeared altogether.

In 1945, as the Battle of the Reich wore on, dozens of new units were created. Almost none of them had significant fighting power. Several of these units were panzer divisions, but in name only. They included Panzer Divisions Holstein, Silesia, Jueterbog, Muencheberg, Feldherrnhalle, and Clausewitz, among others. There was little they could do, however. The German panzer division, however, fought to the end. Rommel's old 7th Panzer Division, for example, fought to its last tank, as did the 13th Panzer Division in Budapest, while the 12th and 14th Panzer Divisions, isolated in the Courland Pocket, saved Army Group North more than once against overwhelming odds. They could not stave off "Final Victory," however. As late as April 26, 1945, OKW commended the 17th Panzer Division and especially its 27th Panzer Division for destroying or capturing 103 Soviet tanks and assault guns and 104 guns in Silesia between March 15 and April 10.[45] Four days later, on April 30, Hitler committed suicide. For the next 11 days, every division that could do so fled to the west, in an effort to surrender to the Anglo-Americans, rather than to the Russians. The last panzer divisions lay down their arms on May 9, leaving behind a legacy that endures to this day.

## NOTES

1. Matthew Cooper and James Lucas, *Panzer: The Armored Force of the Third Reich* (New York, 1976): 7 (hereafter cited as "Cooper and Lucas").

2. The term *Kampfwagen* referred only to tanks with turrets that turned—i.e., not to assault guns, even if they were mounted on tank chassis. Kampfwagen (or *Kampfpanzer* from 1941 on) included the PzKw I–VI in all of their variations and all belonged to the panzer troops.

3. A holder of the Pour le Mérite, Alfred von Vollard-Bockelberg became chief of the Army Personnel Office in 1929 and retired in 1933 as a general of artillery. Recalled to active duty in 1939, he held a number of noncombat posts, the most notable of which was Military Commandant of Paris. He retired again in 1940. Arrested by the Soviets in 1945, he disappeared and was never seen again. Erich von Tschischwitz (1870–1958), who held the Pour le Mérite with Oak Leaves, retired as a general of infantry in 1927.

4. After Napoleon decisively defeated the Prussian Army at Jena and Auerstadt in 1806, King Frederick Wilhelm III appointed an Army Reform Commission, headed by Major General Count Wilhelm von Scharnhorst, a Hanoverian and chief of staff to the commander in chief of the Prussian Army. Scharnhorst had foreseen the disastrous defeat. The most prominent members of the commission were Count August Wilhelm Anton Neidhardt von Gneisenau, a South German from the tiny principality of Ansbach,

and Karl von Clausewitz, the Prussian director of the War Academy, whose massive philosophy *On War* is still required reading at many service schools throughout the world. Scharnhorst died of wounds suffered at the Battle of Leipzig in 1813, which threw Napoleon's decimated army out of Germany and back to the borders of France. See T. N. Dupuy, *A Genius For War: The German Army and General Staff, 1807–1945* (Fairfax, Va., 1984), pp. 17–42.

5. Moltke, chief of the General Staff from 1857 to 1888, decisively defeated the French Army at Sedan in 1870, captured Emperor Napoleon III (1870) and took Paris (1870). Schlieben was chief of the General Staff from 1891 until his death in 1912.

6. The Treaty of Versailles outlawed the German General Staff. Instead of disbanding it, however, Seeckt merely camouflaged it under the name *Truppenamt* (Troop Office).

7. James S. Corum, *The Roots of the Blitzkrieg: Hans von Seeckt and German Military Reform* (Lawrence, Ks., 1992), p. 124, citing *Heeresdienstvorschrift 487*, Part 2, pp. 42–69 (hereafter cited as "Corum").

8. Ibid, p. 127.

9. Konstantin von Altrock was born in Breslau in 1861 and received his commission in 1881. A General Staff officer since 1901, he was promoted to major general when World War I broke out and commanded the 60th Infantry Brigade (1914–15) and 28th Reserve Division (1918). He retired in 1919.

10. Corum, p. 127.

11. Completely overshadowed by Guderian in the 1930s, Volckheim led a panzer regiment in World War II and rose to the rank of colonel. He became commander of the Panzer School in 1941.

12. Brandt later became a lieutenant colonel in the SS. He was still writing highly technical articles on armor and AFVs (armored fighting vehicles) for the *Militaer Wochenblatt* in the 1940s.

13. Corum, pp. 130–31. Baron Werner von Fritsch was an artillery officer who was promoted rapidly. He was a colonel general in 1938 when Hitler dismissed him on trumped-up charges of homosexuality. In reality, Hitler suspected Fritsch of being an anti-Nazi and wanted him out of the way, so he could "Nazify" the armed forces. Fritsch apparently committed suicide during the Siege of Warsaw in 1939 by deliberately exposing himself to Polish fire.

14. Ibid, p. 130.

15. Otto von Stuelpnagel (b. 1878) retired from the army as a lieutenant general in 1931. In 1935, he returned to active duty as commandant of the Luftwaffe's Air War Academy. Promoted to general of fliers in 1936, he was forced into retirement by Hermann Goering in 1938. Recalled to active duty in the army in 1939, he served as military governor of France from 1940 to 1942, when he retired again, this time as a general of infantry. Arrested as a war criminal in 1945, he committed suicide in his cell in Paris in early 1948.

16. Roger Edwards, *Panzer: A Revolution in Warfare, 1939–1945* (London, 1989): 28 (hereafter cited as "Edwards, *Panzer*").

17. Oswald Lutz was born in Oehringen, Bavaria, on November 6, 1876. He joined the service as a Fahnenjunker in a Bavarian Army railroad battalion in 1894. Commissioned second lieutenant in the 1st Bavarian Engineer Battalion in 1896, he fought in World War I and served in the Reichsheer. Lutz was promoted to lieutenant colonel in 1923, colonel in 1928, major general on April 1, 1931, lieutenant general on February 1, 1933, and general of panzer troops on November 1, 1935. He was abruptly dismissed

from active duty in February 1938. He was temporarily recalled on September 22, 1941, to head a minor special staff, but he was retired again on May 31, 1942, and was never reemployed. He died in Munich in 1944. Wolf Keilig, *Die Generale des Heeres* (Friedberg: 1983): 213 (hereafter cited as "Keilig").

18. Werner Haupt, *A History of the Panzer Troops*, Edward Force, trans. (West Chester, Pa., 1990): 24 (hereafter cited as "Haupt, *Panzer*").

19. Reichenau later commanded the 10th Army in Poland and the 6th Army in Belgium, France, and Russia. He died as the result of a heart attack suffered on the Eastern Front in January 1942.

20. Heinz Guderian, *Panzer Leader*, Constantine Fitzgibbon, trans. (New York, 1957; reprint ed., New York, 1972): 19 (hereafter cited as "Guderian").

21. Hammerstein had replaced Blomberg as chief of staff in 1929. He became commander in chief of the Army in 1930. A known anti-Nazi and a member of the anti-Hitler conspiracy, Hammerstein briefly commanded the ad hoc Army Detachment A in late 1939, but otherwise was never reemployed. He died in 1943. Adam commanded Army Group C on the West Wall during the Sudetenland crisis of 1938. He so badly annoyed Hitler in this capacity that he was never reemployed. He died in 1948. Schleicher, who served 57 days as chancellor of Germany (1932–33), was murdered by the Gestapo in 1934.

22. Cooper and Lucas: 21.

23. Haupt, *Panzer*: 18.

24. Paulus later commanded the 6th Army and was largely responsible for the Stalingrad disaster. He was promoted to field marshal on January 31, 1943—the day he surrendered to the Soviets.

25. Army Group 4 was activated on April 1, 1937.

26. Hitler quashed all attempts to court-martial Blomberg, made sure he received his full retirement, and sent him on an around-the-world trip. All expenses were paid by the Nazi Party. He even promised to return Blomberg to active duty when World War II started. By the time the war began, however, Hitler had learned how much the straitlaced Prussian Officer Corps resented Blomberg for making a whore their "first lady." Hitler sent word back to Blomberg that he could not reemploy him until he divorced his wife. That settled the matter, as far as Blomberg was concerned, and he was never reemployed.

27. Keitel played a discreditable role in the Blomberg affair by turning incriminating evidence over to Hermann Goering. He was promoted to colonel general in late 1938 and to field marshal on July 19, 1940. Commander in chief of OKW throughout the war, he was executed as a war criminal at Nuremberg on October 16, 1946.

28. Oswald Lutz died in Munich in 1944.

29. An example of Halder's animosity toward Guderian can be seen in the latter's mobilization assignment. In case of war, Halder decreed, Guderian would assume command of a reserve infantry corps. Guderian used his influence with the Fuehrer to get this assignment changed. Halder remained chief of staff until September 1942, when he was sacked by Hitler and never reemployed. He ended the war in a concentration camp.

30. Haupt, *Panzer*: 45.

31. This figure excludes the Panzer Lehr Regiment, which became part of the Home Army.

32. Reinhardt was promoted to general of panzer troops effective June 1, 1940.

33. General of Cavalry Ewald von Kleist (1881–1954), a Prussian nobleman and life-

long cavalry officer, was chosen by OKH to command the panzer forces, under the assumption that his conservative nature would be a counterbalance to Guderian's rashness. Despite his background and lack of experience in armored operations, Kleist performed reasonably well. He later commanded the 1st Panzer Group (subsequently Army) and Army Groups A and South Ukraine. Promoted to field marshal on February 1, 1943, he was dismissed by Hitler on March 31, 1944, and never reemployed. Handed over to the Yugoslavs and then the Russians after the war, he died in a Soviet prison camp.

Hermann Hoth (b. 1885) was another infantry officer who did well in the panzer branch, subsequently commanding the 3rd Panzer Group (1941), 17th Army (1941–42), and 4th Panzer Army (1942–43), all on the Eastern Front. Promoted to colonel general in 1940, he was dismissed by Hitler in late 1943 and never reemployed. He was sentenced to 25 years imprisonment after the war, but this sentence was subsequently reduced and he was a free man by the mid-1950s. Hoth retired to Goslar and was 85 years of age at the time of his death on January 25, 1971.

34. Haupt, *Panzer*: 68

35. These figures exclude 230 Pz Bef Wg (PzKw III command vehicles).

36. Erich Fellgiebel was the officer responsible for designing a radio that could take the punishment of a rough tank ride and continue to operate. This communications genius was named chief signals officer for the High Command of the Armed Forces when the war broke out. He had been chief of the Signals Troops Inspectorate since 1934. He was thus chief signals officer for both the army and OKW. Promoted to general of signals troops in 1940, he was deeply involved in the plot to assassinate Adolf Hitler and was hanged on September 4, 1944. Fellgiebel had been born in Breslau in 1886 and joined the army as a Fahnenjunker (officer cadet) in a telegraph battalion in 1905.

37. Albert Seaton, *The Russo-German War, 1941–45* (New York, 1970): 96 (hereafter cited as "Seaton").

38. Guderian: 230–31. Kurt Zeitzler succeeded Halder as chief of the General Staff in September, 1942, and was replaced by Guderian himself on July 21, 1944. Like Halder, Zeitzler ended up in a concentration camp.

39. Under this arrangement, mounted and motorcycle troops were transferred to the infantry and were not part of the Panzer Inspectorate. The assault gun units came under the artillery branch.

40. The 500th, 501st, 502nd, 503rd, and 504th Heavy Panzer Battalions were created from scratch under the direction of Wehrkreis VI in Muenster. The 505th was from the 5th Panzer Division, the 506th was formed from the II/33rd Panzer Regiment, the 507th was from the I/4th Panzer Regiment, the 508th was from III/4th Panzer Regiment, the 36th Panzer Regiment provided cadres for the 509th Heavy Panzer Battalion, and the 510th was formed from survivors of the 14th Panzer Division. All operated as independent units until they were destroyed or surrendered, save the 509th. It was made part of the Fuehrer Begleit Division in late 1944.

41. Haupt, *Panzer*: 108.

42. John Desch, "The 1941 German Army/The 1944–45 U.S. Army: A Comparative Analysis of Two Forces in Their Primes," in *Hitler's Army: The Evolution and Structure of German Forces* by the Editors of Command Magazine (Conshohocken, Pa., 1995): 86–87.

43. Werner Haupt, *Das Buch der Panzertruppen, 1916–1945* (Friedberg, 1989): 115.

44. Haupt, *Panzer*: 121.

45. Ibid: 125.

# CHAPTER 2

# The Wehrkreise

The unsung hero of the German war effort in World War II was undoubtedly the *Wehrkreise*—the German military districts. They performed their tasks so efficiently that they kept the German Army in the field against most of the rest of the world for six years, despite the "genius" of the Fuehrer, but operated so quietly that many historians have never even heard of them.

The Wehrkreise were responsible for the organization and administration of German territory, as defined by the Third Reich. This task included implementing the German draft, including registration, conscription, and the actual call-up and induction of men; mobilization; training new recruits, noncommissioned officers, and officer candidates; providing advanced training to all ranks, including senior officers; administering training facilities, military schools, and military installations within the Reich; furnishing trained replacements to field units; forming new combat, combat support, and service support units of all branches; forming new higher headquarters; the development and testing of new weapons; providing field replacement units to the combat divisions; and emergency defense of home territory. With all of these responsibilities, the Wehrkreise had considerably more responsibility than its American counterparts, the U.S. Army's military districts; for that reason (i.e., because they are hardly comparable), the words Wehrkreise and *Wehrkreis* (its singular form) will not be translated into English in this book.

The Wehrkreise date back to Imperial times. During World War I, German mobilization was so rapid and efficient that it earned the begrudging admiration of the entire world, although the role played by the Wehrkreise generally was not known outside of Germany. Indeed, in the Wehrkreise, the Second Reich, the Reichsheer, and the Third Reich best fulfilled the long-standing General Staff axiom: "Great accomplishments, small display. More reality than appearance."

When the Reichsheer was created after the Treaty of Versailles, the Army Command (Seeckt) reduced the number of Wehrkreise to seven, numbered I to VII. They were both corps headquarters and territorial commands. By August 1939, there were 15 Wehrkreise, numbered I to XIII, XVII, and XVIII. Each had two components: a primary (field command) component, which was a corps headquarters; and a deputy component. Upon mobilization, on August 27, 1939, the German Army divided into two almost mutually exclusive parts, which for the most part dealt with distinctly different tasks throughout the war. The primary component, which was directly concerned with military operations, became a corps headquarters (or, in some cases, an army headquarters) and was part of the field army (*Feldheer*). The part left behind came under the deputy corps commander (or Wehrkreis commander), whose responsibilities were outlined above.

When war broke out, the High Command of the Army (OKH) established a separate headquarters at Zossen to direct the field army. To control the Wehrkreise, it created the *Ersatzheer*, the Replacement Army, which was also known as the Home Army. It occupied the huge building complex on the Bendlerstrasse in Berlin, which formerly housed the Ministry of War. Its commander, General of Artillery Friedrich "Fritz" Fromm, held the title Chief of Army Equipment and Commander in Chief of the Replacement Army (*Chef der Heeresruestung und Befehlshaber des Ersatzheeres*). It was responsible for keeping the rest of the army in the field by providing trained replacements, organizing and transporting new units to the front(s), and providing the field armies with equipment and supplies, as well as the military administration of the Zone of Interior. Later its functions were expanded to include the administration of certain occupied territories.

In mid-1939, as the army prepared to mobilize for the invasion of Poland, the XIV, XV, and XVI Corps (which controlled Germany's motorized, light, and panzer divisions, respectively) had no territorial responsibilities and thus no deputy components. Likewise, XIX Corps in Vienna controlled the 2nd Panzer and 4th Light Divisions, but had no territorial components or responsibilities. When these corps mobilized, there were no deputy components to leave behind. Table 2.1 shows the Wehrkreise and their headquarters. No Wehrkreis XIV, XV, XVI, or XIX were ever created.

In October 1939, after Poland was conquered, two new Wehrkreise were created to occupy this territory: XX and XXI. (There were significant numbers of ethnic Germans or Volksdeutsche in these regions, so the areas in question were largely—but by no means exclusively—foreign territory.) Later, Wehrkreise Bohemia and Moravia (*Boehmen und Maehren*) and General Government (*Generalgouvernement*) were added in the former Czechoslovakia and Poland, respectively. These were distinctively non-German areas, but nevertheless came under the command of the Replacement Army. Later, as the war progressed and the Third Reich expanded, new areas of occupied territory came under the command of administrative area headquarters (*Oberfeldkommandodanturen*) and

**Table 2.1**
**The Wehrkreise and Their Territorial Responsibilities**

| Wehrkreis | Headquarters | Territorial Extent |
|---|---|---|
| I | Koenigsberg | East Prussia; extended in 1939 to include Memel and portions of northern Poland |
| II | Stettin | Mecklenburg and Pomerania |
| III | Berlin | Altmark, Neumark and Brandenburg |
| IV | Dresden | Saxony and part of Thueringia; part of northern Bohemia was annexed later |
| V | Stuttgart | Wuerttemberg and part of Baden; extended in 1940 to include Alsace |
| VI | Muenster | Westphalia and the Rhineland; parts of eastern Belgium were added later |
| VII | Munich | Southern and central Bavaria |
| VIII | Breslau | Silesia; the Sudetenland was added in late 1938 and parts of Moravia and southwestern Poland were added later |
| IX | Kassel | Hessen and part of Theuringia |
| X | Hamburg | Schleswig-Holstein and northern Hanover; part of Danish Slesvig was added in 1940 |
| XI | Hanover | Burnswick (Braunschweig), Anhalt, and most of Hanover |
| XII | Wiesbaden | Eifel, the Palatinate, and the Saar; part of Hessen; Lorraine (including Metz and Nancy) was added after the fall of France |
| XIII | Nurenberg | Northern Bavaria; part of western Bohemia was added in 1938 |
| XVII | Vienna | Northern Austria; extended in 1939 to include the southern districts of the former Czechoslovakia |
| VIII | Salzburg | Southern Austria; extended in 1941 to include the northern parts of Slovenia |
| XX | Danzig | The former Danzig Free State, the former Polish Corridor, and the western part of East Prussia |
| General Gouvernement | Warsaw | Created in 1943 and included central and most of southern Poland |
| Bohemia and Moravia | Prague | Created in late 1942 and included most of what was formerly Czechoslovakia |

*Note*: The pre-war XIV, XV, XVI, and XIX Corps had no deputy components and no territorial responsibilities. No Wehrkreise bearing these numbers ever existed during World War II.

The territorial adjustments made by Reichsfuehrer-SS Himmler (the commander in chief of the Replacement Army after July 20, 1944) are not included in this table and were relatively minor in any event.

subarea headquarters (*Feldkommandanturen*), which were not part of the Home Army.

From 1939 to 1942, the Replacement Army controlled all replacement and training units, including the panzer and mobile troops. Despite the unsavory role he played in the July 20, 1944, attempt to assassinate Adolf Hitler and overthrow the Nazi regime, it must be admitted that Friedrich Fromm did an excellent job commanding the Replacement Army. Hitler himself recognized this on July 19, 1940, when he promoted Fromm to colonel general. He also decorated Fromm with the Knights' Cross. This award was almost unique in the history of the Wehrmacht, because it was normally reserved only for those who distinguished themselves in combat or in directing very large operations against hostile forces; indeed, in 1940, it was only one cut below being the German equivalent of the Congressional Medal of Honor.

A detailed description of the call-up and induction of individual recruits will be covered later in another book. Suffice it to say that, in Germany, the system worked well. Training was, in a sense, conducted by the division to which the recruit or volunteer was assigned. When a regiment went to war, it left behind a battalion cadre at its home station. This battalion bore the number of the regiment and was known as its *Ersatz* (replacement or replacement training) battalion. Its primary mission was to receive recruits, train them, and send them on to the field regiment as trained replacements. Similarly, independent battalions (such as a division's panzer reconnaissance unit) would leave behind replacement training companies.

Later in the war, transfer companies (*Marschkompanien*) were formed. They were units of trained replacements ready to depart for the field units.

The first major change in the Wehrkreise system occurred in October 1942, when almost all of the replacement training battalions were broken into two components: an induction and replacement unit (which retained the name Ersatz) and a new training battalion, called the *Ausbildungseinheit*. The job of the Ersatz was to receive the new recruits from the conscription offices, issue them their equipment, give them a short military indoctrination course, and forward them to their training units as quickly as possible. The Ausbildungseinheit units (which bore the same number as their sisters, the Ersatz units) trained the recruits and sent them on to their affiliated field units.

The purposes of this measure were to use training units as occupation troops and to provide a reserve pool of partially trained emergency units in occupied areas, for use as needed. By the fall of 1942, Germany's manpower was growing short, but the demands of the front continued to increase. By sending training units to the field armies' rear areas, combat divisions were released for frontline duty. Training units were also used to deal with partisans. This arrangement had the added advantage of allowing the training cadres to conduct more realistic training than would have been possible inside Germany. Large numbers of training units were sent to France, the Low Countries, Denmark, Poland, the Baltic States, and, of course, Russia. Later, they were sent to northern Italy as well.

The Ersatz battalions in Germany which retained their training elements were called replacement training (*Ersatz- und Ausbildungsbataillone*) battalions. They amounted to about one-third of all of the original Ersatz units.[1]

Beginning in the latter part of 1942, the training units in occupied territories became part of reserve divisions, which were still part of the Replacement Army. The divisional headquarters of these units were usually upgraded replacement division headquarters or special administrative division staffs (*Divisionskommando z.b.V.*). Other special administrative division staffs were created within the Wehrkreise to assist in the replacement function. Three motorized or panzer reserve divisions were formed in this process.

As we have seen, Heinz Guderian's Inspectorate of Panzer Troops became an independent command, responsible directly to the Fuehrer and not to OKH, in February 1943. Among its other tasks, the Inspectorate was responsible for providing replacements and training for all mobile troops. To accomplish this task, Guderian created a Panzer Troops Command (*Kommander der Panzertruppen*) in every Wehrkreis. Although primarily responsible only to the Inspectorate, it also coordinated its activities with the Wehrkreis commander and his staff, which supplied it with recruits and which assisted it in administrative matters.

Panzer Troops Command III (located in Wehrkreis III) provides a good example of how the panzer commands were set up. In December 1943, it included the panzer troops command staff, a brigade-level staff, located at Kuestrin; the 5th Panzer Replacement Battalion at Neuruppin; the 83rd Panzer Grenadier Replacement Regiment (3rd, 8th, and 9th Panzer Grenadier Replacement Battalions), located at Schwedt/Oder; the 3rd Motorized Grenadier Replacement Regiment (8th, 29th, and 50th Motorized Replacement Battalions), located at Frankfurt/Oder; the 3rd Panzer Reconnaissance Replacement Battalion at Freienwalde; the 4th Panzer Reconnaissance Replacement and Training Battalion at Stahnsdorf; the 3rd Tank Destroyer (*Panzerjaeger*) Replacement Battalion at Potsdam; the 43rd Replacement and Training Battalion at Spremberg; and the I Feldherrnhalle Grenadier Replacement Battalion at Gueterfelde (in Wehrkreis XX). The training units for this command were with the 233rd Reserve Panzer Division in France.[2]

In 1943 and 1944, almost all of the reserve divisions were absorbed by older divisions or were caught up in combat. Their training functions, therefore, reverted back to the Ersatz units of the Home Army and the Panzer Inspectorate. In early 1945, for example, Panzer Troops Command V headquartered at Stuttgart and controlled the 7th Panzer Replacement and Training Battalion at Boeblingen; the 5th Panzer Grenadier Replacement and Training Regiment at Ludwigsburg; the 25th Panzer Grenadier Replacement and Training Regiment at Stuttgart-Zuffenhausen; the 5th Tank Destroyer Replacement and Training Battalion at Karlsruhe; the 86th Panzer Grenadier Signal Replacement and Training Battalion at Stuttgart-Zuffenhausen; 25th Motorized Howitzer Replacement and Training Company at Stuttgart-Zuffenhausen; and possibly the 61st

Heavy Artillery Replacement and Training Battalion (Motorized) and the 260th Motorized Replacement and Training Artillery Battalion as well.[3]

The Wehrkreise system was not disrupted by the coup attempt of July 20, 1944. The fact that Fromm was replaced by Heinrich Himmler also had little negative impact on the system that served Germany so well. Himmler, in fact, instituted some positive chances by simplifying paperwork and increasing the Replacement Army's influence at Fuehrer Headquarters, making it easier for the army to retain personnel formerly earmarked for the navy or the Luftwaffe.

In short, the establishment of the Panzer Inspectorate did not significantly disrupt the Wehrkreise system. Working with the Wehrkreise and the Replacement Army, the Inspectorate continued to provide trained replacements and new units for the panzer forces until the end of the war. Most of the training installations actually continued to function until the Allied tanks rolled up to their front doors.

## NOTES

1. U.S. War Department Technical Manual *TM-E 30–451*, "Handbook on German Military Forces" (Washington, D.C., 1945): I-63. The figure cited is for infantry units, but the proportion was about the same in panzer units.

2. Georg Tessin, *Verbaende und Truppen der deutschen Wehrmacht und Waffen-SS im Zweiten Weltkrieg, 1939–1945* (Osnabrueck, 1973–81), Volume 2: 175 (hereafter cited as "Tessin").

3. Military Intelligence Division, U.S. War Department, "The German Replacement Army (Ersatzheer)" (Washington, D.C., 1945): 93–94, on file at the U.S. Army War College, Carlisle Barracks, Pennsylvania. Hereafter cited as "RA."

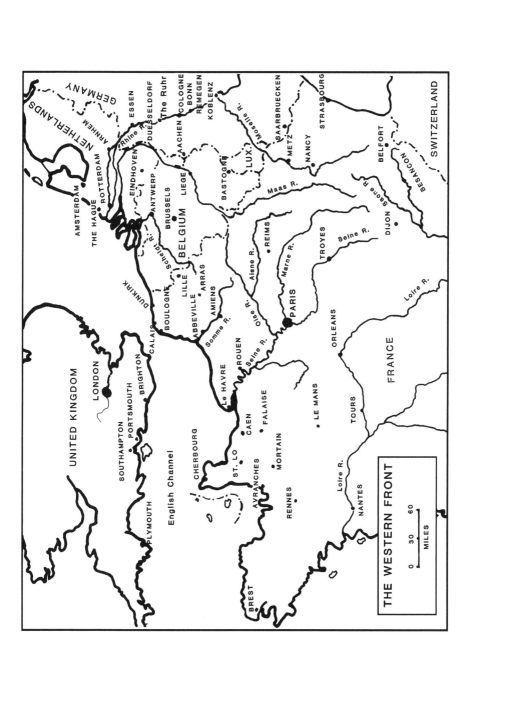

THE WESTERN FRONT

0   30   60
MILES

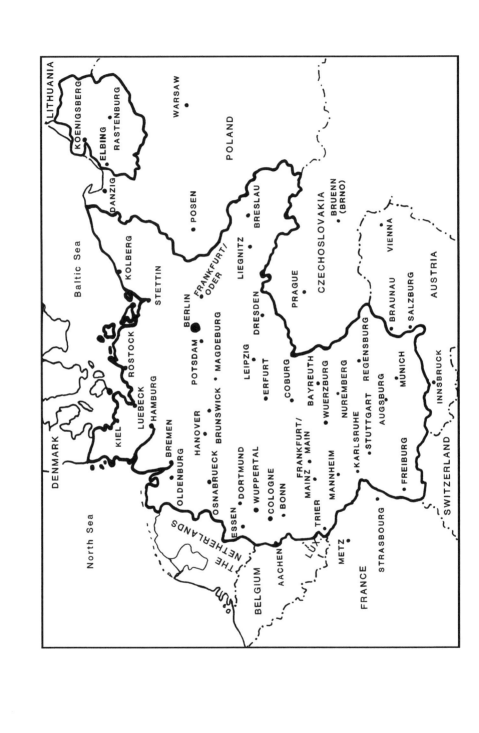

ICELAND

NORWAY

SWEDEN

FINLAND

ESTONIA

IRELAND

DENMARK

LATVIA

LITHUANIA

U. K.

E. Pr.

SOVIET UNION

GERMANY

POLAND

LUX.

FRANCE

SWITZ.

HUNGARY

PORTUGAL

SPAIN

ITALY

YUGOSLAVIA

RUMANIA

Sardinia

BULGARIA

ALB.

GREECE

Sicily

MOROCCO

ALGERIA

TUNISIA

0        200

MILES

Crete

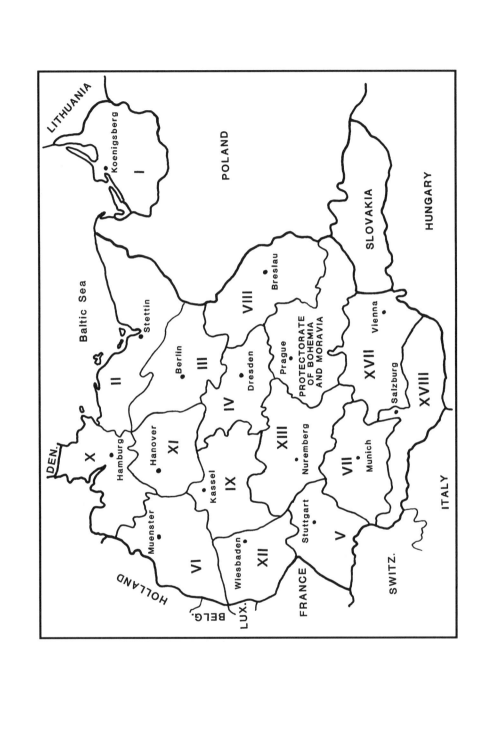

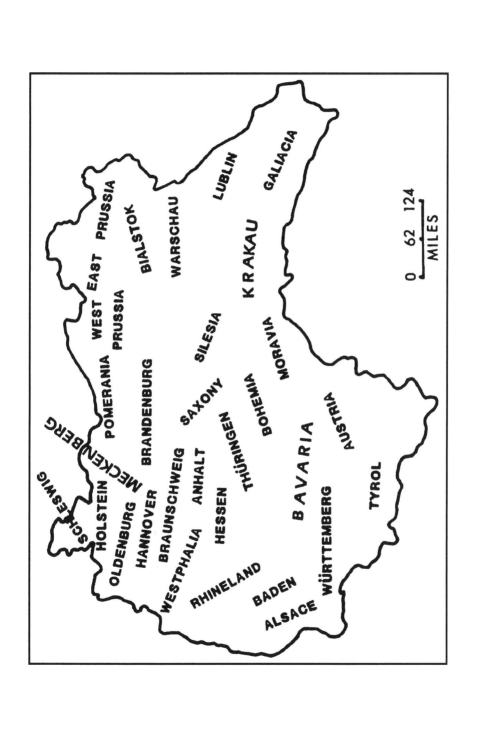

SCHLESWIG
HOLSTEIN
MECKENBERG
POMERANIA
WEST PRUSSIA
EAST PRUSSIA
BIALSTOK
WARSCHAU
LUBLIN
GALIACIA
OLDENBURG
HANNOVER
BRANDENBURG
PRUSSIA
KRAKAU
BRAUNSCHWEIG
ANHALT
SAXONY
SILESIA
WESTPHALIA
HESSEN
THÜRINGEN
MORAVIA
BOHEMIA
RHINELAND
BADEN
BAVARIA
AUSTRIA
ALSACE
WÜRTTEMBERG
TYROL

0   62  124
MILES

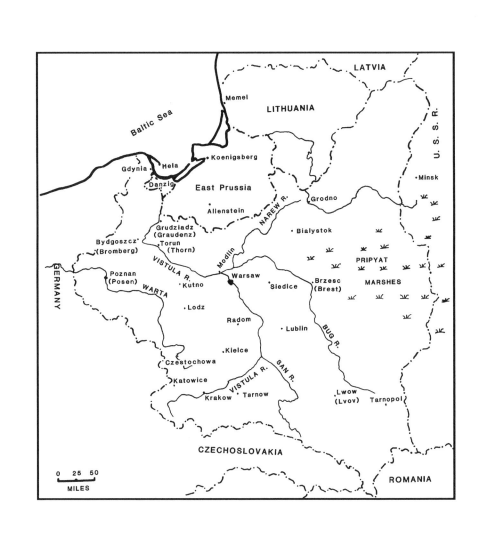

LATVIA

Baltic Sea

Memel

LITHUANIA

Koenigsberg

Gdynia · Hela

Danzig

East Prussia

Minsk

Allenstein

Grodno

NAREW R.

Grudziadz
(Graudenz)

Bialystok

Bydgoszcz
(Bromberg)

Torun
(Thorn)

VISTULA R.

Modlin

PRIPYAT

Poznan
(Posen)

WARTA

· Kutno

Warsaw

Siedice

Brzesc
(Brest)

MARSHES

GERMANY

· Lodz

Radom

Lublin

BUG R.

· Kielce

Czestochowa

Katowice

VISTULA R.

SAN R.

Krakow · Tarnow

Lwow
(Lvov)

Tarnopol

CZECHOSLOVAKIA

0   25  50

MILES

ROMANIA

U. S. S. R.

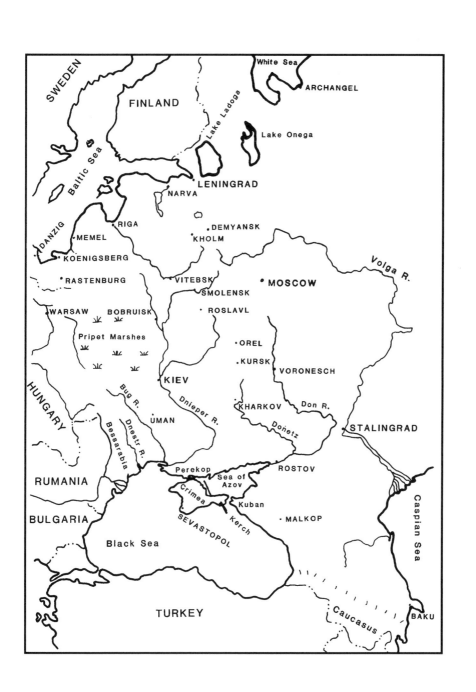

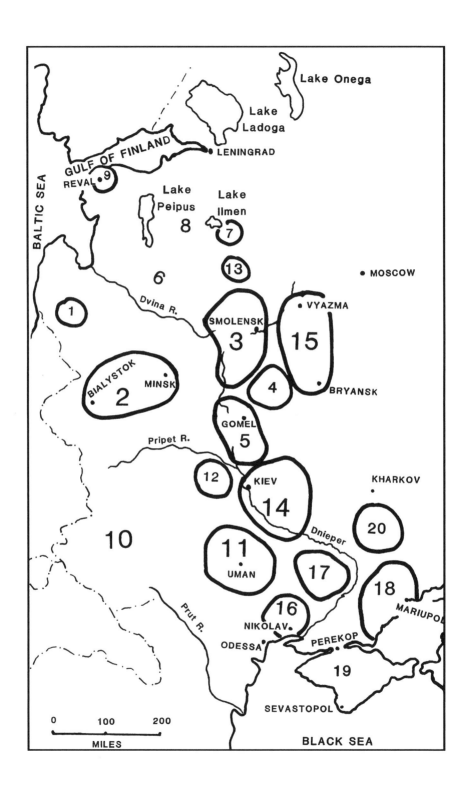

BALTIC SEA

Lake Onega

Lake Ladoga

GULF OF FINLAND

• LENINGRAD

REVAL • ⑨

Lake Peipus

Lake Ilmen

8

⑦

• MOSCOW

6

⑬

Dvina R.

① 

SMOLENSK

③

VYAZMA •

⑮

④

BRYANSK •

BIALYSTOK

② MINSK •

Pripet R.

GOMEL •

⑤

⑫

KIEV •

⑭

KHARKOV •

⑳

10

⑪

UMAN •

⑰

⑱

MARIUPOL

⑯

NIKOLAV •

ODESSA •

Prut R.

Dnieper

PEREKOP •

⑲

SEVASTOPOL •

0    100    200

MILES

BLACK SEA

# THE BATTLES OF ENCIRCLEMENT OF THE EASTERN FRONT, 1941

1.  **Rossizny**: 200 tanks
2.  **Bialystok-Minsk**: 290,000 captured, 3,332 tanks, 1809 guns
3.  **Smolensk**: 310,000 men, 3,205 tanks, 3,120 guns
4.  **Roslavl**: 38,000 men, 250 tanks, 359 guns
5.  **Gomel**: 84,000 men, 144 tanks, 848 guns
6.  **Divina**: 35,000 men, 355 tanks, 655 guns
7.  **Staraya Russa**: 53,000 men, 320 tanks, 695 guns
8.  **Luga**: 250,000 men, 1,170 tanks 3,075 guns
9.  **Reval**: 12,000 men, 91, tanks, 293 guns
10. **Galacia**: 150,000 men, 1,970 tanks, 2,190 guns
11. **Uman**: 103,000 men, 317 tanks, 1,100 guns
12. **Zhitomir**: 18,000 men, 142 tanks, 123 guns
13. **Valdai Hills**: 30,000 men, 400 guns
14. **Kiev**: 667,000 men, 884 tanks, 3,718 guns
15. **Vyazma-Bryansk**: 663,000 men, 1,242 tanks, 5,412 guns
16. **Nikolav**: 60,000 men, 84 tanks, 1,100 guns
17. **Dnieper Bend**: 84,000 men, 199 tanks, 465 guns
18. **Mariupol (Sea of Azov)**: 106,000 men, 212 tanks, 672 guns
19. **Crimea**: 100,000 men, 160 tanks, 700 guns
20. **The Donetz**: 14,000 men, 45 tanks, 69 guns

*Note*: Soviet losses in men refers to those captured only; losses in tanks and guns refer to those captured or destroyed.

# PART TWO

# The Panzer Divisions

## NOTES APPLYING TO ALL PANZER DIVISIONS

Independent battalions had their own numerial designations, such as the 37th Panzer Engineer Battalion. Battalions organic to parent regiments were identified by their Roman numerals, followed by the number of their parent regiment. For example, the III Battalion, 73rd Panzer Artillery Regiment would be designated III/73rd Panzer Artillery Regiment. Companies were expressed by their number, followed by the designation of their parent battalion or regiment. The 1st Company of the 2nd Panzer Regiment, for example, was listed as 1/2nd Panzer Regiment. This practice will be used throughout this book.

In the German Army, only corps-level units and above had chiefs of staff. The division Ia (chief of operations) functioned as the divisional chief of staff. He was also referred to as the first general staff officer of the division. The Ib (chief supply officer) was the second general staff officer. Appendix 5 gives a full roster of all German staff officers at the divisional level.

In addition to the units shown under "Composition," each division had several service support-type units, most of which reported to the Ib. They usually included a supply unit, a medical unit, a field post office, a field police unit, as well as bakery, workshop, rations, and other units. They varied slightly from time to time and division to division. They always bore the auxiliary number of the division. In the 23rd Panzer Division, for example, combat support units bore the number 128—as in 128th Panzer Reconnaissance Battalion, 128th Tank Destroyer Battalion, etc. Likewise, the service support units bore the number 128. In the 23rd Panzer Division, they included the 128th Supply Troop (i.e., Company), 128th Medical Troop, 128th Workshop Company, 128th Bakery Company, 128th Butchery Company, 128th Division Rations Office, 128th Field Post Office, 128th Divisional Mapping Office, and the 128th Field Police Company.

# 1st Panzer Division

**COMPOSITION (early 1943):**   1st Panzer Regiment, 1st Panzer Grenadier Regiment, 113th Panzer Grenadier Regiment, 73rd Panzer Artillery Regiment, 1st Motorcycle Battalion, 4th Panzer Reconnaissance Battalion, 37th Tank Destroyer Battalion, 37th Panzer Engineer Battalion, 37th Panzer Signal Battalion, 299th Army Flak Battalion.

**HOME STATION:**   Weimar, Wehrkreis IX

Formed on October 15, 1935, the 1st Panzer Division initially included the 1st *Schuetzen* (Rifle) Brigade (1st Rifle Regiment and 1st Motorcycle Battalion) and the 1st Panzer Brigade (1st and 2nd Panzer Regiments), as well as the 73rd Artillery (later Panzer Artillery) Regiment and assorted divisional troops. The division consisted mainly of Thuringians, with significant numbers of Saxons and Prussians, and (later) with draftees from other parts of Germany. The bulk of its troops came from the 3rd (Motorized) Cavalry Division at Weimar and the II Motor Transport Demonstration Command (*Kraftfahr-Lehrkommando II*) in the Thueringen (Wehrkreis IX) region. The majority of the divisional staff came from the Lehr command, and the operations staff was from the 3rd Cavalry Division. The signal battalion was formed around the 6th (Signal) Company of the 16th Cavalry Regiment. The staff of the rifle brigade was largely taken from the 1st Motorcycle Rifle Battalion at Langensalza, and many of the brigade's men came from the I/16th Cavalry Regiment at Erfurt. The 1st Rifle Regiment was formed in Weimar from the 11th Cavalry Regiment and I/14th Infantry Regiment (Rifle Regiment Meiningen). The staffs of the 1st Panzer Brigade and 1st Panzer Regiment were from I/Motor Transport Demonstration

Command Ohrduf and their personnel were from the 5th and 6th (Prussian) Cavalry Regiments. The 2nd Panzer Regiment at Eisenach was formed from the former 7th Cavalry Regiment Breslau and part of the II/Kraftfahr-Lehrkommando Ohrdruf. That summer the 4th Motorized Reconnaissance Battalion had already been formed from the 4th (Leipzig) Motor Transport Battalion, and the 37th *Panzerabwehr* (Antitank) Battalion formed at Eisenach/Muehlhausen around cadres supplied by the 3/5th Motorized Transport Battalion at Kassel. The artillery regiment (which initially controlled only one organic battalion) was the redesignated Motorized Artillery Lehr Battalion Ohrdruf, but a II Battalion was formed from scratch in the summer of 1936. Both were stationed in Weimar. The 37th Motorized (later Panzer) Engineer Battalion was not created until the summer of 1938 and then only as a company—it did not become a battalion until 1939. The 37th Signal Battalion was formed at Weimar from the signals platoon of the 16th Cavalry Regiment. The division did not establish separate supply, medical, and repair shop units until the spring of 1938. Most of the division's replacements in the prewar period came from Wehrkreis IX (Tuebingen and Hesse).

Initially the 1st Panzer Division was equipped only with hastily produced and completely substandard PzKw Is, which had no main battle gun—only two machine guns in the turret. PzKw IV-As began to arrive in the spring of 1936 and much better PzKw IIIs—the workhorse of the German tank divisions until 1941–42—started to appear that winter. Even so, several of the division's tank battalions were still equipped with obsolete PzKw IIs even as late as 1941.

Each year from 1936 on, each of the division's tank regiments had to provide two to four companies as cadres to other panzer regiments. Around these cadres the 7th, 8th, 15th, 35th, and 36th Panzer Regiments were formed.

The 1st Panzer took part in the occupation of Austria (1938), the Sudetenland (1938), and Prague (1939). It first saw action in the Polish campaign of 1939, when it crossed the Liswarthe River and rolled from the frontier to the suburbs of Warsaw in just eight days. It held and expanded a bridgehead on the east bank of the Vistula until September 15, when it was shifted to the Bzura sector, where it supported the 18th Infantry Division. After Poland surrendered, the division returned to its home bases and then was sent to Dortmund in western Germany at the end of November. It was transferred to the southern Eifel in March and attacked across Luxembourg and southern Belgium in May 1940. It fought in the decisive Battle of Sedan, formed part of the "panzer wedge" in the drive across France, and took part in the early phases of the Battle of Dunkirk, before turning south to help finish off the doomed French Republic. Jumping off on June 10, the 1st Panzer quickly broke through the Weygand Line, despite a fierce tank battle with French B 2s, during which both sides suffered heavy casualties. It quickly crossed the Aisne and the Marne, raced behind the Maginot Line, took Besançon, reached the Swiss frontier on June 17, and stormed Belfort the following day. The division lost only 495 men killed during the Western campaign of 1940. After the French surrendered on June 25, the

1st Panzer Division remained in France (in training areas along the Loire) until September, when it was sent to the Zinten-Sensburg-Allenstein area of East Prussia to reorganize. The 2nd Panzer Regiment was transferred to the newly formed 16th Panzer Division; three companies of the 1st Panzer Regiment were transferred out as cadres for the 18th Panzer Division; the staff of the 1st Panzer Brigade was disbanded; and the newly formed 113th Rifle (Motorized Infantry) Regiment was incorporated into the 1st Panzer Division. During this process, the 1st Panzer Division absorbed the III/69th Motorized Infantry (Schuetzen) Regiment (the new III/1st Rifle Regiment) and the II/56th Motorized Artillery Regiment (a heavy artillery unit), which became III/73rd Panzer Artillery Regiment. The division also added the independent 702nd Motorized Heavy Infantry Howitzer Company, which it assigned to the rifle brigade. Meanwhile, the tank units were largely reequipped with the modern PzKw III tanks, and the tank destroyer and reconnaissance battalions also received the most modern equipment. By the end of the year the division had 155 tanks, of which 85 were PzKw IIIs and 30 were PzKw IVs.

The 1st Panzer Division remained in East Prussia until June 22, 1941, when the invasion of the Soviet Union began. In the Russian campaign of 1941, the division formed part of Army Group North's 4th Panzer Group (later Army). It crossed the Lithuanian frontier and took part in the annihilation of the well-equipped Soviet III Armored Corps at Dunaburg (Dubysa) in June. It breached the Stalin Line near Ostrov on July 5 and nine days later established a bridgehead across the Luga River near Szabsk, which it held despite several desperate Soviet counterattacks. The 1st Panzer was seriously depleted by casualties and by August 16 had only 44 serviceable tanks; nevertheless it pushed on to the Leningrad defensive belt, where it took part in heavy fighting in the Duderhof Hills. Then it was transferred to Army Group Center and, on October 2, 1941, joined the drive on Moscow. It pushed across the Dnieper and took Kalinin, south of the Volga Basin, on October 13. Here it was involved in heavy fighting until the end of November. It took part in the final drive on Moscow later that month and pushed to within 20 miles of the Soviet capital. The 1st Panzer opposed the Russian winter offensive, during which it was partially surrounded and forced to break out. During the Battle of Klin (which ended on December 14), the crews of the 1st Panzer Regiment—which had lost or been forced to abandon all of its tanks—were armed with grenades and fought as infantry.

In 1942, the division fought in several defensive battles on the central sector of the Eastern Front—mainly in the very dangerous Rzhev Salient, which faced major Soviet attacks from three sides. By February, 1942—thanks to the efforts of its maintenance crews—the division was up to a strength of one full tank company (18 PzKw III tanks). The rest of the 1st Panzer Regiment was used to form two ad hoc ski companies. The division continued to fight in the defense of 9th Army's critical northern sector, the Rzhev-Sychevka-Olenin triangle, for the next six months. In the spring, it was finally reequipped to a large extent. Among other things, the 37th Tank Destroyer Battalion received 24 long-barreled 75mm guns and a dozen self-propelled 75mm AT guns, and the panzer regiment received a number of new tanks. In July 1942 the division was reinforced again and added a heavy artillery battalion (IV/73rd Panzer Artillery), but the 1st Panzer Regiment had to give up a battalion to the 16th Panzer Grenadier Division of Army Group South. The following March, 1st Panzer Division also lost its motorcycle battalion.

Despite its reduced size, the division—along with the 102nd Infantry Division—was assigned the task of keeping the *Rollbahn* (9th Army's main supply route) open. Near Pushkeri in early July, the 1st and 2nd Panzer Divisions surrounded two Soviet cavalry corps, two infantry divisions, two mechanized brigades, and some parachute battalions. Joined by German infantry, they crushed the pocket, destroying or capturing 218 tanks, 592 guns, and 1,300 antitank guns in the process. The next month the Soviets broke through east of Sychevka, ripping a 30-mile hole in the 9th Army's front. The 1st Panzer (along with the 5th Panzer Division) again played a major role in closing the line and sealing off the breakthrough. It continued to fend off Soviet attacks and launch local counterattacks until the end of the year; in one two-day period, the division destroyed 65 Soviet heavy and superheavy KV-1 and KV-2 tanks. During the Soviet winter offensive of 1942–43, 1st Panzer Division defended Belyy and kept the vital Sychevka road open in very heavy fighting. In the battle at Bosino, I/1st Panzer Grenadier Regiment lost every officer either killed or wounded, but continued to hold its positions and even counterattacked. It was reinforced with 2nd Company, 1st Panzer Regiment, which destroyed 35 KV-2 and T-34 tanks in two days, but lost its company commander, and two of its three platoon leaders were killed or wounded. Command devolved on Sergeant Georg Schaefer, who destroyed more than 25 T-34s on two consecutive days, breaking the back of the Soviet attack. Shortly thereafter, XXXXI Panzer and XXX Corps restored the front and sealed off the Soviet spearheads, which were subsequently destroyed.

Greatly reduced by losses and transfers, the 1st Panzer was withdrawn for resting and refitting in January 1943. Initially it was sent to Amiens, France, and later to Coetquidan in Brittany, where it was temporarily reequipped with captured French Hotchkiss and Somua tanks. The division was sent to the northern Peloponnisos in Greece in June, because Hitler and the High Command were deceived into thinking that the Allies would land there in July 1943. Their actual target was Sicily. When Italy tried to defect from the Axis in September, the 1st Panzer Division played a major role in rounding up the 11th Italian Army, which put up little resistance. Meanwhile, in May 1943, the division added the 299th Army Motorized Flak Artillery Battalion to its table of organization and, in October, it was given enough PzKw V (Tiger) tanks to equip a battalion. It also received about 100 Panthers (PzKw VIs) and was again brought up to full strength. The following month it returned to the Russian Front, fighting on the southern sector as part of the 1st Panzer Army—except for the I/1st Panzer Regiment, which was stationed north of Trieste as a mobile reserve for

OB Southwest; it did not rejoin the division until October. Meanwhile, the rest of the 1st Panzer Division took part in the Battle of the Kiev Salient, the Battle of Zhitomir (which it captured on the night of November 17–18), the counteroffensive west of Kiev (November–December 1943), and the subsequent battles around Zhitomir and Berdichev (late 1943–early 1944). For the next year, the 1st Panzer Division would serve as a "fire brigade" for the 1st and 4th Panzer Armies, rushing from one crisis to another, as the German front reeled. In February 1944, the 1st Panzer Division spearheaded the attempt to rescue the XI and XXXXII Corps, which were surrounded at Cherkassy. It could not penetrate the last six miles to the pocket but was still successful in saving about half of the trapped Germans. The next month, the 1st Panzer rescued the 96th and 291st Infantry Divisions from the Soviet spring offensive of 1944. The division's losses had already been very heavy. As of March 14, 1944, its panzer grenadier battalions were at 25 percent of their authorized strength, as was the case with its medium flak batteries and the 1st Panzer Reconnaissance Battalion. The artillery regiment was in better shape: its light batteries were at 50 percent strength and its heavy batteries were at 75 percent of their authorized strength, while the 37th Panzer Engineer Battalion was at 30 percent strength and the 1st Panzer Regiment had between 50 and 60 operational tanks.

The division formed part of the Kamenez Pocket (the "Hube Pocket") in April 1944 (when the 1st Panzer Army was encircled and forced to fight its way out); it also fought in the battles of Brody (where it rescued part of the XIII Corps), the Dnieper Bend, the north Ukraine, the eastern Carpathians, in the defense of the San and Vistula Rivers, and in eastern Poland in 1944. In August and September 1944 it was involved in heavy defensive fighting against the Russian Baranov bridgehead, west of the Vistula, and it was transferred south to defend the Carpathian passes in the vicinity of Dukla (west of Grosswardein, Hungary) at the end of September. During the defense of Hungary, the 1st Panzer kept the 8th Army's retreat route open and spearheaded several counterattacks against Soviet breakthroughs and was cited for its counterattack against the Russians at Debrecen.

From December 1944 until the end of March 1945, the 1st Panzer Division held defensive positions south of Szekesfehervar (southeast of Lake Balaton), blocking the Soviet route to Graz and Vienna. Despite its reduced numbers, the 1st Panzer Division spearheaded the German effort to rescue the IX SS Mountain Corps (more than 30,000 men), which was encircled in Budapest and, on January 28, 1945, reached a point only 10 miles southwest of the garrison's perimeter. Hitler, however, refused to allow the garrison to break out, and the chance to save it was lost. The division then fell back to the area around Szekesfehervar. Much of the 1st Panzer was subsequently destroyed here in January, February, and March 1945, where the entire 6th Army was decimated. The division itself was encircled at Jenoe (south of Szekesfehervar) on March 20, 1945, and had to fight its way out, but with very heavy casualties; despite its losses, however, the remnants of the 1st Panzer continued fighting in the defense of Graz, in the retreat into Austria, and in the defense of Styria until the end of the war. As late as April 26, 1945, it was still launching counterattacks. It was in the Hartberg, Styria, area of Austria when the war ended, but it managed to extricate itself from the Soviets and head for the west. The division crossed the Line of Demarcation southeast of Linz and managed to surrender to the Americans at Mauerkirchen in Upper Bavaria on May 8, 1945. They dissolved the 1st Panzer Division on May 13. Most of the soldiers were released and sent home by the end of July.

Commanders of the division included Lieutenant General Baron Maximilian von Weichs (assumed command October 1, 1935), Major General/Lieutenant General Rudolf Schmidt (assumed command October 1, 1937), Major General/ Lieutenant General Friedrich Kirchner (November 3, 1939), Major General/ Lieutenant General Eugen Walter Krueger (July 17, 1941), Colonel Oswin Grolig (August 8, 1943), Colonel Walter Soeth (September 9, 1943), Krueger (resumed command, September, 1943), Major General Richard Koll (January 1, 1944), Colonel/Major General Werner Marcks (February 20, 1944), Colonel/ Major General/Lieutenant General Eberhard Thunert (September 18, 1944), Colonel Helmut Huppert (April 23, 1945) and Thunert (late April 1945–end).

## COMMANDERS

Baron Maximilian von Weichs (1881–1954) joined the Bavarian Army as a Fahnenjunker (officer cadet) in 1900. He spent much of his pre–World War II career in cavalry, commanding the 18th Cavalry Regiment (1928) and the 2nd Cavalry Division at Weimar (1933) before assuming command of the 1st Panzer Division. He was chosen for this post by Colonel General Ludwig Beck, chief of the General Staff, because Beck thought his cautious and conservative nature would be an effective counterweight to the blitzkrieg theories of Heinz Guderian et al.—theories which Beck considered revolutionary and impractical. Weichs was never an effective armored officer, although he proved to be a capable commander of marching infantry and horse-drawn formations. In 1937 he took over command of the XIII Military District and XIII Corps at Nuremberg and rose to the command of the 2nd Army in 1940. He led this force in France, Yugoslavia, and Russia until he fell ill during the Battle of Moscow in December 1941. In January 1942 he was briefly commander in chief of Army Group South following the death of Field Marshal Walter von Reichenau on January 17. From July 1942 to July 1943 he was commander in chief of Army Group B on the Russian Front and was involved in the Stalingrad disaster. Placed in Fuehrer Reserve for a brief period in the summer of 1943, Baron von Weichs was reemployed in August 1943 as commander in chief, Southeast (i.e., the Balkans) and, as such, commanded Army Group F during the retreat from southeastern Europe. He was retired on Hitler's orders on March 25, 1945: the Fuehrer had always mistrusted von Weichs because of his strong Catholic leanings.

He was promoted to general of cavalry (1936), colonel general (1940), and to field marshal (February 1, 1943). Almost alone of Hitler's field marshals, Baron von Weichs was not tried as a war criminal.

Weichs' friend and successor as commander of the 1st Panzer Division was Rudolf Schmidt (1886–1957), a Berliner who had begun his military career as a Fahnenjunker in the infantry in 1906. He was promoted to lieutenant general (June 1, 1938), general of panzer troops (June 1, 1940), and colonel general (January 1, 1942). He commanded the XXXIX Motorized (later Panzer) Corps in France and Russia (1940–41), was acting commander of the 2nd Army during the Battle of Moscow (once again replacing Weichs) and was commander of the 2nd Panzer Army on the Russian Front from December 26, 1941, to July 10, 1943. Although popular with Hitler, he was highly critical of the Nazi regime and was relieved of his command two days before the Battle of Kursk began, because some of his letters containing anti-Nazi statements fell into the Fuehrer's hands after the Gestapo arrested Schmidt's brother on an unrelated matter. Despite the fact that he was an excellent commander, Schmidt was never reemployed.

Friedrich Kirchner (1885–1960) was promoted to lieutenant general on April 1, 1940, and became a general of panzer troops on February 1, 1942. He commanded the LVII Panzer Corps from November 15, 1941, until the end of the war. (OKH looked upon him as a good armored corps commander but not army commander material, so they simply left him where he was.) Kirchner had started his career as an officer cadet in the infantry in 1906, but transferred to the cavalry in 1911. Prior to assuming command of the 1st Panzer Division, Kirchner commanded the 11th Cavalry Regiment (1933–34), the 1st Rifle Regiment (1934–38), and the 1st Rifle Brigade. He held the Knight's Cross with Oak Leaves and Swords.

Walter Krueger (1892–1973) joined the army as an infantry officer cadet in 1909, but transferred to the cavalry after receiving his commission in 1911. He became a lieutenant general on October 1, 1940, and a general of panzer troops on May 1, 1944. He served as acting commander of the LXVIII Corps (October 1943) and commander of the LVIII Panzer Corps (January, 1944-March 25, 1945). Earlier, Krueger had commanded the 10th Cavalry Regiment (1937–39), the 171st Infantry Regiment (1939), and the 1st Rifle Brigade (1940–41). He ended the war as commander of Wehrkreis IV.

For an overview of the career of Oswin Grolig, see 25th Panzer Division.

For a sketch of the career of Walter Soeth, see Commanders, 3rd Panzer Division.

Richard Koll was born in Kolberg in 1897. He entered the army as a cadet in the 4th Telegraph Battalion in 1914 but was commissioned only six weeks later, due to the outbreak of World War I. He served in the Reichsheer (the 100,000-man army of the Weimar Republic), led the II/11th Panzer Regiment (1937–40) and 11th Panzer Regiment (1940–43) and was a staff officer at OKW

(1943) before assuming command of the 1st Panzer. Promoted to major general on August 1, 1943, he returned to the motorization staff at OKW and remained there until the end of the war. He was promoted to lieutenant general in 1945.

Werner Marcks (b. 1891), a Berliner, a veteran of the Afrika Korps, and a strong Nazi, joined the army in 1910 and was commissioned in the artillery in 1911. He had previously led the 19th Antitank Battalion (1939–41) and the 115th and 104th Panzer Grenadier Regiments (1941–42) in Africa and was briefly acting commander of the 90th Light Division in Libya in July 1942. He was assigned to the staff of the Panzer Inspectorate from October 1942 until he assumed command of the 1st Panzer Division. Promoted to major general on April 1, 1944, he later commanded the 21st Panzer Division on the Eastern Front and was in Soviet prisons until 1955. Marcks was promoted to lieutenant general on April 20, 1945. He died in 1967.

Eberhard Thunert was born in 1899 and joined the army as an infantry Fahnenjunker in early 1918. He later served in the Reichsheer, was commissioned in the 6th Infantry Regiment in 1920, and was Ia (chief of operations) of the 5th Panzer Division (1938–40) when World War II began. Thunert later was Ia of the XIV Motorized (later Panzer) Corps (1940–41), was chief of staff of the XIV Panzer (1942–43), and was chief of staff of the LVIII Reserve Panzer (subsequently Panzer Corps) in 1943–44. Transferring from the staff to the line, he led the 394th Panzer Grenadier Regiment of the 3rd Panzer Division from June to September 1944. He was promoted to major general on January 1, 1945, and to lieutenant general on May 1, 1945—the day after Hitler committed suicide. After the war he resided in Bad Godesberg, a resort town near Bonn.

Helmut Huppert (1916–1961) commanded the I/1st Panzer Grenadier Regiment (early 1943), the 1st Panzer Reconnaissance Battalion (1944) and the 1st Panzer Grenadier Regiment (1945).

## NOTES AND SOURCES

Like the other antitank battalions, the 37th Antitank Battalion (Panzerabwehr-Abteilung 37) was redesignated 37th Tank Destroyer Battalion (Panzerjaeger 37) on April 1, 1940. The Luftwaffe 83rd Light Motorized Flak Battalion was attached to the division for the Polish and French campaigns.

The 1st Panzer Brigade was disbanded in late 1942 and the 1st Rifle was dissolved in May, 1943.

The 1st Panzer Regiment was fully equipped with PzKw IVs and PzKw V (Panther) tanks by the end of January 1944.

In 1945, in the last weeks of the war, the 1009th Replacement Grenadier Battalion of Panzer Division Tatra was transferred to the 1st Panzer Division.

The incredibly brave Sergeant Schaefer was awarded the Knight's Cross. He was killed in action on October 13, 1944.

Jacques Benoist-Mechin, *Sixty Days That Shook the West: The Fall of France* (New York, 1963): 68 (hereafter cited as "Benoist-Mechin"); Paul Carell, *Hitler Moves East, 1941–1943* (Boston, 1965; reprint ed., New York, 1966): 24, 79, 336, 398 (hereafter cited as "Carell 1966"); Christopher Chant et al., *Hitler's Generals* (New York, 1979): 102 (hereafter cited as "Chant et al."); Christopher Chant, ed., *The Marshall Cavendish Illustrated History of World War II* (New York, 1979): Volume 15: 2057 (hereafter cited as "Chant 1979"); Guy Chapman, *Why France Fell: The Defeat of the French Army in 1940* (New York, 1968): 347–48 (hereafter cited as "Chapman"); Paul Joseph Goebbels, *The Goebbels Diaries*, Louis P. Lochner, ed. and trans. (New York, 1948; reprint ed., New York, 1971): 414; Theodor Hartmann, *Wehrmacht Divisional Signs, 1938–1945* (London, 1970): 60–61 (hereafter cited as "Hartmann"); Wolf Keilig, *Die Generale des Heeres* (Friedberg, 1983): 169–89, 217, 346 (hereafter cited as "Keilig"); Robert M. Kennedy, *The German Campaign in Poland (1939),* United States Department of the Army *Pamphlet 20-255* (Washington, D.C., 1956): 74 (hereafter cited as "Kennedy"); Charles B. MacDonald, *The Siegfried Line Campaign* (Washington, D.C., 1963): 300 (hereafter cited as "MacDonald 1963"); Erich von Manstein, *Lost Victories* (Chicago, 1958): 488, 526 (hereafter cited as "Manstein"); Otto E. Moll, *Die deutschen Generalfeldmarshaelle, 1939–1945* (Rastatt/Baden, 1961): 252 (hereafter cited as "Moll"); Horst Riebenstahl, *The 1st Panzer Division*, Edward Force, trans. (West Chester, Pa., 1990): 1 ff.; Peter Schmitz, Klaus-Juergen Thies, Guenter Wegmann, and Christian Zweng, *Die deutschen Divisionen, 1939–1945* (Osnabrueck, 1993), Band (Volume) 1: 33–37 (hereafter cited as "Schmitz et al."); Seaton: 360, 367; Rolf Stoves, *Die Gepanzerten und Motorisierten deutschen Grossverbaende: Divisionen und selbstaendige Brigaden, 1935–1945* (Friedberg, 1986): 11–16 (hereafter cited as "Stoves, *Gepanzerten*"); Rolf O. G. Stoves, *Die 1. Panzerdivision, 1935–1945: Die deutschen Panzerdivision in Bild* (Friedberg, n.d.): 1 ff.; Tessin, Volume 2: 29–31; RA: 144; United States Military Intelligence Service, "Order of Battle of the German Army, 1942" (Washington, D.C., 1942): 55 (hereafter cited as "OB 42"; subsequent editions only changed by the year designation and will be cited as such, e.g., "OB 43" would indicate "Order of Battle of the German Army, 1943"); OB 43: 198; OB 45: 286; Earl F. Ziemke, *Stalingrad to Berlin: The German Defeat in the East* (Washington, D.C., 1966): 225–38 (hereafter cited as "Ziemke"). For a detailed description of the Balkans campaign, see U.S. Department of the Army *Pamphlet 20-260*, "The German Campaign in the Balkans (Spring 1941)" (Washington, D.C., 1953). Also see Franz Thomas, *Die Eichenlaubtraeger 1940–1945* (Osnabrueck: 1977–98), 2 volumes.

# 2nd Panzer Division

**COMPOSITION (1943):**   3rd Panzer Regiment, 2nd Panzer Grenadier Regiment, 304th Panzer Grenadier Regiment, 74th Panzer Artillery Regiment, 2nd Motorcycle Battalion, 5th Panzer Reconnaissance Battalion, 38th Tank Destroyer Battalion, 38th Panzer Engineer Battalion, 38th Panzer Signal Battalion.

**HOME STATION:**   Wuerzburg, Wehrkreis XIII; later Vienna, Wehrkreis XVIII

Formed at Wuerzburg on October 15, 1935, 2nd Panzer Division included the 2nd Schuetzen (Rifle) Brigade (2nd Rifle Regiment and 2nd Motorcycle Battalion), the 2nd Panzer Brigade (3rd and 4th Panzer Regiments), the 74th Panzer Artillery Regiment (two battalions), and assorted divisional units, all of which had been added to the division by 1937 except the 273rd Army Antiaircraft (Flak) Battalion, which became part of the division in 1942. The Headquarters, 2nd Panzer Brigade was dissolved in late 1942 and the 2nd Rifle Brigade HQ ceased to exist in the summer of 1943, as the division was reduced by casualties and transfers to the point that it became superfluous. Meanwhile, in 1938 the division was transferred to Vienna after participating in the annexation of Austria. By the start of the war, most of the men of the unit were Austrians. The 2nd Panzer suffered heavy losses in central Poland in 1939 and took part in the French campaign of 1940, where it formed part of Guderian's XIX Motorized Corps. It fought in Luxembourg, northern France, and southern Belgium, and captured Abbeville on the English Channel in May, thus isolating the main Allied armies (the French 1st and 7th Armies and the British Expeditionary Force) in the Dunkirk Pocket and sealing the doom of France. The 2nd Panzer Division subsequently pursued the disintegrating Allied armies across the Aisne and took part in the surrounding of the French Maginot Line divisions in the Belfort Gap region. After the French capitulated, the 2nd Panzer returned to the Reich, but was sent to Poland in September.

In late 1940 the division gave up the 4th Panzer Regiment plus other cadres to the newly authorized 13th Panzer Division and added the 304th Panzer Grenadier Regiment to its own table of organization. It now included the 3rd Panzer Regiment (which had been enlarged to three battalions), and the 2nd and 304th Rifle Regiments (two battalions each), the 74th Panzer Artillery Regiment (three battalions), the 2nd Motorcycle, 5th Motorized Reconnaissance, 38th Tank Destroyer, and 38th Signal Battalions. The reorganized Austrian tank division was sent to Romania in March 1941, and participated in the Balkans campaign that spring. Along with the 6th Mountain Division, the Austrian *Panzertruppen* took Athens in April, after defeating the British Expeditionary Force. Subsequently, the 2nd Panzer Division was sent to Bavaria to refit and spent the summer in Poland and southwest France before being transported to the Russian Front in September. Despite heavy fighting, elements of the unit managed to reach as far as Khimki, a small river port five miles from Moscow, and the 5th Panzer Reconnaissance Battalion even reported being able to see the Kremlin itself, before they were thrown back by the start of the Soviet winter offensive of 1941–42. The division fought at Klin, Karmanowo, Bjeloje, and in the Rzhev Salient, where it suffered heavy casualties.

In 1942, the 5th Reconnaissance Battalion was reorganized and became the 24th Motorcycle Battalion; it was also transferred to the 24th Panzer Division. Later, the 2nd Motorcycle Battalion (which remained with the division) became the 2nd Panzer Reconnaissance Battalion. The 2nd Panzer Division also lost two of its three tank battalions, which were sent south to join the main German thrust of 1942 against the Volga and the Caucasus. (In March 1943, a new I/3rd Panzer Regiment was created—this one equipped with Panther tanks.) Remaining on the central sector, the battered and depleted division took part in the defensive fighting of 1942, the Rzhev withdrawal (1943), the Battles of Kursk, Orel, Kiev, Gomel, and the middle Dnieper battles early in the winter of 1943–44, where it suffered heavy casualties. Withdrawn to Amiens, France, to rest and refit in early 1944, the division absorbed the 507th Heavy Panzer Battalion (equipped with Tiger tanks) into its ranks, and I/3rd Panzer Regiment was equipped with Panthers. It was also exceptionally well trained by General von Luettwitz for combat against the Anglo-Saxons, especially in night tactics, which came in very handy in the months ahead. The division was ordered to Normandy on June 10 and, taking advantage of night, early morning fog, and camouflage, covered an average of 60 miles per 24 hours over a badly damaged road network without being detected—despite total Allied domination of the air. This was an incredible feat for a German division during the Normandy campaign. As a result, the 2nd Panzer was able to surprise the veteran British 7th Armoured Division and recapture Villers-Bocage, and the very important Hill 174 (June 15–16). It then held a sector around Caumont and formed a mainstay of the German defense until the end of June, when it was shifted to the Vire sector. The division had inflicted heavy casualties upon the invaders, but also suffered high losses itself—including all of its regimental commanders and most of its battalion commanders. General von Luettwitz continued to command the division, despite being wounded. The 2nd Panzer took part in the unsuccessful counterattack at Mortain in August and, with only 25 tanks left, was surrounded at Falaise in August. Breaking out with heavy losses, it was withdrawn from the line. By September 1, it had 27 tanks (mostly replacements), 12 guns, and 1,600 men. The division reformed at Bitburg and at Wittlich in the Eifel area of western Germany, where it temporarily absorbed the remnants of the 352nd Infantry Division. It was sent back into combat in the Ardennes offensive in December, where it spearheaded the German attack and advanced further than any other unit. It was smashed when the Allies counterattacked.

In the last campaign the 2nd Panzer was fighting against the Americans in 1945 and was down to a strength of only four tanks, three assault guns, and 200 men. The survivors of the old division were grouped with Panzer Brigade Thueringen and fought on the middle Mosel at Hunsrueck/Rhine and at Karlsbad-Pilsen. It ended the war defending Fulda in April 1945. It surrendered to the Americans at Plauen and Koetzing in May 1945.

Its commanders included Colonel/Major General/Lieutenant General Heinz Guderian (assumed command October 1, 1935), Major General/Lieutenant General Rudolf Veiel (March 1, 1938), Colonel Vollrath Luebbe (January 16, 1942), Major General Baron Hans-Karl von Esebeck (February 17, 1942), Major General Arno von Lenski (June 1, 1942), Colonel Karl Fabiunke (August 20, 1942), Colonel/Major General/Lieutenant General Luebbe again (September 5, 1942), Lieutenant General Baron Heinrich von Luettwitz (February 1, 1944), Colonel Count Eberhard von Nostitz (September 1, 1944), Colonel/Major General Henning Schoenfeld (September 5, 1944), Colonel/Major General Meinrad von Lauchert (December 13, 1944), Colonel Oskar Munzel (March 20, 1945), and Colonel Heinrich-Wilhelm Stollbrock (April 4, 1945–end).

## COMMANDERS

Heinz Guderian (1888–1954)—the father of the blitzkrieg—was Germany's leading advocate of mobile, armored warfare before World War II and greatly influenced Hitler in that direction. He was promoted to major general on August 1, 1936, and to lieutenant general on February 1, 1938. Shortly thereafter he was given command of the XVI Motorized Corps and, in 1939, the XIX Motorized (later Panzer) Corps. He distinguished himself in Poland (1939), France (1940), and in the early stages of the Russian campaign (1941), where he commanded the 2nd Panzer Group (later Army). Promoted to general of panzer troops in late 1938 and to colonel general on July 19, 1940, he was relieved by Hitler for the German failure before Moscow and held no further commands, but was inspector general of panzer Troops (1943–44) and acting chief of the General Staff of the Army (July 21, 1944–March 1945), a job for which he was intellectually and temperamentally unsuited. The outspoken Guderian was again relieved by Hitler after a bitter argument in March 1945 and surrendered to the Western Allies in northern Italy the next month. Later he wrote a book, *Panzer Leader*, which has been translated into many languages. Although a highly valuable historical document, it should be read very carefully and not every word should be accepted at face value—especially Guderian's alleged opposition to Hitler and the Nazis. As chief of the General Staff, for example, he did nothing to prevent the spread of Nazi doctrine with the army—in fact, quite the opposite is true. Guderian's first order as chief of the General Staff, for example, was to outlaw the traditional army salute and to order the adoption of the Nazi (Hitler) salute in its place. He also acted to expel anti-Hitler conspirators from the army, so that they could be tried (and usually hanged) by civilian authorities. Despite this, however, Guderian was an outstanding field commander and a brilliant tactician.

Rudolf Veiel (b. 1883), a Wuerttemberger, entered the army as a Fahnenjunker in the 19th Ulam Regiment in 1904, fought in World War I, and served in the Reichswehr. He was promoted to lieutenant general on October 1, 1938, and to general of panzer troops on April 1, 1942. After leading the XXXXVIII Panzer Corps in Russia (1942), he became commander of Wehrkreis V (September, 1943). Veiel was arrested for complicity in the July 20, 1944, attempt to kill Hitler and overthrow the Nazi regime, but was never executed. Freed by the Allies at the end of the war, he retired to Stuttgart, the city of his birth, where he passed away in 1956.

Vollrath Luebbe (b. 1894) joined the 103rd Infantry Regiment as a Fahnenjunker in 1912. He fought in World War I, served in the Reichsheer, and was commander of the 13th Cavalry Regiment (1938–41) when World War II broke out. He later commanded the 2nd Rifle Brigade (1941–42) before assuming command of the 2nd Panzer Division. Apparently Luebbe's handling of the 2nd Panzer left something to be desired, for—after years of commanding motorized and armored formations—he was transferred back to the infantry in early 1944. He led the 81st Infantry Division and the 443rd Infantry Divisions (1944–45) on the Eastern Front and surrendered to the Soviets at the end of the war. Like many "Eastern" generals who fell into Russian hands, he was not released from prison until 1955. Luebbe was promoted to major general on October 1, 1942, and to lieutenant general exactly one year later.

Baron Hans-Karl von Esebeck (1892–1955), a Wuerttemberger, joined the 3rd Guards Ulam Regiment as an officer cadet in 1911. He earned his commission in 1913, fought in World War I, and served in the Reichsheer. Later he commanded the 1st Cavalry Regiment (1936–39), the 6th Rifle Brigade of the 6th Panzer Division (1939–41), and the 15th Rifle Brigade (1941), before assuming command of the 15th Panzer Division in North Africa. He was wounded in the Siege of Tobruk in 1941 and, upon his recovery, was placed in charge of the 11th Panzer Division (1941) and then the 2nd Panzer. He subsequently commanded the XXXXVI Panzer Corps (late 1942–43) and the LVIII Panzer Corps (1943–44), and was acting commander of Wehrkreis XVII in Vienna in mid-1944. A general of panzer troops since February 1944, Esebeck was arrested in connection with the July 20, 1944, attempt on Hitler's life, and spent the rest of the war in prison. An excellent armored commander, he spent the rest of his life in relative poverty. He died in Dortmund on January 5, 1955.

For a sketch of Arno von Lenski's career, see 24th Panzer Division.

Karl Fabiunke (1893–1980) enlisted in the Imperial Army in 1911 and, as a sergeant, commanded a platoon in World War I. He earned his commission in the 3rd Artillery Regiment in 1922. After commanding a battalion of forward observers (1936–39), he assumed command of the 74th Panzer Artillery Regiment when war broke out and, as senior regimental commander in August 1942, assumed command of the division in the absence of General Luebbe. Promoted to major general in late 1943, he led the 129th Infantry Division (late 1943–early 1944) and the 144th Artillery Command (1944). He was wounded on August 28, 1944, and was unemployed for the rest of the war.

Baron Heinrich von Luettwitz (1896–1969), a cavalry officer and a skilled rider, was on the German equestrian team in the 1936 Olympics. When his team failed to win the gold medal, however, Luettwitz fell into unofficial disgrace and spent the next several years in professional obscurity; he was not, for example, allowed to participate in the French campaign (1940), which he spent languishing in Poland. (He had not been allowed to go to the front during the Polish campaign of 1939 until the outcome was already decided; then he was critically wounded by a sniper three days later.) He did not come into his own until the invasion of Russia (1941). Thereafter he was promoted rapidly: to colonel (1941), major general (December 1, 1942), lieutenant general (June 1, 1943) and general of panzer troops (November 1, 1944). In the process he rose from battalion to corps command in three years, successively leading the I/11th Rifle Regiment (1940–41), 59th Panzer Grenadier Regiment (1941–42), 20th Rifle Brigade (1942), 20th Panzer Division (1942–44), 2nd Panzer Division (1944), and XXXXVII Panzer Corps (1944–45). Perhaps he was promoted too rapidly. Luettwitz was an excellent divisional commander, both on the Eastern and Western Fronts, and it is difficult to imagine anyone doing better than he in the Battle of Normandy, where he saved the remnants of his division and continued to lead it despite being wounded. His conduct as commander of the XXXXVII, however, left much to be desired, especially during the Siege of Bastogne (December 1944), when he tried unsuccessfully to bluff the American commander into a premature surrender. Later, after he had been significantly reinforced, he was still unable to take the place, despite the fact that the odds were heavily in his favor and the Allied air forces were grounded by poor weather. General von Manteuffel, the commander of the 5th Panzer Army, considered relieving Luettwitz of his command and probably would have, except that he considered Luettwitz' senior divisional commander—Lieutenant General

Fritz Bayerlein—to be even less desirable than Luettwitz. The Baron surrendered the remnants of XXXXVII Panzer Corps to the Americans when the Ruhr Pocket collapsed in April 1945. Heinrich should not be confused with his first cousin, General of Panzer Troops Baron Smilo von Luettwitz, who commanded the 26th Panzer Division, XXXXVI Panzer Corps and 9th Army on the Eastern Front.

Count Eberhard von Nostitz (the chief of staff of the LVII Panzer Corps) became acting commander of the division on September 1, 1944, when General von Luettwitz was hospitalized due to wounds suffered in Normandy. He had previously served as Ia of the 7th Panzer Division on the Eastern Front (1943).

Henning Schoenfeld (b. 1894) was promoted to major general on December 1, 1944. A Pomeranian, he joined the cavalry in 1912 and was commissioned in 1913, but was discharged as a *Charaktersitik Rittmeister* (honorary captain of cavalry) in September, 1918—two months before the end of World War I. Schoenfeld rejoined the army in 1934 (the year after Hitler came to power) and served as commander of the 20th Reconnaissance Battalion (1939–40), an inspector of mobile troops at OKH (1940–43), and as commander of the 949th Infantry Regiment (1943–44). His contacts at OKH probably explain why he was given command of the prestigious 2nd Panzer. During the Battle of the Bulge and only 15 days after his promotion to major general, Schoenfeld was relieved of his command. He held no further appointments.

Meinrad von Lauchert (b. 1905) was promoted to major general on March 1, 1945. Considered an exceptionally brave and talented young tank officer even by German standards, he was unable to prevent the 2nd Panzer from being slaughtered by the Americans and British during the Battle of the Bulge. He did, however, push the advance as far as it would go and came within five miles of reaching the Meuse River—the high water mark of the German advance. A holder of the Knight's Cross with Oak Leaves, Lauchert rose from captain in 1935 to major general ten years later. In the process he commanded II/35th Panzer Regiment (1935–38), I/35th Panzer Regiment (1938–43), Panzer Regiment Grafenwoehr (1943), 15th Panzer Regiment (1943–44), and 2nd Panzer Division. He settled in Stuttgart after the war and died there in 1987.

Major General Oskar Munzel (b. 1899), a Pomeranian, joined the cavalry in 1917 and was commissioned six days before World War I ended. He served in the Reichswehr and was a staff officer in the Army Personnel Office in 1938. In 1941 he assumed command of a battalion in the 6th Panzer Regiment and, at the end of the year, took command of the regiment itself. He returned to Germany in early 1943 and directed courses of instruction at various tank training schools before becoming acting commander of the 14th Panzer Division on the Eastern Front in September 1944. He was transferred to the 1st Panzer Army in January, 1945 and commanded an ad hoc *Kampfgruppe* (battle group) until March, when he took over the 2nd Panzer. Munzel was named Higher Panzer Officer at *OB West* (a term referring to the Supreme Commander, Western Front, or his headquarters) on April 6, 1945, and ended the war in this post. He later became a general in the West German Armed Forces (the *Bundeswehr*), serving for a time as inspector of panzer troops. After the war he wrote *Die deutschen Panzer Truppen bis 1945*, a history of the panzer branch.

Colonel Stollbrock was an acting commander only. He had previously commanded the 36th Panzer Grenadier Regiment and had only recently been promoted to full colonel when he assumed command of the division in early April, 1945.

## NOTES AND SOURCES

The 273rd Army Antiaircraft Artillery Battalion was added to the division's table of organization on March 25, 1943.

John C. Angolia, *On the Field of Honor* (San Jose, Calif., 1979–80), Volume 1: 273 (hereafter cited as "Angolia, *Field*"); Martin Blumenson, *Breakout and Pursuit* (Washington, D.C., 1960): 295, 422, 505, 549 (hereafter cited as "Blumenson 1960"); Martin Blumenson, *Salerno to Cassino* (Washington, D.C., 1969): 42 (hereafter cited as "Blumenson 1969"); Dermont Bradley, Karl-Friedrich Hildebrand, and Markus Roevekamp, *Die Generale des Heeres, 1921–1945*, Volume 3 (Osnabrueck, 1994): 391 (hereafter cited as "Bradley et al."); Carell 1966: 180, 336; Paul Carell, *Scorched Earth* (Boston, 1971): 26–37, 309 (hereafter cited as "Carell 1971"); Chant 1979, Volume 14: 1859–61; Chant et al.: 66; Chapman: 347–48; Hugh M. Cole, *The Ardennes: The Battle of the Bulge* (Washington, D.C., 1965): 177–80 (hereafter cited as "Cole 1965"); Edwards, *Panzer*: 74; Guderian: 25–29; Gordon A. Harrison, *Cross-Channel Attack* (Washington, D.C., 1951): Map VI (hereafter cited as "Harrison"); Keilig: 84, 117, 211–12, 236, 309, 354; Kennedy: 74, Map 7; Andris J. Kursietis, *The Wehrmacht at War* (Soesterberg, The Netherlands, 1999): 77–78; Charles B. MacDonald, *The Last Offensive* (Washington, D.C., 1973): 93, 257, 259 (hereafter cited as "MacDonald 1973"); Manstein: 482–83; F. W. von Mellenthin, *German Generals of World War II* (Norman, Okla., 1977): 199 (hereafter cited as "Mellenthin 1977"); Kurt Mehner, *Die Geheimen Tagesberichte der deutschen Wehrmachtfuehrung im Zweiten Weltkrieg 1939–1945* (Osnabrueck, 1984–1995): Volume 4: 382; Volume 5: 329; Volume 12: 458 (hereafter cited as "Mehner," followed by the appropriate volume number); Oskar Munzel, *Die deutschen Panzer Truppen bis 1945* (Herford and Bonn, 1965); Horst Scheibert, *Die Traeger des deutschen Kreuzes in Gold* (Friedberg, n.d.): 364 (hereafter cited as "Scheibert"); Schmitz et al., Volume 1: 125–27; Hans Speidel, *Invasion, 1944* (New York, 1968): 42; Friedrich von Stauffenberg, "Panzer Commanders of the Western Front," unpublished manuscript in the possession of the author (hereafter cited as "Stauffenberg MS"); Tessin, Volume 2: 105–08; RA: 220; OB 42: 55; OB 43: 199; OB 45: 286–87; Martin Windrow, *The Panzer Divisions* (London, 1985): 6 (hereafter cited as "Windrow"). Guderian also wrote the book *Achtung! Panzer!* (published in 1937), which outlined his basic concepts of armored warfare and was considered revolutionary at the time.

# 3rd Panzer Division

**COMPOSITION (1943):** 6th Panzer Regiment, 3rd Panzer Grenadier Regiment, 394th Panzer Grenadier Regiment, 75th Panzer Artillery Regiment, 3rd Motorcycle Battalion, 3rd Panzer Reconnaissance Battalion, 543rd Tank Destroyer Battalion, 39th Panzer Engineer Battalion, 39th Panzer Signal Battalion, 314th Army Flak Artillery Battalion.

**HOME STATION:** Berlin, Wehrkreis III

Known as the "Bear Division" from its emblem, the Berlin Bear, the 3rd Panzer Division was activated at the Wuensdorf Maneuver Area, Berlin, on October 15, 1935. At that time it included the 3rd Rifle Brigade (3rd Rifle Regiment and 3rd Motorcyle Battalion), the 3rd Panzer Brigade (5th and 6th Panzer Regiments), and the 75th Motorized (later Panzer) Artillery Regiment (two battalions), as well as divisional troops. Its men came from a wide variety of sources, including *Kraftfahr-Lehrstab Zossen* (Motor Transport Demonstration Command Zossen), the cavalry regiments of the 1st Cavalry Division, elements of the 3rd Cavalry Division, elements of the 2nd, 3rd, and 6th Motor Transport Battalions, and from the provincial police (*Landespolizei*). Its men were mainly Prussians. During the years 1937–39, volunteers from the 6th Panzer Regiment formed the cadres for the 88th Panzer Battalion of the Condor Legion, which fought in the Spanish Civil War on the side of General Franco. The 3rd Panzer took part in the Anschluss and then the Polish campaign of 1939, where it formed part of Guderian's XIX Corps, attacking from Pomerania to Thorn in northern Poland, and then southeast to Brest-Litovsk. The 3rd also distinguished itself in France in 1940 as part of Hoepner's XVI Motorized Corps. It fought in

53

the Battle of the Albert Canal and in the battles south of Brussels, as well as the pursuit after the fall of Dunkirk, which ended in the capitulation of France. In late 1940 the division supplied the 5th Panzer Regiment to the 5th Light (later 21st Panzer) Division, and received the 394th Rifle (later Panzer Grenadier) Regiment in exchange. Like the other panzer divisions that were similarly reduced in the winter of 1940–41, the Bear Division lost about half its tank strength. It also added the 543rd Tank Destroyer Battalion. Its original antitank battalion, the 39th, was separated from the division and sent to Libya in early 1941 and was destroyed in Tunisia in May 1943. Like the other antitank battalions assigned to the Panzerwaffen, it had been redesignated a tank destroyer battalion (Panzerjaeger-Abteilung) on April 1, 1940.

The 3rd Panzer invaded Russia on June 22, 1941, and seized the Koden Bridge on the frontier by a coup de main. Under the command of future Field Marshal Walter Model, it took part in the Battle of the Bialystok-Minsk Pocket, the Smolensk encirclement, and the Dnieper River crossings before being sent to the southern sector, where it helped trap several Russian armies, comprising more than 700,000 men, in the Kiev area. Later it took part in the drive on Moscow and fought in the Battle of Tula, Guderian's unsuccessful attempt to seize the Soviet capital from the south. During the Soviet winter offensive of 1941–42 it acted as a "fire brigade," fighting in the Orel and Kursk sectors, and in March 1942 held Kharkov against massive Soviet attacks. That summer the division took part in the Caucasus campaign and suffered heavy losses in the battles around Mozdok. It escaped from the Kuban by crossing the Sea of Azov over the ice after Rostov was threatened in January 1943. It fought in the battles of Kursk and Belgorod in July and suffered heavy losses in the Kharkov battles of autumn 1943. It also took part in the battles of the Dnieper Bend (September 1943–January 1944), where it again distinguished itself, and in the fighting around Cherkassy and Uman in the winter of 1943–44. It was surrounded at Kirovograd on January 5, 1944, but broke out—followed by four other divisions—on January 10. Remaining in the line despite its casualties, the 3rd Panzer fought at Kiev and in the retreats through Ukraine and east Poland. It fought its way out of the encirclement in Romania, took part in the Hungarian campaign, and ended the war fighting in the Steiermark region of Austria, on the southern sector of the Eastern Front. Following Hitler's death on April 30, 1945, and prior to the actual German capitulation, the 3rd Panzer Division managed to disengage itself from the Russians and head west, so its men could avoid Soviet captivity. They were successful in this effort and surrendered to the Americans at Enns.

The commanders of this division included Lieutenant General Ernst Fessmann (assumed command October 1, 1935), Colonel Friedrich Kuehn (June, 1937), Fessmann (July, 1937), Lieutenant General Baron Leo Geyr von Schweppenburg (October 12, 1937), Major General Horst Stumpff (October 7, 1939), Geyr again (October 31, 1939), Stumpff again (February 15, 1940), Major General Kuehn again (September, 1940), Lieutenant General Model (November 13, 1940), Major General/Lieutenant General Hermann Breith (October 2, 1941), Colonel Baron Kurt von Liebenstein (September 1, 1942), Major General/Lieutenant General Franz Westhoven (October 1, 1942), Major General Fritz Bayerlein (October 25, 1943), Colonel Rudolf Lang (January 5, 1944), Lieutenant General Wilhelm Philipps (May 25, 1944), Colonel/Major General Wilhelm Soeth (January 1, 1945), and Colonel Volkmar Schoene (April 19, 1945).

## COMMANDERS

Ernst Fessmann was born in Bavaria in 1881 and entered the service in 1900 as an officer cadet. Prior to assuming command of the 3rd Panzer, he had spent most of his career as a cavalryman and rose to the command of the 17th Cavalry Regiment in 1926. Many historians dismiss Fessmann as just a cavalry officer who was given command of one of the first panzer divisions, even though there were tank officers better qualified than he. He had, however, served on the staff of the 7th Kraftfahr Battalion (1921–22), commanded the 7th Battalion from 1924 to 1926, and commanded the motorized battalion of the 2nd Artillery Regiment (1931–34) and the Panzer Lehr Brigade (1934–35). Fessmann therefore had considerably more experience with motorized units than most historians realize. He was given command of the tank division by Ludwig Beck, the highly conservative chief of the General Staff, as a counterweight to the perceived rashness of Heinz Guderian, the "father" of the blitzkrieg. (Beck thought tanks should only be used as infantry support vehicles and did not approve of the idea of panzer divisions at all.) Fessmann was not as reactionary as Beck nor as revolutionary as Guderian. He retired as a general of panzer troops in 1937. Recalled to active duty when the war broke out, he commanded the 267th Infantry Division (1939–41) and a special staff at Frankfurt/Oder (1941–42). He retired for the second and final time in 1942 and was discharged in 1943. He settled in Pullach and died on October 25, 1962.

Friedrich Kuehn (1889–1944) was promoted to major general on July 1, 1940, to lieutenant general on July 1, 1942, and to general of panzer troops on April 1, 1943. He led the 14th and 3rd Panzer Brigades (1939–40) before assuming command of the 3rd as an acting commander. He later led the 15th Panzer Division (1940–41) and the 14th Panzer Division (1941–42). He was named chief of army motorization in September 1942, and chief of armed forces motorization in February 1943. He was killed during an air raid on Berlin on February 15, 1944. Kuehn began his career as an infantry Fahnenjunker in 1909.

Baron Leo Geyr von Schweppenburg (1886–1974), a Wuerttemburger and German military attaché to London, Brussels, and The Hague in the 1930s, entered the army as a Fahnenjunker in the 26th Dragoon Regiment in 1904. He led the XXIV Motorized (later Panzer) Corps (1940–42), the XXXX Panzer Corps (1942), and the LVIII Panzer Corps (1942–43). He was appointed commander of Panzer Group West (which later became the 5th Panzer Army) in October 1943 and led it in the opening days of the Normandy campaign. An aristocratic snob, Geyr did not get along well with Field Marshal Rommel (the Desert Fox), who was the son and grandson of school teachers and was thus below Geyr socially (or so he felt), even though Rommel was superior to him in rank. Their relationship improved somewhat after the battle began. Geyr was severely wounded by Allied bombers on June 9, 1944, and his chief of staff was killed. Recovering from his wounds in late June, he returned to Normandy, only to be relieved of his command on Hitler's orders in early July. He succeeded Guderian as inspector general of panzer troops shortly thereafter. After the war, Geyr became a military historian. He died at Irschenhausen, Upper Bavaria, on January 27, 1974. The baron's record as a general on the Eastern Front was very good; on the Western Front he was much less successful, largely because he did not take Allied air superiority into proper account. His headquarters, for example, was hardly camouflaged at all and was an inviting target for Allied fighter-bombers on June 9. Although he professed to be an anti-Nazi and did, in fact, detest them, Geyr refused to join the anti-Hitler conspiracy as early as 1938, on the grounds that his troops would not obey orders which went counter to those of the Fuehrer. Geyr was commander of the 3rd Panzer Division at the time.

Horst Stumpff (b. 1887) joined the 54th Infantry Regiment in the standard manner (as an officer cadet) in 1907. He commanded the 3rd Panzer Brigade (1938–39) before taking charge of the division. Promoted to lieutenant general on February 1, 1941, he later commanded the 20th Panzer Division (1940–41) but could not stand up to the rigors of the Eastern Front. Unemployed from October 14, 1941, until the spring of 1942, he was inspector of Recruiting Area Koenigsberg (1942–44) and inspector general of panzer troops in the Replacement Army (1944). His success at this job led to his promotion to general of panzer troops on November 9, 1944. Stumpff died in Hamburg in 1958.

Walter Model (1891–1945), a field marshal as of March 1, 1944, was born into a family of extremely modest means. He entered the service as an infantry officer cadet in 1909. After fighting in World War I and serving in the Reichsheer, he switched over to the motorized/armored branch in the 1930s and became an expert on the technical matters of armament. He served as chief of the Training Department of the Defense Ministry and chief of the Technical Department of the Army in the 1930s. Model was chief of staff of Wehrkreis IV and later IV Corps (1938–1939) and chief of staff of the 16th Army (1939–40) during the campaign in France. He did not come into his own, however, until the Russian campaign, where he distinguished himself as an extremely energetic commander and excellent tactician (except at Kursk, where he was largely responsible for the German defeat). He commanded the 9th Army (1942–January 1944), Army Group North (January–March 1944), Army Group North Ukraine (April–June 1944), and Army Group Center (June–August 1944). Sent to the

West, he was less successful. Briefly commander in chief of OB West (i.e., of the Western Front) in August 1944, he was commander of Army Group B from September 1944 until it was destroyed in the Ruhr Pocket in April 1945. He played a major part in the Allied defeat at Arnhem in September. Model committed suicide in a wooded area near Duesseldorf in April 1945 rather than surrender and for years lay in an unmarked grave.

Although tactically brilliant, Model tended to oversupervise and was often too harsh in dealing with subordinate commanders, although never with enlisted men. A strongly Catholic and yet pro-Nazi officer, he was drinking heavily by the end of the war.

Hermann Breith (1892–1964) started his career as an infantry cadet in 1910. He was promoted to lieutenant general on November 1, 1942. Brieth left the 3rd Panzer to take charge of the III Panzer Corps, which he led on the Eastern Front until the end of the war. Prior to commanding the division, Breith had commanded 36th Panzer Regiment (1936–40), was commander of the 5th Panzer Brigade (1940–41), and was briefly general of mobile troops at OKH (1941). Although not as good a divisional or corps commander as Model, he was nevertheless very effective in both jobs. He was promoted to general of panzer troops on March 1, 1943.

For a sketch of Baron Kurt von Liebenstein's career, see 21st Panzer Division.

Franz Westhoven was promoted to lieutenant general on April 1, 1943. Born in the Rhineland in 1894, he joined the army in the usual manner (as a Fahnenjunker or officer cadet) in 1913. He served for a long period in the powerful Army Personnel Office (1934–40), was commander of the 1st Rifle Regiment (early 1941–42), and commanded the 3rd Rifle (later Panzer Grenadier) Brigade (February–October 1942). Westhoven was wounded in action on October 20, 1943, and command devolved upon Colonel Ernst Wellmann, but only for a few hours, until Bayerlein arrived. After his recovery, Westhoven served as an advisor to General Geyr von Schweppenburg, the commander of Panzer Group West (1944); deputy inspector general of panzer troops (1944–45), again under his friend Geyr; and commander of tank schools (1945).

Ernst Wellmann (1904–1970), a holder of the Knight's Cross with Oak Leaves, commanded the 3rd Panzer Grenadier Regiment (1942–44).

For the details of Fritz Bayerlein's career, see Commanders, (130th) Panzer Lehr Division.

Born in Wuppertal in 1894, Wilhelm Philipps entered the army in 1913 as an officer cadet in a foot artillery regiment. Before assuming command of the 3rd Panzer, General Philipps was associated with the weapons and equipment manufacturing office of the OKH Ordnance Department and commanded the 11th Panzer Regiment (1937–39). He returned to OKH after leaving the 3rd.

A native of Holstein, Wilhelm Soeth was born in 1903 and joined the 6th Infantry Regiment in 1921. He promoted to major general on January 30, 1945.

He had previously commanded the II/56th Artillery Regiment (1938–43), the 73rd Panzer Artillery Regiment (1943–44), and the 1131st Grenadier Brigade (1944). He lived in Hamburg in the 1950s.

## NOTES AND SOURCES

The 3rd Panzer was one of the three original panzer divisions in the German Army. Ironically, its divisional symbol was the peace symbol, worn by many American antiwar demonstrators, draft dodgers, hippies, and other unwashed persons in the 1960s and 1970s.

In 1942, the 75th Artillery Regiment added a III Battalion, the 314th Army Flak Artillery Battalion joined the division, and the 3rd Motorcycle Battalion became the 3rd Panzer Reconnaissance Battalion; meanwhile, the III/6th Panzer Regiment was dissolved and its men and equipment transferred to the division's other two tank battalions.

Benoist-Mechin: 241; Bradley et al., Volume 3: 452–53; Volume 4: 267–28; Carell 1966: 9, 474, 488, 491, 512, 546–50; Carell 1971: 19, 48, 142; Chapman: 347–48; Hartmann: 61–62; Keilig: 23, 51, 89, 106, 191, 326, 340; Manstein: 488, 525; Mehner, Volume 5: 329; Georg Meyer, "Geyr, Leo," in David G. Chandler and James Lawton Collins, Jr., eds., *The D-Day Encyclopedia* (New York, 1994): 274–78 (hereafter cited simply as "*D-Day Encyclopedia*"); Leo Geyr von Schweppenburg, "Panzer Group West (Mid 43–5 July 44"), United States Army Military History Institute, Carlilse Barracks, Pa. *MS # B-258 and MS # B-466* (hereafter cited as "Geyr MS"); Schmitz et al., Volume 1: 215–17; Stoves, *Gepanzerten*: 25–31; Tessin, Volume 2: 173–74; RA: 46; OB 42: 55, 199; OB 45: 287. Also see Richard Brett-Smith, *Hitler's Generals* (San Rafael, California, 1976): 176–78 (hereafter cited as "Brett-Smith"), for an account of Geyr von Schweppenburg's career.

# 4th Panzer Division

**COMPOSITION (1943):**   35th Panzer Regiment, 12th Panzer Grenadier Regiment, 33rd Panzer Grenadier Regiment, 103rd Panzer Artillery Regiment, 34th Motorcycle Battalion, 7th Panzer Reconnaissance Battalion, 49th Tank Destroyer Battalion, 79th Panzer Engineer Battalion, 79th Panzer Signal Battalion.

**HOME STATION:**   Wuerzburg, Wehrkreis XIII

The peacetime 4th Panzer Division was formed at Wuerzburg in 1938 and consisted mainly of Bavarians, with draftees from other parts of Germany. Initially it consisted of the 4th Rifle Brigade (12th Rifle Regiment at Meiningen) and the 5th Panzer Brigade at Bamberg (including the 35th Panzer Regiment at Bamberg and 36th Panzer Regiment at Schweinfurt), along with the two battalion 103rd Artillery (later Panzer Artillery) Regiment at Meiningen, and assorted divisional troops, including the 7th Motorized (later Panzer) Reconnaissance Battalion, 79th Engineer Battalion, 79th Signal Battalion, and the 49th Antitank (later Tank Destroyer) Battalion. In the Polish campaign the 4th Panzer Division distinguished itself by penetrating from Germany to the outskirts of Warsaw in just eight days, although it could not take the city and lost about half its tanks in the attempt—most of them during street fighting in the Polish capital. The following month (October 1939) it received the 33rd Rifle (later Panzer Grenadier) Regiment from the 13th Motorized Infantry Division and the 34th Motorcycle Battalion from the 2nd Infantry Division. Both were assigned to the 4th Rifle Brigade.

Sent to the lower Rhine in late 1939, the 4th Panzer Division spearheaded the invasion of southern Holland in May 1940 and captured the critical frontier city of Maastricht. Then (along with 3rd Panzer Division) it pushed the French mobile forces east to the Dyle, effectively isolating the Netherlands, the conquest of which was completed by the 18th Army a few days later. The 4th Panzer then participated in the Dunkirk campaign, took part in the battle of the Weygand Line, and helped finish off France in June 1940. Its losses were negligible. Returning to Germany in November, it lost the 36th Panzer Regiment plus some cadres to the 14th Panzer (formerly 4th Infantry) Division that winter; simultaneously, it added a third battalion to its artillery regiment. In January 1941 it acquired 20 new PzKw IV-Es. Four months later, the division was sent to East Prussia and, as part of Army Group Center, the 4th Panzer crossed into Russia in June 1941 and fought at Minsk, Gomel, Bryansk, Vyasma, and other bitterly contested points on the road to Moscow. By mid-November, it had only 50 operational tanks left. In December 1941 it attempted to encircle the strategic city of Tula, southeast of Moscow, but failed, suffering heavy losses in the attempt. Remaining on the central sector of the Russian Front until 1944, it defended the Kirov sector (1942) and the Orel sector (1942–early 1943), fought in the Kursk and Dnieper campaigns (1943–early 1944), in the Bobruisk and Kovel battles (1944), and in the unsuccessful attempt to check the Soviet summer offensive of 1944. Reorganized in 1941, 1942, and 1943, the division in 1944 included the 12th and 33rd Panzer Grenadier Regiments (two battalions each), the 4th Reconnaissance Battalion, the 35th Panzer Regiment (two battalions), the 103rd Panzer Artillery Regiment, the 290th Army Flak Battalion (added in 1942), and other divisional troops, including the 103rd Field Replacement Battalion and the 84th *Versorgunstruppen* (Supply Troop). The division lost its brigade headquarters in 1942.

In November 1944, the 4th Panzer Division was isolated in the Courland Pocket but was evacuated by sea to northern Germany in early 1945. Now in remnants, the 4th Panzer underwent a partial refit at Danzig, but could not be completely rebuilt. It took part in the West Prussian and Vistula campaigns of 1945—the last of the war. It ended the conflict isolated on the Frischen Nehrung, along with the remnants of the 2nd Army, and its survivors surrendered to the Soviets in May 1945.

The 4th Panzer Division was an outstanding unit even by German Army standards, and it was the most heavily decorated of all the German tank divisions.

Commanders of the 4th Panzer included Major General/Lieutenant General Georg-Hans Reinhardt (assumed command November 10, 1938), Major General Ritter Ludwig von Radlmeier (February 5, 1940), Major General Joachim Stever (April 6, 1940), Colonel Baron Hans von Boineburg-Lengsfeld (May 15, 1940), Stever (resumed command, May 19, 1940), von Boineburg-Lengsfeld again (July 24, 1940), Major General/Lieutenant General Baron Willibald von Langermann-Erlenkamp (September 7, 1940), Major General Dietrich von Saucken (December 24, 1941), Major General Heinrich Eberbach (March 2, 1942), Lieutenant Colonel Otto Heidkaemper (acting commander, March 2, 1942), Eberbach (April 4, 1942), Colonel Edgar Hielscher (June 23, 1942), Eberbach (resumed command, July 3, 1942), Colonel/Major General Dr. Erich Schneider (November 24, 1942), Lieutenant General von Saucken (May 31, 1943), Major General Hans Junck (acting commander, January 21, 1944), Saucken again (February 1944), Major General/Lieutenant General Clemens Betzel (May 1, 1944), Saucken again (June 1944), Betzel (June 1944), Colonel Hans Christern (December 21, 1944), Betzel (December 28, 1944), Colonel Ernst Wilhelm Hoffmann (acting commander, March 27, 1945) and Major General Hans Hecker (April 1, 1945).

## COMMANDERS

Georg-Hans Reinhardt (1887–1963), who was promoted to lieutenant general on October 1, 1939, joined the army in 1907 as an infantry Fahnenjunker and rose to the rank of colonel general on June 1, 1942. A solid, dependable and competent commander, he led the XXXXI Motorized (subsequently Panzer) Corps in France and Russia (1940–41) and the 3rd Panzer Army from late 1941 until the fall of 1944. Named commander of Army Group Center on August 16, 1944, Hitler relieved him of his command on January 25, 1945, because Reinhardt demanded permission to abandon East Prussia in order to avoid being isolated there. Reinhardt would have been replaced in any case: he had suffered a serious head wound a few hours before, but word had not yet reached Fuehrer Headquarters when Hitler sacked Reinhardt. A holder of the Knight's Cross with Oak Leaves and Swords, Reinhardt had commanded the 1st Rifle Brigade before the war.

Ludwig von Radlmeier (1887–1943) was one of the intellectual founders of the concept of the blitzkrieg and was writing articles advocating armored warfare long before Guderian. Radlmeier entered the Bavarian Army as an infantry Fahnenjunker in 1908 and commanded the 6th Panzer Brigade (1938–39), 5th Panzer Brigade (1939–40), and 4th Panzer Division (1940). Promoted to major general in 1938, his health was not robust, and he was forced to give up command of the division after only a week. He returned to duty that fall as an inspector in the Home Army, but was forced to give up even this position in the spring of 1941. He was nevertheless promoted to lieutenant general in 1942, the year before his death.

Johann Joachim Stever (1889–1945), a Berliner, joined the Prussian Army in 1908 as an infantry officer cadet and was chief of staff of XV Motorized Corps by 1938. Not a huge success as commander of the 4th Panzer Division, he was given command of the Saxon 336th Infantry Division in late 1940—a serious demotion. He led his new unit on the Eastern Front until March 1942, when he either fell ill or was wounded. When he returned to duty that summer, he was named *Oberfeldkommandantur 399* (OFK 399)—a military territorial command (hereafter translated as military area command) in occupied Russia. Apparently this was also too much for his health, for he was unemployed by the end of

1943 and officially retired in 1944. A lieutenant general since June 1941, he was picked up by the Soviets at the end of the war and disappeared. He has not been seen or heard from since and was almost certainly murdered by the Soviets.

For Baron von Boineburg-Lengsfeld's career, see Commanders, 23rd Panzer Division.

Baron Willibald von Langermann-Erlenkamp (1890–1942) was a cavalry officer who became a capable armored officer. Commissioned in the 5th Dragoon Regiment in 1910, he became commander of the 4th Cavalry Regiment in late 1935, was named Higher Cavalry Officer I in 1938, and then became inspector of cavalry and transport troops. He was named commander of Special Administrative Division Staff 410 in late 1939—a real backwater post. Three days before the invasion of France began, he was given command of the elite 29th Motorized Infantry Division in France—a surprising appointment, given Langermann's background and the fact that he had been promoted to major general less than three months before. He nevertheless proved himself to be a skillful commander of mobile formations in the conquests of Belgium and France, and was rewarded for his success by being given command of the 4th Panzer Division. On January 8, 1942, he was named commander of the XXIV Panzer Corps on the Eastern Front, followed a week later by a promotion to lieutenant general. He became a general of panzer troops on June 1, 1942. Baron von Langermann was killed in action during the Battle of Stalingrad on October 3, 1942.

A Wuerttemberger, Heinrich Eberbach (b. 1895) was born in Stuttgart and joined the Imperial Army as an infantry cadet in 1914. He was discharged in 1919 after Germany lost World War I. He then joined the poice and remained there until 1935, rising to the rank of major. He rejoined the army when Hitler reintroduced conscription in 1935. He received command of the 35th Panzer Regiment in late 1938. After fighting in Poland and France, Eberbach was given command of the 5th Panzer Brigade of the 4th Panzer Division in July 1941 and took over the division on January 6, 1942. He was promoted to major general on February 1 and to lieutenant general on January 1, 1943. On August 1, 1943, he became a general of panzer troops and took charge of XXXXVIII Panzer Corps on October 1. On July 5, 1944, he replaced Geyr von Schweppenburg as commander of Panzer Group West (which was then upgraded to 5th Panzer Army). Eberbach held this post from July 5 to August 21, 1944, when he was named commander of the 7th Army. He held his new command only ten days. He was captured on August 31, 1944, during the German retreat from France. He died in Norzingen in 1992 at age 95.

Otto Heidkaemper was acting divisional commander in the absence of General Eberbach and simultaneously Ia (chief operations officer) of the division. Previously he had served on the staff of Rommel's 7th Panzer Division.

Edgar Hielscher was the chief of operations (Ia) of the 4th Panzer Division in the summer of 1942. He was acting commander of the division in the absence of General Eberbach, who was gone for about a week.

Erich Schneider (1881–1948), a Hessian artillery officer with an advanced engineering degree, was a ballistics expert and spent much of his career in the Ballistics Branch. He commanded the 103rd Panzer Artillery Regiment of the 4th Panzer Division (June 1940–early 1942) before assuming command of the division. Promoted to major general on January 1, 1943, he returned to the Weapons Office on June 1 and was promoted to lieutenant general a month later. In 1944 he was the head of the Experimental and Testing Group of the Army Ordnance Office. His last post was as commander of the 14th Panzer Grenadier Division on the Eastern Front and in East Prussia (December 28, 1944–March 20, 1945). He was without an assignment at the end of the war. Schneider held the Knight's Cross with Oak Leaves.

Dietrich von Saucken (b. 1892) was an East Prussian cavalry officer who possessed incredible courage and the skill to match. As late as March 1945 he categorically (and rudely) refused to obey one of Hitler's orders to the dictator's face—and got away with it. Saucken joined the army as an infantry cadet in 1912 but soon transferred to the mounted branch. He led the 2nd Cavalry Regiment (1937–late 1940), the 4th Rifle Brigade (1940–December 1941) and the 4th Panzer Division only briefly (December 27, 1941–January 2, 1942). Seriously wounded, he did not return to active duty until August 24, 1942, as commander of the School for Mobile Troops. Reassuming command of the division on May 31, 1943, shortly after his promotion to lieutenant general, he became deputy commander of the III Panzer Corps (May 1944), commander of the XXXIX Panzer Corps (June 1944), the Grossdeutschland Panzer Corps (December 1944), and the 2nd Army in East Prussia (March 1945). Saucken was the last man to receive the Knight's Cross with Oak Leaves and Swords. Promoted to general of panzer troops on August 1, 1944, he surrendered his army to the Soviets in May 1945 and spent the next 10 years in Communist prison camps. He lived in Bavaria in the 1970s and died on September 27, 1980.

Clemens Betzel, a Bavarian, was a reserve major in 1940. He commanded the II/93rd Artillery Regiment (1939–41) and the 103rd Panzer Artillery Regiment of the 4th Panzer Division (late 1941–spring 1944), before taking charge of the 4th Panzer Division as senior regimental commander in May 1944. Promoted to major general on July 1, 1944 and to lieutenant general on January 1, 1945, he led the 4th until March 27, 1945, when he was killed in action near Danzig (now in Poland) on the Eastern Front.

Hans Junck (b. 1893) joined the army in 1913 and was a department chief in the Army Personnel Office when the war began. He went to the field in 1943 and successively commanded the 609th Artillery Regiment, Arko 125, the 4th Panzer and the 253rd, 299th and 265th Infantry Divisions. At the end of the war, he was commandant of the isolated fortress of St. Nazaire. He was promoted to lieutenant general in early 1945.

For information on Hans Christern, see 7th Panzer Division.

Ernst Wilhelm Hoffmann (1904–1991), a Bavarian, was the former commander of I/12th Rifle Regiment (1940–42) and the 12th Panzer Grenadier Regiment (1944). He held the Knight's Cross with Oak Leaves.

Hans Hecker (1895–1979) was born in Duisburg and joined the army as an artillery Fahnenjunker in late 1914, but transferred to the engineers in 1915. He remained in the engineers during the interwar years and commanded the 29th Motorized Engineer Battalion of the 29th Motorized Division (1938–41) in Poland, France, and Russia. Hecker was named engineer commander, Panzer Army Afrika, in early 1942 and distinguished himself commanding a battle group in the capture of Bir Hacheim, during which he was wounded when his command vehicle struck a mine. In February, 1943, he was named commander of the 29th Motorized Division, a new unit (the original 29th had been destroyed at Stalingrad), but only very briefly. Later he commanded the 345th Motorized Infantry Division (1943), the Panzer School at Krampnitz (1943), and the 3rd Panzer Grenadier Division in Italy (1944). After serving as acting commander of the 26th Panzer Division (1944), he was commander of the 3rd Panzer Grenadier Regiment (1944) and the 4th Panzer (1945). Hecker managed to escape Soviet captivity; exactly how is not revealed by the records. Apparently he boarded one of the last ships to leave the area in May, 1945.

## NOTES AND SOURCES

Benoist-Mechin: 241; Bradley et al., Volume 5: 221–22; Carell 1966: 69, 79, 80, 136–37; Carell 1971: 35, 591–94; Chant 1979, Volume 2: 217, Volume 14: 1931; Chapman: 347–48; Edwards, *Panzer*: 74; Keilig: 32, 44, 131, 160, 197, 292, 333; Manstein: 487, 538; Mehner, Volume 4: 382, Volume 5: 329, Volume 10: 520, Volume 11: 367, Volume 12: 458; Schmitz et al., Volume 1: 289–91; Gerhard von Seemen, *Die Ritterkreuztraeger 1938–1945* (Friedberg, 1976): 56 (hereafter cited as "Seemen"); Stauffenberg MS; Stoves, *Gepanzerten*: 37–43; Tessin, Volume 2: 242–44; OB 42: 56; OB 43: 199–200; OB 45: 288.

# 5th Panzer Division

**COMPOSITION (1943):** 31st Panzer Regiment, 13th Panzer Grenadier Regiment, 14th Panzer Grenadier Regiment, 116th Panzer Artillery Regiment, 55th Motorcycle Battalion, 8th Panzer Reconnaissance Battalion, 53rd Tank Destroyer Battalion, 89th Panzer Engineer Battalion, 85th Panzer Signal Battalion.

**HOME STATION:** Oppeln, Wehrkreis VIII

Originally a peacetime division, the 5th Panzer fought well throughout its existence and was six times cited for distinguished conduct in combat on the Eastern Front. Organized in November 1938 after the annexation of the Sudetenland, the division's troops were mainly Silesians and Sudeten Germans. It initially consisted of the 13th and 14th Rifle (Schuetzen) Regiments, the 8th Panzer Brigade (15th and 31st Panzer Regiments), the 116th Panzer Artillery Regiment (two battalions), the 8th Motorized (later Panzer) Reconnaissance Battalion, the 53rd Antitank Battalion, the 77th Panzer Signal Battalion, the 89th Panzer Engineer Battalion, and assorted divisional troops. When Germany mobilized in August 1939, the 5th Rifle Brigade was activated and took charge of the 13th and 14th Rifle Regiments, which it controlled until November 1942, when it was dissolved. (Strength reductions in the panzer divisions—which were the result of reorganizations and casualties—made the panzer and rifle brigades superfluous in the panzer divisions and they were dissolved or converted into other types of headquarters in 1942 and 1943.) The 5th Panzer Brigade was transferred to the 3rd Panzer Division in January 1941 but was dissolved 13 months later. The 15th Panzer Regiment was transferred to the newly formed 11th Panzer Division in September 1940, at the same time the 116th Panzer Artillery Regiment absorbed the II/48th Artillery Regiment as its third battalion.

Meanwhile, the division played a minor and "inconspicuous" role in the Polish campaign of 1939 and a "prominent" part in the French campaign of 1940, according to Allied intelligence evaluations. It took part in the conquest of Belgium, the destruction of the French armies around Lille in the Dunkirk Pocket, and the capture of Rouen. It pushed almost all the way to the Spanish frontier before the armistice was signed. The 5th Panzer remained in France until January 1941, when it was sent to Romania. In April and May it was involved in the Balkans campaign, fighting in both Yugoslavia and Greece, including a sharp battle with (and victory over) the 2nd New Zealand Division at Molos. Sent to Russia and Army Group Center in July, the division took part in heavy fighting all the way to the gates of Moscow, including the battles of Vyasma and Istria. Remaining on the central sector, it faced the Soviet winter offensive of 1941–42 and fought in the defensive battles of 1942–43, including Rzhev, the Rzhev withdrawal, Vyasma, Spas-Demjansk, and Gshatsk. It suffered heavy losses near Orel during the unsuccessful Kursk offensive.

Later in 1943 it fought in the battles on the middle Dnieper and in the summer of 1944 it counterattacked against the massive Russian offensive, inflicting considerable casualties on the Soviets near Bobruisk, Kovel, and Minsk. The 5th Panzer was unable to turn the tide and save the trapped elements of the 4th and 9th Armies and, with the remnants of Army Group Center, took part in the retreats across White Russia and Poland, briefly fought in Courland, and retreated into East Prussia, where it fought in the battles of Koenigsberg and Pillau. It was still fighting, isolated on the Samland peninsula in mid-April, when the German Navy was ordered to transport it back to the West. This operation was not finished when the war ended. The bulk of the division was in Pomerania or Bornholm, Schleswig-Holstein when the Third Reich capitulated. Much of the 5th Panzer managed to surrender to the Western Allies, although a significant portion was still on the Hela peninsula and had to surrender to the Russians. The 5th was one of the best German divisions in World War II, and as late as July 1944 the Soviet High Command advised its generals that the best way to deal with the 5th Panzer was to avoid it whenever possible.

Commanders of this division included Lieutenant General Heinrich von Vietinghoff gennant Scheel (assumed command November 24, 1938), Lieutenant General Max von Hartlieb gennant Walsporn (October 18, 1939), Lieutenant General Joachim Lemelsen (May 29, 1940), Major General Ludwig Cruewell (June 6, 1940), Lemelsen (July 4, 1940), Major General/Lieutenant General Gustav Fehn (November 25, 1940), Major General Eduard Metz (August 8, 1942), Colonel Johannes Nedtwig (February 1, 1943), Major General Ernst Felix Faeckenstedt (July 5, 1943), Major General/Lieutenant General Karl Decker (September 7, 1943), Lieutenant Colonel Heinrich-Walter von Bronsart von Schellendorff (December 30, 1943), Decker (resumed command, January 30, 1944), Colonel/Major General Rolf Lippert (October 16, 1944), Major General

Guenther Hoffmann-Schoenborn (February 19, 1945), Major General Karl Koetz (April 1, 1945), and Colonel of Reserves Hans Herzog (April 9, 1945).

## COMMANDERS

Heinrich von Vietinghoff (1887–1952) was a tough, solid East Prussian soldier—extremely capable but not brilliant. He spent most of his career in the infantry, entering the service as a *Faehnrich* (senior cadet–sometimes translated as "ensign") in the 2nd Guards Grenadier Regiment in 1906. A better infantry than armored commander, Vietinghoff did not earn any special laurels commanding the 5th Panzer in Poland in 1939. He later led XIII Corps in the West (1939–40), XXXXVI Panzer Corps in the Balkans and Russia (1940–42), the 9th Army in Russia (September–December 1942), and the 15th Army in France (late 1942–September 1943) before being sent to Italy. He fought his most famous battles there as commander of the 10th Army (September 1943–January 1945) or as acting commander in chief of Army Group C (October–December 1944). He was named commander of Army Group Courland in January 1945 but returned to Italy as OB Southwest (Supreme Commander, Southwest)—this time on a permanent basis—in March 1945. Field Marshal Kesselring relieved him of his command at the end of April for being involved in unauthorized surrender negotiations. A few days later, Vietinghoff surrendered to the Allies. He was promoted to general of panzer troops in 1940 and to colonel general in September 1943. An excellent commander at all levels, General von Vietinghoff is best known for his very skillful retreats before the Americans and British in Italy (1943–44).

Max von Hartlieb gen. Walsporn (1883–1959) joined the army as an infantry cadet in 1904. A rather early convert to mobile warfare, he commanded the 2nd Rifle Regiment (1934–35), the 2nd Panzer Brigade (1935–38), and the 5th Panzer Brigade (1938–39) before assuming command of the 5th Panzer Division. His performance as divisional commander in Belgium and France left much to be desired, however, and his corps commander, General Hoth, was not at all satisfied with him. Hartlieb was relieved of his command on May 29 and, a month later, was placed in charge of Special Administrative Divisional Staff 179 in Weimar—a definite demotion. From this point his career was effectively ruined and he received no further promotions. He later commanded Korueck 585 (a rear-area headquarters) (1942), Military Area Command 226 (1943–44) and Special Divisional Staff 601 (1944–45)—all in the East. He was wounded by partisans in May 1942 and did not return to duty until February 1943. General Hartlieb was unemployed at the end of the war.

Joachim Lemelsen (1888–1954), a Berliner, entered the service as an artillery Fahnenjunker in 1907. He was commander of the Artillery Lehr (Demonstration) Regiment in 1934 and later was a course commandant at the Infantry School at Dresden (1935–38), and commander of the 29th Motorized Infantry

Division (1938–40). Named commander of the 5th Panzer Division in the last days of the French campaign (in part because he was close at hand), he was promoted to general of artillery on August 1, 1940. (Later, on June 4, 1941, he changed his branch affiliation and became a general of panzer troops.) Lemelsen led XXXXVI Panzer Corps (1940–43) in Russia, was acting commander of the 10th Army in Italy (October–December 1943), and commanded the 1st Army in France (May–June 5, 1944) and the 14th Army in Italy (1944). He was demoted to deputy army commander in Italy in December 1944. Lemelsen held the Knight's Cross with Oak Leaves. A pro-Nazi, Lemelsen was an excellent motorized divisional commander and did well leading panzers in Russia. He was less successful as an army commander in Italy.

For a sketch of Ludwig Cruewell's career, see 11th Panzer Division.

A Franconian, Gustav Fehn was born in Nuremberg in 1892. He joined the army as an infantry officer cadet in 1911. During World War II, Fehn commanded the 33rd Infantry Regiment (1938–40), 4th Rifle Brigade (1940), 5th Panzer Division (1940–42), XXXX Panzer Corps in Russia (late 1942), and the Afrika Korps in Libya (December 1942–January 1943). On January 15, 1943, he was seriously wounded and evacuated to Germany. He did not recover until July, when he became acting commander of the XXVI Panzer Corps. Later he commanded the XXI Mountain Corps (1943–44) and the XV Mountain Corps (1944–45). He was promoted to lieutenant general (August 1, 1942) and to general of panzer troops (November 1, 1942). He was murdered by Yugoslavian partisans on June 5, 1945.

Eduard Metz, a Bavarian artillery and General Staff officer, was born in Munich in 1891 and entered the service in 1912. He was Ia of Group Command I (1938–39), Ia of the 10th Army (1939), chief of staff of XIV Panzer Corps (1939–41), liaison officer between the Romanians and the 11th Army (1941), and commander of the German Army Mission to Romania (1942). Metz took command of the 5th Panzer Division on August 10, 1942, and was apparently wounded in action on February 12, 1943, for he held no assignments for several months. After leaving the 5th Panzer, Metz directed Harko 302 (the 302nd Higher Artillery Command) (September 1943–January 1945) and was promoted to lieutenant general on January 1, 1944. He was apparently without an assignment at the end of the war.

Johannes Nedtwig (b. 1894), a native of Pomerania, joined the army as a war volunteer in 1914 and received a reserve commission in the infantry in 1916. He left the service in 1921 (when the army was reduced to 100,000 men) but returned to active duty in 1934. He was commander of the 1st Panzer Regiment (1938–40), served on the staff of the 2nd Army (1940), and was commander of the tank school (1940–43) before taking over command of the 5th Panzer Division as a colonel. Promoted to major general on August 1, 1943, he later commanded the 156th Reserve Division (1943), the 73rd Infantry Division (1943–44), and the 454th Security Division (1944). Captured by the Russians when his division was overrun on July 22, 1944, Nedtwig spent the next 11 years in

Soviet prisons. His assignments after leaving the 5th Panzer, coupled with the fact that he was not promoted to lieutenant general, are sure indications that someone in authority was not satisfied with his performance as commander of the 5th Panzer Division.

Ernst Felix Faeckenstedt, a Saxon, was born in Dresden in 1896 and entered the service as an infantry Fahnenjunker when World War I broke out. Remaining in the service between the world wars (mainly in the cavalry), he was Ia of III Corps (1938–39), chief of staff of III Corps (later III Panzer Corps) (1939–42), and chief of staff of the 1st Panzer Army (1942–43) before assuming command of the 5th Panzer Division. Later he returned to Germany as chief of staff of Wehrkreis VI (1943–44) and Wehrkreis XII (1944–45). He was promoted to lieutenant general on September 1, 1943, and was a prisoner-of-war until 1948. He died in 1961.

Karl Decker was born in Pomerania in 1897 and entered the army as a Fahnenjunker a few weeks after World War I broke out. From 1919 to 1935 he served in the Reichsheer. An excellent panzer officer and combat leader, he commanded the 1st Antitank Battalion (1936–40), I/3rd Panzer Regiment (1940–41), 3rd Panzer Regiment in Russia (1941–43), 21st Panzer Brigade (1943), 5th Panzer Division (1943–44), and XXXIX Panzer Corps (1944–45). He was promoted rapidly: lieutenant colonel (1939), colonel (1942), major general (1943), lieutenant general (June 1, 1944), and general of panzer troops (January 1, 1945). Trapped in the Ruhr Pocket and despairing over the fact that Germany had lost the war, General Decker took his own life on April 21, 1945, rather than surrender to the Americans.

Heinrich Bronsart von Schellendorff normally commanded the 13th Panzer Grenadier Regiment (1943–44). Promoted to colonel in 1944, he led the 111th Panzer Brigade on the Western Front in the fall of 1944. He was killed in action on September 22, 1944. Bronsart was posthumously promoted to major general and was awarded the Oak Leaves to his Knight's Cross. Bronsart had entered the service as a Fahnenjunker in the 6th Cavalry Regiment in 1925. He did not join the motorized branch until late 1939, when, as a captain, he was named commander of the 36th Motorized Reconnaissance Battalion. He also commanded the 36th Motorcycle Battalion (1942).

Rolf Lippert (1900–1945) was a native of Leipzig. He entered the army as a Fahnenjunker in the infantry at the tail end of World War I but was not commissioned until 1922, by which time he had transferred to the cavalry. He was commander of the 216th Reconnaissance Battalion when the war began. Later he commanded the 9th Reconnaissance Battalion (1940–41), the 15th Bicycle Training Battalion (1941–43), the Grossdeutschland Panzer Regiment (1943), the 31st Panzer Regiment, and the 5th Panzer Division. Promoted to major general on January 1, 1945, Rolf Lippert was killed in action at Bielefeld on April 1, 1945.

A young officer, Guenther Hoffmann-Schoenborn was born in Posen (now Poland) in 1905. He enlisted in 1924 and was commissioned in the 3rd Artillery

Regiment in 1928. A captain and battery commander in the 42nd Artillery Regiment when the war began, Hoffmann later commanded the 191st Assault Gun Battalion (1940–43), the 2nd Artillery Lehr Regiment (1943), the Assault Gun School at Burg (1943–44), and the 18th Volksgrenadier Division (1944–45). During the Battle of the Bulge, Hoffmann was primarily responsible for encircling and destroying the U.S. 106th Infantry Division in the Schnee Eifel, the worst disaster to befall the American Army in Europe during World War II. He was wounded and evacuated from East Prussia in April 1945. An assault gun specialist, he was the first artillery officer to receive the Knight's Cross with Oak Leaves (1941). He died in Bad Kreuznach, the Rhineland, in 1970.

Karl Koetz was born in 1908 and, like Hoffmann-Schoenborn, was an infantry officer who rose rapidly. He was a lieutenant in 1937 and a company commander when the war broke out. Later he commanded II/463rd Infantry Regiment (1941–43), 185th Infantry Regiment (1943–44), 349th Infantry Division (1944–45), and the 21st Infantry Division in East Prussia (1945). His chief qualification for command of the 5th Panzer Division seems to have been that he was a competent general and his own division had already been virtually destroyed, through no fault of his own. Koetz, however, was ill and no doubt exhausted from four years on the Eastern Front. Although he was named commander of the 5th Panzer, it is questionable if he ever assumed the post. If he did, he only commanded the division for a week, and had to be relieved for reasons of health. He retired to Duesseldorf.

Hans-Georg Herzog was a reserve officer. A first lieutenant commanding 1/13th Rifle Regiment in 1942, he was rapidly promoted thereafter. Herzog was a captain commanding II/14th Panzer Grenadier Regiment in September 1943. A major in 1944, he was a lieutenant colonel commanding the 14th Panzer Grenadier in March 1945. He was apparently promoted to colonel when he assumed command of the division. Herzog was severely wounded in the last days of the war, but remained in command of the division. He held the Knight's Cross with Oak Leaves. Born in 1912, Herzog was still alive in 1990.

## NOTES AND SOURCES

The division added the 228th Army Flak Artillery Battalion in 1942.

Angolia, *Field*, Volume 2: 59; Benoist-Mechin: 304; Bradley et al., Volume 2: 284–85; Volume 3: 395–97; Volume 5: 126–27; Carell 1966: 175, 330; Carell 1971: 309, 591–92; Chant 1979: 53; Edwards, *Panzer*: 75; Keilig: 64, 85–86, 126, 147, 179, 207, 224, 238; Kennedy: 74; Mellenthin 1977: 176–77; Mehner, Volume 5: 329; Volume 6: 545; Volume 7: 354; Volume 12: 458; Schmitz et al., Volume 1: 361–71; Stoves, *Gepanzerten*: 52; Tessin, Volume 2: 293–94; RA: 130; OB 42: 56; OB 43: 200; OB 45: 288.

# 6th Panzer Division

**COMPOSITION (1943):** 11th Panzer Regiment, 4th Panzer Grenadier Regiment, 114th Panzer Grenadier Regiment, 76th Panzer Artillery Regiment, 57th Panzer Reconnaissance Battalion, 41st Tank Destroyer Battalion, 57th Panzer Engineer Battalion, 82nd Panzer Signal Battalion.

**HOME STATION:** Wuppertal, Wehrkreis VI

Created as the 1st Light Brigade at Wuppertal on October 12, 1937, the 6th Panzer was composed of Westphalians and Rhinelanders. It was expanded to divisional size in the spring of 1938, with relatively little increase in its strength. The new division initially contained the 11th Panzer Regiment, the 4th Mechanized Cavalry Regiment (four battalions), the 76th Motorized Artillery Regiment (two battalions), the 6th Reconnaissance Battalion, the 41st Panzer Abwehr (Antitank) Battalion, the 57th Engineer Battalion, and the 82nd Signal Battalion. On April 1, 1939, the IV/4th Mechanized Cavalry was separated from its regiment and became the 6th Motorcycle Battalion.

As was the case with virtually every prewar German division, the 1st Light was very well dispersed. The mechanized cavalry regiment was divided between bases at Iserlohn and Wuppertal, the reconnaissance battalion was at Krefeld, the artillery units' barracks were at Wuppertal and in the Senne Maneuver Area, the antitank companies were billeted at Iserlohn, the engineers were at Muelheim (in the Ruhr), and the 11th Panzer Regiment garrisoned at Paderborn.

In preparation for Hitler's 1938 operations against the Sudetenland, the division was temporarily given the 65th Panzer Battalion—a move which was made permanent in late 1939. Thus reinforced, the 1st Light Division took part in the

71

occupation of theSudetenland in October 1938 and in the bloodless conquest of Czechoslovakia in April 1939. Almost immediately thereafter the Wehrmacht gave the 11th Panzer Regiment and 65th Panzer Battalion about 130 Skoda-built Czech tanks, which were designated PzKw 35 (t). Although they only weighed 10.5 tons, they were superior to all of the German tanks of that day except the PzKw III.

The division fought in southern Poland in 1939, after which the High Command of the Army (Oberkommando des Heeres or OKH) determined that the light divisions were too unwieldy to be of optimum effectiveness; consequently, the 1st was converted into a panzer division, as were the 2nd, 3rd, and 4th Light Divisions, which became the 7th, 8th, and 9th Panzer Divisions, respectively. The 1st Light was redesignated the 6th Panzer Division on October 18, 1939, and consisted of the newly formed 6th Rifle Brigade (which controlled the 4th and 114th Rifle Regiments and the 6th Motorcycle Battalion), the 11th Panzer Regiment, the 65th Panzer Battalion, the 76th Panzer Artillery Regiment, and associated divisional troops. Although the new tank divisions were smaller than the panzer divisions created earlier and were equipped with Czech-made 35 (t) tanks, they performed very creditably in the West. (The Czech tanks were major maintenance challenges—largely because the technical manuals which accompanied them were written in Czech, which the German mechanics could not read.) The 6th Panzer fought its way through Belgium, pushed across the Meuse, and played a prominent role in the drive to the English Channel, during which it pushed forward 217 miles in nine days, and overran and captured the British 145th Infantry Brigade at Cassel. It took part in the conquest of Flanders and in the subsequent drive to the south, advancing from the Aisne River to the Swiss border. Sent back to Germany, it gave up large cadres to help form the 16th Panzer Division, but incorporated the 114th Rifle Regiment (formerly the 243rd Infantry Regiment of the 60th Infantry Division) and a third artillery battalion into its table of organization. The division now had a total of 239 tanks but only 12 were PzKw IIIs—and even they were inferior to the Soviet T-34, KV-1, and KV-2 tanks they would soon have to face.

In September 1940, the 6th Panzer Division was sent to East Prussia and subsequently to Poland, where it remained until June 1941, when it crossed into the Soviet Union. The 6th broke through the Stalin Line, crossed the Dvina, fought in the Battle of Ostrov, and crossed the Luga—an advance of 500 miles in three weeks. Here OKH ordered it to halt to allow supplies and infantry units to catch up, and the division did not resume its drive on Leningrad until August 8. By this time the Soviets had partially recovered, and the fighting was even more severe, but on September 9 elements of the division took the Duderhof hill southwest of the city and signaled that it could see St. Petersburg and the sea. Hilter, however, ordered that the city not be taken—he preferred to starve it into submission. He transferred the 6th Panzer Division (along with most of the rest of Army Group North's armor) to Army Group Center in October, and the 6th became part of the drive on Moscow. It was involved in the exceptionally hard-fought battles of Vyasma, Kalinin, Klin, and Moscow. Temperatures fell to minus 22 degrees Fahrenheit and all of the Czech tanks—which featured pneumatic clutches, brakes, and steering controls—failed in the bitter cold. On December 6, Stalin unleashed his winter offensive of 1941–42, and four days later the 6th Panzer lost only its remaining tank—a vehicle which had appropriately been dubbed "Anthony the Last." Due to the terrible weather, motorized vehicles could not be started unless warmed up first by improvised stoves. Since very few of these were available, the men often resorted to using open fires or applying blow torches directly to the engine blocks. The results were predictable and more than one vehicle exploded or was burned up, and at least one village was accidentally burned to the ground (along with a German convoy) when the fires could not be extinguished.

By the end of the year virtually every motorized vehicle in the division had been lost or abandoned, and the division had appropriated more than 1,000 Russian *panje* wagons (two-wheeled carts). The men of the unit now referred to their division as the "6th Panzer of Foot," and the soldiers of the 11th Panzer Regiment were organized as a battalion and fought as marching infantry. The division nevertheless remained in the line and kept the vital Rzhev-Vyasma Road—the lifeline of the German 9th Army—open, despite repeated attacks from greatly superior enemy forces. By the end of January 1942, the 6th Panzer Division had fewer than 1,000 combat effectives remaining and only three operational guns. With the help of replacements (made up of stragglers, the survivors of other mauled divisions and men drafted from disbanded supply units), the 6th Panzer launched a "Snail Offensive" through the heavy snow and slowly pushed the Russians back 10 to 15 miles from the road, taking more than 80 villages in the process.

The Russian thaw began in March 1942, and in April the 6th Panzer was transferred back to northwestern France, which seemed like fairyland to one survivor. In addition, every man in the division was given a furlough. The division also received thousands of new replacements and was practically rebuilt. The 11th Panzer Regiment was reduced to two battalions, but they were equipped with about 160 excellent Mark III (PzKw III) tanks, armed with long-barreled 50mm guns. At the same time, the 65th Panzer Battalion was disbanded (its survivors were transferred to the 11th Panzer Regiment) and the 6th Rifle Brigade Headquarters was dissolved. The division also absorbed the remnants of the 22nd Panzer Division and was reorganized. It now included the 4th and 114th Panzer Grenadier Regiments (two battalions each), the 11th Panzer Regiment (two battalions), and the 76th Panzer Artillery Regiment (three battalions). Meanwhile, it received the 298th Army Flak Artillery Battalion and the 41st Tank Destroyer Battalion, while the 6th Motorcycle Battalion was amalgamated with the 57th Reconnaissance Battalion to form the 6th Panzer Reconnaissance Battalion, which included both reconnaissance vehicles and armored half-tracks. The 76th Panzer Artillery Regiment retained its three battalions (two equipped with a dozen 105mm howitzers and one with 12 150mm howitzers). All of its guns were towed by trucks—the regiment would not receive self-propelled guns until the following spring.

After the Anglo-Americans landed in French North Africa, the 6th Panzer Division was ordered to southern France. Meanwhile, however, the southern sector of the Eastern Front collapsed and the German 6th Army was surrounded in Stalingrad. Much to the chagrin and disappointment of the men of 6th Panzer, their trains were diverted from the south of France to the Eastern Front, where the division spearheaded the attack whose aim was to rescue the trapped army. In the Battle of Kotelnikovo, the division destroyed a mixed Soviet armored and cavalry brigade, which included one regiment mounted on camels. Led by Colonel Walter von Huenersdorff, the commander of the 11th Panzer Regiment, the division established a bridgehead across the Myschkowa despite strong opposition, but was finally halted at Bolwassiljewka, 29 miles south of the city, in very heavy fighting under extreme conditions. It was at this point that Hitler refused to allow the Stalingrad garrison to break out and sacrificed 6th Army on the altar of his own inflexibility. Under heavy attack in danger of being encircled, the 6th Panzer Division was finally forced to retreat on December 23. It had already lost more than half its tanks.

After the retreat from the Volga, the 6th Panzer Division fought in the retreat from the Don, in the Donez, and in the Kharkov counteroffensive, where it formed one wing of a pincher while the II SS Panzer Corps formed the other. They successfully encircled the city on March 14, 1943. The following month, I/11th Panzer Regiment was sent to Germany, to reequip with new PzKw V Panther tanks. This left the division with only one tank battalion (II/11th Panzer), equipped mainly with PzKw IVs. Due to the vicissitudes of war, the I Battalion would not return to the division for 20 months. Meanwhile, the 6th Panzer Division fought in Operation Citadel (the Battle of Kursk), at Belgorod, and in the 4th Battle of Kharkov, during which the division held the city for 10 days, despite massive Soviet assaults. By the time it withdrew from the city on August 23, it had destroyed its 1,500th Soviet tank.

Unable to hold on the Dnieper, the 6th Panzer Division and the remnants of Army Group South fell back to the west, where Field Marshal Erich von Manstein temporarily reinforced the division with the 503rd Heavy Panzer Battalion (34 Tiger tanks) and II/23rd Panzer Regiment (47 Panthers). Along with the II/11th Panzer, these units formed Heavy Panzer Regiment Baake under Colonel Franz Baake, the commander of the 11th Panzer Regiment. The 6th Panzer Division then launched a violent counterattack, destroying 268 Soviet tanks and 156 guns in a single thrust. A few days later Baake led the relief attack on Cherkassy and saved about half the men trapped in the Cherkassy (Korsum) Pocket in February 1944. The division then continued its retreat across Ukraine.

The following month brought yet another crisis. While the 6th Panzer Division was fighting in the unsuccessful defense of Tarnopol, another Soviet thrust to the south encircled the entire 1st Panzer Army (200,000 men in 18 divisions, including the 6th Panzer) in the Kamenets-Podolsk area, east of the Dniester. The army commander, General Hans Valentin Hube, formed a floating pocket and ordered Panzerkampfgruppe Baake (Panzer Battle Group Baake) to spearhead the breakout attempt. It did so successfully, reaching German lines near Buczacz on April 7, 1944. Despite its losses and near exhaustion, the 6th Panzer Division remained in the line, fighting in the successful German attempt to stabilize the front in Galicia.

At last withdrawn to Tarnopol and then to Germany to rest and refit in May 1944, the 6th Panzer was reorganized as a "Panzer Division 44" or 1944-style panzer division, which meant it lost 2,000 men from its table of organization. It had to give up its attached Panther and Tiger units as well, and its remaining tank companies were reduced from an establishment of 22 panzers to 17. The Staff and II/114th Panzer Grenadier Regiment were equipped with armored personnel carriers, but the I Battalion remained motorized. The regiment did form an unofficial (and illegal) III Battalion, which was a volunteer squadron of Cossack cavalrymen.

The 6th was hastily sent to the central sector of the Eastern Front shortly after the Russians surrounded the bulk of the 4th and 9th armies at Bobruisk and Minsk. With the Russians approaching the Baltic Sea, the 3rd Panzer Army was in danger of being cut off in Lithuania. The 6th Panzer Division was sent to East Prussia to keep the corridor open, which it did—rescuing 5,000 German soldiers encircled at Vilna in the process. Afterward (in late August 1944) it was sent to the Narew River in northern Poland, where it was assigned the task of conducting a mobile defense for southern East Prussia. During these battles it destroyed its 2,400th Soviet tank. Later, the now burned-out division was sent to Hungary, where it fought in the battles around Budapest, in the Lake Balaton counteroffensive, in the retreat into Austria, and in the Battle of Vienna. The battered but veteran tank division was encircled or cut off several times during the retreat from Hungary but managed to fight its way out each time. In April 1945 it held the *Reichsbruecke* in Vienna (the last bridge across the Danube) against repeated Red Army attacks and allowed many Germans—both soldiers and civilians—to escape. On April 14 the city fell, and the 6th Panzer Division withdrew to the north. It ended the war north of Bruenn, Moravia, on the southern sector of the Eastern Front. During the war, this excellent division suffered very heavy losses: 7,068 killed, 24,342 wounded, and 4,230 missing—35,640 casualties in all. Its maximum strength never exceeded 17,000 men and was usually considerably less. The remnants of the 6th Panzer surrendered to the U.S. 3rd Army but were handed over to the Soviets, and most of the former panzertruppen spent the next 10 years in Russian prison camps.

Commanders of the 1st Light/6th Panzer Division included Major General/ Lieutenant General Erich Hoepner (October 12, 1937), Major General Friedrich Wilhelm von Loeper (assumed command August 1, 1938), Major General/Lieutenant General Franz Werner Kempf (assumed command October 10, 1939), Major General Franz Landgraf (January 6, 1941), Major General/Lieutenant

General Erhard Raus (April 1, 1942), Landgraf (resumed command, September 16, 1941), Raus again (November 23, 1941), Colonel/Major General Walter von Huenersdorff (February 7, 1943), Colonel Wilhelm Crisolli (acting commander, July 25, 1943), Colonel/Major General/Lieutenant General Baron Rudolf von Waldenfels (August 22, 1943), Colonel Walter Denkert (acting commander, March 13, 1944), Waldenfels (returned March 29, 1944), Colonel Friedrich-Wilhelm Juergens (acting commander, November 23, 1944), and Waldenfels again (January 18, 1945-end). Colonel Max Sperling reportedly served as acting divisional commander in July 1944.

## COMMANDERS

Erich Hoepner (1886–1944) was promoted to lieutenant general on January 30, 1938. Later he advanced to general of cavalry (1939) and to colonel general (1941). He went on to command the XVI Motorized Corps in Poland (1939) and France (1940), and the 4th Panzer Group (subsequently Army) in Russia (1941). Hoepner was promoted to colonel general in 1941. He was relieved of his command by Adolf Hitler for ordering an unauthorized retreat in January 1942. He played an active role in the attempt to kill Hitler on July 20, 1944, and was executed by hanging on August 6. During the Sudetenland crisis of 1938, Hoepner actively planned to use the 1st Light (later 6th Panzer) Division against Hitler and the SS. His Ib (chief supply officer) was Captain (later Colonel) Count Claus von Stauffenberg, who placed the bomb under Hitler's table and narrowly missed assassinating him on July 20, 1944. An East Prussian, Hoepner began his career as a a Faehnrich (senior officer cadet or ensign) in the dragoons in 1905.

Friedrich Wilhelm von Loeper (b. 1888) had previously commanded the 64th Infantry Regiment and the 4th Rifle Regiment. His leadership of the 1st Light Division in Poland was not deemed successful, and he never rose above divisional command as a result. In October 1939 he was transferred to the command of the 81st Infantry Division—a demotion. Later he led the 10th Infantry Division (late 1940–42), the 178th Panzer Replacement Division (1942–44), Panzer Division Tatra (1944–45), and Infantry Division Ludwig (1945). He was promoted to lieutenant general in September 1940. As a youth, Loeper was educated at various cadet schools and was commissioned directly into the infantry in 1906 as a result.

Franz Werner Kempf (1886–1964), an East Prussian, was promoted to lieutenant general on July 31, 1940, and to general of panzer troops in April 1941. He led XXXXVIII Panzer Corps in Russia (1941–early 1943) and Army Detachment Kempf (subsequently 8th Army) until August 1943, when he fell afoul of Hitler and was relieved. In late 1944 he was placed in charge of German troops in the Vosges Mountains on the French frontier. An early mechanized warfare pioneer, Kempf developed the first German armored cars. He had commanded the ad hoc Panzer Division Kempf (a mixed army-SS unit) in the Polish campaign. Despite Hitler's opinion, Kempf was a good to excellent field commander at every level.

A Bavarian, Franz Landgraf was born in Munich in 1888, was educated at various cadet schools, and entered the Bavarian Army as a Faehnrich in 1909. Originally an infantry officer, he was an early convert to the armored branch and was commander of the 7th Panzer Regiment in 1936. He subsequently led the 4th Panzer Brigade (1939–41) before assuming command of the 6th Panzer Division. His health was broken on the Eastern Front during the winter battles of 1941–42. Transferred back to Germany, he was given command of the 155th Reserve Panzer Division on May 1, 1942, but his physical condition forced his early retirement on October 1, 1942—only a month after he was promoted to lieutenant general. His health continued to deteriorate and he died in Stuttgart in 1944.

Erhard Raus (b. 1889), an Austrian infantry officer, joined the German Army when it annexed his country in 1938. He was then a full colonel with 25 years service in the Austro-Hungarian Empire or its successor state. In the Third Reich, he served as chief of staff of Wehrkreis XVII (1938–39), chief of staff of XVII Corps (1939–40), commander of the 4th Rifle Regiment (1940–41), and commander of the 6th Rifle Brigade (1941–42) before assuming command of the 6th Panzer. A major general since September 1, 1941, he was promoted to lieutenant general on January 1, 1943, and subsequently to general of panzer troops (May 1, 1943) and colonel general (August 15, 1944). He later commanded XI Corps (1943), XXXXVII Panzer Corps (1943), 4th Panzer Army (1943–44), 1st Panzer Army (1944), and 3rd Panzer Army in Poland and eastern Germany (1944–45). He also served as acting commander of Army Group North Ukraine in the summer of 1944. On March 12, 1945, an irrational Hitler took a sudden dislike to him and relieved him of his command. He was never reemployed. An excellent commander, Raus held the Knight's Cross with Oak Leaves and Swords. He died on April 3, 1956.

Born in Cairo, Egypt, in 1898, Walter von Huenersdorff served in a Hussar regiment in World War I. A General Staff officer, he was Ia, 1st Panzer Division (1938–39); on the staff of Group Command 6 (1939); Ia, 253rd Infantry Division (1939); Ia, II Corps (1939–41); and chief of staff of the 3rd Panzer Group (later Army) (1941–42). Seen as a rising young star in the army, the talented Huenersdorff was given command of the 11th Panzer Regiment on July 1, 1942, and the division itself when General Raus was promoted to corps commander. Also to his credit, Huenersdorff was a fervent opponent of Nazism and was a member of the anti-Hitler conspiracy. Promoted to major general on May 1, 1943, Huenersdorff was shot in the head at Kursk on July 14, 1943, and died three days later. His young wife, a volunteer nurse, served as his nurse while he lay dying.

Wilhelm Crisolli (1895–1944), a Berliner, was commanding a cavalry battalion when World War II broke out. Transferring to the motorized service, he led III/8th Rifle Regiment (1940), 8th Rifle Regiment (1940–42), and 13th Rifle

Regiment (1942). He was then used as an interim divisional commander, temporarily leading the 13th Panzer (late 1942–43), 16th Panzer Grenadier (1943), 333rd Infantry (1943) and 6th Panzer. Crisolli was finally given a permanent divisional command—the fourth class 20th Luftwaffe Field Division—on November 25, 1943, and was promoted to major general on February 1, 1944. He was killed in an ambush by Italian partisans on October 12, 1944.

Baron Rudolf von Waldenfels (b. 1895) was promoted to major general on November 1, 1943, and to lieutenant general on June 1, 1944. A Bavarian, he was educated at various cadet schools and joined the cavalry as a Fahnenjunker when World War I broke out. He subsequently commanded I/17th Cavalry Regiment (1936–39), 10th Reconnaissance Battalion (1939–40), 24th Reconnaissance Battalion (1940), 4th Rifle Regiment (1941–42), and 6th Rifle Brigade (1942). Between commanding the 24th Reconnaissance and 4th Rifle, he underwent motorized warfare training with the 69th Rifle Regiment. After commanding the Panzer Troop School at Paris (1942–43), Waldenfels took charge of the 6th Panzer and (except for minor breaks) led it for the rest of the war.

For the details of Walter Denkert's career, see 19th Panzer Division.

For Max Sperling's career, see 9th Panzer Division.

Friedrich-Wilhelm Juergens commanded the II/2nd Rifle Regiment during the invasion of France, where he earned the Knight's Cross. He later commanded the 14th Panzer Division (1945).

## NOTES AND SOURCES

I/11th Panzer Regiment was attached to the 8th Panzer Division for most of 1944, during which it suffered heavy casualties. It was then sent to Grafenwoehr Maneuver Area and brought up to strength before rejoining its parent division in November 1944. The 4th Company of the battalion never rejoined the division. It was sent to Magdeburg, was reequipped with captured U.S. Sherman tanks, and fought in the Battle of the Bulge as part of SS Colonel Skorzeny's 150th Panzer Brigade.

During the period July–October 1944, the I/Grossdeutschland Panzer Regiment was on detached duty with the 6th Panzer Division.

For a sketch of Colonel Baake's career, see Panzer Division Feldherrnhalle 2.

Angolia, *Field*, Volume 2: 107–08; Bradley et al., Volume 2: 478–79; Carell 1966: 23–24, 236, 267; Carell 1971: 66, 81–83, 123, 530; Chapman: 347; Alan Clark, *Barbarossa: The Russian-German Conflict, 1941–45* (New York, 1965): 266 (hereafter cited as "Clark"); Harrison: 141; Hartmann: 63–64; Keilig: 62, 68, 153, 196, 208, 361; Kennedy: map 7, 74, 133; Manstein: 389, 499; Mehner, Volume 6: 545 Helmut Ritgen, *The 6th Panzer-Division, 1937–45* (London, 1982, reprinted ed., London, 1985), ff. 1. Horst Scheibert, *Bildband der 6. Panzer-Division, 1939–1945* (Bad Nauheim, 1958): ff. 1; Schmitz et al., Volume 2, *Die Divisionen 6–10*: 23–26; Seaton: 327; Seemen: 182; Tessin, Volume 2: 31; Volume 3: 18–22; RA: 100; OB 42: 56; OB 43: 200; OB 45: 289. Colonel Ritgen, author of *6th Panzer Division*, served in the division from 1938 to 1943. A major in 1945, he was captured in the Ruhr Pocket.

# 7th Panzer Division

**COMPOSITION:**   25th Panzer Regiment, 6th Panzer Grenadier Regiment, 7th Panzer Grenadier Regiment, 78th Panzer Artillery Regiment, 7th Motorcycle Battalion, 37th Panzer Reconnaissance Battalion, 42nd Antitank (later Tank Destroyer) Battalion, 58th Panzer Engineer Battalion, 83rd Panzer Signal Battalion.

**HOME STATION:**   Gera, Wehkreis IX

Formed at Gera in 1938 as the 2nd Light Division, its men came from Thuringia, which was not noted for the fighting qualities of its soldiery; nevertheless, the 7th Panzer turned out to be an outstanding combat unit. Called the Ghost Division, it initially included the 66th Panzer Battalion and the 6th and 7th Mechanized Cavalry (*Kavallerie-Schuetzen*) Regiments, as well as the 7th Reconnaissance Regiment (two battalions), the 78th Artillery Regiment (two battalions), the 58th Engineer Battalion, and the 42nd Antitank Battalion.

Like most of the prewar German divisions, the 2nd Light was not concentrated in a single base but was scattered all over the map. The division staff, the I/7th Mechanized Cavalry, and the antitank battalion were based at Gera, but the I/6th Mechanized Cavalry was billeted at Rudolstadt, and the II/7th Mechanized was at Jena, along with the artillery regiment. The 58th Engineer Battalion's barracks were in Riesa/Elbe, and the I/7th Reconnaissance Regiment (a motorcycle battalion) was found at Kissengen, while its sister battalion, the II/7th Reconnaissance—an armored car unit—was at Meiningen. The signals company was based in Erfurt. (The division did not receive a full signals battalion until late October 1939, after the Polish campaign.) The division also had a light antiaircraft (*Fla*) company, which was on detached duty from the Luftwaffe.

79

When the war broke out, the tank battalion of the 2nd Light Division was equipped only with very poor PzKw I and PzKw II light tanks. (The latter had only a 20mm main battle gun while the former had no main battle gun at all—only machine guns.) The rest of the division, however, was much better equipped. As part of the 10th Army (the main German strike force), the division fought its way through the Polish frontier defenses (September 1–3, 1939), helped overrun the Warta district, and pushed on to the suburbs of Warsaw, before being recalled to help deal with the only significant Polish counteroffensive of the campaign. The 2nd Light fought in the Radom encirclement (September 8–12), where the bulk of the Polish Army was destroyed. It then pushed north to the Bzura before turning east again, to take part in the drive to the Vistula and the Siege of Warsaw. Warsaw capitulated on September 27. The division remained in Poland until October 1, when it returned to the Reich to reorganize and reequip as a panzer division.

The 7th Panzer Division was officially formed from the 2nd Light Division at Gera on October 18, 1939. By November 1, the newly formed staff of the 25th Panzer Regiment had joined the division, along with its newly created I and II Battalions. The 66th Panzer Battalion was absorbed by the regiment and became III/25th Panzer. Meanwhile, Headquarters, 7th Reconnaissance Regiment was dissolved, I/7th Reconnaissance became the 7th Motorcycle Battalion, II/7th Reconnaissance Regiment became 7th Reconnaissance Battalion, and the 6th and 7th Mechanized Cavalry Regiments were officially redesignated Schuetzen (motorized or rifle) regiments in March 1940. Both were placed under the newly activated Staff, 7th Rifle Brigade.

Despite some improvement, the 7th Panzer Division was still poorly equipped in 1940, insofar as tanks were concerned. As of April 12, 1940, it had only three panzer battalions instead of the standard four. More seriously, the 25th Panzer Regiment had no PzKw IIIs—the best tank in the German arsenal before 1943. It was equipped with 72 poor PzKw IIs, 37 nearly useless PzKw Is, and 23 Panzer Kw IVs, whose short-barreled 75mm main battle gun seriously limited its effectiveness. Its main tank was the Panzer 38 (t)—a Czech tank manufactured at the Skoda plant before Hitler occupied Czechoslovakia in 1938. The division also had a new commander: Major General Erwin Rommel, who would soon achieve fame as "the Desert Fox."

The 7th Panzer was in the thick of the fighting during the invasion of France and Belgium and suffered more casualties than any other German division in the West in 1940, losing 2,610 men (682 killed, 1,643 wounded, and 285 captured or missing). It also lost 42 tanks, 16 of which were of German manufacture. The division, however, also distinguished itself to a greater extent than almost any other division in the campaign. It successfully pushed past the Meuse in a contested river crossing, smashed its way through Belgium and France, and overran and destroyed the French 1st Armored Division, taking more than 10,000 prisoners and destroying more than 100 French tanks, 30 armored cars, and 27 field guns in 48 hours, at a cost of 35 killed and 59 wounded. Along with the SS Motorized Division Totenkopf, it repulsed the major Allied counter-attack of the campaign at Arras, overran the French 31st Motorized Division, cut off the escape of major French and British forces at Cherbourg, and took 30,000 more prisoners, including five admirals. In all, the Ghost Division took 97,468 prisoners, shot down 52 aircraft, destroyed another 15 on the ground, and captured a dozen more. It captured the commander of the French Atlantic Fleet, most of the British 51st Highland Division (including its commander), and about 20 other generals. It also captured or destroyed 277 field guns, 64 antitank guns, 458 tanks and armored cars, 4,000 to 5,000 trucks, 1,500 to 2,000 cars, more than 300 buses, and a huge amount of other equipment.

The 7th Panzer was engaged in occupation duties in the Bordeaux region until February 1941, when it was sent to East Prussia, along with much of the rest of the German Army. It crossed into Russia in June and fought in the battles of the Minsk Pocket, the Stalin Line, the Dvina crossings, Smolensk, the Dnieper crossings, Vitebsk, Vyasma, Klim, and Moscow. By October 13, the 78th Panzer Artillery Regiment alone reported destroying 263 Soviet tanks, 124 guns, 69 antitank guns, 760 trucks, 48 bunkers, four airplanes, five ammunition depots, six locomotives, and an armored train. Losses, however, were also heavy. By November 15, the division had lost 290 killed, 783 wounded, and 45 captured or missing: 1,118 men in all. Then came the Russian winter and the Soviet winter offensive of 1941–42. By January 23, 1942, the I/6th Rifle Regiment was down to a strength of 5 officers, 25 NCOs, and 161 men; the II Battalion of the same regiment had only 17 officers, 72 NCOs, and 328 men, while the II/7th Rifle Regiment had been reduced to 7 officers, 54 NCOs, and 293 men. Normally, each battalion had some 700 men. At one time, the 25th Panzer Regiment had only five operational tanks left: four Panzer 38 (t)s and a PzKw IV, and the bulk of the battalion was sent into battle as an ad hoc infantry unit. Many of the panzers were immobilzed by a repair parts shortage—the German supply lines had almost totally failed. Locked (with the rest of 9th Army) in the pitiless struggle for the Rzhev Salient, the II/6th Rifle Regiment lost so many men it had to be disbanded, as was one of the tank battalions; the 25th Panzer Regiment was reduced to four companies, and the survivors of the 37th Reconnaissance Battalion were absorbed by the 7th Motorcycle Battalion. From June 22, 1941, to January 23, 1942, the 7th Panzer Division had lost 2,055 killed, 5,737 wounded, 313 missing or captured, and 1,089 sick—mostly from frostbite or lice-related diseases. Total casualties were 9,203, of which 336 were officers. (The division started the campaign with about 400 officers and 14,000 men.) As of May 27, the division had only 8,589 officers and men remaining—and most of these had not been with the division when the campaign began.

As a result of its losses, the division was sent back to southern France in May 1942 to rest and refit. Here it was at last reequipped with modern tanks of German manufacture, including 35 PzKw III-Js and 30 PzKw IV-Gs. At the same time the 7th Rifle Brigade was dissolved and the rifle regiments were redesignated panzer grenadier. In November of that year it took part in the occupation of Vichy France, driving all the way to Marseilles and Toulon on the Mediterranean coast. Sent to the southern sector of the Russian Front after Stalingrad was encircled, the 7th Panzer defended against heavy Soviet attacks aimed at Rostov in early 1943. It entered the campaign with 95 tanks—20 of which were totally obsolete. Between January 7 and February 27, 1943, the division destroyed or captured 354 Soviet tanks, 124 guns, 276 antitank guns, 70 mortars, 414 trucks, and assorted other equipment. It had lost 12 tanks itself. Later it fought in the Don and Donez withdrawals, at Izjum and the Battle of Kharkov. The 7th Panzer Division suffered particularly heavy losses in Operation Citadelle, Hitler's last major offensive in the East. By the end of the battle, it was down to a strength of 15 tanks and had an infantry strength of three battalions. After Kursk, the 7th Panzer was a Kampfgruppe; it nevertheless fought well in the battles around Belgorod, Kiev, and Zhitomir, where it was twice cited for distinguished conduct. German losses were also heavy. The I/ 7th Panzer Grenadier, for example, lost 2,144 men between January 1 and October 31, 1943—more than three times its original strength.

In November, the division took heavy casualties in the Kiev withdrawal and fought in the Tarnopol area until March 1944, when it was overrun and the 1st Panzer Army encircled. The remnants of the division broke out, but not a single Tiger tank survived the battle. As of April 21, 1944, the once mighty 7th Panzer Division had a total fighting strength of 1,872 men, nine guns, eleven antitank guns, and nine tanks—one of which was a captured Soviet T-34. Clearly a Kampfgruppe—the German term for a burned-out division of approximately regimental combat value—the 7th nevertheless fought on and opposed the Russian summer offensive of 1944 as a part of Army Group Center, fighting at Minsk and Lida. Escaping disaster, it was again officially cited for distinguished conduct in August 1944, for its action in the Battle of Raseiniai in Lithuania. Part of the 7th Panzer was trapped in the Memel bridgehead on October 10 and was evacuated by sea to Pillau on October 22. Reassembling at the Arys Maneuver Area in East Prussia, the 7th Panzer Division fought in the Battle of Elbing and was heavily engaged when the Russian winter offensive of 1944–45 hit the Vistula sector. The Ghost Division was trapped and pinned against the coast in the Gotenhafen-Danzig area in early 1945. Although the German Navy managed to evacuate it by sea to Swinemuende, all of its vehicles and tanks had to be left behind. The 7th Panzer nevertheless took part in the Berlin campaign in April 1945. Most of its men managed to escape to Allied lines and surrendered to the British at Schwerin on May 3.

Commanders of the 2nd Light/7th Panzer included Lieutenant General Georg Stumme (assumed command October 1, 1938), Erwin Rommel (February 2, 1940), Major General/Lieutenant General Baron Hans von Funck (February 7, 1941), Colonel Wolfgang Glaesemer (August 16, 1943), Major General Baron Hasso von Manteuffel (August 23, 1943), Major General Adalbert Schulz (January 16, 1944), Colonel/Major General/Lieutenant General Dr. Karl Mauss (January 30, 1944), Colonel Gerhard Schmidhuber (acting commander, May 2, 1944),

Mauss (returned, June 1944), Colonel Hellmuth Maeder (acting commander, October 1, 1944), Mauss (November 1944), Colonel Max Lemke (acting commander, January 4, 1945), Mauss (January 23, 1945), and Colonel Hans Christern (March 23, 1945).

## COMMANDERS

Georg Stumme (1886–1942) entered the Imperial Army as a Fahnenjunker in the artillery in 1906 and was commissioned the following year. Later he transferred to the cavalry and was promoted to general of cavalry on June 1, 1940. He had his rank changed to general of panzer troops in 1941 and led XXXX Panzer Corps in France, the Balkans, and Russia (1940–42). A man who enjoyed a good time and took full advantage of all of the pleasures of life, Stumme was a good divisional and corps commander, but his direction of Panzer Army Afrika in 1942 left much to be desired. He was court-martialed for a serious security violation in Russia in 1942 and was imprisoned for a time, but then was pardoned and made acting commander of Panzer Army Afrika in Egypt, after Erwin Rommel reported sick. (Stumme and his chief of staff had impressed Hermann Goering, the president of the court-martial, with their military bearing and with the fact that they assumed full responsibility for their failing, without making excuses.) General Stumme had a problem with high blood pressure and died of a heart attack on October 23, 1942, while in action against an Australian attack.

Erwin Rommel (1892–1944) had brilliant career which is well known. He spent virtually his entire prewar career in the infantry or mountain troops branches and did not transfer to the armored branch until 1940, when he was already a major general. Rommel entered the service as an officer cadet in the infantry in 1910 and earned the *Pour le Mérite* in World War I. In the 1920s he wrote a book about his experiences, *Infantry in the Attack*, which became a bestseller in Nazi Germany and led to temporary duty assignments at Fuehrer Headquarters while he was commandant of the Infantry School at Weiner Neustadt. He commanded the Fuehrer's Bodyguard Battalion in the Sudetenland, the occupation of Czechoslovakia, and in the Polish campaign, and used his high standing with Hitler to obtain command of the 7th Panzer Division. Later he commanded the Afrika Korps (1941), Panzer Group Afrika (1941–42), Panzer Army Afrika (1942–43), Army Group Afrika (1943), and Army Group B in northern Italy and then France (1943–44). Promoted to field marshal in 1942, he won incredible victories against overwhelming odds in Africa and conducted a brilliant defensive campaign in Normandy in 1944. He committed suicide on October 14, 1944, after the Gestapo and Hitler discovered that he was in sympathy with the conspirators of July 20. In exchange for his suicide, the Nazis agreed to spare his family. Hitler kept his end of the bargain. Frau Rommel died in the 1970s and his only child, Manfred, was mayor of Stuttgart in 1983.

Baron Hans von Funck (1891–1979), former military attaché to Madrid during the Spanish Civil War (1936–39), was military attaché to Lisbon when World War II broke out. Originally a cavalryman, Funck had transferred to the mobile troops in the 1920s and was promoted quickly: major general (January 1, 1941), lieutenant general (September 1, 1942), and general of panzer troops (March 1, 1944). He led the 5th Panzer Regiment (1939–early 1940), 3rd Panzer Brigade (1940–41), and 5th Light Division (1941). Ironically, he was initially selected over Erwin Rommel to be chief German commander in North Africa but was passed over because he took a pessimistic view of the situation there, did not want the post, and made a poor impression on Hitler when he briefed him on the African situation in early 1941. Since he had temporarily lost the opportunity to command a corps, OKH gave him command of the famous 7th Panzer Division as sort of a consolation prize. Funck subsequently led the 7th Panzer Division (1941–43), XXIII Corps (1943–44), and the XXXXVII Panzer Corps (1944) on the Eastern and Western Fronts, where he proved to be an excellent handler of armored units in emergency situations. He was nevertheless sacked by Hitler in early September 1944 and, except for a brief administrative post in Wehrkreis XII, was never reemployed. The fact that he was a very able and experienced tank officer did not outweigh the fact that Hitler was prejudiced against the aristocracy and disliked Funck personally. Also, the baron had undergone a messy divorce in the early 1930s and Hitler held this against him. Funck was arrested by the Communists at the end of the war and spent 10 years in Soviet prison camps. He was 88 years old at the time of his death.

Wolfgang Glaesemer commanded the 460th Infantry Regiment as a lieutenant colonel in 1942. He was commander of the 6th Panzer Grenadier Regiment on August 16, 1943, when General von Funck collapsed due to wounds and exhaustion. Glaesmer commanded the division until Baron von Manteuffel, Funck's permanent replacement, arrived.

Baron Hasso Eccard von Manteuffel (1897–1978) was another cavalry officer who rose rapidly in the panzer branch. A major in 1939, he was a general of panzer troops in 1944, despite missing both the Polish and French campaigns. Meanwhile, Manteuffel commanded the 3rd Motorcycle Battalion (1940), I/7th Rifle Regiment (1941), 6th Rifle Regiment (1941–42), and 7th Rifle (later Panzer Grenadier) Brigade (1942), all in the 7th Panzer Division. Later he briefly commanded the ad hoc Division Manteuffel in Tunisia (1943). He was commander of the Grossdeutschland Panzer Division (1944) before being promoted to general of panzer troops and elevated directly from divisional to army command in August 1944. He led the 5th Panzer Army on the Western Front (1944–45) during the Battle of the Bulge and the 3rd Panzer Army in the East (1945) during the Battle of Berlin. A Prussian, von Manteuffel held the Knight's Cross with Oak Leaves, Swords, and Diamonds. One of the best commanders in the German Wehrmacht, he was only forty-eight years old in 1945.

Adalbert Schulz was born in Berlin in 1903. He joined the Berlin police in the 1920s and was a lieutenant when he was inducted into the army. Retaining his rank, he was given command of a company in the 25th Panzer Regiment in

1937. Three years later he became a major and a battalion commander in the same regiment. In March 1943 he was given command of the regiment, followed by rapid promotions to lieutenant colonel (1943), colonel (1943), and major general (January 1, 1944)—three promotions in less than a year. An incredibly brave officer and a talented one, Schulz held the Knight's Cross with Oak Leaves, Swords, and Diamonds. He was killed in action near Schepetowka on the Eastern Front on January 28, 1944, after having commanded the 7th Panzer Division for only 28 days.

Dr. Karl Mauss (1898–1959), who was also rapidly promoted, entered the service as a war volunteer in 1914 and was given a battlefield commission in 1915. Discharged from the service in 1922, he served with the Freikorps and returned to the army as a captain in 1934. A company commander in an infantry regiment when the war began, he later commanded II/69th Infantry Regiment (1939–42) and the 33rd Panzer Grenadier Regiment (1942–44). A holder of the Knight's Cross with Oak Leaves and Swords, Mauss was promoted to major general on January 1, 1944, and to lieutenant general on October 1, 1944. He was seriously wounded near the end of the war and had not recovered at the time of the surrender. He settled in Hamburg and died on February 9, 1959.

For an outline of Gerhard Schmidhuber's career, see 13th Panzer Division Commanders.

For an outline of Hellmuth Maeder's career, see Fuehrer Grenadier Division, Commanders.

Max Lemke was born at Schwedt/Oder in 1895. He entered the service as a war volunteer in the cavalry in 1914, and was discharged as a reserve second lieutenant at the end of the war. He returned to duty as a reserve Rittmeister (captain of cavalry) in 1937. During World War II, he was adjutant of an infantry regiment (1939), commander of the 218th and 17th Reconnaissance Battalions (late 1939–43), and commander of the 25th Panzer Grenadier Regiment (early 1943–45). He became commander of the 1st Hermann Goering Parachute Panzer Division at the end of January and was promoted to major general on April 20, 1945.

Hans Christern, the last commander of the 7th Panzer Division, had previously served in the 5th Panzer Division and had commanded the II/31st Panzer Regiment (1941).

## NOTES AND SOURCES

Fla and Flak units were two different things. Fla units were equipped with relatively light, anti-aircraft guns (usually 20mm guns). Flak units were equipped with heavy duty 88mm anti-aircraft cannons (*Fliegerabwehrkanone*).

The Panzer Kw II weighed about 9.35 tons, as opposed to 29.7 tons for the British Mark IIA Matilda and approximately 24.5 for the PzKw III (with slight variations according to model). The PzKw VI Tiger weighed 62.7 tons, the PzKw VI Tiger II weighed 74.8 tons, and the Russian T-34 weighed 34.4 tons. The American M4A3 Sherman tank weighed 37.1 tons.

Colonel Karl Rothenburg, a reserve officer who earned the *Pour le Mérite* in World War I, commanded the 25th Panzer Regiment in France, where he won the Knight's Cross. He was killed in action in Russia on June 28, 1941. Thereafter the 25th Panzer Regiment was semiofficially known as the Rothenburg Regiment.

The 7th Motorcycle Battalion was redesignated 7th Reconnaissance Battalion on April 25, 1943. The 296th Army Flak Battalion was assigned to the 7th Panzer Division in 1943.

Angolia, *Field,* Volume 1: 103–04; Werner Brehm, *Mein Kriegstagebuch 1939–1945: Mit der 7. Panzer-Division 5 Jahre in West und Ost* (Kassel, 1953), 1 ff.; Carell 1966: 80, 334, 623; Carell 1971: 39, 66, 208, 510; Chapman: 347; Keilig: 99, 201, 214, 219, 339; Kennedy: 74, Map 10; Manstein: 298–99; Hasso von Manteuffel, *Die 7. Panzer-Division im Zweiten Weltkrieg* (Friedberg, 1986); Mellenthin 1977: 211; Mehner, Volume 7: 354, Volume 12: 458; Samuel W. Mitcham Jr. and Gene Mueller, *Hitler's Commanders* (Lanham, Md., 1992): 148; Hermann Plocher, "The German Air Force versus Russia, 1943," United States Air Force Historical Studies Number 153 (United States Air Force Historical Division, Aerospace Studies Institute, Maxwell Air Force Base, Alabama, 1965): 335; Scheibert: 117; Schmitz et al., Volume 2: 69–78; Stauffenberg MS; Tessin, Volume 2: 106–07, Volume 3: 60–62; OB 42: 57; OB 43: 201; OB 34: 289–90; Windrow: 7. For a description of Manteuffel's career, see John S. D. Eisenhower, *The Bitter Woods* (New York, 1969). For the story of the 7th Panzer's campaign in France, see Erwin Rommel, *The Rommel Papers,* B.H. Liddell Hart, ed. (New York, 1953) and Desmond Young, *Rommel: The Desert Fox* (New York, 1965) (hereafter cited as "Young"). Also see Samuel W. Mitcham Jr., *Triumphant Fox: Erwin Rommel and the Rise of the Afrika Korps* (Briarcliff Manor, NY, 1984). For Rommel's career, see Young, David Fraser, *Knight's Cross: A Life of Field Marshal Erwin Rommel* and Samuel W. Mitcham Jr., *The Desert Fox in Normandy* (Westport, Conn., 1996). For a highly negative version, see David Irving, *The Trail of the Fox* (New York, 1977).

# 8th Panzer Division

**COMPOSITION:** 10th Panzer Regiment, 8th Panzer Grenadier Regiment, 28th Panzer Grenadier Regiment, 80th Panzer Artillery Regiment, 8th Motorcycle Battalion, 59th Panzer Reconnaissance Battalion, 43rd Antitank (later Tank Destroyer) Battalion, 59th Panzer Engineer Battalion, 59th Panzer Signal Battalion.

**HOME STATION:** Cottbus, Wehrkreis III

The 8th Panzer Division was formed in 1938 as the 3rd Light Division. At the time it included the 67th Panzer Battalion, the 8th and 9th Mechanized Cavalry Regiments, and the 8th Reconnaissance Regiment. It fought in Poland in 1939 and in the winter of 1939–40 returned to Cottbus, where it was converted to a tank division. On October 16, 1939, it was redesignated 8th Panzer Division and absorbed the 10th Panzer Regiment—an East Prussian unit—as well as the newly formed HQ, 8th Rifle Brigade, which directed the 8th Rifle Regiment and 8th Motorcycle Battalion. The 8th Panzer Division also lost one of its two reconnaissance battalions to the 10th Panzer Division. Later, on January 1, 1941, the 10th Panzer Regiment absorbed the 67th Panzer Battalion, which became III/10th Panzer Regiment. Meanwhile, equipped mainly with inferior Czech tanks, the division was part of Reinhardt's XXXXI Motorized Corps in Belgium and France and suffered heavy losses in the Battles of the Meuse Crossings. Later it took part in the destruction of the French 1st and 7th Armies and the final mopping up campaign in France in June 1940. It remained in France until March 1941, when it was sent east and, in April 1941, it took part in the Yugoslav campaign as part of the 1st Panzer Group. It assembled north of Lake

Balaton, Hungary, by April 7, crossed the Dvina on April 10, pushed to the outskirts of Belgrade by April 12, and seized Sarajevo against neglible resistance on April 15. Here it received the surrender of the Yugoslav 3rd Army. Yugoslavia capitulated two days later.

Quickly transferred to East Prussia, the 8th Panzer Division invaded Russia as part of Manstein's LVI Panzer Corps and spearheaded the German sweep through the Baltic states. Within days it secured the bridges over the Dving River and fought a series of fierce battles to hold and extend the bridgehead. By order of the vacillating High Command, the 8th Panzer had to push along the swampy Mshaga River—terrain totally unsuited for armored operations. By mid-July, battle losses and wear and tear had reduced the division's tank strength from 175 to 80. On August 5, just as the Battle of Luga was beginning, the division was withdrawn into Army Group North's reserve and—over the objections of the division's commander—was ordered to clear the communications zone of partisans. This was also a terribly inefficient way to employ an armored division.

In early October 1941, the 8th Panzer Division was returned to the front and reassumed its proper role, taking part in the battles of the Volkhov River bridgeheads and the drive on Tikhvin. As part of Army Group North, it helped check Stalin's winter offensive of 1941–42 in the Volkhov sector. The next year it fought in the defensive battles of Army Groups North and Center (including Kholm, Orel, and Smolensk) and was transferred to the southern sector of the Eastern Front after the Kursk attacks failed. In October 1943 it sustained heavy losses in the withdrawal from Kiev. It was more or less continuously in combat in 1944, fighting at Zhitomir in northern Ukraine, at Tarnopol, at Brody, in southern Poland, at Lemberg, in the Carpathian withdrawal, and in Slovakia. The 8th Panzer was sent to Hungary in December and retreated to Austria in 1945. It ended the war in Moravia on the central sector of the Eastern Front and surrendered to the Soviets at Deutsch-Broad on May 10, 1945.

Commanders of the 8th Panzer Division included Major General/Lieutenant General Adolf Kuntzen (assumed command, November 10, 1938), Major General/Lieutenant General Erich Brandenberger (February 21, 1941), Major General Walter Neumann-Silkow (acting commander, April 15 to May 25, 1941), Brandenberger (returned to command, May 25, 1941), Major General Werner Huebner (acting commander, December 8, 1941), Brandenberger (January 29, 1942), Major General Joseph Schroetter (August 6, 1942), Colonel Herbert von Wagner (November 14, 1942), Brandenberger (returned November 27, 1942), Major General/Lieutenant General Sebastian Fichtner (January 17, 1943), Lieutenant General Friedrich von Scotti (acting commander, June 1943), Fichtner (returned, July 1943), Lieutenant Colonel Albert Kleinschmidt (September 3, 1943), Colonel Dr. Karl Mauss (September 9, 1943), Colonel/Major General Gottfried Froelich (September 20, 1943), Colonel/Major General Werner Friebe (April 1, 1944); Colonel Friedrich-Wilhelm von Mellenthin (July 16, 1944),

Froelich again (July 20, 1944), and Colonel/Major General Heinrich Georg Hax (January 22, 1945–end).

## COMMANDERS

Adolf Kuntzen (b. 1889) entered the army as a Fahnenjunker in 1909. He was promoted to lieutenant general on April 1, 1940. He later commanded LVII Panzer and LXXXI Corps (late 1941–42 and 1942–September 1944, respectively). He was promoted to general of panzer troops in July 1941. A solid and dependable commander, Kuntzen was nevertheless one of the officers Hitler held responsible for the loss of France in 1944 (without justification in Kuntzen's case). He was placed in Fuehrer Reserve on September 4, 1944, and was never reemployed.

Erich Brandenberger (1892–1955) joined the Bavarian Army as an artillery Fahnenjunker in 1911. After successfully commanding the 8th Panzer Division, he served as commander of XVII and XXIX Corps in Russia (1943–44) and the 7th Army on the Western Front (October 1944–February 1945). Sacked by Field Marshal Model due to a personality conflict, he was given command of the 19th Army in southwestern Germany on March 25, 1945, and led it until the end of the war. He was promoted to lieutenant general on August 1, 1942, and was made a general of artillery in August 1943. Brandenburger was a steady and dependable commander—but not a flashy one. A thorough study of the German and Allied records and the Stauffenberg papers have convinced me that Brandenberger was one of the best army-level field commanders Germany had on the Western Front in the 1944–45 period. Despite tremendous pressure and often with a mediocre team, he always reacted with speed and an incredible calmness, which transferred itself downward. He only very rarely made a mistake. In my view, he was even slightly better than Baron von Manteuffel as an army commander, although Manteuffel was the better panzer division commander. Brandenberger died in Bonn in 1955. Prior to commanding the 8th Panzer, he was chief of staff of Frontier Command Eifel (1939) and chief of staff of XXIII Corps (1939–41). Brandenberger was wounded by shrapnel on December 8, 1941, and did not resume command until March 21, 1942.

For the details of Walter Neumann-Silkow's career, see 15th Panzer Division.

Werner Huebner (b. 1886) joined the Imperial Army as a Fahnenjunker in the infantry in 1908. After serving in World War I and the Reichsheer, he led the 25th Infantry Regiment (1938–41) and the 12th Rifle Brigade of the 12th Panzer Division (1941). He assumed command of the 8th Panzer when General Brandenberger was wounded. Later he commanded the 61st Infantry Division (1942–43) and the 416th Infantry Division (1943) and was commandant of fortifications in East Prussia (1943–44). He was commandant of Stettin in 1945. Huebner was promoted to lieutenant general on January 1, 1943.

Joseph Schroetter was born in Cologne in 1891. He was educated in various cadet schools, entered the service as an infantry officer cadet in 1912, fought in World War I, and served in the Reichswehr. He obtained an advanced degree in engineering in 1926. Schroetter spent most of his World War II career in staff positions with OKH or OKW. Considered an expert on motorized troops, he was promoted to major general in 1942 and to lieutenant general in 1944. He was commander of the 8th Rifle Brigade (his only permanent command of the war) when General Brandenberger was wounded, so Schroetter took temporary command of the division. He was the field army's General of Motorized Troops at OKW until June 10, 1944, when he was relieved of his post for reasons not disclosed by the records. Quite likely, Hitler took a dislike to him. Never reemployed, he settled in Frankfurt am Main after the war.

Herbert von Wagner previously commanded the 14th Motorized Artillery Regiment (1942).

Sebastian Fichtner (1894–1950) was promoted to lieutenant general on August 1, 1943. A Bavarian engineer officer and a player of some skill in army politics, he was a lieutenant colonel, colonel, and major general in the powerful Army Personnel Office (HWA) from 1937 to September 15, 1942, when he was placed in Fuehrer Reserve at the same time Hitler sacked Colonel General Franz Halder, the chief of the General Staff. Fichtner's contacts at OKH (the High Command of the Army) explain why he was given command of the prestigious 8th Panzer Division. Although many other officers had much better claims to the command than he, one must conclude that he did a pretty good job as a divisional commander and, in fact, thoroughly deserved his promotion to lieutenant general. Apparently wounded in action on November 6, 1943 (German personnel records are, as usual, unclear on this point), he was unemployed for six months; then he was given command of Armaments Inspection Staff XIII on April 1, 1944. He was arrested on July 25, 1944, for complicity in Colonel Count Claus von Stauffenberg's failed attempt to assassinate Hitler five days earlier. Fichtner, however, was able to "beat the rap" and was released in September. He was never reemployed.

Friedrich von Scotti (b. 1889) joined the army as an artillery Fahnenjunker in 1907. He served in World War I and in the Reichsheer. During the World War II era, he commanded the 14th Artillery Regiment (1936–38), the 35th Artillery Command (1939–41), the 227th Infantry Division (1941–43), Harko 304 (1943–44), and Harko 306. Promoted to lieutenant general in early 1941, he was apparently wounded on January 13, 1945, and was never reemployed. General von Scotti settled in Karlsruhe.

Albert Kleinschmidt was Ia of the 8th Panzer Division (July 1942–February 1944).

Dr. Karl Mauss was the commander of the 7th Panzer Division. He led the 8th Panzer for only 11 days, until General Froelich arrived.

Gottfried Froelich was promoted to major general on December 1, 1943. Born in Dresden in 1894, this Saxon joined the army when World War I broke out and was commissioned second lieutenant in the artillery in 1915. Remaining in the peacetime army, Froelich commanded the 76th Panzer Artillery Regiment of the 6th Panzer Division (1938–39), 78th Panzer Artillery Regiment (1939–43), and 36th Infantry Division (1943), before assuming command of the 8th Panzer. He was absent for three months, recovering from wounds or illness (April–July 1944) and was hospitalized again on January 22, 1945 after General Balck relieved him of his command for a lack of aggressiveness in the Hungarian campaign. This cost him his promotion to lieutenant general. Froelich led the ad hoc Corps Group von Tettau in March and early April 1945 and was leader of Higher Artillery Command 3rd Panzer Army on the Eastern Front at the end of the war. He surrendered to the British. Released from prison in 1948, he died at Heidenheim on July 30, 1959.

A Silesian, Werner Friebe (b. 1897) started his career as a war volunteer in 1914 and was commissioned in a fusilier (infantry) regiment in 1916. He became a major general on June 1, 1944. During World War II, Friebe served as Ia, 20th Infantry Division (1938–41), chief of staff of the XXXXVIII Panzer Corps (1941–late 1942), chief of a commanders' training course (1943–44), commander of the 8th Panzer Division (1944), and chief of staff of Wehrkreis III in Berlin (1944–45). However, he was a poor tank division commander. On July 15, 1944, during operations along the Bug River, he deviated from his instructions and moved his division along a main road in broad daylight. As a result, the 8th Panzer Division suffered devastating casualties. General Hermann Balck, the commander of the XXXXVIII Panzer Corps, was furious when he learned what had happened, and relieved Friebe of his command on July 17. Friebe was not reemployed until September, when he was made chief of staff of Wehrkreis III—a major demotion. He did, however, escape Soviet captivity as a result. Released from Allied prisoner of war camps in 1948, Werner Friebe died in Stuttgart in 1962. His older brother Helmut was a lieutenant general and acting commander of the LXIV Corps at the end of the war.

Friedrich-Wilhelm von Mellenthin was born in Breslau in 1904 and entered the army as a Fahnenjunker in the cavalry in 1924. Commissioned in 1928, he was on the General Staff of III Corps when World War II broke out. During the war, he served as Ia of the 197th Infantry Division (1940), as a staff officer with 1st Army (1940–41), and as chief intelligence officer of Panzer Army Afrika (1941–42). Evacuated due to illness, he was named chief of staff of XXXXVIII Panzer Corps, a post he held when he was acting commander of the 8th Panzer Division. Later he was chief of staff of 4th Panzer Army (1944), Army Group G (1944), and 5th Panzer Army (1945). Promoted to major general on December 1, 1944, Mellenthin also briefly commanded the 33rd Panzer Regiment of the 9th Panzer Division (1944). Captured in the Ruhr Pocket, he emigrated to South Africa, where he founded a very successful airline. He was still alive and quite active in the mid-1980s. His memories, *Panzer Battles*, are considered a classic of World War II literature.

Heinrich Georg Hax was born in Berlin in 1900. He joined the army as a Fahnenjunker in 1918 but World War I ended before he could obtain his commission, which he finally received in the elite 9th Infantry Regiment in 1922. A General Staff officer, Hax served as Ia, 2nd Infantry Division (1938–39), Ia, Army Group South (1939–42), and chief of staff of LVI Panzer Corps (1943–44). He was not employed from September 1942 until January 1943, suggesting that he was wounded or that he fell from Hitler's grace at the same time as did General Halder. Hax commanded the 111th Panzer Grenadier Regiment (1944–45) before taking command of the division. He was promoted to major general on April 1, 1945. He surrendered the division to the Americans near Pilsen on May 9, 1945, but was later handed over to the Russians and spent the next 10 years in Soviet prisons. Following his release, Hax joined the Bundesheer as a brigadier general, was promoted to major general, commanded the 3rd Panzer Division (1956–58) and 5th Panzer Grenadier Division (1958–59) of the West German Army. He retired in 1961 and died in Koblenz in 1969.

## NOTES AND SOURCES

The 8th Panzer Division was reorganized on January 1, 1941, when the 67th Panzer Battalion became III/10th Panzer Regiment and the 80th Panzer Artillery Regiment absorbed the 645th Artillery Battalion, which became its III Battalion. At the same time, however, the 8th and 28th Rifle Regiments lost their III Battalions. The 8th Rifle Brigade was dissolved in the fall of 1942, and the 8th Motorcycle Battalion was converted into a panzer reconnaissance unit. The division added the 286th Army Flak Artillery Battalion in early 1943. In December 1944, the 8th Rifle (now Panzer Grenadier) Regiment was redesignated 98th Panzer Grenadier Regiment.

Bradley et al., Volume 4: 95–97; Volume 5: 217–18; Carell 1966: 21–22; Chapman: 347–48; Keilig: 89, 97, 131, 193; Kennedy: 74, Map 7; Manstein: 182; F. W. von Mellenthin, *Panzer Battles*, H. Betzler, trans., L. C. F. Turner, ed. (Norman, Okla., 1956; reprint ed., New York, 1984): 339–43; Mellenthin 1977: 214; Mehner, Volume 6: 545; Harrison E. Salisbury, *The 900 Days: The Siege of Leningrad* (New York, 1969): 95 (hereafter cited as "Salisbury"); Schmitz et al., Volume 2: 119–27; Stauffenberg MS; Stoves, *Gepanzerten*: 66–67; Tessin, Volume 2: 175, Volume 3: 99–100; RA: 46; OB 42: 57; OB 43: 201; OB 45: 290–91.

# 9th Panzer Division

**COMPOSITION (1942):** 33rd Panzer Regiment, 10th Panzer Grenadier Regiment, 11th Panzer Grenadier Regiment, 102nd Panzer Artillery Regiment, 9th Motorcycle Battalion, 9th Panzer Reconnaissance Battalion, 50th Tank Destroyer Battalion, 86th Panzer Engineer Battalion, 85th Panzer Signal Battalion.

**HOME STATION:** Vienna (later St. Poelten), Wehrkreis XVII

On April 1, 1938, shortly after Germany annexed Austria, the German Army formed the 4th Light (later 9th Panzer) Division in Vienna. It initially included the 33rd Panzer Battalion and the 10th and 11th Motorized Cavalry Regiments, as well as the 9th Reconnaissance Regiment (two battalions), the 102nd Motorized Artillery Regiment (two battalions), the 86th Motorized Engineer Battalion, the 50th Antitank Battalion, the 3rd Company of the 38th Signal Battalion, and assorted divisional service support units. The I/9th Reconnaissance was a motorcycle unit. The 4th Light took part in the invasion of Poland in 1939, fighting on the right flank of Army Group South. It attacked out of Slovakia and pushed its way over the San River (September 10), captured Krakowiec (September 12), and established a bridgehead over the Bug in the vicinity of Krylow (September 14). Turning west again, the 4th Light blocked the escape route of the Polish Army and took tens of thousands of prisoners. On October 24, the division entrained for Salzburg and returned home to Wehrkreis XVII. That winter it was converted to an armored division and redesignated 9th Panzer. As of January 3, 1940 (the date it was converted into a tank unit), the 9th Panzer included the newly activated 9th Rifle Brigade (10th and 11th Rifle Regiments [two battalions each], the 59th Motorcycle Battalion, and the I/9th

93

Reconnaissance Regiment), the 33rd Panzer Battalion, the 102nd Panzer Artillery Regiment, and assorted divisional units, including the II/9th Reconnaissance Regiment, the 50th Antitank Battalion, 85th Signal Battalion, and the 86th Engineer Battalion. On February 2, 1940, the Headquarters, 33rd Panzer Regiment was created from the staff of Panzer Regiment Conze (a Panzer Lehr or training regiment) and the III/5th Panzer Regiment. Simultaneously, the 33rd Panzer Battalion became II Battalion, 33rd Panzer Regiment, and Panzer Training Battalion Wuensdorf was absorbed by the regiment, forming the bulk of its I Battalion.

The 9th Panzer Division fought in the Western campaign of 1940, in which it played a major role in knocking the Netherlands out of the war in six days, despite the fact that it was equipped with inferior Czechoslovakian tanks. The division then took part in the battles around Antwerp, Brussels, Arras, and Dunkirk. After Dunkirk fell, the 9th Panzer became part of Panzer Group von Kleist in the pursuit operations that finished off France. It broke through the Weygand Line, pushed to the gates of Paris, and crossed the Oise, Aisne, Marne, and Loire, taking thousands of prisoners in the process. The 9th Panzer covered more ground than any other division in the Western campaign and was near Lyon when the French surrendered. It returned to Vienna in July, where it absorbed the II/3rd Panzer Regiment, which became the III Battalion of the 33rd Panzer Regiment. Meanwhile, the 102nd Panzer Artillery Regiment added a III Battalion. The 59th Motorcycle Battalion was converted to a reconnaissance unit and became 9th Reconnaissance (later Panzer Reconnaissance) Battalion. The division was then sent to Poland with the XXXX Panzer Corps in September.

In the spring of 1941, the 9th Panzer was shipped to Romania and took part in the blitzkrieg through the Balkans. It formed the spearhead of the 12th Army and successfully separated the Greek forces from those of Yugoslavia. Then it pushed back the main British, Greek, and Australian forces through Macedonia until they were in full retreat; the division was then recalled to Romania for the invasion of the Soviet Union. As part of Army Group South, the division crossed the border on June 28, broke through the Stalin Line on July 7, swept through Ukraine, was involved in the encirclement of Uman, took Krivoy Rog and Nikopol (on August 16 and 17, respectively), and captured the huge Dnieper River dam at Dnepropetrovsk on August 25. The 9th Panzer Division formed the spearhead of 1st Panzer Group's (von Kleist's) drive to encircle Kiev from the south, while Guderian's 2nd Panzer Group drove behind the city from the north. They linked up on September 15, encircling five Soviet armies. Some 667,000 Soviet prisoners and 900 tanks were captured in the operation. After the Kiev Pocket was crushed, the 9th Panzer was assigned to Guderian's panzer army for the advance on Moscow. It took part in the Bryansk encirclement and—after being delayed by the Russian mud—captured Kursk on November 2. The division was finally halted near Tim. Still on the southern sector, the 9th Panzer faced the Soviet winter offensive of 1941–42, successfully holding its sector east of Schtschigry in heavy fighting until the attacks ended in March 1942.

During the spring lull of 1943, the 102nd Panzer Artillery Regiment lost its IV (antiaircraft) battalion, which it had received in 1942. This unit was redesignated the 287th Army Flak Artillery Battalion and became part of the divisional troops on April 20, 1943. More seriously, 9th Rifle Brigade was dissolved in December 1942, and now 33rd Panzer Regiment lost two of its three battalions, one of which (I/33rd Panzer) was reequipped with PzKw VI Tiger tanks and was sent to France, where it became part of OB West's reserve. Then the division was sent to Orel, where it was engaged in the Battle of Kursk from July 5 to 13, 1943, when the offensive was finally abandoned. The 9th Panzer had gained little ground but had suffered heavy casualties in the fighting.

Following the failure of Operation Citadel, the 9th Panzer covered the withdrawal of the 9th and 2nd Panzer Armies north of Orel and Kirov, and then fought a series of mobile defensive actions east of Bryansk near the end of August. Returning to the southern sector, it was in heavy combat in the retreat to the Mius, in the Battles of Stalino, Zaporozh'ye, Krivoy Rog, and Odessa, and the retreat behind the Dnieper. By January 1944, it was down to a strength of 13 tanks, and its infantry and artillery units were also very much reduced. Still in the line, it conducted a slow retreat across the Ingulez and Ingul. Finally pulled out of the fighting in April, when it was sent to Avignon in southern France to rebuild. Here it absorbed the 155th Reserve Panzer Division on May 1, 1944, and engaged in training for a time. In January 1944, it received the 51st Panzer Battalion—equipped with PzKw V Panther tanks—which became the new II Battalion, 33rd Panzer Regiment. Between April and June, it received a total of 74 PzKw IVs, 20 assault guns, and 15 Panthers, as well as 31 obsolete PzKw IIIs and 200 soft-skinned vehicles. Eventually it was posted to an area on the Rhone River northwest of Marseilles, and when the Allies landed it had a strength of 12,768 men. It helped cover the retreat of Army Group G from southern France, and in early August was rushed to the disintegrating 7th Army in Normandy, just in time to be involved in the Battle of Falaise. Although it avoided encirclement, it suffered ruinous losses just the same, and on August 12 had a strength of one grenadier battalion, one battalion of self-propelled guns, and five tanks. It then took part in the retreat across the Seine, fought in the eastern suburbs of Paris, and then formed blocking positions along the Marne. By late August it was in Mons, Belgium, with a strength "equivalent of a company, with no tanks and no guns left in running order," according to the U.S. Army's Official History. By September 2, it had been reinforced to a strength of 1,700 grenadiers (up from a low of 140 in mid-August) and two batteries of commandeered 105mm self-propelled guns, but it still had no tanks. As of the first week of September, it was merged with the 2nd Panzer Division for tactical purposes. Remaining in the line, it took part in the Battles of Arnhem and Aachen, and other Siegfried Line fighting, where it lost another thousand men—about two-thirds of its remaining combat strength. Its counterattacks against American forces near Aachen from September 11 to 15 led to the relief of the divisional commander and his chief of operations. When the division was sent into Army Group B's reserve around the end of September, its authorized versus actual strength was:

|  | Authorized | Actual |
|---|---|---|
| Staff Company | 14 tanks | 5 tanks |
| 33rd Panzer Regt. | 800 men, 120 tanks | 150 men, 1 tank |
| 10th Panzer Gren. Rgt. | 1110 men | 216 men |
| 11th Panzer Gren. Rgt. | 1100 men | 246 men |
| 102nd Panzer Artillery Rgt. | 1055 men, 86 guns | 600 men, 20 guns |
| 9th Panzer Recon. Battalion | 640 men | 50 men |
| 287th Flak Battalion | 780 men, 24 guns | 430 men, 10 guns |
| 81 Panzer Signal + 86th Panzer Engineer + 50th Antitank Battalions (combined) | 850 men | 234 men |

The 9th Panzer Division was hurriedly sent to Arnhem during Operation Market-Garden, but the battle was nearly over when it arrived. Transferred to Bracelen, west of the Ruhr River, the division was rehabilitated once more during the first three weeks of October, receiving 11,000 replacements and 178 armored vehicles, at least 50 of which were late-model PzKw V Panther tanks. (These reinforcements included the 105th Panzer Brigade, sent by Wehrkreis VIII, which the 9th Panzer absorbed on September 27.) It also received 30 105mm and 150mm self-propelled howitzers and 240 soft-skinned vehicles. Soon it was back at the front, checking an American armored advance in the Peel Marshes, although it lost 30 Panthers in the process.

Reassembling on the eastern bank of the Ruhr, the 9th Panzer Division mustered a strength of more than 10,000 men, 28 Panthers, 14 PzKw IVs, 30 assault guns, 42 howitzers, and 204 other vehicles, including several self-propelled guns. Reinforced with the 506th Heavy Panzer Battalion (28 Tiger tanks) and elements of the 15th Panzer Grenadier Division, the 9th Panzer fought a six-day battle with the elite 2nd U.S. Armored Division in the Puffendorf-Immendorf sector in mid-November. The 9th inflicted 1,300 casualties on the Americans and knocked out 76 tanks (40 of which were salvageable), but lost 1,100 men and 86 tanks itself. (Thirty German tanks were later salvaged.) From November 16 to December 14, in heavy fighting, it prevented the U.S. 1st Army from breaking through the Rhine plain; during the fighting around Geilenkirchen, the 9th Panzer destroyed its 2,325th enemy tank.

In December the 9th Panzer played a prominent role in the Battle of the Bulge but suffered heavy losses when Hitler refused to allow a timely retreat. Despite repeated heavy casualties, the division's morale never flagged. It distinguished itself once more in the Eifel fighting of early 1945 and again in the Battle of the Erft River in February, when it was down to a strength of 29 tanks and 16 assault guns. Still, in late February, it launched a spirited but unsuccessful counterattack against the U.S. bridgehead on the Rhine at Remagen. By this time it had only 600 men and 15 tanks left. On March 6, 1945, during the Battle of Cologne, the 9th Panzer was attacked by strong Allied forces and finally collapsed; its commander, Major General Baron Harald Gustav von Elverfeldt, was killed in action. The remnants of the once-proud division were forced into the Ruhr Pocket, where they surrendered to the U.S. Army in April. One small battle group under Major Halle, the divisional adjutant, managed to break out of the encirclement and joined the 11th Army in the Harz Mountains. On April 26, 1945, OB West ordered this unit disbanded. Its men were absorbed by other divisions in the 11th Army. The 9th Panzer Division had ceased to exist.

The last commander of the division was Colonel Helmuth Zollenkopf, its senior regimental commander, who was captured in the Ruhr. Previous commanders included Major General/Lieutenant General Dr. Alfred Ritter von Hubicki (assumed command April 1, 1938), Major General Johannes Baessler (April 15, 1942), Colonel Heinrich-Hermann von Huelsen (July 25, 1942), Major General/Lieutenant General Walter Scheller (August 4, 1942), Colonel/Major General Erwin Jolasse (July 22, 1943), Colonel Johannes Schulz, PhD (October 9, 1943), Jolasse (returned November 27, 1943), Colonel Walter Boemers (December 1, 1943), Jolasse again (returned, January, 1943), Colonel Max Sperling (acting commander, August 10, 1944), Major General Gerhard Mueller (September 2, 1944), Major General Baron Harald Gustav von Elverfeldt (September 16, 1944), and Zollenkopf (March 6, 1945). Major General Friedrich Wilhelm von Mellenthin was acting divisional commander from December 28, 1944, until February 1945, because General von Elverfeldt had been wounded in a fighter-bomber attack.

## COMMANDERS

Dr. Alfred Ritter von Hubicki, an Austrian, was born in Hungary in 1887. He joined the Austro-Hungarian Army, was an artillery Fahnenjunker in 1905 and served in it or its successor, the Austrian Army, until March 1938, when Austria was absorbed by the Third Reich. By this time Hubicki was a major general and commander of the Austrian Motorized Division. Judged sufficiently politically reliable by the Nazis, Hubicki was allowed to transfer into the Heer as a major general. He took command of the 4th Light the day it was created. He was promoted to lieutenant general on August 1, 1940, and oversaw the unit's conversion into the 9th Panzer Division. On sick leave from April 25 to August 1, 1942, Hubicki later commanded the ad hoc Corps Schelde (1942) and LXXXIX Corps in occupied France (1942–43). Promoted to general of panzer troops on October 1, 1942, he headed a special staff at OKH (1943–44) before becoming chief of the German Military Mission to Slovakia (July 26, 1944-early 1945). He retired on March 31, 1945 and died in 1971.

Johannes Baessler (1892–1944) entered the Imperial Army as an infantry lieutenant in January 1914 and fought in World War I. Remaining in the Reichsheer, he became Ia of the 1st Panzer Division in 1935 and was a colonel commanding the 4th Panzer Regiment in 1938–39. Later he served as chief of staff of XI Corps (1939–42), commander of the 9th Panzer Division (April–October, 1942), and commander of the 14th Panzer Division (November 1–26, 1942). Seriously wounded in the Stalingrad fighting, he did not return to duty until July 20, 1943, when he was given command of the 242nd Infantry Division (a static unit) at Toulon in southern France. Obviously OKH felt he could no longer stand up to the rigors of the Eastern Front. Surrounded in Toulon by the Allied invasion of southern France, Baessler conducted a spirited defense of the city and naval base against the French and Americans, despite overwhelming odds and the third-class nature of his troops. He was critically wounded on August 26. The Allies returned him shortly after the city fell but he never regained his health, dying in Vienna on November 27, 1944. He was promoted to major general on February 1, 1942, and to lieutenant general on February 1, 1944.

For a sketch of General von Huelsen's career, see 21st Panzer Division.

A Hanoverian infantry officer, Walter Scheller (1892–1944) began his career as an infantry officer cadet in 1911. After serving in World War I and the Reichsheer, he commanded the 66th Infantry Regiment (1938–39), was chief of staff of Wehrkreis X (1939–40), and commanded the 8th Rifle Brigade (1940–41), 11th Panzer Division (1941–42), and 9th Panzer Division (1942–43). He was severely wounded at the end of Operation Citadel. Not judged a successful tank division commander, Scheller was transferred back to the infantry after he recovered. He was acting commander of the 334th Infantry Division (1943), commander of the 337th Infantry Division (1943–44), and commander of Military Area Command 399 (1944). In June 1944 he was named commander of Brest-Litovsk, one of Hitler's "fortresses" on the Eastern Front. Scheller was killed in action when the Soviets stormed the place on July 22, 1944. He had been promoted to lieutenant general on January 1, 1943.

Erwin Jolasse was born in Hamburg in 1892 and entered the service as an infantry Fahnenjunker in 1911. He was discharged in 1919 (after Germany lost World War I) and for many years was a civilian instructor pilot for the clandestine air units of the German Army. He returned to active duty as a captain in 1934. Prior to assuming command of the 9th Panzer Division, Jolasse commanded II/39th Infantry Regiment (1936–40), 52nd Infantry Regiment (1940–42), and 18th Panzer Brigade (1942–43). He was wounded in action in April 1943 and permanently lost the use of his left arm. Promoted to major general on October 1, 1943, he was wounded by machine gun fire 19 days later and temporarily replaced by Colonel Schulz. He resumed command the day after Schulz was killed and held it until August 10, 1944, when he was wounded again—this time critically. Jolasse did not return to active duty until January 1945, when he was given command of a battle group at Breslau. He was named commander of the 344th Infantry Division on the Eastern Front in March and was promoted to lieutenant general on April 20, 1945. He managed to escape the debacle in the East and was living at Kochel am. See, West Germany, in 1958.

Dr. Johannes Schulz (1892–1943) was an engineer officer who entered the service in 1910. After fighting in World War I, he was discharged from the Reichsheer as a captain in 1920. He returned to active duty at the same rank in 1934. Schulz commanded the 70th Engineer Battalion (1938–39), served on the staff at OKH (1939–43), and commanded the 10th Panzer Grenadier Regiment of the 9th Panzer Division from March 4 to October 9, 1943. On October 9 he was suddenly named acting divisional commander when General Jolasse was wounded. Schulz was killed in action near Krivoy Rog on November 27, 1943, and was posthumously promoted to major general.

Walter Boemers was normally commander of the 102nd Panzer Artillery Regiment.

Max Sperling was normally the commander of the 11th Panzer Grenadier Regiment. He was acting commander of the 9th Panzer Division on November 27–28, 1943, and from August 12 to September 2, 1944. As a major, he was commander of the 10th Panzer Reconnaissance Battalion on the Eastern Front in 1941. He had previously served with the 10th Panzer Division in France (1940).

Gerhard Mueller was relieved of the command of the 9th Panzer Division by General Bandenberger on September 16, along with his chief of operations, Lieutenant Colonel Wilhelm Friedel. For a sketch of his career, see 116th Panzer Division.

Baron Harald Gustav von Elverfeldt (1900–45) was considered a rising young star in the German Army and was indeed a brilliant General Staff officer and an equally capable division commander. Commissioned in 1919, he served as Ia of the 3rd Light (later 8th Panzer) Division (1938–40), Ia of the XV Panzer Corps (1940–41), chief of staff of LVI Panzer Corps (1941–43), chief of staff of the 9th Army (January–August, 1943), chief of staff of the 17th Army (1943–44), and an instructor at the War Academy in Berlin (1944) before taking command of the 9th Panzer. He was even singled out for commendation by Hitler in 1944—a rare honor indeed for any German Army general in the fifth year of the war. Elverfeldt was posthumously awarded the Oak Leaves and promoted to lieutenant general.

A career staff officer, Friedrich Wilhelm von Mellenthin was born in Breslau in 1904. He entered the service as a Fahnenjunker in 1924 and was commissioned second lieutenant in the 7th Cavalry Regiment in 1928. During World War II, he served on the staff of the III Corps (1939), was Ia of the 197th Infantry Division (1940), was on the staff of 1st Army in occupied France (1940–41), and was chief intelligence officer (Ic) of Panzer Group (later Army) Afrika (1941–42). Returning to Germany after being wounded, Mellenthin was chief of staff of XXXXVIII Panzer Corps in Russia (late 1942–44), chief of staff of the 4th Panzer Army (1944), and chief of staff of Army Group G (1944). Sacked by General Guderian for insubordination (with little justification), it is unclear how long Mellenthin actually commanded the 9th Panzer. He was named chief of staff of the 5th Panzer Army on March 5, 1945, and was captured after the Ruhr Pocket collapsed. Later he immigrated to Johannesburg, South Africa, where he became a very prosperous businessman and airline owner. He was still alive and riding horses every day in the 1980s. His book, *Panzer Battles*, is considered a classic of World War II literature.

Colonel Helmuth Zollenkopf had previously commanded the 114th Rifle Regiment as a lieutenant colonel in 1942–43.

## NOTES AND SOURCES

The 5th Reserve Panzer Grenadier Regiment (35th and 86th Battalions) of the 155th Reserve Panzer Division was absorbed by the 10th Panzer Grenadier Regiment; the 25th Reserve Grenadier Regiment (Motorized) (119th and 215th Battalions) was absorbed by the 11th Panzer Grenadier Regiment. The HQ, 9th Rifle Brigade became the 9th Panzer Grenadier Brigade on July 5, 1942, but was dissolved on December 15, 1942. Casualties rendered it unnecessary. In 1942, the 33rd Panzer Regiment was given the honorary title "Prinz Eugen."

Bradley et al., Volume 1: 168–69; Blumenson 1960: 422, 501; Carell 1966: 125; Carell 1971: 26–34; Chant 1979, Volume 14: 1855; Volume 16: 2133; Chapman: 347–48; Harrison: 240, 244, Map VI; Carl Hans Hermann, *68 Kriegsmonate: Der Weg der 9. Panzerdivision durch zweiten Weltkrieg* (Vienna, 1975): 1 ff.; Carl Hans Hermann, *Die 9. Panzerdivision, 1939–1945* (Friedberg, n.d.): 1 ff.; Keilig: 18, 81, 152, 297, 316; Kennedy: 74, Map 7; MacDonald 1963; 69, 74, 95, 242–44, 567; MacDonald 1973: 34, 163, 191, 221, 370; Manstein: 52; Mellenthin 1977: 155; Mehner, Volume 4: 383; Volume 5: 329; Volume 7: 354; Scheibert: 479; Stauffenberg MS; OB 42: 57–58; Tessin, Volume 2: 243–44, Volume 3: 136–39; OB 43: 202; OB 45: 291; Ziemke 1966: 241.

# 10th Panzer Division

**COMPOSITION (1942):**  7th Panzer Regiment, 69th Panzer Grenadier Regiment, 86th Panzer Grenadier Regiment, 90th Panzer Artillery Regiment, 10th Motorcycle Battalion, 90th Panzer Reconnaissance Battalion, 90th Tank Destroyer Battalion, 90th Panzer Engineer Battalion, 90th Panzer Signal Battalion.

**HOME STATION:**  Vaihingen/Filder, Wehrkreis V

The 10th Panzer Division was formed in Prague on April 1, 1939, as a composite unit, made up of a number of previously established active duty formations from throughout Germany. It initially included the 86th Motorized Infantry Regiment from the 29th Motorized Infantry Division at Muehlhausen; the 8th Panzer Regiment from the 4th Panzer Brigade at Boeblingen; the I Battalion, 8th Reconnaissance Regiment from the 3rd Light Division at Stettin; and the II/29th Artillery Regiment from the 29th Motorized Infantry Division at Erfurt.

The 10th Panzer was hurriedly transferred to Pomerania in August and was thrown into the Polish campaign of 1939 before its organizational and training process was complete and before it received all of its units; for that reason it was in reserve during much of the operation. During the initial fighting in the drive across the Polish Corridor and in northern Poland it did quite well, however, in spite of the fact that it had to direct the 4th Panzer Brigade, the 7th Panzer Regiment, and several SS combat units with which it had never before worked and with which it was totally unfamiliar. That winter it completed its organization, absorbing the 69th Motorized Infantry Regiment of the 20th Motorized Infantry Division, but without its I and III Battalions. It also absorbed the 4th Panzer Brigade and I/20th Artillery Regiment and incorporated the newly formed 10th Rifle Brigade into its table of organization.

101

As of April 1, 1940, the division consisted of the 10th Rifle Brigade (69th and 86th Rifle Regiments), the 4th Panzer Brigade (7th and 8th Panzer Regiments), the 90th Panzer Artillery Regiment (two battalions), and assorted divisional troops. The 10th Panzer Division played a vital role in the French campaign. As part of Guderian's XIX Motorized Corps it broke through the French lines at Sedan and penetrated all the way to the English Channel. After helping clear the Flanders ports of Allied troops, the 10th was involved in the mopping-up operations in the West. After spending a winter on occupation duty and in training, the 10th Panzer was sent to Russia in June 1941 and fought in the battles of the Minsk Pocket, Smolensk, Vyasma (Vjasma), and the drive to Moscow. It was heavily engaged against the Russian winter offensive of 1941–42 and held Juchnow against repeated attacks from January to April 1942. The division suffered such heavy losses that it was sent to the Amiens area of France in May 1942 to rest and rebuild. In August 1942 it was hurriedly sent to Dieppe, where it played a minor role in crushing an Anglo-Canadian amphibious attack. Still in France when the Allies landed in North Africa, it spearheaded the German occupation of Vichy France in November 1942 and was then rushed to Tunisia as fast as transport became available. Elements of the division were primarily responsible for Eisenhower's failure to take Tunis in 1942. The 10th Panzer also provided the U.S. Army with some of its most embarrassing moments in World War II during the Battle of the Kasserine Pass; however, when the Axis front collapsed in May 1943, the division was trapped and destroyed. It surrendered on May 12 and was never rebuilt.

Its commanders included Major General Georg Gawantka (May 1, 1939), Major General/Lieutenant General Ferdinand Schaal (July 15, 1939), Major General/Lieutenant General Wolfgang Fischer (assumed command, August 2, 1941), Colonel Guenther Angern (acting commander, August 8, 1941), Fischer (returned, August 27, 1941), Colonel Nikolaus von Vormann (acting commander, November 19, 1942), Fischer (returned, December, 1942), and Lieutenant General Baron Friedrich von Broich (February 5, 1943).

## COMMANDERS

Georg Gawantka was born in Berlin in 1891 and entered the service as a Fahnenjunker in the cavalry in 1910. After fighting in World War I and serving in the Reichswehr, he was commander of the 2nd Rifle Regiment (1935–38), the 3rd Rifle Brigade (1938), and the 2nd Rifle Brigade (1938–39). Promoted to major general in 1938, he died suddenly in Prague on July 14, 1939.

Ferdinand Schaal (b. 1881), a native of Brunswick, joined the 22nd Dragoons as a Fahnenjunker in 1908. A veteran cavalry officer who had previously commanded the 1st Panzer Brigade (1935–39), he was promoted to lieutenant general on April 1, 1939. He was named commander of the Afrika Korps in September 1941; however, he had been in Libya less than a month before he fell ill and had to be returned to Europe. Promoted to general of panzer troops effective October 1, 1941, Schaal was acting commander of the XXXIV Corps and commander of the LVI Panzer Corps in Russia (late 1941–42), during which his health was severely strained. Later he was Military Plenipotentiary and Commander of Wehrkreis Bohemia and Moravia (1943–44). He was arrested on July 21, 1944, for his part in the attempt to assassinate Adolf Hitler and spent the rest of the war in prison.

Wolfgang Fischer (1888–1943) began his career as an infantry Fahnenjunker in 1910. A colonel in 1939, he commanded the 69th Infantry Regiment (1938–39) and the 10th Rifle Brigade (late 1939–41) before assuming command of the 10th Panzer Division. Fischer was promoted to major general on August 1, 1942 (the day before he took command of the 10th Panzer Division) and to lieutenant general on November 1, 1942. Considered one of the best tank division commanders in the Wehrmacht, Fischer distinguished himself in Tunisia before being killed in action on February 1, 1943, when his command car hit a mine and blew off his left arm and both of his legs. He bled to death while writing a farewell letter to his wife. He was posthumously promoted to general of panzer troops.

For sketches of the careers of Guenther Angern and Nikolaus von Vormann, see Commanders, 16th and 23rd Panzer Divisions, respectively.

Baron Friedrich von Broich was a veteran cavalry officer who lacked Fischer's ability in leading armored units; his performance was merely adequate and was sometimes short of that. His handling of tank units in the Kasserine offensive, for example, left much to be desired. Born in Strasbourg, Alsace, in 1896, Broich began his service as a Fahnenjunker in the 9th Ulan Regiment in 1914. During the World War II era, he was commander of the II/6th Cavalry Regiment (1938–38), the regiment itself (1938-late 1939), the 21st Cavalry Regiment (1939–40), the 22nd Cavalry Regiment (1940), the 1st Cavalry Brigade in Russia (1941), the 24th Panzer Grenadier Brigade (1941–42), and the ad hoc Division Broich in Tunisia before assuming command of the 10th Panzer. He was severely wounded in the spring of 1943 but continued to command the 10th Panzer Division until Axis supply lines collapsed. He surrendered it to the British on May 12, 1943. Broich was promoted to major general on January 1, 1943 and to lieutenant general effective May 1, 1943. Released from the POW camps in 1947, he died at Leoni (near Starnberg) on September 24, 1974.

## NOTES AND SOURCES

During the Polish campaign, most of the division fought under the name Panzer Verband Ostpreussen or Panzer Division Kempf.

Angolia, *Field*, Volume 2: 45–46; Benoist-Mechin: 68; Bradley et al., Volume 2: 279–80; Carell 1966: 80; Chant 1979, Volume 16: 2232; Chapman: 347–48; Keilig: 91, 292; Kennedy: 74, Map 7; Manstein: 34, 488; Mehner, Volume 6: 545; Schmitz et al., Volume 2: 241–46; Tessin, Volume 3: 170–71; OB 42: 58; OB 45: 292; Windrow: 8. Also see W. G. F. Jackson, *The Battle for North Africa, 1940–43* (New York, 1975), for a more detailed description of the 10th Panzer's campaign in Tunisia (hereafter cited as "Jackson").

# 11th Panzer Division

**COMPOSITION (1943):**   15th Panzer Regiment, 110th Panzer Grenadier Regiment, 111th Panzer Grenadier Regiment, 119th Panzer Artillery Regiment, 231st (later 11th) Panzer Reconnaissance Battalion, 231st Tank Destroyer Battalion, 231st Panzer Engineer Battalion, 341st Panzer Signal Battalion.

**HOME STATION:**   Sagan, Wehrkreis VIII

The 11th Panzer—a Silesian unit—was formed from the 11th Motorized Infantry Brigade (110th and 111th Rifle Regiments), which had fought in France; the 15th Panzer Regiment of the 5th Panzer Division; and the 61st Motorcycle, 231st Reconnaissance, and 61st Antitank (subsequently Tank Destroyer) Battalions from the 231st Infantry Division. The 341st Signal Battalion was contributed by the 311th Infantry Division, the 209th Engineer Battalion came from the 209th Infantry Division, and the 119th Artillery Regiment was created from a variety of sources: the staff from the 746th Artillery Regiment, I Battalion from the I/4th Artillery Regiment (4th Infantry Division), the II Battalion from the III/677th Artillery Regiment, and the III Battalion was the former I/643rd Artillery Regiment (an army General Headquarters unit). The new division was formed in the Neuhammer Maneuver Area but was sent to Poland in December 1940 and to Romania in January 1941. It first saw action in the Balkans in April 1941 and (along with the SS Motorized Division Leibstandarte Adolf Hitler) claimed credit for the capture of Belgrade.

   The 11th Panzer Division crossed into Russia with Army Group South in July, fought at Zhitomir, Uman, and Kiev, and was sent to Army Group Center for the Battle of Moscow. It held the Gshatsk (Gzhatsk) sector from January to

104

May 1942 as part of the 4th Panzer Army. Sent south in June, it fought at Orel and Voronesh, on the Don and in the Donez. Although it took part in the drive on Stalingrad, it avoided the encirclement that trapped the 6th Army in November; nevertheless, it suffered heavy losses from the Soviet winter offensive of 1942–43, in the Stalingrad relief effort, and in the subsequent retreats. The 11th Panzer (now a Kampfgruppe) played a minor role in halting the Russians east of Rostov and thus kept the escape route of Army Group A opened. By early 1943 the division had been reorganized again, losing the 11th Rifle Brigade HQ (dissolved in early 1943), but adding a III Battalion to the 15th Panzer Regiment by absorbing II/35th Panzer Regiment (4th Panzer Division). The 61st Motorcycle was coverted into the 231st Panzer Reconnaissance Battalion at the end of 1942 and the 277th Army Flak Artillery Battalion became part of the division on April 20, 1943. Thus reinforced, the 11th Panzer fought at Kharkov, at Kursk, and at Belgorod, and suffered heavy losses at Krivog Rog and Kremenchug in the fall of 1943. It was surrounded, along with several other divisions, at Cherkassy (Korsun) in February 1944. It broke out, but with such appalling losses in life and equipment that it had to be almost completely rebuilt. It absorbed the remnants of the 416th Grenadier Regiment of the 123rd Infantry Division (which had also been smashed on the Eastern Front) and was sent to the Libourne area of southern France, where it absorbed the personnel of the 273rd Reserve Panzer Division.

The 11th Panzer remained in the West and was stationed at Toulouse for a time. In July 1944, it conducted delaying operations up the Rhone Valley against the Allied forces that had landed in southern France. It fought in Alsace and took part in the defense of the Belford Gap and in the subsequent withdrawal to the Saar, before being sent to the Ardennes in December 1944. By the time the Battle of the Bulge began, the division had only 3,500 men left and only 800 of these were infantry, despite the fact that it had absorbed the remnants of the 113rd Panzer Brigade on September 23. After the failure of this, Hitler's last offensive in the West, the 11th Panzer Division was reinforced and sent into the Battle of the Saar-Moselle Triangle and again suffered serious losses. The following month it tried to overrun the U.S. bridgehead at Remagen but was down to a strength of 4,000 men, 25 tanks, and 18 pieces of artillery, and was repulsed; nevertheless, it was one of the strongest panzer divisions left on the Western Front. Kesselring ordered it transferred to Army Group G on the southern sector of the front in March, so it escaped encirclement in the Ruhr Pocket and fought in the Black Forest until the end of the war. The remnants of this veteran combat division, which had distinguished itself in a dozen battles, surrendered to the U.S. 90th Infantry Division near Wallern on May 2, 1945.

Commanders of the 11th Panzer included Major General Ludwig Cruewell (assumed command August 1, 1940), Colonel Guenther Angern (acting commander from August 15, 1941), Major General Baron Hans-Karl von Esebeck (assumed command August 24, 1941), Major General Walter Scheller (October 20, 1941), Major General/Lieutenant General Hermann Balck (May 16, 1942),

Lieutenant General Dietrich von Choltitz (March 3, 1943), Major General Johann Mickl (May 11, 1943), Colonel/Major General/Lieutenant General Wend von Wietersheim (August 8, 1943), Colonel Friedrich von Hake (May 7, 1944), Major General Baron Horst Treusch von Buttlar-Brandenfels (January 1945), and Wietersheim again (May 3, 1945).

## COMMANDERS

Ludwig Cruewell (1892–1958), an excellent tactical commander, was promoted to lieutenant general on September 1, 1941, shortly after he gave up command of the 11th Panzer. Later he was promoted to general of panzer troops and led the Afrika Korps in a brilliant manner during Operation Crusader. Had Rommel listened to his advice, it is unlikely the British would have broken the Siege of Tobruk in December 1941. Rommel named him deputy commander of Panzer Army Afrika in early 1942. Cruewell was captured when the British shot down his airplane over the Gazala Line on May 29, 1942. He did not see Germany again until 1948. Previously Cruewell had been commander of the 6th Panzer Regiment (1937–38), a branch chief at OKH (1939), and on the staff of the 16th Army (1939–40). He began his military career as a Fahnenjunker in the 9th Dragoon Regiment in 1911.

For the details of General Angern's career, see 16th Panzer Division, Commanders.

Hans-Karl von Esebeck (1892–1955) was born in Potsdam and served in the cavalry from 1911 to 1939. He assumed command of the 6th Rifle Brigade in March, 1939, however, and spent the entire war in the mobile branch, commanding the 6th Rifle (1939–41), the 15th Rifle Brigade (1941), and the 15th Panzer Division of the Afrika Korps (1941). Wounded near Tobruk by a shell splinter, he was sent to Russia after he recovered (despite the fact that Rommel wanted him back) and led the 11th Panzer. Later he commanded the 2nd Panzer Division (1942), was deputy commander of the XXXXVI Panzer Corps (1942–43), and served as commander of LVII Panzer Corps (1943–44) and Wehrkreis XVII (1944). Arrested for his part in the July 20, 1944, attempt on Hitler's life, he spent the rest of the war in concentration camps. After the war, he lived in relative poverty. An excellent armored commander, Baron von Esebeck is another example of a German cavalry officer who successfully made the transition to motorized warfare. Prior to the war, Esebeck commanded the 1st Cavalry Regiment (1936–39).

For the details of Walter Scheller's career, see 9th Panzer Division, Commanders.

Hermann Balck (b. 1893), a Prussian from Danzig, entered the army as an infantry Fahnenjunker in 1913. He distinguished himself as commander of the 1st Rifle Regiment in France in 1940. Later he commanded the 3rd Panzer Regiment (1940–41) and the 2nd Panzer Brigade (1941). After a tour of duty with the Office of Mobile Troops at OKH, he led the 11th Panzer, was acting commander of the Grossdeutschland Motorized Infantry Division (1943), and served as commander of the XXXX Panzer Corps (1943), XXXXVIII Panzer Corps (1943–44), 4th Panzer Army (late 1944), Army Group G on the Western Front (1944), and 6th Army in the East (late 1944–end). He was awarded the Knight's Cross with Oak Leaves, Swords, and Diamonds and was promoted to lieutenant general on January 1, 1943, and to general of panzer troops on November 1, 1944. He moved to Stuttgart after the war and died at Erbenbach-Rockenau on November 29, 1982, less than two weeks prior to his 89th birthday. He was buried at Asperg, near Ludwigsburg.

Dietrich von Choltitz (b. 1894), a Silesian, was an infantry officer most of his career. During World War II, he commanded III/16th Infantry Regiment (1939–40), 16th Infantry Regiment (1940–42), and 260th Infantry Division (1942). After a short staff tour at OKH (1942), he was deputy commander of XXXXVIII Panzer Corps (1942), acting commander of XVII Corps (1942–43), commander of the 11th Panzer Division (1943), deputy commander of XXXX-VIII Panzer Corps again (1943), and commander of LXXXIV Corps on the Western Front. Unjustly sacked by Field Marshal Guenther von Kluge for the Normandy debacle, he was almost immediately named Wehrmacht commander of greater Paris by Adolf Hitler, who ordered him to destroy the city. This Choltitz would not do. He surrendered Paris to the Allies on August 24, 1944—23 days after his promotion to general of infantry. After being released from prison, he retired to Baden-Baden. As a youth, Choltitz was a page in the Saxon court. He was educated at various cadet schools and began his military service as a Faehnrich (senior officer cadet) in the 107th Infantry Regiment in 1914. He died at Baden-Baden on November 5, 1966.

Johann Mickl (1893–1945) served in the Austro-Hungarian or Austrian armies from 1914 to 1938, when he was absorbed into the Wehrmacht. He served as commander of the 42nd Antitank Battalion (1938–40), 7th Rifle Regiment (1940–41), 155th Infantry Regiment (1942–43), and then as commander of the 11th Panzer. Transferred to Yugoslavia, he commanded the Croatian 392nd Infantry Division from August 13, 1943, until the end of March 1945, when he was killed in action near Karlobey on the Eastern Front. Mickl was promoted to major general on March 1, 1943, and to lieutenant general on April 1, 1944.

Wend von Wietersheim (1900–75) was one of the best (and youngest) divisional commanders to serve on the Western Front. Even Adolf Hitler thought highly of him. A native of Neuland/Loewenberg, Wietersheim entered the service as a Fahnenjunker in 1918 and was commissioned in the 4th Hussars the following year. He assumed command of the 11th Panzer as a colonel and was promoted to major general on November 1, 1943, and to lieutenant general on July 1, 1944. Prior to getting his division, Wietersheim was adjutant of the 3rd Panzer Division (1938–40), commander of the 1st Motorcycle Battalion (1940–41), and commander of the 113th Panzer Grenadier Regiment (1941–43). He was apparently wounded in the last stages of the Battle of the Bulge and did not recover until the end of the war. He resumed command of the division just in time to surrender it. Wietersheim held the Knight's Cross with Oak Leaves and Swords.

For details on Friedrich von Hake's career, see 13th Panzer Division, Commanders.

Like Wietersheim, Baron Horst Treusch von Buttlar-Brandenfels was born in 1900, but he did not approach Wietersheim's talent as a leader. Also a cavalry officer, Treusch served on the staff of OKH (1937–39), was Ia of the 81st Infantry Division (1939–40), was Ia of Group XXI (later the Army of Norway) (April 1941–42), and was a member of the staff of the chief of operations at OKW (i.e., he was a member of Colonel General Alfred Jodl's staff). While at OKW (a distinctly pro-Nazi organization), Treusch insisted that the orders of the Fuehrer and OKW be obeyed without question—whether they made sense or not. As the Soviets closed in on Berlin, however, Treusch made sure that he was given his first command of the war—and on the Western Front. Certainly there were many officers better qualified for this post. Treusch was promoted to major general on January 1, 1944. In 1955 he was living in Kassel, the city of his birth.

## NOTES AND SOURCES

In the spring of 1944, the Headquarters, 11th Panzer Division absorbed the staff of the 273rd Reserve Panzer Division. The 110th Panzer Grenadier Regiment absorbed the 92nd Reserve Panzer Grenadier Regiment (12th Reserve Panzer Grenadier and 20th Reserve Motorized Battalions); the 111th Panzer Grenadier Regiment absorbed the 73rd Reserve Motorized Grenadier Regiment (with the 40th Reserve Panzer Grenadier and the 41st Reserve Motorized Grenadier Battalions); the 11th Panzer Reconnaissance Battalion absorbed the 7th Reserve Panzer Reconnaissance Battalion; the 15th Panzer Regiment absorbed the 25th and 35th Reserve Panzer Battalions; and the 119th Panzer Artillery Regiment absorbed the 167th Reserve Panzer Artillery Regiment.

Angolia, *Field*, Volume 1: 163–64; Blumenson 1960: 535; Carell 1966: 118, 330, 649; Carell 1971: 47, 123; Clark: 261; Hugh M. Cole, *The Lorraine Campaign* (Washington, D.C., 1950): 217, 237, 450, 527 (hereafter cited as "Cole 1950"); Harrison: 244, Map VI; Hartmann: 64; Keilig: 60, 84, 227, 348, 370; MacDonald 1973: 118, 126, 142, 221, 345, 467; Manstein: 389, 526; Mellenthin 1977: 183; Schmitz et al., Volume 3, *Die Divisionen 11–16*: 17–28; Stoves, *Gepanzerten*: 85; Tessin, Volume 3: 202–03; OB 43: 202; OB 45: 292.

# 12th Panzer Division

**COMPOSITION:** 29th Panzer Regiment, 5th Panzer Grenadier Regiment, 25th Panzer Grenadier Regiment, 2nd Panzer Artillery Regiment, 12th Panzer Reconnaissance Battalion, 508th Tank Destroyer Battalion, 32nd Panzer Engineer Battalion, 2nd Panzer Signal Battalion.

**HOME STATION:** Stettin, Wehrkreis II

The 2nd Infantry Division—the forerunner of the 12th Panzer—was created at Stettin in the Reichsheer organization of 1921. Its personnel were Prussians. In 1934–35 it was reorganized to include the 5th, 25th, and 92nd Infantry Regiments, and in 1936–37 it was again reformed, this time as a motorized infantry division. In the summer of 1939 its 92nd Motorized Infantry Regiment was attached to the 60th Motorized Infantry Division, a separation that was made permanent in 1940. Meanwhile, the 2nd Motorized fought in northern Poland and in France, where it was part of Gustav von Wietersheim's XIV Motorized Corps. In the fall of 1940 it returned to Stettin and was reorganized as a panzer division. As of October 5, 1940, it included the newly formed Staff, 12th Rifle Brigade (5th and 25th Rifle Regiments and 22nd Motorcycle Battalion), the 29th Panzer Regiment (three battalions), and assorted divisional troops. The following year it fought in Russia, taking part in the Minsk encirclement, the crossing of the Dnieper, and the Battle of Smolensk, as well as the drive on Leningrad and the Battle of Mga on the northern sector. Hit hard by the Soviet winter offensive of 1941–42, it was withdrawn to Estonia to rest and refit.

Soon back in action, the 12th Panzer took part in the battles south of Leningrad in 1942, fighting at Volchov, Lake Ladoga, and Nevel, before being sent to Roslavl on the central sector of the front late in the year. Here it was reorganized in 1943 and lost its brigade headquarters. The division now consisted of the 29th Panzer Regiment, 5th and 25th Panzer Grenadier Regiments, 2nd Panzer Artillery Regiment, 12th Panzer Reconnaissance Battalion, 2nd Tank Destroyer Battalion, 32nd Panzer Engineer Battalion, 2nd Panzer Signal Battalion, 303rd Army Flak Battalion, and assorted divisional service support troops. The 12th Panzer fought at Vitebsk in February, at Orel in March, and at Kursk in July 1943, and later took part in the Battles of Bryansk and Gomel, and in the defense of the middle Dnieper (autumn 1943). Transferred back to Army Group North in January 1944, it arrived too late to prevent the Soviets from breaking the Siege of Leningrad, but it did distinguish itself in the retreat across the Baltic states. That summer it tried to prevent the encirclement of the 4th and 9th Armies, but it failed and was driven into the Courland Pocket in September. It fought in all six battles of the Courland Pocket and was still there when the war ended. Most of its survivors spent the next 10 years in Soviet captivity.

Commanders of the 2nd Infantry/12th Panzer Division included Major General/Lieutenant General Paul Bader (April 1, 1937), Major General Josef Harpe (October 5, 1940), Major General/Lieutenant General Walter Wessel (January 15, 1942), Colonel/Major General/Lieutenant General Baron Erpo von Bodenhausen (March 1, 1943), Colonel Hans-Joachim Kahler (acting commander, early 1944), Bodenhausen (resumed command, 1944), Colonel Gerhard Mueller (acting commander, June–July 1944), Bodenhausen (autumn, 1944), and Colonel Horst von Usedom (April 12, 1945).

## COMMANDERS

Paul Bader (b. 1883) was promoted to lieutenant general on January 1, 1938. He had enlisted in the army as an artilleryman in 1903 and served in it for 41 years. Bader became a Fahnenjunker in 1905 and earned his commission the following year. During the World War II era, he commanded the 2nd Infantry Division (Motorized) (1937–40) and LXV Corps Command (1941), was Military Commander, Serbia (1941–43), and commanded the XXI Mountain Corps (1943–44) before retiring in early 1944. He died in 1971.

Josef Harpe (1887–1968) was promoted to lieutenant general on January 15, 1942. He had previously led the 3rd Panzer Regiment (1935) and was Ia of the 1st Panzer Brigade. Later he commanded this unit (1939–40). After leaving the 12th Panzer, he led XXXXI Panzer Corps (1942–43), 9th Army (late 1943–44), 4th Panzer Army (1944), Army Group North Ukraine (June–August, 1944), and Army Group A (from September 1944). Despite his pro-Nazi sentiments, he was relieved of command on January 17, 1945, five days after the Russian winter offensive of 1944–45 began, because Hitler needed a scapegoat. Harpe was nevertheless given another command—5th Panzer Army—shortly thereafter. It was destroyed in the Battle of the Ruhr Pocket, where Harpe himself

surrendered in April 1945. He had begun his military career as an infantry Fahnenjunker in 1909. He retired to Nuremberg.

Walter Wessel (1897–1943) was promoted to lieutenant general on January
1, 1943. He joined the army in the summer of 1911 and was commissioned in
the infantry the following year. He commanded the III/15th Infantry Regiment
(1937–39), the 15th Infantry Regiment (1939–41), and the 12th Panzer (1942–
43). He joined the staff of the Inspector of Panzer Troops on March 1, 1943,
and was killed in an accident near Morano, Italy, on July 20, 1943. Wessel held
the Knight's Cross with Oak Leaves.

Baron Erpo von Bodenhausen (1897–1945) was promoted to major general
on May 1, 1943, and to lieutenant general exactly six months later. He was
named acting commander of the L Corps on April 12, 1945; simultaneously he
retained command of the division, with Colonel von Usedom acting as his deputy and de facto divisional commander. Bodenhausen committed suicide in early
May 1945, just as the Courland Pocket surrendered. A cavalry officer, he had
previously commanded the II/8th Cavalry Regiment (1938–40), the 28th Rifle
Regiment (1940–42), and the 23rd Rifle Brigade (1942). He was cited for distinguished leadership in 1944.

Hans-Joachim Kahler (b. 1908) briefly commanded the division in 1944, no
doubt when Baron von Bodenhausen was on leave. Originally an officer cadet
in the cavalry, Kahler commanded the 5th Panzer Grenadier Regiment (1943–
44) and the Grossdeutschland Panzer Grenadier Brigade (1944–end).

For the details of Gerhard Mueller's career, see 116th Panzer Division.

Horst von Usedom (1906–1970), acting commander of the 12th Panzer Division and its last commander, was normally commanding officer of the 108th
Panzer Grenadier Regiment (1944–45). He was a Saxon.

## NOTES AND SOURCES

In 1942, the III/29th Panzer Regiment was transferred to the 13th Panzer Division and
became III/4th Panzer Regiment. At the same time, the 22nd Motorcycle Battalion became the 2nd Panzer Reconnaissance Battalion, the 303rd Army Flak Battalion was
transferred to the division, and the former I/28th Panzer Regiment was transferred to the
division as the 508th Tank Destroyer Battalion.

Paul Adair, *Hitler's Greatest Defeat* (London, 1994): 134; Bradley et al., Volume 1:
176–78; Volume 2: 432–43; Carell 1966: 26, 69, 80; Carell 1971: 591–94; Keilig: 16,
38–39, 368; Kennedy: 10B, 74, Map 7; Kursietis: 92–93; Manstein: 131–32, 538;
Mehner, Volume 4: 383; Volume 6: 545; Volume 12: 458; Salisbury, 275; Scheibert:
382; Schmitz, Volume 3: 60; Stoves, *Gepanzerten*: 88–89; Tessin, Volume 3: 202–04;
OB 42: 58–59; OB 43: 208; OB 45: 293–94; Windrow: 9; Ziemke: 258.

# 13th Panzer Division

**COMPOSITION (1943):** 4th Panzer Regiment, 66th Panzer Grenadier Regiment, 93rd Panzer Grenadier Regiment, 13th Panzer Artillery Regiment, 13th Panzer Reconnaissance Battalion, 13th Tank Destroyer Battalion, 13th Panzer Engineer Battalion, 13th Panzer Signal Battalion.

**HOME STATION:** Magdeburg, Wehrkreis XI

The 13th Panzer was initially formed in October 1934 as Infantry Command IV. It was redesignated 13th Infantry Division on October 15, 1935. Initially it included the 33rd, 66th, and 93rd Infantry Regiments. In the winter of 1936–37 it was converted to a motorized infantry unit and was officially designated as such on October 12, 1937. In the summer of 1939, it gave up the 33rd Infantry Regiment to the 4th Panzer Division. The 13th Motorized took part in the conquests of Poland and France and distinguished itself in both campaigns, fighting in southern Poland as part of the 10th Army (the main German strike force). In the Western campaign of 1940 it again took part in the main thrust, pushing across Belgium to Calais in May. Later it fought at Amiens and was near Lyon when the French surrendered. Initially returning to Germany in July, it was transferred to Poland with XXXX Panzer Corps, but was then transported to Vienna, Wehrkreis XVII (Austria) that fall. Here it was reorganized and on October 11, 1940, and was converted into the 13th Panzer Division. It included the 13th Rifle Brigade (66th and 93rd Rifle Regiments [two battalions each] and the 43rd Motorcycle Battalion); 4th Panzer Regiment (two battalions); the 13th Panzer Artillery Regiment (three battalions); and the usual divisional support and service support troops.

The 13th Panzer spent the winter of 1940–41 in Romania but was not used in the Balkans campaign. It was sent to Silesia in May 1941 and crossed into Russia with Army Group South in June. The 13th was very heavily engaged, almost from the beginning. It fought in the battles of Lubin and Uman, in the breakthrough of the Stalin Line at Hulsk, and in the drive on and encirclement of Kiev. It captured Kremenchug and, on August 25, established the first German bridgehead across the vast Dnieper River at Dnepropetrosk. It then participated in the Battle of the Chernigovka Pocket (on the Sea of Azov), and in the captures of Mariupol, Taganrog, and Rostov, which the Soviets retook a short time later. Losses within the 13th Panzer were heavy and stress was high. By November 1941, its divisional commander and two of its regimental commanders were suffering from nervous exhaustion. After helping halt the Soviet winter offensive of 1941–42 on the Mius River, the 13th Panzer took part in the recapture of Rostov (in heavy fighting) and Ewald von Kleist's drive on the Caucasus oilfields in 1942. The 13th Panzer crossed the Terek River at Ischerskaja (within 15 miles of Grozny), where they faced heavy Soviet counterattacks. The division's forward battle group destroyed 33 Soviet T-34 and KV-1 tanks in two days, but Colonel Herbert Olbrich, the commander of the 4th Panzer Regiment, was killed in the fighting. The division's vanguards then pushed on to capture Elchetovo, the "Gateway to the Caucasus," on September 27, but could advance no further. It was encircled by a major Soviet counteroffensive in November, but broke out without particularly heavy losses. Most of the division escaped isolation in the Kuban before the Russians retook Rostov, although part of it was cut off and had to be evacuated later via the Crimea.

By this time the division had only 18 operational panzers left. Reunited in the Crimea under the command of the resurrected 6th Army, the 13th was given a battalion of Panther tanks and new, improved models of the PzKw IV, as well as several self-propelled antitank guns, and was sent to Ukraine, where it fought near Kharkov and Zaporozh'ye. By August 1943, it had a strength of only seven tanks when it was surrounded at Melitopol, along with the 336th Infantry and 15th Luftwaffe Field Divisions and Headquarters, XXIX Corps. Outnumbered more than 7 to 1, the 13th Panzer led the ensuing breakout on August 30 and reached German lines on September 2. Remaining at the front, the battered but veteran tank division continued covering the corps' retreat as Stalino was abandoned. It then fought its way back to the Dnieper, was in the Battle of the Nikopol bridgehead, and was involved in the subsequent retreat to Krivoy Rog.

In 1944, the division was partially refitted and received an infusion of new tanks. Back at the front, it took part in the Cherkassy relief attempt, and in the retreats to the Bug and Dniester (Dnestr). It suffered heavy losses when the Romanians defected from the Axis in September 1944 and the 13th Panzer suddenly found itself cut off behind enemy lines. The division had only 40 tanks left when the breakout began and lost almost all of them. Elements of the division managed to fight their way back to German lines; other remnants (including one led by General Troeger, the divisional commander) retreated into Bulgaria, where they were interned and handed over to the Soviets. Withdrawn to reform in October, the 13th absorbed the recently formed 110th Panzer Brigade, which included the 2110th Panzer Battalion (four companies of Panther tanks), the 2110th Panzer Grenadier Battalion (five companies of mechanized infantry, equipped with half-tracks), the 2110th Engineer Company, and assorted brigade support units. Simultaneously, it was redesignated 13th Panzer Division Feldherrnhalle—FHH for short.

Even though it was still well below its authorized strength, the division was sent back into action on the southern sector of the Eastern Front (now in Hungary) in November. As of December 1944, the 13th Panzer Division had only 3,000 men and about 20 PzKw IV and V tanks. Most of the division was encircled at Budapest in December and was destroyed during the siege or in the subsequent (largely unsuccessful) breakout attempt in February. The remnants of the division (about 300 to 500 men) that escaped were reformed under the command of Lieutenant Colonel of Reserves Wilhelm Schoening and, as Kampfgruppe Schoening, formed the nucleus of the Panzer Division Feldherrnhalle 2, which was activated on February 24, 1945. This division was also unofficially referred to as the 13th Panzer Division, even though it was a separate division (see Panzer Division Feldherrnhalle 2).

Commanders of the 13th Infantry/Panzer Division included Major General/ Lieutenant General Paul Otto (assumed command, October 1, 1934), Lieutenant General Moritz von Faber du Faur (August 21, 1939), Otto (resumed command, September 7, 1939), Lieutenant General Friedrich-Wilhelm von Rothkirch und Panthen (November 1, 1939), Major General Walter Duevert (June 14, 1941), Colonel/Major General Traugott Herr (November 29, 1941), Colonel Walter Kuehn (acting commander, October 1, 1942), Major General/Lieutenant General Hellmut von der Chevallerie (November 1, 1942), Colonel Wilhelm Crisolli (December 1, 1942), Chevallerie again (May 15, 1943), Colonel/Major General Eduard Hauser (September 1, 1943), Colonel/Major General Hans Mikosch (December 23, 1943), Colonel Friedrich von Hake (May 18, 1944), Lieutenant General Hans Troeger (May 25, 1944), Colonel/Major General Gerhard Schmidhuber (September 9, 1944), and Lieutenant Colonel of Reserves Wilhelm Schoening (February 12, 1945).

## COMMANDERS

Paul Otto (b. 1881) was promoted to lieutenant general on January 1, 1937. He had entered the service as an infantry Fahnenjunker in 1901 and was commander of the 21st Infantry Regiment in 1932. Later he served as Infantry Fuehrer IV and deputy commander of the 4th Infantry Division (1934–35), commander of the 13th Motorized (1935–39), chief of the German Army Mission to Slovakia (1939–42), and commander of Wehrkreis IX. He retired as a general of infantry in 1943.

Moritz von Faber du Faur (1886–1971) was born in Stuttgart. He entered the service as a volunteer in 1904 and was commissioned int he dragoons in 1906. He fought in World War I, was retained in the Reichsheer, and was a colonel commanding the 8th Cavalry Regiment in 1933. From 1936 to August 1939, Faber was German military attaché to Belgrade; meanwhile, he was promoted to major general (1937) and lieutenant general (1939). After leaving the 13th, Faber commanded the 586th and 588th Rear Area Commands (1939–40), was military commander of the Bordeaux region (1940–42), and was commander of the 593rd Rear Area Command (1942). He ended his career as commander of Recruiting Area Innsbruck (1943–44).

Friedrich-Wilhelm von Rothkirch und Panthen (1884–1953) entered the service as a Fahnenjunker in the 8th Dragoon Regiment and was discharged as a major in 1922. A "retread," he reentered the army as a major in late 1933. He then rose rather rapidly, to lieutenant colonel (1935), colonel (1937), major general (1938), and lieutenant general (August 1, 1941), commanding the 49th Infantry Regiment (1937–39) and the 13th Motorized/Panzer Division in the process. On July 26, 1941, however, his health collapsed or he was wounded—the German records (as usual) do not say which. He was probably wounded; in any case, a brilliant career was cut short. Rothkirch did not return to active duty for more than a year and did not hold another field command. He commanded the 148th Reserve Division from April 1 to October 1, 1943, and then retired. He died in Trier on December 24, 1953.

Walter Duevert (b. 1893) was another case of a brilliant career cut short. An artillery officer, he carried the seeds of great potential and it was thought that he would rise to the highest positions in the German Army—and indeed he was on his way. He served as chief of staff of Wehrkreis IX (1936–37), commanded the 28th Artillery Regiment (1937–38), was chief of staff of VI Corps (1939–41), and commanded the 13th Panzer Division (1941–42). However, the strain of the Russian Front—especially during the Soviet winter offensive of 1941–42—proved too much for General Duevert and he broke down completely on February 16. Some people recover after such ordeals (as did Kesselring's chief of staff, General Siegfried Westphal, for example); others do not. Duevert never made it all the way back. On July 1, 1942, he was given command of another panzer division (the 20th), but had to be relieved in October. This time he did not return to duty for eight months, when he was given command of the 265th Infantry Division in occupied France. After D-Day, however, it was obvious that Duevert would never again be able to stand up under the strain of a combat command. He was relieved on July 27, 1944, and was never reemployed. He retired at the end of November 1944 and died in Duesseldorf on February 4, 1972.

Traugott Herr (1890–1976) joined the Imperial Army as an officer cadet in the infantry in 1911. He commanded the III/33rd Infantry Regiment (1937–39), the 13th Replacement and Training Regiment (1939), the 66th Rifle (or Motorized Infantry) Regiment of the 13th Motorized Division (1939–40), the 13th Motorized Infantry Brigade (1940–41), and the 13th Panzer Division (1941–

42). He was promoted to major general on April 1, 1942, and to lieutenant general on December 1, 1942. Herr was seriously wounded on October 31, 1942, and saw no further service until June 25, 1943, when he assumed command of the LXXVI Panzer Corps in Italy (1943–45). A general of panzer troops from September 1, 1943, he was acting commander of the 14th Army in Italy (November–December 1944) and commander of 10th Army (1945), which he surrendered to the Western Allies at the end of the war in Italy. A holder of the Knight's Cross with Oak Leaves and Swords, General Herr was an excellent panzer commander.

Colonel Dr. Walter Kuehn was normally commander of the 13th Panzer Artillery Regiment.

For the details of Hellmut von der Chevallerie's career, see 273rd Reserve Panzer Division, Commander.

For a sketch of Wilhelm Crisolli's career, see 6th Panzer Division.

Eduard Hauser (1895–1961) was promoted to major general on December 1, 1943, and to lieutenant general on June 1, 1944. A former staff officer with Guderian's XIX Panzer Corps (1939–40), he commanded the 18th Panzer Regiment (1940–41) and 25th Panzer Regiment (1941–43) before assuming command of the 13th Panzer. He was seriously wounded in December 1943. After recovering, Hauser commanded Special Purposes Divisional Staff 605 (*Division. Stab 605 z.b.V.*), known as Kampfgruppe Hauser, on the Eastern Front from June 1944 until April 30, 1945. This unit consisted of a collection of ad hoc formations under 4th Army and was hardly considered a prized command. Hauser lived in Garmisch after the war. A Bavarian by birth, he entered the service as a Fahnenjunker in the 17th Bavarian Infantry Regiment in 1914.

Hans Mikosch (b. 1898) entered the army as a war volunteer in 1914 and was commissioned in an engineer battalion in 1916. He made himself a reputation as commander of the 51st Engineer Battalion, which so effectively reduced the strategic Belgian fortress of Eben Emael in 1940. Promoted to colonel (1942), major general (January 1, 1944), and lieutenant general (March 16, 1945), he was acting commander of the 10th Panzer Grenadier Division (1943) before commanding the 13th Panzer. A better engineer than he was a tank officer, Mikosch later was commandant of Boulogne, directed Higher Engineer Command XIII, and was commander of fortifications in East Prussia (1944–45). He was captured by the Red Army on April 8, 1945, and spent the next 10½ years in Soviet prisons. He died in Westphalia in 1993.

Friedrich Erdmann von Hake was commander of the 4th Panzer Regiment (1943–44). Prior to that, he had commanded the 13th Panzer Reconnaissance Battalion. He briefly commanded the 11th Panzer Division in 1944.

Hans Troeger (b. 1896) was also an engineer, joining the army as a Fahnenjunker in 1915. He was a relatively early convert to the idea of motorized warfare. Troeger was adjutant to the higher cavalry officer in the Office of Mobile Troops at OKH (1938–39), commander of the 64th Motorcycle Battalion (1940–41), commander of the 103rd Rifle Regiment (1941–42), acting commander of the 27th Panzer Division (1942–43), commander of the School for Panzer Troops (1943), commander of the 25th Panzer Division (1943–44), and commander of the 13th Panzer. He was interned in Bulgaria in September 1944, was handed over to the Russians, and remained in Soviet prisons until 1955.

Gerhard Schmidhuber (1894–1945) was an excellent commander of armored formations and a forceful human being. He was promoted to major general on October 1, 1944, and was killed during the Budapest breakout on February 11, 1945, after distinguishing himself during the siege. It was reportedly Schmidhuber who ended the Holocaust in Budapest. A Saxon, he had enlisted in the army in 1914 and was discharged as a reserve second lieutenant in 1920. He returned to active duty as a captain in 1934 and was a company commander (2/ 103rd Infantry Regiment) in 1938. Later he commanded II/103rd Infantry Regiment (1939–42) and 304th Panzer Grenadier Regiment (1943–44), was deputy commander of the 7th Panzer Division (1944) and commander of the 13th. He held the Knight's Cross with Oak Leaves.

As a reserve major in 1944, Wilhelm Schoening commanded I/Fusilier Regiment Feldherrnhalle (Motorized). By the fall of that year, he was commanding the 110th Panzer Brigade FHH in Hungary. By January 21, 1945 (when he received his Knight's Cross with Oak Leaves), Schoening was acting commander of the 66th Panzer Grenadier Regiment. He was promoted to lieutenant colonel of reserves shortly thereafter. Born in East Prussia in 1907, he died in Bochum in 1987.

## NOTES AND SOURCES

As was usual, not all of the divisional units of the 13th Panzer Division had the same home station as the divisional headquarters. The home station for the 66th Rifle (later Panzer Grenadier) Regiment was Burg, the 93rd Panzer Grenadier's home station was Stendal, and the 4th Panzer Regiment's home base was Wiener Neustadt. The divisional staff, the divisional support troops, and the 13th Panzer Artillery Regiment were all based at Magdeburg.

On October 11, 1940, the 13th Panzer Artillery Regiment absorbed the I/49th Artillery Regiment, which became its III Battalion.

In 1942, the division gained the 275th Army Flak Artillery Battalion, the 43rd Motorcycle became the 13th Panzer Reconnaissance Battalion, and the 4th Panzer Regiment gained a III battalion (the former I/29th Panzer Regiment), which it lost again the following year.

During the Caucasus campaign, the 13th Tank Destroyer Battalion was equipped with Marder IIIs—75mm self-propelled antitank guns mounted on PzKw II chassis. Two of the Marders destroyed 33 Soviet T-34 and KV-1 tanks in three days.

In May 1944 the division absorbed the 1030th Panzer Grenadier Regiment Feldherrnhalle. The following month it received another large shipment of replacements from Replacement and Training Brigade Feldherrnhalle.

The 110th Panzer Brigade was formed on July 19, 1944.

Angolia, *Field*, Volume 1: 226–27; Benoist-Mechin: 133; Bradley et al., Volume 3: 229–30; Volume 5: 196–98, 345–47; Carell 1966: 300–01, 533; Carell 1971: 153, 537;

Chant 1979, Volume 15: 2057; Chapman: 347–48; Keilig: 17–18, 59, 76, 130, 137, 227, 250, 285, 303, 349; Kennedy: 74; Manstein: 398; Mehner, Volume 3: Seite 5; Volume 4: 382; Volume 5: 330; Volume 6: 545; Volume 11: 351; Schmitz et al., Volume 3: 85–96; Seaton: 197–98 (citing Franz Halder, *Kriegstagebuch*, Volume III: 319), 483, 500; Seemen: 53, 307; Stoves, *Gepanzerten*: 94; Tessin, Volume 3: 263–64, 266–68; Thomas, Volume 2: 279; RA: 172; OB 42: 59; OB 43: 201–03; OB 44: 283; OB 45: 294.

# 14th Panzer Division

**COMPOSITION (1943):** 36th Panzer Regiment, 103rd Panzer Grenadier Regiment, 108th Panzer Grenadier Regiment, 4th Panzer Artillery Regiment, 14th Panzer Reconnaissance Battalion, 4th Tank Destroyer Battalion, 13th Panzer Engineer Battalion, 4th Panzer Signal Battalion, 276th Army Flak Battalion.

**HOME STATION:** Dresden, Wehrkreis IV

Formed at Dresden as the 4th Infantry Division in the Reichswehr organization of 1921, the 14th Panzer division included the 52nd, 103rd, and 108th Infantry Regiments by 1935. It fought well in Poland and in the French campaign of 1940, where it followed up the decisive tank breakthrough at Sedan. In August and September of that year it was reorganized as the 14th Panzer Division, receiving the 36th Panzer Regiment from the 4th Panzer Division but giving up the 52nd Motorized Infantry Regiment to the 18th Panzer Division. It also received the newly formed Staff, 14th Rifle Brigade and the 64th Motorcycle Battalion (which was formed from the 7th Machine Gun Battalion), but both of its infantry (now Schuetzen [rifle or motorized infantry]) regiments lost their III Battalions. As of August 15, 1940—the day the 14th Panzer Division was officially activated—it included the 36th Panzer Regiment (two battalions), the 14th Rifle Brigade (103rd and 108th Rifle Regiments and the 64th Motorcycle Battalion), the 4th Panzer Artillery Regiment (three battalions), and assorted divisional troops, including the 40th Panzer Reconnaissance Battalion, the 13th Panzer Engineer Battalion, etc. That winter, it was sent to the Koenigsbrueck and Milowitz Maneuver Areas to train.

The following March, the new tank division was sent to Hungary and was involved in the Balkans campaign of April, fighting in Yugoslavia. It then returned to the Reich and was at Doeberitz (a primarily infantry training facility near Berlin) when Operation Barbarossa, the invasion of the Soviet Union, began. The 14th Panzer was soon sent east and was in action in July. It fought in the drive across Ukraine, in the Battles of Kiev, Kholm, and Dnepopetrovsk, in the closing and crushing of the Chernigovka Pocket on the Sea of Azov, in the push across the Mius, and in the capture of Rostov, suffering severe losses in the process. After the Russian winter offensive of 1941–42 had been checked, the division fought in the Battle of Kharkov, and in drive across the Don and to the Volga. It was surrounded with the 6th Army in Stalingrad in November 1942 and was destroyed there in January 1943.

The 14th Panzer Division was resurrected by the 1st Army in Brittany, France, in the spring and summer of 1943. It included the 36th Panzer Regiment (three battalions), the 103rd and 108th Panzer Grenadier Regiments (two battalions each), 4th Panzer Artillery Regiment (three battalions), 64th Motorcycle Battalion, 4th Tank Destroyer Battalion, 13th Panzer Engineer Battalion, 4th Panzer Signal Battalion, 276th Army Flak Battalion, and the divisional service support troop units. The division returned to southern Russia in time to take part in the Battle of Kiev that autumn. In more or less continuous retreat after that, it fought at Krivoy Rog, Kirovograd, in the Dnieper Bend battles, and at Jassy. During these battles, the division suffered such heavy losses that it had to be rebuilt in the summer of 1944. That September (after fighting in southern Ukraine) it was sent to the northern sector of the front and was soon isolated in the Courland (Kurland) Pocket. It opposed all six major Soviet attempts to eradicate Army Group North (later Courland) and played a major role in saving the German 18th and 16th Armies. After Berlin fell, much of the 14th Panzer (along with parts of the 11th Infantry Division) was returned to Germany on the last available shipping before Army Group Courland capitulated, and thus many of its men escaped Russian captivity. These two units were selected because they had been the "firefighters" of the army group when the Russians tried unsuccessfully to crush the pocket in 1944–45. The rest of the division surrendered to the Red Army on May 9 and 10, 1945.

Commanders of the 4th Infantry/14th Panzer Division included Major General/Lieutenant General Eric Hansen (assumed command November 10, 1939), Major General Heinrich von Prittwitz und Gaffron (October 1, 1940), Major General Friedrich Kuehn (March 22, 1941), Major General Ferdinand Heim (July 1, 1942), Colonel Baron Hans von Falkenstein (acting commander, November 1, 1942), Major General Johannes Baessler (November 16, 1942), and Colonel/Major General Martin Lattmann (November 26, 1942), who surrendered the division at Stalingrad. Colonel Guenther Ludwig briefly served as acting divisional commander in January 1943. Commanders of the second 14th Panzer Division were Colonel/Major General Friedrich Sieberg (April 1, 1943), Colonel Karl-Max Graessel (October 29, 1943), Colonel/Major General/Lieutenant General Martin Unrein (November 5, 1943), Colonel Oskar Munzel (acting commander, September 15, 1944), Unrein (November 15, 1944), Graessel (again acting commander, March 25, 1944), Unrein (May 7, 1944), Colonel Werner Mummert (September 1, 1944), Colonel Oskar Munzel (September 5, 1944), Unrein (returned, November 25, 1944), Colonel Friedrich-Wilhelm Juergen (February 1, 1945), Graessel (February 24, 1945), and Colonel Walter Palm (March 20, 1945).

## COMMANDERS

Eric Hansen (1889–1967) was promoted to lieutenant general on August 1, 1939. He commanded the division in Poland, before it was converted into a panzer unit. Later a general of cavalry (1940), he commanded LIV Corps on the Eastern Front (1941–43) before taking charge of the German Military Mission to Romania (1943). Simultaneously Military Commander, Romania, he was captured in September 1944 and was not released until 1955. He retired to Hamburg, the city of his birth. Hansen was a good, solid infantry commander but was ill-suited to the task of directing a military mission in a foreign country. His military career began in 1907, when he entered the 9th Dragoons as a Fahnenjunker. He is sometimes confused with General of Artillery Christian Hansen, who commanded X Corps and the 16th Army on the northern sector of the Eastern Front (1941–44).

For the details of Heinrich von Prittwitz und Gaffron's career, see 15th Panzer Division, Commanders.

Friedrich Kuehn (1889–1944) was a longtime tank officer and an expert on motorization. He began his career as a Fahnenjunker in the infantry in 1909. He was commander of the 4th Panzer Regiment (1935–38), commandant of the Panzer School (1938–39), commander of the 14th Panzer Brigade (late 1939-early 1940), commander of the 3rd Panzer Brigade (1940), acting commander, 3rd Panzer Division (1940), commander of the 15th Panzer Division (1940–41), and commander of the 14th Panzer (1941–42). He was promoted to major general (July 1, 1940), lieutenant general (July 1, 1942), and general of panzer troops (April 1, 1943). Named General for Army Motorization in 1942, he became Chief of Armed Forces Motor Transport Vehicles and Chief of Army Motorization on February 23, 1943. General Kuehn was killed during an Allied bomber attack on Berlin on February 15, 1944.

Ferdinand Heim (b. 1895) entered the Imperial Army as an officer cadet in 1914. An artilleryman by trade, he served as chief of staff of XVI Motorized Corps (1939–40), as a branch chief at OKW (1940), and as chief of staff of the 6th Army (1940–42) before taking over the 14th Panzer. He was named commander of the XXXXVIII Panzer Corps on November 1, 1942. The corps was a technical disaster. Ordered to prevent the encirclement of Stalingrad, most of Heim's tanks broke down almost immediately, and the corps itself barely escaped encirclement. An enraged Hitler ordered Heim arrested on November 26. He was subsequently court-martialed and imprisoned. Eventually released, Heim was named commandant of Boulogne and surrendered it to the Canadians on September 23, 1944. Released from captivity in early 1948, he died in Ulm on November 14, 1977.

Baron Hans von Falkenstein was born in Dresden in 1893 and entered the service in 1912 as an infantry Fahnenjunker. He commanded the 7th Machine Gun Battalion (1937–40), the 103rd Infantry Regiment (1940–41), and the 14th Rifle Brigade (1942). After serving as acting commander of the 14th Panzer (November 1942), he was not reemployed for four months, suggesting that he was wounded during the Battle of Stalingrad. There is also considerable indication that his performance as commander of the 14th Panzer Division did not live up to expectations. He returned to active duty in February 1943 as acting commander of the 707th Infantry Division, but was never given command of another motorized unit. Later he commanded the 45th Infantry Division (1943), 24th Infantry Division (1944), and Recruiting Area Dresden (1944–45). Promoted to major general and lieutenant general (both in 1943), Falkenstein spent 10 years in Soviet prisons (1945–55) and died in Hanover in 1980.

For the details of Johannes Baessler's career, see 9th Panzer Division, Commanders.

Martin Lattmann (b. 1896) was promoted to major general on January 1, 1943. He surrendered the remnants of the division to the Soviets at the end of that month. In captivity, Lattmann soon went over to the Communists. He was released from prison in 1948 and was serving in East Germany in the 1950s. Lattmann had previously commanded I/110th Artillery Regiment (1938–39) and 430th Artillery Battalion (1939), served on the artillery staffs of the 1st Army (1939–40) and an artillery school (1940–42), and commanded the 16th Panzer Artillery Regiment (1942). He had started his career as an artillery Fahnenjunker in 1914. His brother, a colonel, was Rommel's chief artillery advisor in 1944.

Colonel Guenther Ludwig, commander of the 4th Panzer Artillery Regiment (1942–43), was captured at Stalingrad.

Friedrich Sieberg (1896–1943) was promoted to major general on June 1, 1943. He was mortally wounded on October 29, 1943, and died in the Kirovograd hospital on November 3. Prior to commanding the division, Sieberg led I/10th Panzer Regiment (1938–39), 10th Panzer Regiment (1939–40), and directed a tactics course at the Panzer Troops School (1940–43). He was posthumously promoted to lieutenant general—a sign that he was highly thought of at higher headquarters. He had begun his career as an infantry officer cadet in 1914.

Colonel Karl-Max Graessel was normally commander of the 108th Panzer Grenadier Regiment.

For a sketch of Martin Unrein's career, see Panzer Division Clausewitz Commander.

For a sketch of Oskare Munzel's career, see 2nd Panzer Division Commanders.

For an outline of Werner Mummert's life, see Panzer Division Muencheburg Commanders.

For more information on Friedrich-Wilhelm Juergen, see 6th Panzer Division.

## NOTES AND SOURCES

The 14th Panzer Division was reorganized in 1942. The 36th Panzer Regiment received a III Battalion (the former III/7th Panzer Regiment [10th Panzer Division]), the 40th Panzer Reconnaissance Battalion absorbed the remnants of the 64th Motorcycle Battalion, and the 276th Army Flak Artillery Battalion joined the division as IV/4th Panzer Artillery Regiment. The 14th Rifle Brigade was disbanded in Stalingrad on November 15, 1942.

Bradley et al., Volume 3: 412–13, Volume 5: 105–06, 240–42; Carell 1966: 301, 490, 495, 564, 599; Rolf Grams, *Die 14. Panzer-Division 1940–1945* (Bad Nauheim, 1957), 1 ff.; Keilig: 85, 125, 191, 323, 352; Kennedy: 10B, 74; *Kriegstagebuch des Oberkommando der Wehrmacht (Wehrmachtfuehungsstab)* (Frankfurt am Main, 1961), Volume II: 1453 (hereafter cited as "KTB OKW"); Manstein: 482, 487; Mellenthin 1956; 225; Mehner, Volume 5: 330; Volume 9: 396; Volume 12: 458; Scheibert: 122; Schmitz et al., Volume 3: 125–37; Stoves, *Gepanzerten*: 95–100; Tessin, Volume 3: 298–99; Juergen Thorwald, *Defeat in the East* (New York, 1980): 288; RA: 72; OB 42: 59; OB 43: 204; OB 45: 295.

# 15th Panzer Division

**COMPOSITION:** 8th Panzer Regiment, 115th Panzer Grenadier Regiment, 33rd Panzer Artillery Regiment, 33rd Panzer Reconnaissance Battalion, 33rd Tank Destroyer Battalion, 33rd Panzer Engineer Battalion, 33rd Panzer Signal Battalion.

**HOME STATION:** Landau, Wehrkreis XII

The 15th Panzer was formed on April 1, 1936, as the 33rd Infantry Division of the peacetime army. Its home base at that time was Darmstadt, and it initially included the 104th, 110th, and 115th Infantry Regiments. The division was stationed in the Saar during the "Phoney War" of 1939–40 and took part in the Western campaign of 1940, fighting in the Ardennes and Belgium, and pushing across the Somme to the Loire. The 33rd was on occupation duty in France until September 1940, when it was sent back to Wehrkreis XII and converted into the 15th Panzer Division. It received the 8th Panzer Regiment but gave up the 110th Infantry Regiment to the 112th Infantry Division. Its horses were transferred to Wehrkreis IX and were incorporated into the 129th Infantry Division. As of November 1, 1940 (the day the 15th Panzer Division was officially activated), the division consisted of the 15th Rifle Brigade, which included the 104th Rifle Regiment (Staff, I and II Battalions of the former 104th Infantry Regiment); 115th Rifle Regiment (Staff, I and II Battalions of the 115th Infantry Regiment); and the 15th Motorcycle Battalion (the former III/104th Infantry Regiment). The 8th Panzer Regiment had only two battalions, and the 647th Heavy Artillery Battalion (an Army GHQ unit) functioned as the IV Battalion

124

of the 33rd Panzer Artillery Regiment. In the spring of 1941, it was sent to Libya to form one of the two divisions of Erwin Rommel's Afrika Korps. That summer it gave up the 104th Panzer Grenadier Regiment to the 5th Light Division, which was reorganizing as the 21st Panzer Division. Shortly thereafter, a III Battalion (the former 2nd Machine Gun Battalion) was added to the 115th Panzer Grenadier Regiment and the 15th Motorcycle Battalion was transferred to the 21st Panzer Division as III/104th Panzer Grenadier Regiment.

The 15th Panzer fought in all the campaigns on the North African Front except the first: it arrived too late to be on hand when Rommel captured Benghazi in April 1941. The division took part in the unsuccessful attacks on Tobruk in April and May 1941, helped defeat the British relief attempts aimed at Tobruk that summer (Operations Brevity and Battleaxe), and was severely mauled in heavy fighting in Operation Crusader (November 18–December 7, 1941), which was called the Winter Battle by the Germans. Down to a handful of tanks, it retreated into Libya. Reinforced by shipments of panzers from Europe in January 1942, the 15th Panzer fought in Rommel's Second Cyrenaican campaign and helped retake Benghazi.

Later in 1942, it was involved in the battles of the Gazala Line, the capture of Tobruk, and the invasion of Egypt. It was checked and virtually destroyed in the El Alamein battles. By the time Rommel retreated in early November 1942, the 8th Panzer Regiment had lost all of its tanks, and its regimental commander, the legendary Colonel Wilhelm "Willi" Teege, was dead; the 33rd Panzer Artillery Regiment had only seven guns left. The 15th Panzer retreated through Egypt, Libya, and into Tunisia. Here it received shipments of new tanks and the 504th Heavy Panzer Battalion, a Tiger unit, which was incorporated into the division as III/8th Panzer Regiment. Then it turned to attack again, this time at the Kasserine Pass, where it gave the U.S. Army a costly and embarrassing defeat. Finally checked, the division was destroyed in the final collapse in North Africa in May 1943. It went into its last battle with its petrol tanks full of Tunisian wine—the only fuel available.

Its commanders included Major General Ritter Hermann von Speck (assumed command March 1, 1938), Major General Rudolf Sintzenich (assumed command April 29, 1940), Major General Friedrich Kuehn (October 5, 1940), Major General Heinrich von Prittwitz und Gaffron (October 1, 1940), Colonel Hans-Karl von Esebeck (April 13, 1941), Colonel Maximilian von Herff (May 15, 1941), Major General Walter Neumann-Silkow (May 26, 1941), Colonel Erwin Menny (December 6, 1941), Major General Gustav von Vaerst (December 9, 1941), Colonel Eduard Crasemann (May 28, 1942), Major General Heinz von Randow (July 15, 1942), Vaerst again (August 25, 1942), and Colonel/Major General/Lieutenant General Willibald Borowietz (November 18, 1942).

The survivors of the 15th Panzer Division (many of whom were in hospitals in Europe when Army Group Afrika collapsed) were incorporated into the newly formed 15th Panzer Grenadier Division, which later fought in Sicily,

Italy, the final stages of the German retreat from France, the Battle of the Bulge, and in the last battles in Germany. It surrendered to the British at the end of the war.

## COMMANDERS

Ritter Hermann von Speck (1888–1940), a native of Munich, entered the Bavarian artillery as a Fahnenjunker in 1907. He performed with such bravery during World War I that he received the Max Joseph Order and, with it, a knighthood and the title "Ritter." Looked upon as a future senior general, Speck commanded the 33rd Infantry Division (1938–40), was named acting commander of the XXXXIII Corps on May 1, 1940, and on June 5 was given command of the XVIII Mountain Corps. Nine days later he was killed in a firefight near Pont sur Yonne. He was the senior German officer killed in the French campaign. For reasons never made known to me, he was posthumously promoted to general of artillery on December 15, 1944—during the Battle of the Bulge and four and a half years after his death.

Like Speck, Rudolf Sintzenich (1889–1948) was from Munich. He joined the 11th Bavarian Infantry Regiment as a Fahnenjunker in 1908. During World War II, he commanded the 61st Infantry Regiment (1935–40), the 33rd Infantry Division (1940), the 132nd Infantry Division (1940–42), the 147th Reserve Division (1942), and the 467th Replacement Division (1944–45). He also served as an inspector in the Munich Recruiting Area (1943–44). Although a competent divisional commander, Sintzenich was not looked upon as corps commander material. He was promoted to lieutenant general on January 1, 1943. He died in Munich.

For a summary of Friedrich Kuehn's career, see 14th Panzer Division, Commanders.

Heinrich von Prittwitz und Gaffron (1889–1941) was killed in action by an antitank shell near Tobruk on April 10, 1941. Considered an officer of considerable promise, he was posthumously promoted to lieutenant general. Originally a cavalry officer, Prittwitz was an early transfer to the Panzerwaffe and had already commanded the 2nd Panzer Regiment (1935–38), 2nd Panzer Brigade (1938–39), and 14th Panzer Division (1940–41).

Hans-Karl von Esebeck was severely wounded by a shell splinter near Tobruk in the summer of 1941. For details on his previous and subsequent career, see 2nd Panzer Division, Commanders.

Maximilian von Herff was born in Hanover on April 17, 1893, the descendant of an old Hessian family. He was commissioned second lieutenant in the 115th (1st Hessian) Life Guards Infantry Regiment and served with it throughout World War I. Retained in the Reichswehr, he was promoted slowly (as was typical of a small army) and was a first lieutenant in the 18th Cavalry Regiment in 1926. Promoted to captain in 1928, he became a lieutenant colonel in early

1939 and a full colonel in 1941. The commander of the 115th Rifle Regiment in the desert, Herff was acting commander of the 15th Panzer Division for 13 days after General Esebeck was wounded. He was awarded the Knight's Cross in June, 1941; shortly thereafter he transferred to the SS, where he became chief of Himmler's personnel office and rose to the rank of *Obergruppenfuehrer* (General of SS). Herff was captured by the British at the end of the war and would almost certainly have been convicted as a war criminal, had he not died in a Scottish prison on September 6, 1945.

As a colonel, Walter Neumann-Silkow (1891–1941) had served as commander of the 7th Reconnaissance Battalion (1938–40) and the 8th Rifle Brigade (1940–41) and was acting commander of the 8th Panzer Division (1941). He was promoted to major general on April 1, 1941. Neumann-Silkow, whose mother was Scottish, was mortally wounded on December 7, 1941, and died two days later. An outstanding officer who was both loved and respected by his men, Neumann-Silkow's death was a severe blow to the morale of the 15th Panzer Division. He was posthumously promoted to lieutenant general.

For details on Erwin Menny's career, see 18th Panzer Division, Commanders.

An outstanding tank commander, Gustav von Vaerst was born in 1894 and joined the 14th Hussar Regiment as a Fahnenjunker in 1912. He commanded the 2nd Rifle Regiment (1938–39) and the 2nd Rifle Brigade (1939–41) before assuming command of the 15th Panzer Division. He was wounded in late May 1942, and did not return to action until August. He was acting commander of the Afrika Korps during the Battle of Alam Halfa Ridge and Eduard Crasemann again assumed acting command of the division (see below). Vaerst was promoted to lieutenant general on December 1, 1942, and to general of panzer troops in March 1943. He led the 5th Panzer Army in Tunisia until it surrendered on May 12, 1943.

Colonel Eduard Crasemann, commander of the 33rd Panzer Artillery Regiment (1941–43), succeeded Vaerst as acting commander of the division on two occasions. Later—as major general—he led the 26th Panzer Division on the Italian Front. See 26th Panzer Division, Commanders.

For a sketch of Heinz von Ranclow's career, see 21st Panzer Division, Commanders.

Willibald Borowietz (1893–1945) was promoted to major general on January 1, 1943, and to lieutenant general on May 1, 1943. A Fahnenjunker in the 156th Infantry Regiment when World War I broke out, he was twice wounded in 1914 and rose to the command of a machine gun company by 1916. A battalion adjutant in 1918, he was discharged from the service in January 1920 and joined the Breslau police, where he rose to the rank of major. Borowietz rejoined the army as a member of the motorized branch in late 1935 and served on the staff of the chief of Mobile Troops (1935–39). During the war, he was commander of the 50th Antitank Battalion (1941–42), 10th Rifle Regiment (1941), 10th Panzer Grenadier Brigade (1942) and 15th Panzer Division (1942–43). Although he served well in lesser positions, his performance as a divisional commander was adequate but less than stellar. General Borowietz died in an accident in a prisoner-of-war camp at Clinton, Mississippi on July 1, 1945.

## NOTES AND SOURCES

Initially (1936), the 104th Infantry Regiment was stationed at Landau, the 110th Infantry Regiment was at Heidelberg, and the 115th Infantry Regiment was posted to Darmstadt, as was the 33rd Artillery Regiment and the divisional support units. The I/69th Artillery Regiment was attached to the division in the 1930s.

The 104th Rifle Regiment was not officially transferred to the 21st Panzer Division until September 1, 1941, but the actual transfer took place much earlier.

Bradley et al., Volume 2: 157–59; Volume 3: 375–76; Paul Carell, *Foxes of the Desert* (New York: 1960) (hereafter cited as "Carell 1960"); David Irving, *Trail of the Fox* (New York, 1977) (hereafter cited as "Irving 1977"); Jackson; Keilig: 46–47, 263, 327, 327; Kursietis: 97; Mellenthin 1956; Mehner, Volume 3: Seite 24; Volume 4: 383; Volume 5: 330; Nikolaus von Preradovich, *Die Generale der Waffen-SS* (Berg am See, 1985): 36; Tessin, Volume 4: 9–11; Volume 5: 24–25; and Young. Also see OB 43: 204 and OB 44b: B5.

# 16th Panzer Division

**COMPOSITION:**   2nd Panzer Regiment, 64th Panzer Grenadier Regiment, 79th Panzer Grenadier Regiment, 16th Panzer Artillery Regiment, 16th Motor-cycle Battalion, 16th Panzer Reconnaissance Battalion, 16th Tank Destroyer Battalion, 16th Panzer Engineer Battalion, 16th Panzer Signal Battalion.

**HOME STATION:**   Muenster (later Wuppertal), Wehrkreis VI

Formed in October 1934 as the 16th Infantry Division, this unit was made up mainly of Westphalians, with some East Prussians interspersed. It initially included the 60th, 64th, and 79th Infantry Regiments, the 16th Artillery Regiment, the 16th Panzer Antitank, 16th Reconnaissance, 16th Signal, and 16th Engineer Battalions, as well as assorted divisional service troops. It was posted on the lower Rhine in 1939 and thus missed the Polish campaign; however, it did well in France the following year. It assembled in the Bitburg area and, on May 10, crossed the border into Luxembourg. It quickly pushed into southern Belgium and then into France, and was present at Sedan, supporting the German armor. Afterward it defended a section of the "Panzer Corridor" against possible French counterattacks. That fall it was sent back to Wehrkreis VI and was converted into a panzer division, receiving the 2nd Panzer Regiment from the 1st Panzer Division and supplying the 60th Infantry Regiment (now motorized) to the 16th Motorized Infantry Division, which was then being formed. Both of its rifle regiments (the 64th and 79th) were two-battalion units, as was the 2nd Panzer. The 16th Panzer Artillery Regiment included the former Staff and II Battalion of the 16th Artillery Regiment; the I Battalion was the former I/76th Panzer Artillery Regiment from the 6th Panzer Division; and the III/16th Panzer Artil-

129

lery Regiment was the former 644th Artillery Battalion. The new tank division also received the 16th Motorcycle Battalion (the former 1st Machine Gun Battalion). The 16th Panzer Division was also transferred to Wuppertal, which became its new home base. The new division had no panzer or rifle brigade headquarters. The 274th Army Flak Artillery Battalion (Motorized) was later added to its table of organization.

The 16th Panzer Division was sent to Romania in January 1941, then to Bulgaria, where it remained in reserve during the Balkans campaign in April. It returned to Germany in late May and spent three weeks in Silesia (south of Breslau), before marching on to Poland from June 16 to 25. It was sent into action on the Eastern Front on June 26, crossing the Bug near Sokai-Krystinopol. It was almost continuously engaged thereafter, fighting against Soviet armor in the Dubno-Verba battles (June 27–July 1), during which it destroyed 243 Soviet tanks. It was heavily engaged in the drive at Kiev and to the Dnieper (July 5–24), in the Battle of Uman (July 25–August 2), in the fierce struggle for the Soviet Black Sea naval base at Nikolaev (August 6–20), and in the encirclement and liquidation of the Kiev Pocket, where 667,000 Soviet soldiers were captured (August 3–September 26). It also secured a bridgehead over the Dnieper River at Kirovograd on September 11. On September 25, before the Battle of Kiev ended, the 16th Panzer Division turned and drove south and east, fighting sharp battles at Novo Moskovsk (September 29), Kamenovatka (October 1), Verkne Tohmak (October 5), and Pologi (October 6). In the process, it destroyed the Soviet 18th Army, killed its commander, and reached the Sea of Azov, trapping several more Russian divisions. Next the 16th Panzer helped overrun eastern Ukraine (October 10–20), fought its way through the Donez (October 21–November 21), and reached the Don on November 20. At this point, the 16th stopped because it had run out of supplies. On November 22, two Soviet armies (10 divisions) attacked the immobilized tank unit at Tschistiakovo. The 16th Panzer Division nevertheless held its positions and was reprovisioned during the battle. It finally retreated on November 28, and Rostov was lost two days later. The 1st Panzer Group retreated to the Mius, where the 16th Panzer held a section of the line against the Russian winter offensive of 1941–42, in often heavy defensive fighting (November 22, 1941–April 26, 1942). Finally pulled back to the Stalino sector in late April, it remained on the defensive in the Donez and conducted antipartisan operations until May 1942, when Stalin launched his spring offensive against the 6th Army east of Kharkov. South of that city and east of the Donets, the 1st Panzer Army launched a hasty counteroffensive, to take the pressure off the 6th Army. The 16th Panzer Division fought the Battle of the Bacaklesa Encirclement from May 17–22, during which it captured 31,500 Russians and destroyed 224 vehicles and 69 tanks.

On July 8, Hitler at last launched his summer offensive of 1942. The veteran division helped clear the middle Don of Soviet troops (July 8–25) and fought in the drive on Stalingrad, fighting battles at Lissitschansk (July 15), Belowodsk (July 16), and Kaimikoff (July 25) along the way. It finally reached the Volga at Rynok north of Stalingrad on August 23. After turning back several attacks, it cleared the steppe north of the city and supported the divisions engaged in street fighting in September, October, and November.

Seriously depleted by casualties—it had only 4,000 men left on November 19—the 16th Panzer Division was replaced in the line at Stalingrad by the 94th Infantry Division in mid-November and was ordered to withdraw to the Donets for refitting. This movement was in progress on November 19, when Stalin launched a massive counteroffensive that encircled the 6th Army in the Stalingrad Pocket on November 23. The main thrust cut across the path of the division's march; the Staff, 16th Panzer Division, the 79th Rifle Regiment, most of the 64th Rifle Regiment, and the 16th Panzer Artillery Regiment were cut off in Stalingrad. The vanguard of the division—including the 16th Tank Destroyer Battalion, the 2nd Panzer Regiment, I/64th Rifle Regiment, and the 16th Panzer Engineer Battalion—were pushed out of Kalach on November 21 and driven westward, away from the pocket. These forces were grouped into two (later three) combat groups under Colonel Rudolf Sickenius, the commander of the 2nd Panzer Regiment.

The rest of the division remained trapped inside the Stalingrad Pocket and was destroyed there. The remnants surrendered at the beginning of February 1943.

A second 16th Panzer Division was formed in Brittany in February and March 1943. It was built around some 3,400 veterans from the original division who escaped the Stalingrad debacle or were wounded and evacuated by air during the siege, as well as 600 Russian "hiwis" (volunteers). The new division also absorbed the 890th Motorized Grenadier Regiment and other GHQ units and replacements from the 7th Army. It included the 2nd Panzer Regiment (three battalions), 64th and 79th Panzer Grenadier Regiments (two battalions each), the 16th Motorcycle Battalion (which became the 16th Panzer Reconnaissance Battalion on April 1), the 16th Panzer Artillery Regiment (three battalions), the 16th Tank Destroyer Battalion, the 16th Engineer Battalion, and the 274th Army Flak Artillery Battalion. Its divisional support units bore the number 16. Sent to the Taranto sector of Italy in June, it was shifted to the Salerno sector just before the Anglo-Americans invaded Italy on September 9 with 450 ships and 169,000 men, supported by 20,000 aircraft. The 16th Panzer at first absorbed the full weight of the invasion and inflicted heavy casualties on the Allied landing forces, which lost almost 7,000 men killed, wounded, or captured by September 18. Over the same period, however, the Germans lost 840 killed, 2,002 wounded, and 630 missing. At least 90 percent of these were from the 16th Panzer Division, which also lost two-thirds of its tank strength—much of it to Allied naval gunfire—in the heavy fighting.

The 16th Panzer Division formed the rearguard of the German 10th Army's retreat to the Avellino-Olfante line, and inflicted a sharp little defeat on the pursuing U.S. VI Corps at Teora (September 24–25). It continued in the line and fought delaying actions against the British 8th Army north of Naples until November 1943, when it was returned to the Eastern Front. The 16th Panzer

was immediately thrown into the attack in the zone where the 2nd and 9th
Armies connected, because a gap had developed between them. After defending
between the Pripet and the Berezina, the division was hurriedly transported
south, where it fought another offensive-defensive battle in the Trogrebitsche
sector (January 4–31, 1944). Next it was hurriedly marched to the zone north
of Uman, from which it took part in the partially successful effort to rescue the
XI and XXXXII Corps at Cherkassy. After part of the encircled forces escaped,
the 16th Panzer returned to the sector north of Uman, where it was engaged in
further defensive fighting (February 20–26).

Like most of the panzer divisions in the East, the 16th was used as a fire
brigade, counterattacking, defending, and then being pulled out and sent to the
next fire. From March 6 to 22, it fought in the Battle of Tarnopol, but was
encircled (along with the rest of the 1st Panzer Army) on March 23. As part of
"Hube's wandering pocket," it broke out and reached German lines on April 10.
Despite its heavy losses and relatively few replacements, the 16th Panzer remained in the line, holding a sector on the Dniester in April, before being sent
to the Delatyn-Kolomea sector to partially rebuild (April 28–May 16). It was
sent back into action on May 17, when the Soviets neared Kolomea, which it
held (along with the Hungarian 25th Infantry Division) until May 30. After
fighting another series of defensive battles south of Hrabkow-Zaniesze, it was
again pulled out of the line on June 8 to complete the refurbishing process.

After partially rebuilding, the veteran division fought along the Bug (July
2–31), retreated deeper into Poland, took part in the unsuccessful counterattacks
against the Baranov bridgehead (August 4–31), and in antipartisan operations
around Daleszycze (September 1–October 15, 1944). Pulled out of the combat
zone on October 15, it was again partially rebuilt by XXIV Panzer Corps, using
corps troops. The 79th Panzer Grenadier Regiment was redesignated 79th Panzer Fusilier Regiment (Corps) and remained with the corps; however, the II
Battalion of the 79th remained in the division as the new III/64th Panzer Grenadier Regiment. The former II/63rd Panzer Grenadier Regiment (of the 17th Panzer Division) became II/79th Panzer Fusilier.

Sent back to the Baranov sector on New Year's Day, 1945, the significantly
reduced division was surrounded—along with the rest of the XXIV Panzer
Corps—when the Soviets launched a massive breakout offensive. Thanks to the
brilliant leadership of General Nehring, the corps commander, it succeeded in
reaching German lines near Glogau on the Oder on January 25.

Finally pulled out of the line on February 1 to rest and reorganize, the 16th
Panzer was back in action on February 8, trying unsuccessfully to check the
Soviet drive on the Neisse. The division fought its last battles in southeastern
Germany and in Czechoslovakia (around Lauban and Brno), where it was at the
end of the war. On May 7, 1945—with Hitler dead and the Third Reich in its
death throes—the 16th Panzer Division divided itself into three groups and
headed for Anglo-Saxon lines, in an effort to avoid Soviet captivity. Group 1
managed to reach Karlsbad, where it surrendered to the Americans. Group 2

was less successful and was forced to surrender to the Red Army at Troppau; and Group 3 (with its men dressed largely in captured Soviet uniforms) evaded the Russians and reached Pilsen, where it capitulated to the Americans. It was, however, quickly handed over to the Russians.

Commanders of the division included Major General/Lieutenant General Gerhard Glokke (assumed command October 1, 1934), Major General Gotthard Heinrici (October 1, 1937), Major General Heinrich Krampf (February 1, 1940), Major General/Lieutenant General Hans Valentin Hube (May 17, 1940), Major General/Lieutenant General Guenther von Angern (September 15, 1942), Lieutenant Colonel Dr. Woermann (February 2, 1943), Colonel Burkhart Mueller-Hildebrandt (February 1943), Colonel/Major General Rudolf Sieckenius (March 5, 1943), Colonel/Major General Hans-Ulrich Back (November 8, 1943), Colonel/Major General/Lieutenant General Dietrich von Mueller (August 1944), Colonel Theodor Kretschmer (acting commander, December 1, 1944), von Mueller (returned, February 28, 1945), Dr. Albrecht Aschoff (April 19, 1945) and Colonel Kurt Treuhaupt (April 20, 1945).

## COMMANDERS

Gerhard Glokke (1884–1944) joined the army in 1903 and was commissioned in the infantry the following year. He commanded the 16th Infantry Regiment before assuming command of the division. He was promoted to major general the day he assumed command of the 16th and to lieutenant general on October 1, 1936. Promoted to general of infantry in 1940, he commanded Wehrkreis VI from the outbreak of the war until his death at Muenster on June 5, 1944.

Gotthard Heinrici (1886–1971) was a solid, dependable, and extremely capable infantry and armored commander; his tenacity in the defense was awesome and the skill with which he conducted retrograde operations became legendary. Because he had none of the charisma of a Patton or a Rommel, he is practically unknown today, but he was one of the best commanders on either side during the war. After commanding the 16th in Poland, Heinrici served as acting commander of VII Corps (1940), acting commander of XII Corps (1940), commander of XXXXIII Corps (1940–42), commander of 4th Army (January 20, 1942–June 4, 1944), commander of 1st Panzer Army (1944–45), and commander in chief of Army Group Vistula (1945). He was promoted to lieutenant general on March 1, 1938, to general of infantry (April 20, 1940), and to colonel general (January 1, 1943). He held the Knight's Cross with Oak Leaves and Swords. An East Prussian by birth, Heinrici began his military career as a Fahnenjunker in the 95th (6th Thueringen) Infantry Regiment in 1905. After his release from British captivity in 1948, Heinrici retired to Waiblingen/Wuerttemberg, where he died at the age of 85.

Heinrich Krampf (b. 1888) was a veteran infantry officer from Bavaria. He commanded the 31st Infantry Regiment (1938–40), 16th Infantry Division (1940–41), 304th Infantry Division (1940–42), Military Area Command 579

(1942–end of 1943) and Rear Area Command, 4th Army (1944–45). He was promoted to lieutenant general on December 12, 1941. He fell ill during the drive through Belgium and was replaced by Hube on May 15, 1940. Krampf was immediately evacuated back to Germany for hospitalization.

As a lieutenant in the infantry, Hans Hube (1890–1944) lost an arm at Verdun in the First World War. He rehabilitated himself and was commanding an infantry company in the trenches when the war ended. The only handicapped officer selected for retention in the Reichsheer, Hube never allowed his handicap to stand in his way and, in fact, became an excellent skier. He was also an outstanding officer at all levels—one of the best Germany produced during World War II. He commanded the Infantry School at Doeberlitz (1935–39), the 3rd Infantry Regiment (1939–40), the 16th Motorized/Panzer Division (1940–42), and the XIV Panzer Corps (1942–43). Ordered out of Stalingrad on Hitler's personal command, Hube refused to go. The Fuehrer had to send in Gestapo agents, who literally forced him into the airplane at gunpoint. He oversaw the reconstitution of the XIV Panzer Corps, which he led with great distinction in the Sicilian campaign. He served briefly in Italy before being sent back to Russia, where he commanded the 1st Panzer Army with great skill and courage (November, 1943–44). After this army was encircled far behind Soviet lines, Hube formed a floating pocket and led it all the way back to German lines—one of the greatest tactical feats of the war. On April 20, 1944—Hitler's birthday— the Fuehrer entertained Hube at Berchtesgaden and decorated him with the Diamonds to his Knight's Cross with Oak Leaves and Swords. Earmarked to command an army group, Hube boarded an airplane to return to Russia the next day, but it crashed shortly after takeoff, killing everyone on board. A great leader of fighting men, Hube was known throughout the German Army as "der Mensch"—"the Man."

Guenther von Angern (1892–1943) was a native of Kolberg, East Prussia. Entering the army as a Fahnenjunker, he served in the infantry during World War I. Later he commanded the 3rd Rifle Brigade (1938–39) and the 11th Rifle Brigade (1939–41). On August 15, 1941, he assumed command of the 11th Panzer Division but held it for only nine days. He was badly wounded on August 24, 1941, and did not return to active duty until September 15, 1942, the day he assumed command of the 16th Panzer Division. Angern was promoted to major general on October 1, 1941, and to lieutenant general on December 1, 1942. He committed suicide on or about February 2, 1943, at the end of the Battle of Stalingrad, to keep from falling into the hands of the Russians.

Lieutenant Colonel Dr. Woermann was the commander of the 64th Rifle Regiment (1942–43). He surrendered the remnants of the division when Stalingrad fell.

Burkhart Mueller-Hillebrandt (b. 1904) entered the service as an officer cadet in 1923 and was commissioned in the 16th Cavalry Regiment in late 1926. A career General Staff officer, he served on the staff of OKH (1938–39), as Ia, 93rd Infantry Division (1939–40), as adjutant to the chief of the General Staff of the Army (General Halder) (1940–42), and as chief of the Organizational Department at OKH (1942). After commanding the reformed 16th Panzer Division (1943), he led the 24th Panzer Regiment (1943–early 1944). Returning to staff duties, he was chief of staff of XXXXVI Panzer Corps (1944) and chief of staff of the 3rd Panzer Army (1944–45). Promoted to major general on March 1, 1945, he later became a general in the *Bundeswehr* (West German Armed Forces) and wrote a number of books and historic studies of the German Army, including the three-volume *Das Heer*, which was very important in its day.

Rudolf Sieckenius (1896–1945) was previously commander of the 2nd Panzer Regiment of the 16th Panzer Division (1941–42) and had distinguished himself in the French campaign while commanding III/25th Panzer Regiment of Rommel's 7th Panzer Division. Promoted to major general on June 1, 1943, he was unjustly made the scapegoat for the German failure to destroy the Allied forces at Salerno and was relieved of his command and sent to the Eastern Front, where he served as acting commander of a number of infantry divisions, but received no further promotions. He was, however, an excellent commander, both of mobile and marching formations. He commanded the 263rd Infantry Division during the Battle of Berlin and was killed in action leading a suicide attack on April 29, 1945. Born in Silesia in 1896, Sieckenius began his service as a war volunteer in the artillery in 1914. He was commissioned second lieutenant of reserves in an infantry regiment in 1917, and was in the police from 1920 to 1936, when he returned to active duty as a lieutenant colonel, commanding the 66th Motorized Antitank Battalion.

Hans-Ulrich Back was promoted to major general on February 1, 1944. For the details of his career, see 232nd Panzer Division.

Dietrich von Mueller (1891–1961) served in the infantry for 10 years before being discharged in the troop reductions of 1920. Returning to active duty as a captain in 1934, he was commander, II/5th Infantry Regiment (1939–40), 5th Replacement and Training Regiment (1940–41), 5th Panzer Grenadier Regiment (1941), and commandant of the Battalion Commanders' School for Panzer Troops, which was located in Paris (1943–44). He joined General Guderian's Panzer Inspectorate Staff in March 1944. Guderian became chief of the General Staff on July 21, 1944, and, the following month, placed his friend von Mueller in charge of the 16th Panzer Division, despite his relatively low rank. Mueller more than justified Guderian's faith in him and was such a brilliant leader that he came to be known as "the second Hube." He was promoted to major general on November 9, 1944, and to lieutenant general on April 20, 1945—OKH was probably not aware that he had been captured by partisans the day before. He was soon handed over to the Russians and was not released from Soviet prisons until 1955. Mueller held the Knight's Cross with Oak Leaves and Swords.

For an outline of Theodor Kretschmer's career, see 17th Panzer Division Commanders.

Dr. Albrecht Aschoff previously commanded II/76th Panzer Artillery Regiment of the 6th Panzer Division.

The last commander of the 16th Panzer was Colonel Kurt Treuhaupt, the former commander of the 146th Panzer Grenadier Regiment (1944–45) and the senior regimental commander of the 16th Panzer Division.

## NOTES AND SOURCES

The home station of the 64th Infantry Regiment was Soest, the 79th was stationed at Muenster, and the 16th Artillery Regiment was based at Hamm. The 60th Infantry Regiment's home station was Luedenscheid.

Command of the elements of the 16th Panzer Division outside the Stalingrad Pocket fell to Colonel Sieckenius, who was wounded in mid-January, 1943. He was replaced by Lieutenant Colonel of Reserves Count Hyazinth Strachwitz, commander of I/2nd Panzer Regiment, who was himself wounded two days later. Command finally devolved on Major Bernhard Sauvant, commander of II/2nd Panzer Regiment. These battle groups were later sent back to France and incorporated into the new 16th Panzer Division.

Angolia, *Field*, Volume 1: 245; Bradley et al., Volume 1: 75–76, Volume 5: 256–58; Kameradschaftsbund 16. Panzer- und Infanterie-Division, *Bildband der 16. Panzer-Division* (Bad Nauheim, 1956): 6, 9–16, 18, 37, 57–58, 88–90, 133–34, 142–44, 158; Blumenson 1969: 86; Carell 1966: 488, 586; Hartmann: 66; Keilig: 12, 16, 59, 133, 184, 234; Kursietis: 98; Manstein: 515; Mellenthin 1956: 225; Mehner, Volume 8: 556; Volume 12: 458; Scheibert: 23, 378; Schmitz et al., Volume 3: 225–35; Stauffenberg MS; Tessin, Volume 6: 30–37; RA: 100; OB 42: 60; OB 43: 205; OB 45: 295; Wolfgang Werthen, *Geschichte der 16. Panzer-Division, 1939–1945* (Bad Nauheim, 1958); Ziemke: 225.

# 17th Panzer Division

**COMPOSITION:** 39th Panzer Regiment, 40th Panzer Grenadier Regiment, 63rd Panzer Grenadier Regiment, 27th Panzer Artillery Regiment, 17th Motorcycle Battalion, 27th Panzer Reconnaissance Battalion, 27th Tank Destroyer Battalion, 27th Panzer Engineer Battalion, 27th Panzer Signal Battalion.

**HOME STATION:** Augsburg, Wehrkreis VII

The 27th Infantry Division—forerunner of the 17th Panzer—was created on October 1, 1936, and initially included the 40th, 63rd, and 91st Infantry Regiments. Its personnel were Swabians who fought extremely well in southern Poland and France. Sent back to Augsburg in October, the division was converted to the 17th Panzer on November 1, 1940. It gave up the 91st Infantry Regiment to the 4th Mountain Division, but received the 39th Panzer Regiment, a two-battalion unit which was created at St. Poelten and Vienna, Wehrkreis XVII (Austria) from the 4th and 33rd Panzer Replacement Regiments. The division now consisted of the 39th Panzer Regiment, the 17th Rifle Brigade (40th and 63rd Rifle Regiments [two battalions each] and the 17th Motorcycle Battalion [the former II/63rd Rifle Regiment]), the 27th Panzer Artillery Regiment (three battalions), and the normal contingent of divisional troops. The 39th Panzer Regiment would receive a III Battalion (the former I/Panzer Lehr Regiment) on August 16, 1941.

Meanwhile, in June 1941, it struck into Russia with Army Group Center, fighting at Brest-Litovsk, the Minsk encirclement, in the Dnieper crossings, Smolensk, and at Tula during the Battle of Moscow. The 17th Panzer Division fought brilliantly; it destroyed 100 Russian tanks in a single day—July 9,

1941—at Orsha, during the Dnieper crossing operations. That winter it was
pushed back to Orel, where it finally checked the Red Army's advance in this
sector. It continued to hold the area around Orel until December 1942, when it
was hastily transferred to the southern sector of the front. By this time, it had
been greatly reduced by a year and a half of almost constant fighting on the
Eastern Front. It had only 30 tanks left and only one or two reconnaissance
vehicles. All of its armored cars had been destroyed or were inoperable and
most of its trucks were undergoing repairs or had been destroyed or abandoned
in front of Moscow during the winter retreat of 1941–42. As a result, one company from each motorized regiment had been converted into foot soldiers or
marching infantry.

The 17th Panzer nevertheless took a very active part in the attempt to relieve
Stalingrad and acquitted itself very well. In the battle of the Yessaulovskii Aksai
bridgehead, for example, it destroyed 21 Soviet tanks in one day (December
18). German casualties were also high because of the terrible cold (down to −22
degrees Fahrenheit) and repeated Russian counterattacks; by December 22, the
63rd Panzer Grenadier Regiment had suffered so many casualties that command
had devolved upon a lieutenant. (Its commander, Lieutenant Colonel Hermann
Seitz, a holder of the Knight's Cross with Oak Leaves, had been killed in action
near Gromoslavka on December 20.) The 17th Panzer Division was then involved in the battle of the Kotelnikovo bridgehead and, by Christmas Eve 1942,
was down to a strength of eight tanks and one antitank gun. It was finally forced
to retreat. During its withdrawal from the Stalingrad sector, several elements of
the division were encircled and had to fight their way out or were rescued by
other elements of the division. During the retreat from the Volga to the Don,
casualties were very heavy and some companies were reduced to a strength of
20 men, but the division's morale never flagged.

After the first of the year, it was reinforced with a shipment of 50 new tanks.
The 17th Panzer took part in the Battle of Rostov (1943), in the retreat into the
Donets and in the 3rd Battle of Kharkov (March 1943). After a rest (imposed
by the spring thaw), the division fought at Kursk (July 1943) and in the subsequent retreats from the Donets, the Dnieper Bend, and northern Ukraine. Meanwhile, the division was reorganized and, in 1943, included the 17th Panzer Reconnaissance Battalion (the former 17th Motorcycle Battalion) and the newly
assigned 297th Army Flak Battalion. The Staff, 17th Panzer Grenadier (formerly
Rifle) Brigade was separated from the division in 1944 and used to form Headquarters, IV Panzer Corps.

In the meantime, in March 1944 the 17th Panzer was encircled with Hube's
1st Panzer Army in Galicia but again broke out. It also fought in all of the
major actions during the retreat across eastern Poland. In September 1944 it was
still resisting west of the Vistula. The battered division was reorganized again
in late 1944—this time as a regimental-sized Kampfgruppe. The Staff, 39th
Panzer Regiment was separated from the division and used to form Headquarters, 108th Panzer Brigade. One of the 39th's battalions was transferred to the

103rd Panzer Regiment and another became part of the new tank brigade, leaving the division with a single tank battalion. The seriously depleted 63rd Panzer Grenadier Regiment was dissolved and most of its men were used to form III/40th Panzer Grenadier Regiment—a bicycle unit. All of its divisional support battalions were reduced to companies. Kampfgruppe 17th Panzer Division now consisted of the I/39th Panzer Regiment (with no regimental headquarters), 40th Panzer Grenadier Regiment, 27th Panzer Artillery Battalion (formerly regiment), 27th Panzer Reconnaissance Company, 27th Panzer Signal Company, and 27th Panzer Engineer Company. With this organization, it opposed the Russian drive east of the Vistula River in the winter of 1944–45, fighting in the battles of the Baranov bridgehead and Goerlitz, and ended the war in the pocket east of Prague. It surrendered to the Soviets on May 11, 1945.

Commanders of the 27th Infantry/17th Panzer Division included Major General/Lieutenant General Friedrich Bergmann (January 1, 1937), Lieutenant General Hans-Juergen "Dieter" von Arnim (October 5, 1940), Major General Ritter Karl von Weber (June 26, 1941), Lieutenant General Wilhelm Ritter von Thoma (July 18, 1941), Colonel/Major General Rudolf-Eduard Licht (November 11, 1941), Major General/Lieutenant General Fridolin von Senger und Etterlin (October 10, 1942), Lieutenant General Walter Schilling (June 17, 1943), Colonel/Major General/Lieutenant General Karl-Friedrich von der Meden (June 22, 1943), Colonel Rudolf Demme (September 20, 1944), Colonel Albert Brux (December 2, 1944) and Major General Theodor Kretschmer (February 1, 1945).

## COMMANDERS

Friedrich Bergmann (b. 1883) was promoted to lieutenant general on March 1, 1938. He commanded the 137th Infantry Division in France (1940) and on the Eastern Front, where he was killed in action on December 21, 1941. He had entered the Bavarian Army as a Fahnenjunker in 1902.

Hans-Juergen von Arnim (1889–1962) was commissioned in the elite 4th Guards Foot Regiment in 1909, having entered the service as a Fahnenjunker the year before. He was given command of the 52nd Infantry Division when the war broke out and was promoted to lieutenant general shortly thereafter. He led the 17th Panzer Division from the fall of 1940 until June 26, 1941, when he was wounded in action and replaced by Ritter von Weber. Later, Armin returned to duty and commanded XXXIX Panzer Corps in Russia (late 1941–late 1942), before being given command of the 5th Panzer Army in Tunisia (December 3, 1942) and Army Group Afrika (March 9, 1943). Meanwhile, he was promoted to general of panzer troops (October 1, 1941) and colonel general (December 3, 1942). He surrendered his army group on May 12, 1943, after his supply lines had totally collapsed. A bit of an aristocratic snob, Armin was nevertheless a good commander at the divisional and corps levels, but commanding an army exceeded his capabilities. As commander of the 5th Panzer Army, his failure to cooperate with Field Marshal Rommel—whom he looked down upon as a commoner and of whom he was jealous—was a contributing factor in the Axis defeat in North Africa. On the other hand, Armin was a humane warrior and treated both his men and his prisoners decently.

Major General Ritter Karl von Weber (b. 1892), a Bavarian infantry officer who had earned the Max Joseph Order and his knighthood during World War I, took over the 17th Panzer as acting commander after Armin was wounded. Weber did not join the armored forces until late 1940 but was nevertheless highly thought of by the German panzer leadership and, indeed, led the division very well until July 18, 1941, when he was mortally wounded during the Battle of Smolensk. He died in the hospital at Krassnyj on July 20.

For a sketch of Ritter Wilhelm von Thoma's career, see 20th Panzer Division, Commanders.

Rudolf-Eduard Licht (b. 1890), who was promoted to major general on February 2, 1942, joined the infantry as a Fahnenjunker in 1911. He was a senior course commander at the War School at Wiener Neustadt in 1938–39, but was given command of the 40th Infantry Regiment when the war broke out. Licht commanded the 17th Rifle Brigade (1941) before rising to the command of the 17th Panzer. Obviously his performance was judged as less than stellar. He was soon sent back to Germany and, on November 1, 1942, Licht was given command of Replacement Division Staff 487—a definite demotion. He was only given command of third- or fourth-class units for the rest of his career, successively directing the 487th Replacement (1942–43), the 21st Luftwaffe Field Division (1943–44), and the 710th Infantry Division. The fact that he was not promoted to lieutenant general until 1944 is further evidence that someone in authority did not think highly of him.

Fridolin von Senger und Etterlin (1891–1963), a veteran cavalry officer, spent much of his career with 1st Cavalry Division, about which he later wrote a book. Senger began his career as an enlisted man in the 76th Field Artillery Regiment but, after attending the University of Frieburg and becoming a Rhodes scholar, earned a reserve commission in 1914 and a regular army commission in the artillery in 1917. Returning to the cavalry in 1920, he was chief of staff of the Cavalry Inspectorate (1934–38), and commanded the 3rd Cavalry Regiment (1938–39), the 22nd Cavalry Regiment (1939–40), and the 2nd Rifle Brigade (1940) before becoming a German delegate to the Italian-French Armistice Commission (1941–42). He briefly commanded the 10th Panzer Grenadier Regiment in occupied France (July–September 1942). After leaving the 17th Panzer in late 1942, Senger—who possessed considerable diplomatic ability—was briefly Wehrmacht Commander in Sicily (1943) and German liaison officer to the Italian 6th Army before taking over the XIV Panzer Corps, which he led on the Italian Front for the rest of the war. He was promoted to lieutenant general on May 1, 1943, and to general of panzer troops effective January 1, 1944.

Walter Schilling was born in West Prussia in 1895 and entered the army as an officer cadet in the engineers in 1914. Later he served on the staff at OKH (1936–39), as Ia of Group Command 3 and 8th Army (1939), as Ia of 2nd Army

(1939), as chief of staff of XXIV Panzer Corps (1941–42), and as chief of staff of 3rd Panzer Army (1942–43). Promoted to lieutenant general on April 1, 1943, he had been commander of the 17th Panzer less than five weeks when he was killed in action near Doljenjaja on July 20, 1943. An excellent General Staff officer, Schilling's abilities as a commander are difficult to judge due to his short tenure.

For the details of Karl-Friedrich von der Meden's career, see 178th Panzer Replacement Division, Commanders.

Rudolf Demme was born in Muehlhausen, Thueringen, in 1894. A war volunteer in 1914, he served in engineer and trench mortar units throughout the war, and earned a reserve commission in 1917. Discharged at the end of 1918, he rejoined the army as a first lieutenant in 1937 and served with the Condor Legion in Spain. By 1940, he was commander of the 208th Engineer Replacement Battalion. Later he commanded the 92nd Panzer Engineer Battalion (1941), the 58th Panzer Engineer Battalion (1941–42) and the 59th Panzer Grenadier Regiment (1943–44), earning the Knight's Cross and Oak Leaves in the process. On December 12, 1944, ten days after giving up command of the 17th Panzer, Demme assumed command of the 132nd Infantry Division, which he led for the rest of the war. Promoted to major general on March 1, 1945, he surrendered to the Red Army on May 5 and spent the next 10 years in Soviet prisons, General Demme died in Meckenheim on January 5, 1975.

Albert Brux had previously commanded the I/66th Rifle Regiment (1941), the 43rd Motorcycle Battalion (1943), and the 40th Panzer Grenadier Regiment (1944), and was promoted from captain to colonel in less than three years. A holder of the Knight's Cross with Oak Leaves, he was captured by the Russians in January, 1945. He was born in Silesia in 1907.

Theodor Kretschmer (b. 1901) joined the Guards Cavalry Rifle Division in 1919 and was commissioned in the 5th Motor Transport Battalion in 1924. He was chief of staff of the XVI Motorized Corps (1938–39), on the staff of OKH (1939–40), was commander of the 65th Panzer Battalion (1940), served on the OKH staff again (1940–42), was commander of the 36th Panzer Regiment (1942), and was a branch chief in the Army Personnel Office (1942–44). After briefly serving with the 16th Panzer Division (late 1944–early 1945), Kretschmer took command of the 17th Panzer Division on February 1, 1945. Promoted to major general on April 1, he surrendered the division to the Red Army on May 11, 1945, and was a prisoner of war in the Soviet Union until late 1955.

## NOTES AND SOURCES

All four of the men who were regimental commanders in the 17th Panzer Division in November 1942 were killed in action during the next two years.

Unlike most armored divisions, the 17th Panzer did not get a flak battalion until 1943. On January 12, 1943, it received the 297th Army Motorized Flak Artillery Battalion, which became the 27th (Flak) Tank Destroyer Battalion on June 20, 1943. It was separated from the division in late 1944 and ended the war fighting in Silesia.

Bradley et al., Volume 1: 97–99, 334–35; Volume 3: 67–68; Carell 1966: 42, 80, 344, 651; Carell 1971: 89, 525; Guderian: 131, 140, 144; Hartmann: 68; Keilig: 30, 187, 220, 299, 364; Kennedy: 74, Map 7; KTB OKW, Volume I: 1146; Kursietis: 98–100; Manstein: 134, 498–99, 515; Mehner, Volume 5: 330; Volume 12: 458; Samuel W. Mitcham Jr., "Arnim," in Correlli Barrett, ed., *Hitler's Generals* (London, 1989): 335–60; Schiebert: 60; Seeman: 46, 98; Ferdinand von Senger und Etterlin, "Senger," in Correlli Barrett, ed., *Hitler's Generals* (London, 1989): 375–92; Frido von Senger und Etterlin, *Neither Fear Nor Hope*, George Malcolm, trans. (New York, 1963; reprint ed., Novato, Calif., 1989): 60–125; Seaton: 330–31; Tessin, Volume 6: 61–65, 251–52; Volume 9: 57; RA: 116; OB 42: 60; OB 43: 205; OB 44: 285; OB 45: 296; Windrow: 10; Ziemke: 225.

# 18th Panzer Division

**COMPOSITION:** 18th Panzer Regiment, 52nd Panzer Grenadier Regiment, 101st Panzer Grenadier Regiment, 88th Panzer Artillery Regiment, 18th Motorcycle Battalion, 88th Panzer Reconnaissance Battalion, 88th Tank Destroyer Battalion, 98th Panzer Engineer Battalion, 88th Panzer Signal Battalion.

**HOME STATION:** Leisnig, Wehrkreis IV

The 18th Panzer was formed at Chemnitz on October 26, 1940, as a result of Hitler's decision to create new armored divisions by weakening older panzer and motorized divisions. The 18th Panzer received two veteran infantry regiments: the 52nd Rifle (or Motorized Infantry) Regiment from the 4th Infantry Division and the 101st Motorized from the 14th Infantry Division. By the end of the year, the new division included the newly formed 18th Rifle Brigade (52nd and 101st Rifle Regiments [two battalions each]); the 18th and 28th Panzer Regiments (two battalions each), both formed on December 6, 1940; the 88th Panzer Artillery Regiment; and assorted divisional troops. The 18th Rifle Brigade also controlled the former I/52nd Regiment, which was reorganized as the 18th Motorcycle Battalion. The Staff of the 88th Panzer Artillery came from the 209th Artillery Regiment. One of its artillery battalions was detached from the 14th Artillery Regiment, and the former 741st Light and 630th Heavy Artillery Battalions became II and III/88th Panzer Artillery Regiment, respectively. On March 1, 1941, the 28th Panzer Regiment was transferred to the 3rd Panzer Division, although part of it was used to form a third battalion for the 18th Panzer Regiment.

The new unit first saw action in Russia, crossing the Bug in underwater tanks originally designed for Operation Sea Lion (the invasion of Britain). It spent the rest of 1941 fighting in a number of battles, including the Minsk encirclement, Smolensk, the Dnieper crossings, Roslavl, Bryansk, Moscow, and Orel, all on the central sector of the Russian Front. It was also involved in the encirclement of Kiev on the southern sector (primarily covering the rear of the 2nd Panzer Group). The 18th Panzer was engaged in particularly heavy fighting in the early weeks of the invasion and, by the end of July, had already lost more than half of its tanks, mostly in the drive on Roslavl. During the first 60 days of the campaign, the 18th Panzer Division lost almost 6,000 men—more than a third of its preinvasion strength. By July 9, the division had only 83 operational tanks—39 percent of its strength just three weeks before. By late July, only 12 of its panzers were still in running order, compared to 212 on June 21.

The 18th Panzer Division faced the Soviet winter offensive of 1941–42 near the Soviet capital with greatly reduced numbers but acquitted itself very well. In January 1942 it launched a particularly brilliant counteroffensive, penetrating Soviet lines and rescuing and then extricating the trapped German garrison at Sukhinichi, despite very heavy odds against it. The division then retreated to Ugra, which it held against heavy attacks. It was still there when the spring thaw came. Casualties, meanwhile, had reduced the unit's strength to 10,459 men by January 25, 1942; of these, only 5,443 were combat effective. The continuous fighting permanently altered the quality of the division. By November 1941 the senior chaplain wrote: "This is no longer the old division. All around are new faces. When one asks about somebody, it is always the same reply: killed or wounded." The replacements (when such were available) were generally of poorer quality than those whom they were called upon to replace.

On June 15, 1942, the division was reorganized, largely because of the heavy casualties it had suffered. The much-depleted 18th Panzer Regiment was disbanded and its staff used to form Headquarters, 9th Panzer Regiment (25th Panzer Division); I/18th Panzer became 160th Panzer Battalion and was sent to the 60th Panzer Grenadier Division; III/18th Panzer Regiment formed the cadre from which the 103rd Panzer Battalion of the 3rd Panzer Grenadier Division was built; and II/18th Panzer remained with the division as the 18th Panzer Battalion—its only tank unit. At the same time the division received the 292nd Army Flak Artillery Battalion but lost the 88th Panzer Reconnaissance Battalion, which was sent to the rear to become a training and demonstration (Lehr) unit for reconnaissance and cavalry troops. A new 88th Panzer Reconnaissance was formed from the 18th Motorcycle Battalion (which ceased to exist) on April 29, 1943. The authorized strength of the division was reduced from more than 17,000 men to about 14,000. This reduction, however, was academic: its actual strength stood at fewer than 7,000 combat effectives.

In the summer of 1942, the 18th Panzer Division was sent to the southern sector of the Eastern Front, where it took part in the initial advances on Stalingrad, but it was soon returned to Army Group Center, with which it fought in the defensive battles around Orel in 1942–43. It took part in several antipartisan operations in the spring of 1943 and fought in the Battle of Kursk in July. The 18th Panzer Division was practically destroyed in this offensive. It had 5,432 combat effectives on July 11 but lost 4,028 men in the next 10 days. Major General Wilhelm von Schleiben, the division commander, reinforced his combat units the only way he could: by disbanding supply units, many of which were now unnecessary in any case. The Replacement Army also sent men to the 18th, but they were generally older, poorly trained recruits who only served to further lower the deteriorating quality of the division.

By mid-September, the 18th Panzer had only four panzer grenadier battalions, each numbering about 130 men—less than the size of a prewar company. Desertions—almost unheard-of before 1943—were now becoming increasingly common. By autumn 1943, the 18th Panzer Division was fighting around Kiev; next it took part in the retreat to the Dnieper, and it suffered such heavy losses in the counteroffensives west of Kiev (in the Bryansk, Orscha, and Vitebsk sectors) that it had to be disbanded on September 29, 1943. Low morale was a contributing factor to this decision. Most of the remnants of the division were incorporated into the 18th Artillery Division, including the divisional staff, the artillery regiment, and the reconnaissance, signal, and antitank battalions. The 18th Panzer Battalion became the 504th Panzer Battalion, a General Headquarters unit controlled by Army Group Center. Most of the 101st Panzer Grenadier Regiment was transferred to the 14th Panzer Grenadier Division.

Commanders of the 18th Panzer included Major General/Lieutenant General Walter Nehring (assumed command, October 26, 1940), Major General/Lieutenant General Baron Karl von Thuengen-Rossbach (January 26, 1942), Colonel/Major General Albert Praun (acting commander, July, 1942), Thuengen (returned August 24, 1942), Major General Erwin Menny (acting commander, September 15, 1942, to approximately the end of 1942), Thuengen (returned at the end of 1942), and Colonel/Major General Karl Wilhelm von Schlieben (April 1, 1943).

The 18th Artillery Division was officially activated on October 1, 1943, and, by the end of the month, included the 88th Artillery Regiment (formerly the 88th Panzer Artillery Regiment of the 18th Panzer Division), and the 288th and 388th Artillery Regiments, which were created from a variety of sources. The division joined the 4th Panzer Army in January 1944 and fought at Vinniza. In March 1944 it was encircled (along with the rest of the 1st Panzer Army) in the Hube Pocket, but succeeded in breaking out and reaching German lines the following month. The 18th Artillery Division was then sent to the rear and was disbanded. The divisional staff was used to form Headquarters, Grossdeutschland Panzer Corps. The artillery regiments were used to form self-standing army artillery brigades. Major General/Lieutenant General Karl Thoholte commanded the 18th Artillery Division throughout its existence.

## COMMANDERS

Walter Nehring (b. 1892) joined the army as an infantry Fahnenjunker in 1911. An early convert to the panzer branch, he commanded the 5th Panzer Regiment (1937–39), was Guderian's chief of staff at XIX Motorized (later Panzer) Corps (1939–40), and was chief of staff of Panzer Group Guderian (1940) before assuming command of the 18th Panzer. Nehring was promoted to lieutenant general on February 1, 1942, and to general of panzer troops on July 1, 1942— only five months later. He then left Russia to command the Afrika Korps (1942) until he was seriously wounded by an Allied fighter-bomber on the night of August 31–September 1, 1942, during the advance on Alma Halfa Ridge. Returning to duty in November, he was commander of the newly formed XC Corps during the initial American drive on Tunis, whose capture he prevented. He earned Goebbels' censure and fell out with the Nazis over the issue of Tunisia, which he felt could not be held in the long run. The fact that subsequent events proved him right and the Fuehrer wrong meant nothing—he was permanently barred from further promotion. From February 1943 to March 1945, he was commander of the XXIV Panzer Corps on the Eastern Front. During Stalin's winter offensive of January, 1945, Nehring's corps was totally surrounded. Outnumbered seven to one, he formed a "floating pocket" and moved through the Soviet rear, beating off dozens of attacks from every quarter against seemingly overwhelming odds until he reached German lines. In the process he saved tens of thousands of civilians from the Soviets; by the time he reached friendly lines, there were more German civilians inside the floating pocket than soldiers holding it. In my view, this was arguably the most brilliant tactical feat performed by any general during the Second World War. As a result, Nehring was given command of the 1st Panzer Army in Czechoslovakia on March 22, 1945—but without a promotion. He surrendered his Staff to the Americans on May 9, 1945. In my opinion, Nehring was the best all-around panzer commander in World War II. He died in Duesseldorf on April 20, 1983, at the age of 90.

A Bavarian, Baron Karl von Thuengen-Rossbach (1893–1944) served in the cavalry during World War I. He was on the staff of the Army Personnel Office (1938), had led the 254th Replacement and Training Regiment (1939–40), the 22nd Cavalry Regiment (1940), and the 1st Rifle Brigade (1940–41), before commanding the 18th Panzer. He was promoted to lieutenant general on January 1, 1943. Not ranked among the great tank commanders (although he ranked higher as a human being), he was given a backwater assignment (command of Recruiting Area Berlin I) (1943–44) after leaving the division. He was hanged on October 24, 1944, for his part in the July 20 plot to assassinate Adolf Hitler.

A Bavarian signals official, Albert Praun was born in Staffelstein in late 1894 and joined the army as a Fahnenjunker in the 1st Bavarian Telegraph Battalion in 1913. After serving in World War I and in the Reichsheer, Praun was commander of the 38th signal Battalion (1935–39), commander, 696th Signal Regiment (1939–40), chief signal officer, 7th Army (1940), chief signal officer, Panzer Group Hoth (1940), and chief signal officer, Panzer Group Guderian (1940). After serving briefly in occupied France, Praun again served Guderian as chief signal officer, 2nd Panzer Army (1940–42). Later he commanded the 482nd and 486th Infantry Regiments, the 4th Panzer Grenadier Brigade and the 18th Panzer Division (1942). Promoted to major general on August 1, 1942, Praun led the 129th Infantry Division (1942–43), before becoming chief signals officer of Army Group Center (1943–44) and commander of the 277th Infantry Division (1944). After Erich Fellgiebel and his deputy were arrested for their part in the July 20, 1944 attempt to kill Hitler, Praun (a lieutenant general since early 1943), was named chief signals officer of OKH and OKW. In this post, Praun boldly approached Ernst Kaltenbrunner, the head of the Reich Security Office, and told him that he should stop arresting signals personnel. He was losing so many highly skilled and irreplaceable men, Praun declared, that it would soon adversely effect the war effort. Remarkably, Kaltenbrunner agreed and there were no further arrests. Albert Praun was promoted to general of signal troops on November 1, 1944, and remained in his post until the end of the war. He surrendered to the Western Allies and was living in Munich in the 1960s.

Erwin Menny (1893–1949), a native of the Saar, was commissioned in the dragoons in 1914. During World War II, he commanded the 81st Rifle Regiment (1939–40), 69th Rifle Regiment (1940–41), and the 15th Rifle Brigade of the Afrika Korps. In this position he played a prominent role in the capture of Tobruk. After leading the 18th Panzer, he was promoted to lieutenant general on October 1, 1943, and successively commanded (or was acting commander) of the 333rd, 123rd, 72nd, and 84th Infantry Divisions. He was captured by the British on the Western Front on August 21, 1944.

Karl Wilhelm von Schlieben (1894–1964) entered the service in August 1914 as an infantry Fahnenjunker. He remained in the Reichsheer and served as adjutant, Wehrkreis XIII (1938–40); commander, 108th Rifle Regiment (1940–42); commander, 4th Rifle Brigade (1942–43); and deputy commander, 208th Infantry Division (February–March, 1943). After the 18th Panzer Division was dissolved, Schlieben was unemployed for three months; then he was given command of the 709th Infantry Division (1943–44)—a static unit in France. This was unquestionably a demotion for him. In action on D-Day, Schlieben directed the 709th and Korps von Schlieben (an ad hoc formation of largely shattered units) in Normandy. He surrendered the "fortress" of Cherbourg to the Americans in late June 1944, earning Hitler's censure. Schlieben was promoted to major general on May 1, 1943, and to lieutenant general on May 1, 1944.

## NOTES AND SOURCES

Angolia, *Field*, Volume 1: 234–35; Omar Bartov, *The Eastern Front, 1941–45: German Troops and the Barbarisation of Warfare* (New York, 1986): 11, 18–21, 35; Carell 1966: 14–15, 68–69, 80, 196; Carell 1971: 26; Keilig: 223, 302, 346; Mehner, Volume 4: 383; Volume 5: 330; Wolfgang Paul, *Geschichte der 18. Panzer-Division, 1940–1943* (Freiburg, n.d.); Stoves, *Gepanzerten*: 120–24; Tessin, Volume 6: 93–95, 97; RA: 72; OB 42: 61; OB 43: 206; OB 45: 297.

Heinz Guderian, the "father" of the Blitzkrieg. One of the early advocates of armored warfare, he commanded the 2nd Panzer Division from 1935 to 1938. During World War II, he commanded the XIX Motorized (later Panzer) Corps (1939–40), Panzer Group Guderian (1940), and the 2nd Panzer Group (later Army) (1940–41). Later he served as inspector general of the panzer force (1943–44) and as acting chief of the General Staff (1944–45). (Courtesy, Colonel Dr. Edmond D. Marino)

Field Marshal Erwin Rommel, the "Desert Fox." Originally a member of the mountain troops branch, Rommel did not convert to the concept of blitzkrieg warfare until after the war began. Once he did join the panzer branch, however, he distinguished himself as commander of the 7th Panzer Division (1940–41), the Afrika Korps (1941), Panzer Group Afrika (1941–42) and Panzer Army Afrika (1941–42). He was forced to commit suicide in the fall of 1944 because of his involvement in the anti-Hitler conspiracy. (Author's Personal Collection)

Not every panzer division commander was as distinguished as Guderian or Rommel. Major General Baron Horst Treusch von Buttlar-Brandenfels was a cavalry officer who spent virtually the entire war in staff positions, mainly with the operations staff of the High Command of the Armed Forces. Using his influence, Treusch managed to arrange to get himself appointed commander of the elite 11th Panzer Division on the Western Front in the last weeks of the war and thus avoided being in Berlin when it was encircled by the Soviets. He earned no particular laurels as commander of the 11th Panzer, but he survived the war. (Author's Personal Collection)

German generals in World War II considered Field Marshal Erich von Manstein (1887–1973) the best general ever produced during the Third Reich era. Although a general of infantry, he was an advocate of motorized warfare and distinguished himself as commander of the LVI Panzer Corps on the Eastern Front in 1941. Later he commanded the 11th Army (1941–42), Army Group Don (1942–43) and Army Group South (1943–44). Hitler, who feared him, forced him into retirement on March 31, 1944. (U.S. National Archives)

General Joachim Lemelsen, circa 1940. An artilleryman since he joined the Imperial Army in 1907, Lemelsen was promoted to general of artillery in 1940, but was named a general of panzer troops the following year at his own request. Lemelsen commanded the 5th Panzer Division on the Western Front in 1940 and the XXXXVII Panzer Corps in the East (1940–43). Later he commanded the 10th, 1st, and 4th Armies in the West and in Italy. (U.S. Army Military History Institute)

Erwin Rommel, the "Desert Fox," shortly after his promotion to field marshal in July, 1942. Rommel is carrying his marshal's baton and is wearing the Pour le Mèrite and the Knight's Cross with Oak Leaves and Swords. (U.S. Army Military History Institute)

Lieutenant General Fridolin von Senger und Etterlin. Originally a horse soldier, Senger was commander of the 3rd Cavalry Regiment when the war began. He later transferred to the Panzerwaffe and led the 17th Panzer Division in the Stalingrad relief attempt during the winter of 1942–43. Senger was later promoted to general of panzer troops and led the XIV Panzer Corps on the Italian Front (1943–45). (U.S. National Archives)

Hitler (right) confers with Field Marshal Werner von Blomberg (center) and General of Artillery Baron Werner von Fritsch (left) during the 1935 maneuvers at Munsterlager. Both Fritsch, the chief of the General Staff of the Army (1934–38), and Blomberg supported the panzer experiment and were advocates of large motorized and armored formations. Both Blomberg and Fritsch were forced to retire in disgrace in 1938. Fritsch was later killed during the Siege of Warsaw in 1939. (U.S. Army Military History Institute)

An American Sherman tank passed an abandoned PzKw IV during the Battle of the Bulge, winter of 1944–45. The panzer was abandoned after it threw its left track. (U.S. National Archives)

Major General Baron Johann von Ravenstein, the commander of the 21st Panzer Division of the Afrika Korps. Ravenstein's brilliant career was cut short on November 29, 1941, when he blundered into a New Zealand brigade and was captured during the Battle of Tobruk. He was nevertheless promoted to lieutenant general in late 1943. Like Rommel, Ravenstein held the Pour le Mèrite from World War I. (U.S. Army Military History Institute)

Lieutenant General Heinrich Kirchheim, who briefly commanded the 5th Light (later 21st Panzer) Division in Libya, May, 1941. Considered an expert on desert warfare, Kirchheim ran afoul of General Rommel during the Battle of Tobruk and was relieved of his command. He served in backwater posts for the rest of the war. (U.S. Army Military History Institute)

A Panzer Mark III on the Western Desert. The PzKw III was the "workhorse" of the German Army in the 1940–42 period. This one is a J Model (PzKw IIIj) and has a long-barreled 50mm main battle gun. (U.S. Army Military History Institute)

A knocked-out Panzer Mark IV (PzKw IV), being inspected by a British officer, North Africa, late 1942. The Mark IV was an excellent medium tank. During the last two years of the war, the panzer divisions often had only two tank battalions. Typically, one was equipped with PzKw IVs, while the other was equipped with Panthers. (U.S. Army Military History Institute)

Major General Erwin Rommel, the commander of the 7th Panzer Division, France, 1940. Rommel later achieved fame as the "Desert Fox." (U.S. National Archives)

Field Marshal Werner von Blomberg, Hitler's minister of war, listened to a lecture from Italian Marshal Pietro Badoglio, Berlin, 1937. An infantry officer by profession, Blomberg nevertheless appreciated the potential of the panzer branch and aided in its development. He was forced to retire in disgrace in 1938 when the Berlin vice squad discovered his much younger second wife had posed for nude photographs. He died in a prison hospital in Nuremberg shortly after the end of the war. (U.S. National Archives)

Colonel General Erwin Rommel, the commander of Panzer Army Afrika, congrat-
ulates General of Panzer Troops Ludwig Cruewell, his deputy commander, on his
birthday in March, 1942. Cruewell commanded the 11th Panzer Division (1940–
41) and the Afrika Korps (1941–42). A few weeks after this photograph was
taken, Cruewell's airplane was shot down and he was captured by the British.
Standing immediately behind Rommel is Lieutenant General (later General of
Panzer Troops) Walter Nehring, the commander of the Afrika Korps. Nehring was
a major behind the scenes force in the creation of the blitzkrieg and one of the
unsung heroes of the Panzerwaffe. During World War II, Nehring was Guderian's
chief of staff in Poland and France (1939–40), commander of the 18th Panzer
Division on the Eastern Front (1941–42), commander of the Afrika Korps until he
was wounded at Alam Halfa Ridge (1942), commander of the XC Corps in Tunisia
(1942–43), and commander of the XXIV Panzer Corps and 1st Panzer Armies
on the Eastern Front (1943–45). He was arguably the best panzer commander
the Germans produced during World War II. (U.S. National Archives)

A German panzer regiment pauses in the desert, circa 1941. The two tanks in the foreground are Panzer Mark IIIs (PzKw III), which are equipped with short barrel main battle guns. Later models had long barrel guns and were much more effective. (U.S. Army Military History Institute)

A PzKw VI "Tiger" tank, knocked out during the fighting in Italy, 1944. It is being inspected by an American soldier. (U.S. National Archives)

The typical German army unit of the first half of World War II. An infantry squad marches on foot while its infantry guns are hauled by horse-drawn wagons. This scene was much more typical of the German Army during World War II than that of a surging panzer formation. Of the 140 German divisions on the Western Front in 1940, only 10 were panzer. The German Army used more than 2,000,000 horses during the Russian campaign. (U.S. Army Military History Institute)

Colonel General Franz Halder, the chief of the German General Staff, 1938–1942. Originally a Bavarian artillery officer, Halder was too conservative to fully appreciate the potential of his panzer divisions. (U.S. National Archives)

Lieutenant General Eberhard Rodt, who, as a colonel, commanded the 66th Panzer Grenadier Regiment, the 2nd Panzer Grenadier Brigade and the 22nd Panzer Division on the Eastern Front, 1941–43. Basically a failure as a tank division commander in the East, Rodt later staged a fine professional comeback and distinguished himself commanding the 15th Panzer Grenadier Division in Italy and the West (1943–45). (U.S. National Archives)

General of Panzer Troops Fridolin von Senger und Etterlin, commander of the XIV Panzer Corps in Italy (1943–45). Earlier, Senger had commanded a rifle brigade in France and the 17th Panzer Division on the Eastern Front (1942–43). (U.S. National Archives)

General of Panzer Troops Hans Valentin Hube, who was known throughout the German Army as "der Mensch" (the Man). No officer was more respected by the German soldiers in World War II than Hube. He had lost an arm at Verdun during World War I but nevertheless rehabilitated himself, and was commanding an infantry company in the trenches of the Western Front when the war ended. (It must be recalled that the facilities for assisting the handicapped in the 1910s were primitive to nonexistent.) Hube was the only handicapped officer selected for retention in the Reichsheer, and he later became quite good at skiing. During the war, Hube distinguished himself as commander of the 16th Panzer Division and XIV Panzer Corps. Trapped at Stalingrad, he refused to obey Hitler's orders to fly out of the pocket; the Fuehrer had to send in a special detachment of Gestapo agents, who took him at gunpoint. In 1943, Hube checked two Allied armies in Sicily with a single panzer corps, and then escaped with his entire command. He was then given command of the 1st Panzer Army on the Russian Front. He is shown here wearing the Knight's Cross with Oak Leaves and Swords. The diamonds were added on April 20, 1944, after he launched a brilliant breakout from a Soviet encirclement and escaped with his entire command (18 divisions). He was killed in an airplane crash the next day. (Imperial War Museum)

Traugott Herr commanded the 13th Panzer Division on the Eastern Front (1941–42). Seriously wounded in late 1942, he was not able to return to active duty until June, 1943, when he assumed command of the LXXVI Panzer Corps in Italy. After distinguishing himself at the corps level, Herr was named acting commander of the 14th Army (late 1944) and commander of the 10th Army (early 1945). A holder of the Knight's Cross with Oak Leaves and Swords, he surrendered the 10th Army to the Anglo-Americans at the end of the war. (U.S. National Archives)

Colonel General Heinrich von Vietinghoff, here a prisoner of war, listens to a U.S. intelligence officer, Italy, 1945. At the beginning of the war, Vietinghoff was commander of the 5th Panzer Division. He later led the XXXXVI Panzer Corps in Russia and held several higher commands. His last post was commander-in-chief of Army Group C and OB Southwest in Italy. (U.S. National Archives)

General of Cavalry Georg Stumme, the commander of the XXXX Panzer Corps, in the Balkans campaign of 1941. At his own request, Stumme's rank was changed to general of panzer troops on June 4, 1941. Stumme, who fully enjoyed the pleasures of life, had previously commanded the 7th Panzer Division. Later he was court-martialled (the senior judge was Hermann Goering) and imprisoned for a security violation, but was reprieved by Goering, who was impressed by his conduct during the trial. Named acting commander of Panzer Army Afrika, he was reported as missing in action on November 24, 1942, the second day of the Second Battle of El Alamein. Stumme had been surprised by Australian troops who had broken through. He jumped on the running board of his car and ordered his driver to flee, and suffered a fatal heart attack as the car sped away. The driver did not see the general collapse. A patrol later recovered his body. (U.S. National Archives)

A towed infantry howitzer battery, on maneuvers, circa 1938. (U.S. Army Military History Institute)

General of Panzer Troops Heinrich Eberbach, who successively commanded the 35th Panzer Regiment, 5th Panzer Brigade, 4th Panzer Division, and XXXXVIII Panzer Corps (1938–44). Eberbach excelled as a tank division and corps commander on the Eastern Front. On July 5, 1944, he assumed command of the 5th Panzer Army in Normandy, where he again proved to be an excellent commander, even in a hopeless situation. On August 30, 1944, while commanding 7th Army in France, his command post was overrun by British armor and he was captured. A very handsome man, much of his nose was shot off during World War I, and he disliked having a photograph taken of his profile. After fighting in two world wars (he was in the infantry in World War I and fought in the trenches), including three years on the Eastern Front, Eberbach died in 1992, at the age of 96. (Author's Personal Collection)

Field Marshal Werner von Blomberg, German minister of defense (later war) from 1933 to 1938. Blomberg's support of the concept of rapid armored warfare was invaluable during the formative years of the panzer forces. (U.S. Army Military History Institute)

# 19th Panzer Division

**COMPOSITION (1943):** 27th Panzer Regiment, 73rd Panzer Grenadier Regiment, 74th Panzer Grenadier Regiment, 19th Panzer Artillery Regiment, 19th Motorcycle Battalion, 19th Panzer Reconnaissance Battalion, 19th Tank Destroyer Battalion, 19th Panzer Engineer Battalion, 19th Panzer Signal Battalion.

**HOME STATION:** Hanover, Wehrkreis XI

The 19th Panzer Division was formed on October 2, 1934, during Nazi Germany's secret military expansion, under the code name "Artillery Command VI." It was not officially activated until October 15, 1935, when it became the 19th Infantry Division. It initially included the 59th, 73rd, and 74th Infantry Regiments. It fought in the Polish campaign of 1939 (where it suffered heavy losses at Bzurs in southern Poland) and in Belgium, where it came up against the British Expeditionary Force. After a few months of occupation duty in France, it was sent back to Hanover in October 1940 and was reorganized as a panzer division, adding the 27th Panzer Regiment and giving up the 59th Infantry Regiment to the 20th Panzer Division. In its final form, the 19th Panzer Division consisted of the 19th Rifle Brigade (73rd and 74th Rifle Regiments [two battalions each] and the 19th Motorcycle Battalion [formerly I/73rd Infantry Regiment]); the 27th Panzer Regiment (I, II, and III Battalions, which were formerly the 11th, 25th, and 10th Panzer Replacement Battalions, respectively); the 19th Panzer Artillery Regiment (three battalions) and the normal contingent of divisional support troops. Sent to Russia in 1941, it fought in the Bialystok and Minsk encirclements and in the Battle of Moscow. In the process it suffered so many casualties that III/27th Panzer Regiment was disbanded on August 8 and

I/27th Panzer was dissolved on March 31, 1942, leaving the division with only a single tank battalion. Despite its reduced numbers, the 19th Panzer Division remained on the central sector in the defensive battles of 1942 and was sent to the critical southern sector in late 1942. In January 1943 it escaped to Army Group Don after the 8th Italian Army, which it had been supporting, collapsed. The division took part in the Donets battles of early 1943 and the Kursk offensive of July, where it suffered heavy casualties near Belgorod and in the subsequent retreats. Meanwhile, on April 29, 1943, the 19th Motorcycle Battalion was converted into a panzer reconnaissance unit and the 272nd Army Flak Artillery Battalion was added to the division. In October 1943, the division absorbed the 138th Panzer Battalion, which was redesignated II/27th Panzer Regiment—giving the division a second tank battalion for the first time in more than a year.

The 19th Panzer was fighting near Kiev in November 1943, was in the battle at Zhitomir the following month, and was heavily engaged in the withdrawal through northern Ukraine. It formed part of General Hube's "Floating Pocket" in March and April 1944, when the entire 1st Panzer Army was surrounded but fought its way out from behind Soviet lines. It also fought in the rather indecisive battles of Shepetovka, Proskurov, and Stanislav (April–June). The division was rushed north after Army Group Center was crushed, and the 19th and two other panzer divisions surprised and destroyed the III Soviet Tank Corps north of Warsaw, thus stalling the Russian summer offensive of 1944. It was cited for this action. In autumn 1944, the 19th Panzer was resisting west of the Vistula. Now at battle group strength, the division retreated through southern Poland and fought in the Battle of the Baranov Bridgehead (January 1945), in the subsequent retreat, and then in the Breslau sector of southeastern Germany. It was finally pushed into Czechoslovakia and ended the war in the Moravian pocket east of Prague, where it surrendered to the Red Army in May 1945.

Commanders of the 19th Infantry/Panzer Division included Major General/Lieutenant General Guenther Schwantes (assumed command March 1, 1938), Major General/Lieutenant General Otto von Knobelsdorff (February 1, 1940), Colonel/Major General/Lieutenant General Gustav Schmidt (January 5, 1942), Colonel/Major General/Lieutenant General Hans Kaellner (August 18, 1943), and Major General Hans-Joachim Deckert (March 1945). Colonel Walter Denkert was acting divisional commander from March 28 until May 1944.

## COMMANDERS

Guenther Schwantes (1881–1942), a native of Kolberg, East Prussia, was promoted to lieutenant general on June 1, 1938. A "retread," he joined the army in 1899 and was commander of the 11th Cavalry Regiment from 1930 to 1933, when he retired a month after his promotion to major general. Recalled to active duty in 1938, he retired again in 1942, no doubt due to poor health. He passed away on August 11, 1942.

Otto von Knobelsdorff (b. 1894) was promoted to lieutenant general on December 1, 1940. A Berliner, he joined the army as an infantry officer cadet in 1905 and served as chief of staff of Corps Command XXXIII (1939–40) before assuming command of the 19th Infantry Division. He oversaw the division's conversion into a tank unit. He later served as acting commander of X Corps (1942), acting commander of II Corps in the Demyansk Salient (1942), acting commander of XXIV Panzer Corps (1942), commander of XXXXVIII Panzer Corps (1942–43), commander of XXXX Panzer Corps (1944), and commander of the 1st Army on the Western Front (September–December 1944). A highly capable panzer commander, especially when given the great odds he usually faced, Knobelsdorff was not a particularly good army commander. He was also an outspoken officer, and his blunt opposition to Hitler's plan to strip 1st Army of its few remaining tanks to reinforce the Ardennes offensive led to his being relieved of his command. He was never reemployed. Knobelsdorff held the Knight's Cross with Oak Leaves and Swords. Later he wrote a history of the 19th Infantry/Panzer Division. He died in Hanover in 1966.

Gustav Schmidt (b. 1894) was promoted to major general on April 1, 1942, and to lieutenant general on January 1, 1943. He was commissioned in the 20th Infantry Regiment just before World War I broke out. Schmidt was commander of the II/59th Infantry Regiment (1937–39), 216th Infantry Replacement Regiment (1939), and 74th Infantry Regiment (1939–40), before assuming command of the 19th Rifle Brigade (1940–42), and later the 19th Panzer Division (1942–43). On August 7, 1943, he led a sizable portion of his command into a Soviet ambush near Beresowka. Schmidt himself was among those killed in action. Seemen (p. 33) and Angolia (Vol. 2: 181) state that Schmidt committed suicide. This was quite possibly his reaction following the Berosowka disaster. Angolia further states that he did so after he was captured. Schmidt held the Knight's Cross with Oak Leaves.

Hans Kaellner (b. 1893) joined the army as a Fahnenjunker in 1915 and was commissioned in the infantry in 1917. Not selected for retention in the Reichsheer, he served in the police from 1920 to 1935, when he returned to active duty as a captain of cavalry. He commanded II/4th Cavalry Regiment (1937–39), 11th Panzer Reconnaissance Battalion (1939–41), 73rd Panzer Grenadier Regiment (1941–42), 19th Panzer Grenadier Brigade (1942–43), and 19th Panzer. Kaellner was only promoted to colonel on March 1, 1942. He was elevated to major general on November 1, 1943, and to lieutenant general on June 1, 1944. On March 22, 1945, he was named acting commander of XXIV Panzer Corps. A few weeks later, on April 18, he was killed in action near Sokolnica, Czechoslovakia. General Kaellner held the Knight's Cross with Oak Leaves and Swords.

Walter Denkert (b. 1897) entered the service as a war volunteer in 1914. He received a reserve commission in the 23rd (Landwehr) Infantry Regiment in 1915 and was discharged from the army in 1919. A Hamburg policeman for the next 16 years, Denkert rejoined the army as a major in 1935. He successively commanded 13/65th Infantry Regiment (1935–38), 52nd Machine Gun Battalion (1938–39), and II/27th Infantry Regiment (1939–40), was on the staff of OKH (1941), and commanded 47th Infantry Regiment (1941) and 8th Infantry Regiment (1941–42). Apparently seriously wounded in September 1942, Denkert held no further appointments until March 1944, when he became acting commander of the 6th Panzer Division. Later he briefly commanded the 19th Panzer (1944) before being given command of the 3rd Panzer Grenadier Division in October 1944. He was promoted to lieutenant general on April 20, 1945. He died in Kiel, the city of his birth, in 1982.

Hans-Joachim Deckert (b. 1904), a Thuringian, joined the army as an officer cadet in 1924 and was commissioned in the 4th Artillery Regiment in 1928. He rose rapidly, serving as a battery officer, a battalion adjutant, commander of a forward observer company (1936–37), serving on the staff of the artillery school at Juterbog (1937–40), on the staff of Harko 302 (1940), as commander of a forward observer battalion (1940–42), on the staff of the artillery school again (1942–43), and as commander of the II/76th Panzer Artillery Regiment (1943), commander of the 76th Panzer Artillery Regiment (1943–44), acting commander of the 15th Panzer Grenadier Division (1944–45), and commander of the 19th Panzer (1945). Released from Soviet captivity in 1955, he died at Bielefeld on March 5, 1988.

## NOTES AND SOURCES

The 19th Rifle Brigade was redesignated 19th Panzer Grenadier Brigade on July 13, 1942. Later, on November 6, 1942, it was taken away from the division and used as a special staff under HQ, 4th Army. In June 1944 it became Staff, 1st Ski Jaeger Division.

Hanover was the home station of the divisional staff, the 73rd Rifle Regiment, and the 19th Artillery Regiment. The 27th Panzer Regiment (Staff and I Battalion) was based at Paderborn, Wehrkreis VI, while the II Battalion's home station was Erlangen (Wehrkreis XIII), and III Battalion was garrisoned at Nauruppin, Wehrkreis III. The 74th Rifle Regiment's base was Hameln and the 19th Motorcycle's peacetime station at Celle.

Angolia, *Field*, Volume 2: 181–82; Benoist-Mechin: 133; Bradley et al., Volume 3: 44–45, 77–79; Carell 1966: 67, 151; Carell 1971: 39, 66; Keilig: 51–52, 66, 68, 161, 175, 304, 318; Kennedy: 74, Map 7; Otto von Knobelsdorff, *Geschichte der niedersaechsischen 19. Panzer-Division* (Bad Nauheim, 1958): 1 ff.; Manstein: 397; Mellenthin 1977: 208; Mehner, Volume 4: 383; Seemen: 33; Tessin, Volume 6: 114–19, 253; RA: 1–72; OB 42: 61; OB 43: 206; OB 44: 286; OB 45: 297; Windrow: 10; Ziemke: 340.

# 20th Panzer Division

**COMPOSITION (1943):** 21st Panzer Regiment, 59th Panzer Grenadier Regiment, 112th Panzer Grenadier Regiment, 92nd Panzer Artillery Regiment, 20th Motorcycle Battalion, 20th Panzer Reconnaissance Battalion, 92nd Tank Destroyer Battalion, 92nd Panzer Engineer Battalion, 92nd Panzer Signal Battalion.

**HOME STATION:** Jena, Wehrkreis IX

Formed at Erfurt on October 5, 1940, when Hitler weakened the existing panzer divisions, the Hessian 20th Panzer received the 59th Motorized Infantry Regiment from the 19th Infantry Division. Its 112th Rifle Regiment drew one of its two battalions from the 59th Infantry Regiment, both of the 19th Infantry Division. The 20th Motorcycle Battalion was the former II/115th Motorized Infantry Regiment, 33rd Infantry Division; the newly formed 21st Panzer Regiment drew its troops from the 7th and 35th Panzer Replacement Battalions at Vaihingen (Wehrkreis V) and Bamberg (Wehrkreis XIII) respectively; and the 92nd Panzer Artillery Regiment drew one battalion from the 19th Artillery Regiment. The 92nd also absorbed the III/697th Artillery Regiment and the 648th Heavy Artillery Battalion to form its II and III Battalions, respectively. The Staff, 20th Rifle Brigade also joined the division. By winter, its composition was: 21st Panzer Regiment (three battalions); 20th Rifle Brigade (59th and 112th Rifle Regiments [two battalions each] and the 20th Motorcycle Battalion); 92nd Artillery Regiment (three battalions); 20th Reconnaissance Battalion; 92nd Tank Destroyer Battalion; 92nd Engineer Battalion; 92nd Signal Battalion; and assorted divisional troops.

The 20th Panzer Division first saw action on the central sector of the Eastern

Front, took part in the Minsk encirclement, stormed Ulla on July 17, took Vitebsk by coup de main (July 10), fought in the encirclement of Smolensk, checked several Soviet attacks aimed at relieving the pocket, and penetrated to the western Dvina. In September, it fought in the indecisive Battle of Vyasma, east of Smolensk, while the bulk of the panzer divisions encircled Kiev. Later that year it crossed the Istya and the Nara, routed a Soviet brigade, and established a bridgehead for the drive on Moscow. It was halted less than 60 miles from the Soviet capital. It faced the full fury of Stalin's winter offensive in December 1941 and narrowly avoided encirclement a number of times. By early February 1942 it had been pushed back to positions east of Desna-Oka, which it held against repeated attacks. In March, when the spring thaw halted all operations, the division was pulled back to Bryansk, to rest, refit, and reorganize.

Because of its high casualties, the I and II Battalions of the 21st Panzer Regiment, the II/112th Rifle Regiment, and the 20th Motorcycle Battalion were all dissolved and their survivors were absorbed by other units in the division; III/21st Panzer Regiment was redesignated 21st Panzer Battalion; and the 21st Panzer Regiment Staff became Staff, 21st Panzer Brigade, even though it only controlled one remaining tank battalion. (The panzer brigade headquarters was sent to Norway in 1943 to form Staff, Panzer Division Norway; and the Staff, 20th Rifle Brigade was taken from the division in March 1943 to form HQ, 20th Bicycle Brigade.) Meanwhile, the 20th Panzer Division remained on the central front from 1942 to 1944, taking part in the defensive battles of 1942 (mainly around Orel), in the preemptive strike against the Soviet 13th Army at Livny (which the 20th Panzer captured on May 10, 1942), and in the capture of Voronezh in mid-July. In early 1943 the division was embroiled in heavy fighting south of Orel, where it checked a major Soviet advance. Later, the division fought in the Kursk offensive (northern sector), and in the battles around Gshatsk, Orel, Toropez, Bryansk, Vitebsk, Nevel, Bobruisk, and Kholm. In June 1944 it was encircled by the massive Soviet offensive and had to fight its way out, with ruinous losses.

Transferred to Army Group South Ukraine (a supposedly quiet sector), the 20th Panzer again suffered heavy casualties when the Romanians defected and the front collapsed. In November 1944 the division (or what was left of it) was in East Prussia, and the following month it was transferred to the Hungarian sector. After pulling back to Austria, the division was sent to Silesia, where it took part in the battles around Breslau, Schweidnitz, and Neisse. It was overrun by the Red Army near Goerlitz in April 1945 and pushed into Bohemia, where it ended the war in the pocket east of Prague in May 1945.

Divisional commanders of the 20th Panzer included Major General/Lieutenant General Horst Stumpff (November 13, 1940), Colonel Georg von Bismarck (September 10, 1941), Major General Ritter Wilhelm von Thoma (October 10, 1941), Major General Walter Duevert (July 1, 1942), Colonel/Major General/ Lieutenant General Baron Heinrich von Luettwitz (October 10, 1942), Lieutenant General Mortimer von Kessel (December 12, 1943), and Colonel/Major

General Hermann von Oppeln-Bronikowski (November 6, 1944). Thoma gave up command of the division on or about May 25, 1942. The acting divisional commander between then and July 1 is not listed in the appropriate records.


## COMMANDERS

Horst Stumpff (1887–1958) joined the army as a Fahnenjunker in 1907. A relatively early convert to the panzer arm, he assumed command of the 3rd Panzer Brigade on New Year's Day, 1938. Later he commanded the 3rd Panzer Division (1939–40) and 20th Panzer Division (1940–41). His health apparently failed in the Russian winter, as his troops drove on Moscow, short-circuiting a promising career. He gave up command of the division on October 14, 1941, and, after six months, returned to duty as an inspector of Recruiting Area Koenigsberg in East Prussia. In 1944 he became General Inspector of Panzer Troops in the Home Army. He was promoted to lieutenant general on February 1, 1941, and to general of panzer troops on November 9, 1944.

For a sketch of the career of Georg von Bismarck, see 21st Panzer Division.

Ritter Wilhelm von Thoma was born in Dachau in 1891 and entered the army as an infantry Fahnenjunker in 1912. He distinguished himself in World War I, winning the Bavarian Max Joseph Order and the royal title "Ritter." He served with the Reichsheer, and led the German tank forces in the Spanish Civil War (1936–39), during which he was involved in more than 100 armored combats. Returning to Germany, he commanded the 3rd Panzer Regiment (1939–40), was general of mobile troops at OKH (1940), and commander of the 17th Panzer Brigade (1940–41). He assumed temporary command of the 17th Panzer Division when General Weber was killed. Named commander of the 20th Panzer Division in October, 1941, he returned to OKH as general of mobile troops in May, 1942. He assumed command of the Afrika Korps on September 1, 1942, and was captured by the British on November 4, 1942, at the end of the Battle of El Alamein. Worn out after fighting three wars and being wounded more than 10 times, von Thoma returned to Dachau and died there in 1948. During World War II, he was promoted to major general (August 1, 1940), lieutenant general (August 1, 1942) and general of panzer troops (November 1, 1942).

For an account of Walter Duevert's career, see 13th Panzer Division, Commanders.

For a sketch of Baron Heinrich von Luettwitz' career, see 2nd Panzer Division, Commanders.

Mortimer von Kessel (b. 1893) joined the Imperial Army as a Fahnenjunker in August 1914 and was commissioned in the 12th Hussars Regiment the following year. During the Hitler era, he commanded the 8th Reconnaissance Battalion (1938–39), was a department chief in the Army Personnel Office (1939–43), commanded the 20th Panzer Division (1943–44), and ended the war commanding the VII Panzer Corps (late 1944–45). He was promoted to lieutenant general on December 1, 1943, and to general of panzer troops on March 1, 1945. He died in Goslar in 1981.

Born in Berlin in 1899, Hermann von Oppeln-Bronikowski was an excellent panzer leader—when he was sober. He joined the 10th Ulam Regiment in 1917 and was commissioned later that year. In the Wehrmacht era he commanded II/10th Cavalry Regiment (1937–39) and the 24th Reconnaissance Battalion (1939–40), was on the staff of the General of Mobile Troops at OKH (late 1940–41), served with Panzer Brigade Eberbach (1941–42), commanded 35th Panzer Regiment (1942) and 204th Panzer Regiment (1942–43), and led 11th Panzer Regiment (1943) and the 100th Panzer Regiment (1943–44) before taking over 20th Panzer Division (October 1944). He was promoted to major general on January 1, 1945. Had it not been for his fondness for alcohol, Oppeln would probably have advanced to much higher rank. He died near Bad Toelz, Bavaria, in 1966.

## NOTES AND SOURCES

The 112nd Rifle Regiment was taken from the division on April 20, 1943, and returned to the Reich, where it formed cadres for Wehrkreis IV's Noncommissioned Officers School and for the 890th Motorized Grenadier Regiment. The 20th Schnelle (Mobile or Rifle) Brigade was taken from the division in May 1944 and became the Staff, 20th Bicycle Brigade.

Carell 1966: 42, 78, 80; Carell 1971: 22, 24, 278, 580; Keilig: 167, 212, 247, 340; Kursietis: 103; Mehner, Volume 3: Seite 7; Volume 5: 330; Volume 6: 546; Stoves, *Gepanzerten*: 138; Tessin, Volume 6: 138–39, 162; Thomas, Volume 1: 359; Volume 2: 132; OB 43: 206–07; OB 44: 286; OB 45: 298; Windrow: 10–11.

# 21st Panzer Division

**COMPOSITION (Africa):** 5th Panzer Regiment, 104th Panzer Grenadier Regiment, 155th Panzer Artillery Regiment, 3rd Reconnaissance Battalion, 39th Tank Destroyer Battalion, 200th Panzer Engineer Battalion, 200th Panzer Signal Battalion.

**HOME STATION:** Berlin, Wehrkreis III

Formed as the 5th Light Division on February 18, 1941, the 21st Panzer received most of its units from the Berlin-Brandenberger 3rd Panzer Division, including the divisional staff (the former Staff, 3rd Panzer Brigade); the 5th Panzer Regiment (two battalions), formerly part of the 3rd Panzer Division; the 3rd Panzer Reconnaissance Battalion; the 39th Tank Destroyer Battalion; and the I/75th Panzer Artillery Regiment. The Staff, 200th Infantry Regiment z.b.V. ("for special purposes") came from Wehrkreis III, while HQ, 155th Panzer Artillery Regiment was a newly formed unit. Its three artillery battalions, which were numbered I, II, and III, were the former 864th Artillery Battalion, I/75th Artillery Regiment, and the 911th Heavy Artillery Battalion, respectively. The other units—the 2nd and 8th Machine Gun Battalions, the 605th Tank Destroyer Battalion and 606th Light Antiaircraft Artillery Battalion—were *Heerestruppe* (i.e., troops given to it on a permanent basis by higher headquarters). Shortly after arriving in the desert, the 8th Machine Gun was converted into the 15th Motorcycle Battalion.

Transported to North Africa in April and May 1941, it (along with the 15th Panzer Division) became one of the two divisions in the famous Afrika Korps. It took part in the capture of Cyrenaica and the drive to the Egyptian frontier (a

157

distance of more than 350 miles!), and the first unsuccessful efforts to take Tobruk (1941). That summer it received the 104th Panzer Grenadier Regiment and a few smaller units from the 15th Panzer Division and was redesignated 21st Panzer. At the same time it handed the 2nd Machine Gun Battalion and HQ, 200th Infantry Regiment over to its sister division. The 21st Panzer Division fought in the Battleaxe and Crusader campaigns (where it lost most of its tanks), the retreat from Cyrenaica in late 1941, and the subsequent counterattack which retook Benghazi. It then again showed its excellent fighting abilities in overrunning the Gazala Line, in the capture of Tobruk, and in the sweep into Egypt. Checked at El Alamein and Alam Halfa Ridge, it was virtually destroyed in the Second Battle of El Alamein in October and November 1942, having only 12 tanks left when the order came to retreat. Withdrawing across Libya, it did not panic and turned to help administer the U.S. Army a notable defeat at Kasserine Pass. One of the best divisions in the German Army, it was not destroyed until its supply lines collapsed completely and all of its ammunition was expended; in fact, it went into its last battle using Tunisian wine for fuel! The 21st Panzer finally surrendered when Tunisia fell in May 1943.

The original 21st Panzer Division underwent a number of organizational changes in its legendary career. The I/104th Rifle Regiment was destroyed at Halfaya Pass in January 1942, so the 15th Motorcycle Battalion was converted into a motorized infantry battalion and was redesignated III/104th Rifle. In 1943, the 609th Light Anti-aircraft (Flak) Battalion was absorbed into the artillery regiment as IV/155th Panzer Artillery Regiment, and the division received the 305th Army Flak Battalion from the Reich.

The division's final reorganization occurred on February 26, 1943, when it gave up the 3rd Panzer Recon Battalion to the 90th Light Division and received the 580th Panzer Reconnaissance in exchange. It also received the 220th Panzer Engineer Battalion from the 164th Light Afrika Division and redesignated it the 200th. The 190th Panzer Battalion of the 90th Light Division was also incorporated into the division as II/5th Panzer Battalion. In April 1943, the 580th Recon became the 21st Panzer Reconnaissance Battalion. As of February 26, 1943, the division consisted of: 5th Panzer Regiment (two battalions), 104th and 47th Panzer Grenadier Regiments (two battalions each), 155th Panzer Artillery Regiment (three battalions), 580th Panzer Reconnaissance Battalion, 39th Tank Destroyer Battalion, 220th (formerly 200th) Panzer Engineer Battalion, and 200th Panzer Signal Battalion.

A second 21st Panzer Division was formed in Rennes, France, in May 1943 from the 931st Mobile Brigade—a bicycle unit. Initially it was designated Mobile Division West, but was renamed 21st Panzer Division on July 15. The new tank division's home station was Wuppertal, Wehrkreis VI, and it included the 100th Panzer Regiment, 125th and 192nd Panzer Grenadier Regiments, 155th Panzer Artillery Regiment, 21st Panzer Recon Battalion, 220th Panzer Engineer Battalion, 200th Tank Destroyer Battalion, 200th Panzer Signal Battalion, and the 305th Army Flak Artillery Battalion. Its troops and units came from a variety of sources. The headquarters staff and the 125th Panzer Grenadier Regiment were from Mobile Brigade West. The 1st and 2nd companies of the recon battalion came from the 931st Motorcycle Company and most of the rest of the battalion came from the Panzer Lehr (Demonstration) Reconnaissance Battalion. The two-battalion panzer regiment drew its men and equipment from the 223rd Panzer Battalion, Panzer Company Paris, and the Panzer Company, LXXXI Corps, all of which were equipped with obsolete French tanks. Most of the artillery regiment came from the 931st Artillery Regiment, while the 192nd Panzer Grenadier Regiment and the 305th Flak Battalion were newly formed. The division included a number of Afrika Korps veterans but was equipped with unreliable light tanks, mostly of foreign (Czech and French) manufacture. It was the only panzer division in France to be rated as unfit for service on the Eastern Front and—although it performed fairly well—the 21st Panzer Division never approached the quality of its predecessor, nor achieved the reputation of the original.

The new division was sent to Hungary in April 1944, when it seemed the Eastern Front was on the verge of collapse, but it was hurried back to France in May and was stationed in the Normandy sector, where Field Marshal Rommel suspected the Allies might land. It was the only panzer division to counterattack the Allies on D-Day, although it struck hours later than it should have and was largely ineffective. More than 50 of its fourth-rate tanks were destroyed by the British, while inflicting little damage on them. One battalion was practically destroyed by British tanks before it could even get within range of the enemy tanks. Although its panzer regiment was smashed, its grenadiers fought doggedly in front of Caen for weeks and played a major role in checking Operation Goodwood, Montgomery's attempt to break the stalemate around Caen (July 18–22). At battle group strength, the 21st Panzer nevertheless saved the 326th Infantry Division from being overrun by the British in late July. It was surrounded in the Falaise Pocket and had to break out, suffering very heavy losses in the process.

When the Normandy campaign began on June 6, 1944, the 21st Panzer Division had 12,350 men, 127 tanks, and 40 assault guns. When it finally retreated across the Seine at the end of August, it had lost all of its armored vehicles and assault guns, and all but 300 of its men. (Some were in hospitals or otherwise later made their way back to the unit.) After the retreat through France, it was pulled out of the line and hastily rebuilt, using poor-quality troops from the 16th Luftwaffe Field Division (which had already been placed under the operational control of the 21st). Sent back to Lothringen, it absorbed the 112th Panzer Brigade (2112th Panzer Battalion and 2112th Panzer Grenadier Regiment), and its tank regiment was redesignated 22nd Panzer. With higher quality tanks but with lower quality infantry, the division was assigned to Army Group G, where it served as a "fire brigade" on the southern sector of the Western Front. It fought in the Saar in late 1944 and in January 1945 the 21st was involved on the drive on Strasbourg and in the fighting in the northern Alsace, before being sent to the Eastern Front in February. By this time, it had only one tank battalion left. The 21st fought in the unsuccessful defenses of Lauban, Goerlitz, and Cottbus, and ended the war in the Halbe Pocket near Berlin, where the bulk of the 9th Army was destroyed. Virtually all of its survivors ended up in Soviet captivity.

Commanders of the 5th Light/21st Panzer included Major General Baron Hans von Funck (assumed command January 1, 1941), Major General Karl Boettcher (February 1, 1941), Lieutenant General Johannes Streich (February 7, 1941), Major General Heinrich Kirchheim (May 16, 1941), Major General Baron Johann von Ravenstein (May 20, 1941), Colonel Gustav-Georg Knabe (November 29, 1941), Boettcher again (December 1, 1941), Colonel Alfred Bruer (February 9, 1942), Colonel/Major General Georg von Bismarck (February 11, 1942), Colonel Baron Kurt von Liebenstein (September 1, 1942), Major General Heinz von Randow (September 18, 1942), Colonel/Major General Hans Georg Hildebrandt (January 1, 1943), Colonel/Major General Heinrich-Hermann von Huelsen (March 15, 1943), Major General/Lieutenant General Edgar Feuchtinger (July 15, 1943), Major General Oswin Grolig (January 15, 1944), Major General Franz Westhoven (March 8, 1944), Feuchtinger (returned May 8, 1944), Colonel Helmuth Zollenkopf (December 25, 1944), and Major General/Lieutenant General Werner Marcks (January 10, 1945).

## COMMANDERS

For an overview of Hans von Funck's career, see Commanders, 7th Panzer Division.

Johannes Streich (b. 1891) and General Erwin Rommel had a mutual distaste for one another, which led to Rommel's relieving Streich of his command for his failure to take Tobruk in May 1941. Streich later commanded a battle group and then the 16th Infantry Division in Russia (1941), again without distinction. Heinz Guderian also had a low opinion of his abilities. Streich was named inspector of mobile troops in 1942 but was transferred out of the mobile branch altogether when Guderian took over the Panzer Inspectorate in 1943. Streich's friends in the Home Army secured his promotion to lieutenant general in late 1943 and he was appointed inspector of Recruiting Area Breslau. In April 1945 he became inspector of Recruiting Area Berlin, but got out of the city ahead of the Russians. Streich, who was born in Holstein, began his military career in a railroad engineering regiment in 1911. He commanded the 15th Panzer Regiment (1935–41) and 5th Panzer Brigade (1941) before assuming command of the 5th Light.

Heinrich Kirchheim (b. 1882) entered the service as a Fahnenjunker in the infantry in 1899. He distinguished himself in World War I, earning the Pour le Mérite, and retired from the Reichsheer as a colonel in 1932, only to be recalled to active duty in 1936 as commander of the Cologne recruiting district. He later commanded Recruiting District Vienna I (1938–39), the 276th Infantry Regiment (1939), and the 169th Infantry Division (1939–41). He was promoted to major general in 1939. Considered an expert on tropical warfare, he was sent to Libya as head of an advisory staff in early 1941, but soon clashed with Erwin Rommel, the "Desert Fox." After Rommel relieved General Streich of the command of the 5th Light Division, he reluctantly replaced him with Kirchheim, the senior officer available. Kirchheim's performance during the Siege of Tobruk did not please him either, so he fired Kirchheim as well. This did Kirchheim's career little harm, as Rommel was feuding with General Halder and OKH at the time. Kirchheim was promoted to lieutenant general in 1942 and directed special staffs at OKH from 1941 until October 15, 1944, when he was placed in charge of the Berlin Recruiting District. Kirchheim retired for a second time at the end of March, 1945, as the Russians approached Berlin. He settled in Luedenscheid after the war. He died in late 1973.

Albert Bruer (1897–1976) was commander of the 155th Panzer Artillery Regiment (1941–43), and was the senior regimental commander of the division.

Johann von Ravenstein (b. 1889 in Silesia) was a much more capable and aggressive officer than Streich and acquired a reputation second only to Rommel's in North Africa in 1941. He began his career as a lieutenant in the 7th Grenadier Regiment in 1907 and earned the Pour le Mérite in World War I, but was discharged (apparently at his own request) as a major in 1920. Resuming his military career in 1934, he led the 4th Rifle Regiment (1938–40) and the 16th Rifle Brigade (1940–41) before replacing Streich as commander of the 21st Panzer. He was promoted to major general on May 20, 1941, and was captured by the New Zealanders on November 28, 1941, during the Crusader battles. He was promoted to lieutenant general while in captivity (1943) and settled in Duisburg after the war, where he became a highly successful businessman. He died in 1962.

As a lieutenant colonel, Gustav-Georg Knabe (1897–1972) commanded the 15th Motorcycle Battalion of the 15th Panzer Division (1941). He later commanded the 104th Panzer Grenadier Regiment.

Karl Boettcher (1889–1975) was an artillery officer most of his career, which began as an officer cadet in 1910. He commanded Arko 104 (104th Artillery Command—Rommel's Panzer Army Artillery) from 1939 until General von Ravenstein was captured; then he took charge of 21st Panzer Division as acting commander—largely because he was the only general available. He did a good job in this position, under the circumstances. In February 1942 (when Colonel von Bismarck arrived in Libya), Boettcher went into Fuehrer Reserve because his health did not stand up to the rigors of the harsh Sahara Desert. Upon recovery he commanded the 345th Infantry Division (November 1942–February 1943), served on the staff of Army Group D in France (1943), and commanded the 326th Infantry Division (1943), the 347th Infantry Division (1943), and Harko 305 (1944–45). He ended the war as General of Artillery "for Special Purposes" Number 4—a divisional level post. He was promoted to lieutenant general in 1942. He died in Kiel in 1975.

Georg von Bismarck (b. 1891) was promoted to major general on March 1, 1942. He distinguished himself in the capture of Tobruk (June 1942). He was killed near Alma Halfa Ridge on September 1, 1942. Bismarck's military career began in 1910 when he joined the 6th Jaeger (light infantry) Battalion as a Fahnenjunker. He commanded the 7th Cavalry Rifle (later Rifle) Regiment (1938–40) and the 20th Rifle Brigade (1940–41) before Rommel (his former division commander in France) arranged for his transfer to Panzer Army Afrika. An armored commander of the first order, Bismarck was posthumously promoted to lieutenant general.

Baron Kurt von Liebenstein was born in Jebenhausen in 1899 and joined the army as a Fahnenjunker in the cavalry in 1916. He was a lieutenant colonel on the OKH staff when the war began. Liebenstein served as Ia of the 10th Panzer Division (1940–41), chief of staff of the 2nd Panzer Army (1941–42), and commander of the 6th Panzer Regiment (1942). After giving up command of the 21st Panzer, Liebenstein assumed command of the 164th Light Afrika Division on December 19, 1942, and led it brilliantly during Rommel's retreat from Egypt and in the Tunisian campaign. Promoted to major general on March 1, 1943, he surrendered his division to the British on May 12, 1943. After the war, Liebenstein became a major general in the West German Army.

Major General Heinz von Randow (b. 1890) was killed in action on December 12, 1942, and, like Neumann-Silkow, was posthumously promoted to lieutenant general. A cavalry officer since he entered the service in 1910, he had commanded the 13th Cavalry Regiment (1937–39), the 1st Cavalry Brigade (1939), the 26th Infantry Regiment (late 1939–41), 2nd Rifle Brigade (1941–42), 17th Rifle Brigade (1942), and 15th Panzer Division (1942).

After being educated at various cadet schools, Hans-Georg Hildebrandt (b. 1896) entered the service as a senior officer cadet (Faehnrich) in the 36th Fusiliers in 1914. Remaining in the Reichsheer after World War I, he was Ia of the XIV Motorized (later Panzer) Corps (1938–40), chief of staff of XXXIX Panzer Corps (1940–42), and commander of the 21st Panzer Division (1943). He was promoted to major general on March 1, 1943. Escaping the Tunisian disaster at the last minute, he was placed in charge of a special missions staff at OKH in August, 1943. Hildebrandt was given command of the 715th Infantry Division in Italy in early 1944 and later headed the German advisory staff to Mussolini's 3rd Italian Infantry Division "San Marco". Hildebrandt was a mediocre divisional commander at best and his performance as commander of the 21st Panzer left much to be desired. He was nevertheless promoted to lieutenant general in 1944. He settled in Frankfurt am Main after the war and died there on January 31, 1967.

Heinrich-Hermann von Huelsen (b. 1895) joined the 4th Guards Regiment of Foot as a lieutenant in 1914. He served in the Reichswehr and commanded the 11th Cavalry Regiment (1938–39), was on the staff of the 11th Army (1939–41), and commanded the 2nd Cavalry Regiment (1941–42) and the 9th Rifle Brigade (1942) before joining the staff of Panzer Army Afrika in 1942. He was an acting commander only. Shortly before Army Group Afrika surrendered, von Huelsen was promoted to major general, effective May 1, 1943. He surrendered the remnants of the 21st Panzer Division to the Allies on May 12, 1943. A native of Weimar, he lived in Kassel after the war.

Edgar Feuchlinger (1894–1960), who helped with the Nazi Party's Nuremberg rallies prior to the start of the war, was a favorite of Adolf Hitler and his cronies. He served in the artillery most of his career (which began in 1914) and commanded a horse-drawn artillery regiment in France (1940) and on the Eastern Front in 1941–42. He worked with the Fuehrer's secret weapons program before assuming command of the 21st Panzer. A poor field commander and a corrupt one, he was nevertheless promoted to major general on August 1, 1943, and to lieutenant general exactly one year later. He had to be fetched out of a Paris nightclub on the night of June 5–6, 1944, to be informed that Allied paratroopers and glider-borne forces were landing in his area of operations. He was relieved of his command and arrested for being away without leave at Christmas 1944, when it was discovered that he went home without permission while his men were battling the Americans on the Western Front. Demoted to private and sentenced to death, Feuchlinger was only saved from execution because of his Nazi Party connections. He lived in Krefeld after the war and died on a trip to Berlin in 1960.

Colonel Helmuth Zollenkopf had previously commanded the 114th Panzer Grenadier Regiment (1942).

Werner Marcks (born in Magdeburg in 1896) was promoted to lieutenant general on April 20, 1945. He was a hard-boiled Nazi sympathizer and a brutal leader. Captured by the Soviets, he remained in Russian prisons until 1955. Marcks joined the infantry as a Fahnenjunker in 1914 and served in the Reichsheer. He commanded the 19th Antitank Battalion (1937–41), 115th Rifle Regiment (1941–42), and 155th Rifle/Panzer Grenadier Regiment (1942). On the staff of the Panzer Troops Inspectorate (1942–44), he later commanded 1st Panzer Division (1944) and 21st Panzer (1945). He died in 1967.

For a sketch of the careers of Generals Grolig and Westhoven, see 25th and 3rd Panzer Divisions, Commanders, respectively.

## NOTES AND SOURCES

Blumenson 1960: 324; Bradley et al., Volume 1: 417–18; Volume 2: 99–101; Volume 3: 457–58; Volume 5: 427–28; Chant 1979, Volume 17: 2277; Cole 1950: 553; Carlo D'Este, *Decision in Normandy* (New York, 1983): 140, 475n (hereafter cited as "D'Este, *Normandy*"); Hartmann: 66–67; Keilig: 35–36, 141, 217, 267, 269, 337; Mehner, Volume 4: 383; Volume 5: 330; Volume 6: 546; Volume 7: 354, 359; Scheibert: 419; Schmitz et al., Volume 3: 185; Tessin, Volume 2: 294–95; Thomas, Volume 2: 59; OB 45: 298; Windrow: 11.

# 22nd Panzer Division

**COMPOSITION:** 204th Panzer Regiment, 129th Panzer Grenadier Regiment, 140th Panzer Grenadier Regiment, 140th Panzer Artillery Regiment, 24th Motorcycle Battalion, 140th Tank Destroyer Battalion, 50th Panzer Engineer Battalion, 140th Panzer Signal Battalion.

**HOME STATION:** Schwetzingen, later Neustadt and Heidelberg, Wehrkreis XII

The 22nd Panzer Division, which was composed mainly of Rhinelanders and Austrians, formed in France in the summer of 1941 and was officially activated on September 25, 1941. It consisted of the 22nd Rifle Brigade (129th and 140th Rifle Regiments and the 24th Motorcycle Battalion), the 204th Panzer Regiment (two battalions), and the 140th Panzer Artillery Regiment, whose three battalions were the former III/337th Artillery Regiment, II/44th Artillery Regiment, and IV/227th Artillery Regiment, respectively. The divisional also had the 22nd Reconnaissance, 140th Tank Destroyer, 50th Engineer, and 140th Signal Battalions, as well as the standard divisional service support units. The panzer regiment came from the independent 100th Panzer Brigade; the 129th Rifle was formed from elements of the 2nd Panzer Division; and the 24th Motorcycle Battalion was formed in Wehrkreis XVII and was made up of Austrians. Both of its rifle regiments had two battalions each. The 204th Panzer Regiment was given a third battalion in 1942, and the 289th Army Flak Artillery Battalion was added to the division that same year. The new division was equipped largely with captured foreign material. The 204th Panzer Regiment, for example, was outfitted mainly with French tanks, Czech-made Skoda 38 (t)s, and obsolete

German-manufactured PzKw IIs and IVs. Some PzKw IIIs were added later. The flak battalion was much better equipped than the rest of the division and included self-propelled 88mm guns and other motorized batteries.

Initially under the command of the 7th Army, the new division was sent to the Crimea on the Eastern Front in February 1942, and was mauled in the Battle of Parpach on March 20. Two months later, however, it performed much better, breaking through the Soviet forces on the Kerch peninsula and quickly sealing the fate of ten Red Army divisions. Transferred north of the Sea of Azov that spring, it fought in the Donets, pushed its way across the Don, and fought at Rostov in July. As of June 15, it had 95 tanks, 63 of which were PzKw 38 (t)s. After the fall of Rostov, the 22nd Panzer Division was transferred to the north, where it operated under the command of Army Group B. It was used to support the Italian 8th Army that fall, and was then moved behind the Romanian 3rd Army. Its armored fighting vehicle strength at this time (August 1942) was at 51 percent, and it had about 80 operational tanks. These included 10 obsolete PzKw IIs, 50 Czech-made Skoda 38 (t)s, 10 PzKw III command vehicles, and only 10 PzKw IVs. Its support and supply units were at 70 percent strength.

In November 1942, the Soviets routed the Romanians, and the 22nd Panzer—operating almost alone—attempted unsuccessfully to prevent the encirclement of the 6th Army. It suffered heavy losses against the overwhelming Soviet onslaught; in the end, the 22nd Panzer Division only barely managed to escape encirclement itself. Casualties were so high in the I/129th Panzer Grenadier Regiment, for example, that command devolved onto a first lieutenant. By December 1942, as it retreated back across on the Chir (a tributary of the Don), the 22nd was a Kampfgruppe. It had perhaps half of its tanks left, and most of these were not up to standards mechanically; in fact, Field Marshal Erich von Manstein, the commander in chief of Army Group Don, called the division "a complete wreck." (During the fall of 1942, when it was placed in reserve behind the 6th Army, its men had used straw to keep the tanks warm. Mice had nested in the straw and had eaten the insulation off the wiring.)

It was on Manstein's recommendation that the 22nd Panzer was ordered to disband on March 3, 1943, after it fought on the Mius and the Donets. It had only 31 tanks left by this time and was commanded by a major. The dissolution was completed on April 7. Part of the division—Group Michalik—had been attached to the 2nd Army in early September 1942. This unit, which included the 140th Panzer Grenadier Regiment, III/204th Panzer Regiment, and I/140th Panzer Artillery Regiment, was incorporated into the 27th Panzer Division in 1943. Most of the rest of the division was absorbed by the 6th Panzer Division or the 23rd Panzer Division. The staff of the I/129th Panzer Grenadier Regiment was used to form the staff of Field Lehr (Demonstration) Battalion of the 23rd Panzer Division; the staff of the 204th Panzer Regiment became Headquarters, 504th Panzer Battalion, and the staff of the 140th Panzer Artillery Regiment became Staff, 732nd Army Artillery Brigade. The III/140th Panzer Artillery Regiment became I/959th Army Artillery Brigade.

Commanders of the division included Major General Wilhelm von Apell (assumed command, September 25, 1941), Colonel Rudolf Kuett (October 1, 1942), Colonel Hellmut von der Chevallerie (October 7, 1942), Kuett again (November 1, 1942), Colonel/Major General Eberhard Rodt (November 8, 1942), and Major Hugo Burgsthaler (March 4, 1943).

## COMMANDERS

Wilhelm von Apell (b. 1892) joined the army as an officer cadet in the light infantry in 1910. After serving in World War I and the Reichsheer, he commanded the 11th Cavalry Rifle Regiment (1938–40) and the 9th Rifle Brigade (1941–42) before taking charge of the 22nd Panzer Division. He fell ill at the end of July 1942 and was temporarily replaced by von der Chevallerie. Not considered a successful divisional commander, he was placed in Fuehrer Reserve in October 1942 and was not reemployed until mid March of the following year, when he became Army Replacement Inspector for Vienna. He was promoted to lieutenant general in 1943 but never again held an important command. General von Apell died in Varnholt (near Baden-Baden) on March 7, 1969.

Rudolf Kuett (1896–1949) joined the Bavarian 17th Infantry Regiment in 1915 and was commissioned the following year. He served in the Reichsheer and was on the staff of OKH (1937–40). He later commanded the 8th Motorcycle Battalion (1941), the 129th Rifle Regiment (1942), and the 22nd Panzer Grenadier Brigade (1942), before becoming acting commander of the 22nd Panzer Division. He returned to brigade command after Rodt assumed command of the division, but was without a post when the 22nd Brigade was dissolved. Unemployed for six months, he was named chief of staff of Wehrkreis XI on April 1, 1943, and held the post until the end of the war. He was promoted to major general on December 1, 1943.

Eberhard Rodt (b. 1895) was a native of Munich. He joined the Bavarian 2nd Ulam Regiment as a war volunteer in 1914 and was commissioned the following year. He served in the Reichsheer and later commanded I/18th Cavalry Regiment (1936–39), 7th Cavalry Regiment (1939), 25th Reconnaissance Battalion (1939–40), 66th Panzer Grenadier Regiment (1942), and 22nd Panzer Division (1942–43). Sent to Italy to recuperate with the remnants of his staff, Rodt was promoted to major general on March 1, 1943. Despite the fact that he had basically failed as a panzer division commander in Russia, Rodt was charged with forming the 15th Panzer Grenadier Division in Sicily out of the survivors of the 15th Panzer Division of the Afrika Korps plus assorted miscellaneous units; he was thus, in effect, given a second chance professionally. Rodt took full advantage of this opportunity by performing brilliantly as a divisional commander in Sicily, Italy, and on the Western Front, and fully justified the confidence his superiors had in him, despite his previous failure in the East. He was promoted to lieutenant general in 1944 and led the 15th Panzer Grenadier until mid-January 1945, when the was wounded by an Allied fighter-bomber. He was still recovering at the end of the war. He died in Munich in late 1971.

Hugo Burgsthaler, Ia of the 22nd Panzer Division, was commander of Kampf-gruppe 22nd Panzer Division during the final stages of its existence. Burgsthaler was later promoted to lieutenant colonel and was named Ia of Panzer Group West, which attempted to hurl the D-Day invasion back into the sea. He was killed by an Allied bombing attack in Normandy on June 9, 1944. He had previously commanded II/204th Panzer Regiment.

For a sketch of Hellmut von der Chevallerie's career, see 273rd Reserve Panzer Division.

## NOTES AND SOURCES

The division's Ia in the summer of 1942 was Major Hans-Georg von Tempelhoff, who was later Ia of Army Group West during the Normandy campaign and the Battle of the Bulge.

Bradley et al., Volume 1: 81–82; Volume 2: 423–24; Carell 1966: 482, 486, 535, 620–21, 650; Keilig: 12, 192; Kursietis: 105; Manstein: 322, 389; Mehner, Volume 5: 330; Volume 6: 546; Samuel W. Mitcham Jr. and Friedrich von Stauffenberg, *The Battle of Sicily* (New York, 1991); Scheibert: 63; Rolf Stoves, *Die 22. Panzer-Division, 25. Panzer-Division, 27th Panzer-Division und 233. Reserve Panzer-Division* (Friedberg, 1985): 10–125 (hereafter cited as "Stoves, *Die 22. Panzer-Division*"); Tessin, Volume 6: 179–80; OB 42: 62; OB 45: 207, 299.

# 23rd Panzer Division

**COMPOSITION:** 201st Panzer Regiment, 126th Panzer Grenadier Regiment, 128th Panzer Grenadier Regiment, 128th Panzer Artillery Regiment, 128th Motorcycle Battalion, 128th Panzer Reconnaissance Battalion, 128th Tank Destroyer Battalion, 128th Panzer Engineer Battalion, 128th Panzer Signal Battalion.

**HOME STATION:** Ludwigsburg (later Reutlingen), Wehrkreis V

The 23rd Panzer Division began forming in the area around Paris, France. Activated on September 21, 1941, it absorbed Colonel Wolfgang Elster's 101st Panzer Brigade (203rd and 204th *Beute* Panzer Regiments) of the 1st Army. (A "Beute-Panzer-Regiment" was one outfitted almost solely with captured foreign weapons and equipment.) The new division consisted mainly of Wuerttemburgers and included the 23rd Rifle Brigade (126th and 128th Rifle Regiments [two battalions each] and the 23rd Motorcycle [later Reconnaissance] Battalion), the 201st Panzer Regiment (three battalions), the 128th Panzer Artillery Regiment (formed from the III Battalions of the 335th, 847th, and 863rd Artillery Regiments), the 128th Tank Destroyer Battalion, the 51st Panzer Engineer Battalion, and the 128th Signal Battalion. The following year the division was also given the 278th Army Flak Artillery Battalion. The 201st Panzer Regiment was redesignated 23rd Panzer Regiment on August 16, 1943.

The regimental artillery staff had been formed in August 1939 as the Staff, 606th Motorized Artillery Regiment z.b.V. ("for special purposes") and had fought in Poland, France, the Balkans, and Russia as an army-level General Headquarters unit. The 51st Engineer Battalion had been formed in Dessau-

Rosslau in October 1937, and also had considerable combat experience in Poland and the West. Under the command of Lieutenant Colonel Hans Mikosch, it had played a pivotal role in the capture of the Belgian fortress of Eben-Emael in 1940.

The division completed its training in autumn 1941 and the following spring (after being reequipped with German tanks) was sent to the Russian Front, where it fought in the fierce battles around Kharkov in May 1942. It took part in the drive across the Don and on toward the Caucasus, and even managed to push across the Terek River. In the fall of 1942 it was sent north, where it took the Volga, and narrowly escaped encirclement near Stalingrad that November. It took part in the 4th Panzer Army's attempt to relieve the city but was unsuccessful. By January 1943 it was down to 20 tanks—about 10 percent of its original strength. It nevertheless took part in the retreat to the Don (December 12, 1942–February 11, 1943), in the fighting in the eastern Donets (February 14–March 4, 1943), and in the retreat to the Mius (March 5–31, 1943).

During its first year in Russia, the 23rd Panzer Division had lost more than 90 percent of its tank strength. It had, however, destroyed about six or seven times as many Soviet tanks as it lost itself. During the period May 13–22, for example, when it was engaged in defensive fighting near Kharkov, it destroyed 136 enemy tanks. The 128th Tank Destroyer Battalion and I/201st Panzer Regiment (attached to VII Corps and not under divisional control) destroyed 86 more. In the liquidation of the Izyum Pocket southwest of Kharkov, the 23rd Panzer Division accounted for 95 additional Soviet tanks. In the Caucasus campaign (June 28–November 21), the division destroyed 349 Soviet tanks, and in the Stalingrad-Don-Donets-Mius fighting (December 14, 1942–March 17, 1943), the division destroyed 282 enemy tanks, bringing its total to 948.

Placed in the new 6th Army's reserve in the spring of 1943 and sent to the Odessa area to rebuild, the 23rd Panzer received a great many replacements and a considerable amount of new equipment. It was also reorganized, losing its brigade headquarters and III/201st Panzer Regiment in the process. The division was involved in heavy fighting that summer and fall, taking part in the defense of and withdrawal from the Mius and middle Donets (July 4–August 17), in the 2nd Battle of Izyum (August 18–26), and in the Donets Bend withdrawal and the retreat to the Dnieper (September 28–December 31, 1943). At the beginning of 1944, it was involved in the defense of southern Ukraine, including the battle of the Nikopol bridgehead. In February 1944 it was cited for its conduct in the fighting west of the Dnieper, where it was encircled near Krivoy Rog in March. Breaking out with heavy losses, the 23rd Panzer was at battle group strength thereafter.

Used as a fire brigade, it fought in such widely separated places as Krivoy Rog, the Crimea, and Nikopol. At last forced to retreat, the 23rd Panzer fell back to the Bug (March 7–26), and Northern Bessarabia and the Carpathian foothills (March 27–May 12). It fought in the Jassy sector (May 30–June 6, 1944), in the fighting around Krosno (July 30–August 1), and in the defense of the Mielec sector (August 2–18). During this time, the 23rd Panzer Division continued to inflict disproportionately heavy casualties on the Russians. During the Battle of Stepanovka alone (July 19–23, 1943), it destroyed 57 Soviet tanks. In the fighting around Izyum (August 16–September 6, 1943), it destroyed 372 more, and knocked out another 47 in the next two weeks. In the Mischurin Rog bridgehead (October 3–14, 1943), it destroyed a further 21 Russian tanks, and smashed another 188 between October 15 and 31. It also destroyed 109 Soviet tanks at Krivoy Rog and in the retreat to the Bug (November 1, 1943–March 9, 1944). In the fighting around Jassy and west of the Pruth, the battered but veteran Westphalian division knocked out another 74 Red Army tanks (April 1–June 1, 1944).

The 23rd Panzer was sent to Poland in mid-August 1944, and took part in attacking the Soviet bridgehead at Sandomierz, on the western bank of the Vistula. Transferred back to Army Group South a month later (following the disaster in Romania), it led the 8th Army's counterattack on Nyiregyhaza (October 23–29, 1944) and took the town, destroying or causing the abandonment of about 600 Soviet tanks—a major German victory for the fifth year of the war. The 23rd Panzer also took part in the counterattack west of Debrecen and was again cited for distinguished conduct in the defensive battles along the Puszla (October 6–27, 1944). It spent November conducting defensive operations between the middle Theiss and the Danube (Donau), before being switched to the Szekesfehervar sector, which it held until March 1945. A large part of the division was trapped in the medieval town of Szekesfehervar (Stuhlweissenburg), when the 6th Army's front in Hungary collapsed, and was destroyed there. The remnants of the 23rd Panzer Division fought at Lake Balaton (late March 1945), at Keszthely (March 28), and north of Radkersburg. The division was overrun near Graz in the spring of 1945, but were still fighting in the Steiermark sector of Austria when Berlin fell and Hitler committed suicide. The 23rd Panzer Division (along with the I Cavalry Corps, to which it was subordinate at the time) disengaged from the Red Army and surrendered to Major Mountjoy of the British 5th Northampton Regiment at Mauterndorf on May 10. Its strength at the time was 2,000 men—about one-sixth what it was in 1942. Later, the survivors of the 23rd were incarcerated by the U.S. 7th Army.

During its combat career, the 23rd Panzer Division lost 7,476 men killed, approximately 20,921 wounded, and 2,883 captured or missing. It destroyed 2,672 Soviet tanks and assault guns during the same period. By any measurement, it was an excellent division.

Commanders of the 23rd Panzer included Major General/Lieutenant General Baron Hans von Boineburg-Lengsfeld (November 1, 1941), Major General Erwin Mack (July 20, 1942), Colonel Fritz von Buch (acting commander, August 26, 1942), Colonel Erich Brueckner (acting commander, September 1942), Boineburg-Lengsfeld again (September 1942), Colonel Joseph Rossmann (acting commander, December 1942), Colonel/Major General/Lieutenant General Nikolaus von Vormann (December 26, 1942), Colonel/Major General Ewald

Kraeber (October 25, 1943), Colonel Heinz-Joachim Werner-Ehrenfeucht (acting commander, November 1–18, 1943), Kraeber (returned November 18, 1943), and Colonel/Major General/Lieutenant General Josef von Radowitz (June, 1944–end).

## COMMANDERS

Baron Hans von Boineburg-Lengsfeld (born in Thuringia in 1889) joined the army in 1910 as an officer cadet in the light infantry. He fought in World War I, served in the Reichsheer, and—during the Wehrmacht era—commanded the 1st Rifle Regiment (1938–39) and 4th Rifle Brigade (late 1939–40), was acting commander of the 4th Panzer Division (1940), and commanded the 7th Rifle Brigade (1940–41), before assuming command of the 23rd Panzer Division. He was promoted to major general on October 1, 1941, but was relieved of his command for a security violation—the same violation that brought General of Panzer Troops Georg Stumme and his chief of staff (Colonel Gerhard Franz) before a court-martial and earned them prison terms. In this incident, these actions were entirely justified, as Stumme, Franz and Boineburg-Lengsfeld had committed gross security violations and were guilty of neglect of duty. Boineburg-Lengsfeld, however, was restored to his command after General Mack was killed and was promoted to lieutenant general on December 1, 1942. Later that month, however, he was run over by a German tank and suffered multiple broken bones, effectively ending his career as a panzer commander. He was, in fact, very lucky to survive. After months in the hospital, he returned to active duty as commandant of greater Paris (1943–44). After Paris fell, he was placed in charge of a special fortress staff under OB West and ended the war as commander of Maneuver Area Bergen (1945). He was deeply involved in the July 20, 1944, plot against Adolf Hitler but he was again very lucky and his involvement was not discovered by the Gestapo. He died in Felsberg-Altenburg (Hessen) on November 20, 1980.

Erwin Mack (b. 1893) joined the 16th Engineer Battalion as a Fahnenjunker in 1911. After serving in World War I and the Reichsheer, he commanded the 5th Construction Engineer Staff (1939–40), was commander of the 413th Engineer Regiment (1940), and was chief engineer officer of 3rd Panzer Group (later Army) (1940–42), before assuming command of the 23rd Panzer Division. An excellent officer by all accounts, General Mack was killed in action in the Caucasus on August 26, 1942.

Fritz von Buch was born in East Prussia in 1876 and joined the Imperial Army as a Fahnenjunker in 1894. He was discharged as a lieutenant colonel in 1920, when the Reichsheer scaled down to 100,000 men. Buch rejoined the army in 1938 and was promoted to colonel in 1940 and to major general in 1943. During World War II, he commanded the 9th Artillery Replacement and Training Regiment (1939–40), the 606th Artillery Regiment (late 1940–41), the 128th Panzer Artillery Regiment (late 1941–December 1942), and Arko 19

(1943). After serving as a tactical instructor for the Luftwaffe ground combat units (1943–44), he was named commander of the Higher Artillery Command, 1st Parachute Army (March 1, 1944). He later commanded the 1st Parachute Army's Schools (1945) before being discharged at the end of March 1945. He died in Kassel in 1959.

Colonel Brueckner was the commander of the 126th Rifle Regiment in 1942.

Josef Rossmann was commander of Arko 121 in December 1942. He later returned to the Army Weapons Office (whence he came), and was promoted to major general in late 1943. He was chief of an office group in the Replacement Army in 1945.

Nikolaus von Vormann was born in West Prussia in 1895. He was educated in various cadet schools, began his service as a war volunteer in 1914, and was commissioned directly into the 26th Infantry Regiment in 1915. He remained in the Reichsheer and was Ia of X Corps and Wehrkreis X in 1938–39. An extremely capable staff officer and field commander, Vormann was OKH's representative at Fuehrer Headquarters during the Polish campaign (1939), was chief of staff of III Corps (1939–40), and served as chief of staff of XXVIII Corps (1940–42) before assuming command of the 23rd Panzer. Later Vormann commanded XXXXVIII Panzer Corps (1943–44) and was acting commander of the 9th Army (1944). He gave up this command on September 21, 1944, apparently because his failure to halt the overwhelming Soviet onslaught earned him the Fuehrer's displeasure. Later Vormann was named Fortress Commander Southeast (1944–45) and commander of the Alpine Fortress (1945). He was promoted to general of panzer troops on June 27, 1944.

Ewald Kraeber was born in Saarbruecken in 1894 and joined the 11th Engineer Battalion as a Fahnenjunker in 1914. Except for a tour as commander of the 33rd Panzer Regiment (1942) and later as commander of the 23rd Panzer Division, Kraeber spent the entire war commanding various tank schools or as a fortress inspector. He was promoted to major general on January 1, 1944.

Heinz-Joachim Werner-Ehrenfeucht (b. 1894) entered the service in 1913 as an infantry Fahnenjunker. After serving in World War I and in the Reichsheer, he was a major when Hitler came to power. An early transfer to the mobile branch, he commanded the 32nd Motorized Antitank Battalion (1935–40) and the 66th Panzer Battalion, was acting commander of the 25th Panzer Regiment (1941), and served as deputy commander of the 23rd Panzer Division (November 1941). He must have fallen ill in late 1941, for he was unemployed or in Fuehrer Reserve for the next year and a half; then he became chief of the systems development branch at OKH—a post which he apparently held for the rest of the war, except for his brief tenure as commander of the 23rd Panzer. He was promoted to major general in December 1944.

Josef von Radowitz (1899–1956) was commissioned in the 20th Dragoons at the end of World War I and was discharged in 1919. He reentered the service in 1924 as a member of the 18th Cavalry Regiment and later served as adjutant of III Corps (and later III Panzer Corps) (1938–42), served on the staff of 2nd

Panzer Army (1942–43), and was commander of the 28th Panzer Grenadier Regiment, 8th Panzer Division (1943–44). He was promoted to major general on September 1, 1944, and to lieutenant general on March 1, 1945. An excellent General Staff officer and field commander, he was a major general in the Bundeswehr (the West German Armed Forces) at the time of his death.

## NOTES AND SOURCES

In 1943, the III/201st Panzer Regiment was dissolved and the motorcycle battalion was converted into the 23rd Panzer Reconnaissance Battalion. On August 16, 1943, the 201st Panzer Regiment was redesignated 23rd Panzer Regiment.

In 1944, the 23rd Panzer Division absorbed the 1031st Motorized Grenadier Regiment.

Bradley et al., Volume 2: 127–28, 310–11; Carell 1966: 491, 512, 550; Chant 1979, Volume 15: 2057; Clark: 266; Edwards, *Panzer*: 76–77; Hartmann: 68; Keilig: 44, 214, 266, 358, 368; KTB OKW, Volume III: 258; Manstein: 330; Mehner, Volume 4: 383; Volume 5: 330; Volume 6: 546; Ernst Rebentisch, *Zum Kaukasus und zu den Tauern: Die Geschichte der 23. Panzer-Division, 1941–1945* (Esslingen, 1963): 1 ff.; Seaton: 494; Tessin, Volume 6: 195–65; RA: 72; OB 42: 62–63; OB 45: 299; Windrow: 11.

# 24th Panzer Division

**COMPOSITION (1945):**   24th Panzer Regiment, 21st Panzer Grenadier Regiment, 26th Panzer Grenadier Regiment, 89th Panzer Artillery Regiment, 24th Panzer Reconnaissance Battalion, 40th Tank Destroyer Battalion, 40th Panzer Engineer Battalion, 86th Panzer Signal Battalion, 283rd Army Antiaircraft Battalion.

**HOME STATION:**   Frankfurt an der Oder, Wehrkreis III

An East Prussian unit, the 24th Panzer was formed on October 1, 1934, as the 5th Cavalry Brigade. It was later redesignated Cavalry Command Insterburg and became the 1st Cavalry Brigade on April 1, 1936. In 1938 it included the 1st and 2nd Cavalry Regiments (five squadrons each) at Insterburg and Angerburg, respectively; the 1st Motorcycle Battalion at Tilsit; the 1st Cavalry Artillery Battalion (three batteries); and divisional troops. When mobilization was declared in August 1939, however, the 1st and 2nd Cavalry Regiments were effectively dissolved, as were all of the German cavalry regiments. The division's squadrons went to war as reconnaissance battalions assigned to various infantry and panzer divisions. The brigade itself was given several reserve formations and fought in the frontier districts of eastern East Prussia and northern Poland during the early part of the Polish campaign.

On October 25, 1939, the 1st Cavalry Brigade was reunited, reorganized, and expanded into the 1st Cavalry Division. Initially it consisted of the 21st and 22nd Cavalry Regiments (two squadrons each), which absorbed six reconnaissance battalions each; and the 2nd Cavalry Artillery Battalion (three batteries), plus associated divisional troops. On February 14, 1940, however, the division

174

was expanded to include the 1st and 2nd Cavalry Regiments (two squadrons each). Simultaneously the 22nd Regiment lost its squadron staffs and assumed direct control over five troops of cavalry. The division also received Staff, 2nd (later 1st) Cavalry Brigade, the 1st Bicycle Battalion, the 1st Cavalry Artillery Regiment (three battalions), the 86th Cavalry Signal Battalion and other divisional support units, which bore the number 40.

By the end of 1939, the new horse division was on the lower Rhine, opposite the Netherlands. On May 10, 1940, it crossed the border and overran most of the northern and eastern Netherlands, whose boggy soil was unsuited for motorized warfare. (It was also not a strategically vital area; therefore, it was not part of Fortress Holland and was only weakly defended.) After the Dutch surrender, the 1st Cavalry was sent south, where it joined the 4th Army and took part in the pursuit of the beaten French Army. It was posted on the Channel coast in July, on the Atlantic coast in August, and was sent to the Generalgouvernement (formerly Poland) in September. It crossed into the Soviet Union on June 22, 1941. As was the case in Poland, the Netherlands, and France, the 1st Cavalry did very well in Russia in 1941, fighting at the Dnieper crossings and at Smolensk, and protecting the southern flank of Guderian's 2nd Panzer Army from Russian attacks out of the Pripet marshes. It was transferred back to Stablack, Eastern Prussia, in the winter of 1941 and converted to a panzer unit. The 1st Cavalry Division's colors were retired on November 28, 1941, an event that was considered historic. The new division, however, retained the nickname of the old: the Leaping Rider Division.

By the time it arrived in Maneuver Area Ohrdruf (Wehrkreis IX), the division included the 24th Panzer Regiment (I and II Battalions—the former 2nd and 21st Cavalry Regiments, respectively); the 21st Rifle Regiment (formerly the 1st Cavalry Regiment); the 26th Rifle Regiment (formerly 22nd Cavalry Regiment); the 4th Motorcycle Battalion (formerly 1st Bicycle); the 89th Panzer Artillery Regiment (formerly 1st Cavalry Artillery Regiment); and the divisional support units, which now bore the designation "panzer" instead of "cavalry." Later that year the 283rd Army Flak Artillery Battalion was assigned to the division.

Meanwhile, the 24th Panzer Division was sent to the 7th Army in northern France in April, but in June joined the 4th Panzer Army on the southern sector of the Eastern Front. It fought in the Battle of Voronezh and pushed across the Don to the Volga and into Stalingrad. It was trapped with the 6th Army when it was encircled in November 1942 and was destroyed when the city fell at the end of January 1943.

A new 24th Panzer was organized in Normandy in March–April 1943 under Headquarters, 15th Army. It absorbed the 891st Panzer Grenadier Regiment (from Wehrkreis IX) and the 127th Panzer Signal Battalion from the defunct 27th Panzer Division. The new division included the 24th Panzer Regiment (three battalions), the 21st and 26th Panzer Grenadier Regiments (two battalions each), the 89th Panzer Artillery Regiment (three battalions), the 24th Panzer

Reconnaissance Battalion, the 86th Signal Battalion, the 40th Tank Destroyer Battalion, the 40th Panzer Engineer Battalion, and the 89th Field Replacement Battalion. Sent to northern Italy in August, it was transferred to the Russian Front as winter approached. It fought in the Battles of Nikopol and Kiev in November, where it suffered heavy casualties. By December II/24th Panzer Regiment had suffered so many casualties that it had to be dissolved (III/24th was redesignated II Battalion). In February 1944 the 24th participated in the Cherkassy relief operation, for which it was officially cited. That spring it again sustained heavy losses in the withdrawal from the lower Dnieper Bend.

By July 1944 the remains of the division were fighting in southern Poland but at Kampfgruppe strength, especially after it was forced to transfer I/24th Panzer Regiment to the 1st Panzer Division during the summer. Transferred to the Hungarian sector, the 24th Panzer took part in the counterattack west of Debrecen and sustained heavy casualties in the unsuccessful defense of Kecskemet. Sent north again, the 24th Panzer Division fought the Russians in Slovakia, Poland, and East Prussia. By January 1945 the only extant combat units left to the division were two tank companies (equipped with Tiger tanks), the 21st Panzer Grenadier Regiment and the 40th Tank Destroyer Battalion. In March the division was reinforced with the 9th Grenadier Regiment (three battalions) of the 23rd Infantry Division, which it controlled until the end of the war. Its survivors surrendered to the Russians in May 1945.

Commanders of the 1st Cavalry-24th Panzer Division included Colonel/Major General/Lieutenant General Kurt Feldt (October 25, 1939), Major General Ritter Bruno von Hauenschild (April 15, 1942), Major General/Lieutenant General Arno von Lenski (September 12, 1942), Major General/Lieutenant General *Reichsfreiherr* (Reichsbaron) Maximillian von Edelsheim (March 1, 1943), Colonel/Major General Gustav-Adolf von Nostilz-Wallwitz (August 1, 1944), and Colonel Rudolf von Knebel-Doeberitz (March 27, 1945).

## COMMANDERS

Kurt Feldt (1887–1970), former commander of the 3rd Cavalry Regiment (1934–38) and 1st Cavalry Brigade (1939), was promoted to major general on February 1, 1940, and to lieutenant general on February 1, 1942. He was later military commander of southwestern France (July 1942–July 1944), Corps Feldt (1944–45), and Corps South Jutland (1945). A West Prussian who had entered the service in 1908, Feldt resided in Berlin after the war.

Ritter Bruno von Hauenschild (1896–1953) entered the Bavarian Army as an artillery Fahnenjunker in 1914. He earned the Pour le Mérite and his knighthood in World War I. After serving in the Reichsheer, he commanded the 9th Reconnaissance Regiment (1938), the 7th Panzer Regiment (1939–41), and the 24th Panzer Division (1942). Apparently wounded the week before Stalingrad was surrounded, he held no assignments for more than a year; then he directed the School for Panzer Troops (late 1943–early 1945). Promoted to lieutenant general in 1944, he assumed command of an ad hoc battle group in Wehrkreis III and was then named Battle Commander of Berlin until March 6, 1945, when he was relieved of his command by Adolf Hitler. He thus escaped Soviet captivity and returned to Munich, where he died eight years later.

Arno von Lenski (b. 1893) fought in World War I, served in the Reichsheer, and commanded the 2nd Cavalry Regiment (1935–39), the 2nd Rifle Regiment (1939–41), the 11th Rifle Brigade (1941), the School for Mobile Troops (1941–42), 2nd Panzer Division (1942), and 24th Panzer (1942–43). Lenski was promoted to lieutenant general on January 1, 1943, and surrendered the survivors of the 24th Panzer Division to the Russians at Stalingrad on February 2, 1943, along with part of the 389th Infantry Division. Later he joined the Communists and served in the Eastern Zone.

Reichsfreiherr (Reichsbaron) Maximillian von Edelsheim was promoted to lieutenant general on March 1, 1944. Born in Berlin in 1897, he entered the service as a Fahnenjunker in the 2nd Guards Ulam Regiment when World War I broke out. Commissioned the following year, he served in the Reichsheer and later commanded the 1st Bicycle Battalion (1938–41), the 22nd Cavalry Regiment (1941–42), the 26th Panzer Grenadier Regiment (1942), and 20th Panzer Brigade (1942). The fact that he held his last appointment for less than a month and was unassigned for more than four months thereafter suggests that he was wounded on the Eastern Front. In any case he rebuilt the 24th Panzer Division (1943–44) and led the XXXXVIII Panzer Corps from September 21, 1944, until the end of the war. A highly capable panzer officer, Reichsbaron von Edelsheim was promoted to major general on June 1, 1943, to lieutenant general on March 1, 1944, and to general of panzer troops on December 1, 1944. He held the Knight's Cross with Oak Leaves and Swords. He died in Konstanz on April 26, 1994, at the age of 96.

Gustav-Adolf von Nostitz-Wallwitz (1898–1945) joined the 12th Field Artillery Regiment as a Fahnenjunker in 1917. Commissioned in 1918, he was retained in the Reichsheer and commanded a battalion in the 216th Artillery Regiment (1939–40) and another in the 12th Artillery Regiment (1940) before assuming command of the 117th Artillery Regiment (1940). He then commanded the 1st Cavalry Artillery Battalion (1940) and the 89th Panzer Artillery Regiment (the divisional artillery regiment) from 1941 to 1944. He was flown out of Stalingrad before the city fell. He led the 24th Panzer Division until March 27, 1945, when he was seriously wounded. He died of his wounds on May 31, 1945—almost a month after the end of the war. Nostitz-Wallwitz was promoted to major general on November 9, 1944.

Rudolf von Knebel-Doeberitz commanded I/21st Rifle Regiment as a captain of cavalry in August 1942 and rose rapidly in rank thereafter.

## NOTES AND SOURCES

The cavalry and Landwehr (reservists in the 35- to 45-year old age group) forces in eastern Prussia/northern Poland in 1939 were commanded by Lieutenant General Georg

Brandt, a veteran cavalry officer and a "retread" who first retired from the army in 1931. He is sometimes erroneously listed as the commander of the 1st Cavalry; in fact he was the leader of Corps Command XXXIII, of which the 1st Cavalry was a part. Brandt retired again in 1942 (this time as a general of cavalry) and committed suicide in 1945.

On October 25, 1939, the I/21st Cavalry Regiment absorbed the 8th, 28th, and 162nd Reconnaissance Battalions; II/21st Cavalry absorbed the 7th, 54th, and 14th Reconnaissance Battalions; I/22nd Cavalry Regiment absorbed the 3rd, 17th, and 173rd Reconnaissance Battalions; and II/22nd absorbed the 21st, 30th, and 156th Reconnaissance Battalions.

In September 1944 the 40th Tank Destroyer Battalion was redesignated 471st Tank Destroyer Battalion. The division was then apparently given a new 40th Tank Destroyer Battalion.

Bradley et al., Volume 3: 277–78; Volume 5: 181–82; Carell 1966: 83, 521, 585; Hartmann: 69–70; Kennedy: 10B, 69, Map 7; Kursietis: 107; Manstein: 139, 143, 487, 525; Mellenthin 1956: 225; Seaton: 336; Dr. F. M. von Senger und Etterlin, *Die 24. Panzer-Division, vormals 1. Kavallerie-Division, 1939–1945* (Vohwinckel-Neckargemuend, 1962); Scheibert: 193; Tessin, Volume 2: 35–36; Volume 4: 211–12; OB 42: 63; OB 45: 300.

# 25th Panzer Division

**COMPOSITION:**   9th Panzer Regiment, 146th Panzer Grenadier Regiment, 147th Panzer Grenadier Regiment, 91st Panzer Artillery Regiment, 25th Panzer Reconnaissance Battalion, 8th Motorcycle Battalion, 87th Tank Destroyer Battalion, 87th Panzer Engineer Battalion, 87th Panzer Signal Battalion.

**HOME STATION:**   Wuppertal, Wehrkreis VI

The Rhinelander-Westphalian 25th Panzer was formed in Norway as Schuetzen-Verband Oslo on May 15, 1941. It was created to spearhead a possible German invasion of Sweden. A full panzer division was not considered necessary to accomplish this task, so the Verband was well understrength and included the 146th Rifle Regiment (three battalions), the 214th Panzer Battalion (which included the 514th Tank Destroyer Company), and the 91st Motorized Battery (four 100mm guns). When the Russian campaign did not end in 1941 as expected, the Verband was redesignated 25th Panzer Division on February 25, 1942, but with little increase in its strength. The divisional staff was formed in Eberwalde (the new division's home station) on February 27 and embarked for Oslo on March 5, and the rifle units were redesignated panzer grenadier units on July 5. The 91st Battery became the 91st Artillery Battalion on July 7, 1942.

Gradually the division was rounded out. The III/146th was converted into the 87th Motorcycle Battalion in October, the 87th Signal Battalion was activated in Cologne on November 1, and the II/193rd Grenadier Regiment was sent to the 146th Rifle Regiment as its III Battalion. In December, the 214th Panzer Battalion became the I/9th Panzer Regiment, and the independent 40th Panzer Battalion was assigned to the new division as II/9th Panzer Regiment. In early

179

January 1943, the Staff, 9th Panzer Regiment was activated. The 87th Tank Destroyer Battalion was formed in March 1943, and on April 7, the 87th Motorcycle became the 25th Panzer Reconnaissance Battalion. On May 15, 1943, the 25th Panzer Division added the 147th Panzer Grenadier Regiment, which initially included only its Staff and I Battalion (the former III/146th Panzer Grenadier Regiment). That same month, it added the 91st Panzer Artillery Battalion (the former 91st Artillery Battalion) and the newly formed II and III Battalions from Wehrkreis XI.

The division first saw action on February 28, 1943, when it clashed with Norwegian partisans near Rjukan. In the latter part of August 1943, it sailed from Oslo to Copenhagen, and on August 28, took part in Operation Tivoliausflug, the disarming of the Danish Army. It left behind in Norway the I/9th Panzer Regiment, which became Panzer Battalion Norway and later formed the nucleus of Panzer Division Norway. Later the division added the 279th Army Flak Battalion to its table of organization.

The 25th Panzer was well below strength until September 1943, when it was transferred to the Arras-Amiens-Cambrai area of northern France. It was further handicapped by the fact that it had to transfer more than 600 vehicles (all relatively new) to the 14th Panzer Division, a Stalingrad unit now in the process of rebuilding. Even more seriously, the 25th Panzer had a disproportionately high number of relatively green recruits and few combat veterans; even so, it was soon on its way to Russia, where it fought on the central and southern sectors for two and a half years, with only one major respite. It suffered heavy losses— largely due to inexperience—in the Kiev battles of October and November 1943. It nevertheless played a significant role in sealing off a major Soviet breakthrough east of Fastov (southwest of Kiev). The division later fought in the counterattacks against the Kiev Salient, along the Kiev-Zhitomir road, and at Vinnitsa, Proskurov, Chortkov, and Stanislav.

By January 1944, the division had suffered such serious losses that it had lost all offensive capabilities and higher headquarters were considering whether to disband it. By the start of 1944, the remnants of the 147th Panzer Grenadier Regiment had been absorbed by its sister regiment; the remaining tank battalion had been practically destroyed, the antitank battalion had been virtually wiped out, and the 91st Panzer Artillery Regiment now amounted to a weak battalion. The 25th Panzer Division again took heavy casualties in the withdrawal across northern Ukraine in March 1944, when it was encircled with 1st Panzer Army in the Hube Pocket. The division had only 8,000 men left in April, when it was sent to Aalborg, Denmark, to rebuild. Here it absorbed the main forces of Panzer Division Norway, which was downgraded to a brigade. No sooner than it was reconstituted, however, than the 25th Panzer fell victim to the "panzer brigade" idea. It and the 233rd Reserve Panzer Division were ordered to transfer 8,300 men to the newly created panzer brigades—an experiment that was ultimately unsuccessful. Panzer Battalion Norway was transferred to the 103rd Panzer Brigade (where it became the 2103rd Panzer Battalion), and the II/9th Panzer Regiment, which had been reequipped with Panthers, was sent to the 104th Panzer Brigade as the 2104th Panzer Battalion. The division also sent sizable cadres to the 109th Panzer Brigade, including most of the staff of the 146th Panzer Grenadier Regiment, which was used to form the brigade staff.

Meanwhile, the 91st Panzer Artillery Regiment was rebuilt. Its I Battalion was made up of III/2nd Motorized Artillery Lehr Regiment from Artillery School 2, and its II Battalion came from the remnants of the original three battalions that survived the battles in the East.

The 25th Panzer Division was posted to the Wildflecken Maneuver Area in Wehrkreis IX in August, where the 25th Panzer Reconnaissance Battalion was partially rebuilt. The situation on the Eastern Front, however, had deteriorated so badly and so rapidly that the 25th was thrown back into action in September, without having received any more significant reinforcements. Its effective strength was now one panzer grenadier battalion, one panzer artillery battalion, and less than one battalion of tanks. Inexperience, however, was no longer a problem. As a Kampfgruppe, it fought at Pultusk (Ostenburg) and in the defense of Warsaw (September 1944). The 87th Panzer Engineer Battalion was assigned to the ad hoc Corps von dem Bach, which tried to crush the Warsaw Uprising, but without success initially. The battalion lost its commander and two company commanders killed by Polish snipers. Later the entire division was committed to the battle (except the panzer regiment, which was attached to Headquarters, IV SS Panzer Corps). It only scored one major success: the engineer battalion captured 218 prisoners in a surprise attack east of Kepa Potocka. On the other hand, the 87th Panzer Engineer and 25th Panzer Reconnaissance Battalions lost 110 killed and 240 wounded in the fighting in the suburbs of the Polish capital. At last pulled out of the Warsaw sector, the Kampfgruppe 25th Panzer Division was sent back to the front, holding a sector facing the Soviet Serock bridgeheads over the Narev. Its artillery regiment, however, was detached to support the 6th Volksgrenadier Division.

On November 6, 1944, the division was finally reinforced. It absorbed the 2111th Panzer Battalion (of the 111th Panzer Brigade) and the remnants of the 104th Panzer Brigade, which included the 2104th Panzer Battalion (four companies, including 25 Panthers), the 2104th Panzer Grenadier Battalion (three companies), and a few companies of brigade support troops. It also received some troops and units from Wildflecken, including Panzer Artillery Battalion Norway and II and III/Panzer Grenadier Regiment Norway; in addition, the 147th Panzer Grenadier Regiment was rebuilt, using men from Panzer School Krampnitz. By November 15, the 2104th Panzer Battalion had become the I/9th Panzer Regiment, and the 2104th Panzer Grenadier Battalion was the new I/147th Panzer Grenadier Regiment. The 2111th Panzer Battalion of the 111th Panzer Brigade became II/9th Panzer Regiment.

That winter, the rebuilt division helped defend the Vistula in Poland and was heavily engaged in the defense of Warsaw in January 1945. Following a massive artillery bombardment, the Russians broke out of their Vistula River bridgeheads on January 14. The 25th and 19th Panzer Divisions immediately launched strong counterattacks, but were ineffectual. By January 18, the division was in remnants but was still resisting east of Lodz (Litzmannstadt). It continued to retreat across central Poland and eastern Germany until mid-February, when it was sent south to join the 4th Panzer Army, which was then defending on the Neisse. By the end of the month, the 25th Panzer Division had lost 622 men killed, 2,318 wounded, and 6,030 missing—a total of 8,970 casualties in six weeks.

Meanwhile, the Red Army was expanding its bridgeheads east of Stettin, so the 25th Panzer Division was sent to Pomerania, to help deal with the latest threat. It was reinforced with the II/2nd Panzer Regiment and was involved in heavy fighting at Sydowsaue, Podejuch, and Finkenwalde. Here it suffered 1,330 more casualties, including 172 killed, 747 wounded, and 411 captured or missing. It retreated across Pomerania in March, fought on the Oder and at Muencheberg, and in April 1945 it was sent to Vienna, along with the Fuehrer Grenadier Division. The move cost Army Group Vistula half its armor on the eve of the Battle of Berlin, and its armor was weak already. The 25th Panzer, for example, was a mere battle group by this time. It had 65 panzers and assault guns (45 of them operational) as of April 1, but its 146th Panzer Grenadier Regiment had only 1,000 men, and the 91st Panzer Artillery Regiment had only 16 guns. Instead of fighting in the Battle of Vienna, however, the 25th Panzer was posted north of the Danube, in 8th Army's reserve, to protect the Austrian oil fields. It fought at Prottes, Hohenruppersdorf, Martinsdorf, and Schrick, and ended the war in Austria, where it surrendered to the Americans, along with part of the 11th Panzer Division and the Feldherrnhalle Panzer Corps. Much of the division, however, was handed over to the Russians, along with the 3rd SS Panzer Division Totenkopf and the Fuehrer Grenadier Division.

The 25th Panzer's divisional commanders included Lieutenant General Johann Haarde (February 25, 1942), Lieutenant General Adolf von Schell (January 1, 1943), Lieutenant General Georg Jauer (November 15, 1943), Major General Lieutenant General Hans Troeger (November 20, 1943), Colonel Kurt Truehaupt (May 10, 1944), Major General Oswin Grolig (June 1, 1944), and Colonel/ Major General Oskar Audoersch (August 19, 1944–end).

## COMMANDERS

Johann Haarde was born in Wilhelmshave in 1889. Joining the army in 1908, he fought in World War I as an infantry officer and served in the Reichsheer. He was commander of the 8th Panzer Regiment (1936–38), 8th Panzer Brigade (1938–41), 100th Panzer Brigade (1941), and 383th Infantry Division (1941– 42), before assuming command of the 25th Panzer. Meanwhile, he was promoted to major general (1939) and lieutenant general (1941). Later he was Military Commander Salonika (Greece) (1943) and was placed in charge of a special staff in late 1943. Here his job was to refurbish decimated Kampfgruppen for

Army Group Center. Both posts were definite steps down for a man who had commanded a panzer division. Haarde was killed in action at Kolberg on February 8, 1945. The fact that he rose no higher than he did—after being a full colonel commanding a panzer regiment as early as 1936—suggests that someone in power in the panzer inspectorate and/or the Army Personnel Office was disappointed with his wartime performance.

Adolf von Schell was born in Magdeburg in 1893. A Fahnenjunker in the 57th Infantry Regiment in 1914, he fought in World War I, served in the Reichswehr, was a staff officer at OKH, and was commissioner of transportation under the Four-Year Plan (1938–42) and as inspector of army motorization (1940–43). Schell was simultaneously undersecretary of state in the Reich's transportation ministry. Deposed as the result of an intrigue (which was common in the Nazi government), the energetic and capable Schell commanded the 25th Panzer Division for almost a year, but fell seriously ill and held no further appointments after that. He was discharged from the service at the end of 1944 and retired to Hanover.

George Jauer (b. 1896) entered the service as a war volunteer in 1914 and earned a reserve commission in the artillery in 1916. One of the few such officers selected for the Reichswehr, he was a staff officer and later branch chief in the Army Personnel Office from 1934 to 1941. He later commanded the 29th Artillery Regiment (1941–42), the Grossdeutschland Artillery Regiment (1942–43), the 25th Panzer Division (as an acting commander only, 1943), 20th Panzer Grenadier Division (1943–44), and the Grossdeutschland Panzer Corps (1945). Jauer ended the war as a general of panzer troops. He died in 1971.

Hans Troeger was promoted to lieutenant general on April 1, 1944. For more details about his career, see 13th Panzer Division.

Kurt Treuhaupt was the senior regimental commander of the 25th Panzer Division and was the commander of the 146th Panzer Grenadier Regiment in 1944.

Oswin Grolig (b. 1894) was a Fahnenjunker in 1913 and was commissioned in the 11th Hussars the following year. He fought in World War I, served in the Reichsheer, and later commanded the 8th Reconnaissance Battalion (1938–40), 33rd Rifle Regiment (1940–42), 1st Rifle Brigade (1942), and Panzer School II (1943). On August 18, 1944, while leading the 25th Panzer Division on the Eastern Front, he was mortally wounded. General Grolig died at Litzmannstadt a few days later.

Oskar Audoersch was born in Rastenburg, East Prussia (the future site of Fuehrer Headquarters) in 1898. He became a Fahnenjunker in the 129th Infantry Regiment in 1916 and a lieutenant in 1917. He earned an advanced engineering degree after the war. After serving in the Reichsheer, he was on the staff at OKH (1938–40), commanded the 394th Rifle Regiment (August, 1940–early 1942), and returned to the OKH staff (1942–44). He left OKH shortly after the unsuccessful attempt on Hitler's life, attended a short divisional commanders' course, and assumed command of the 25th Panzer Division the day after General

Grolig was wounded. Audoersch was promoted to major general on November 9, 1944. He was forced to surrender the division to the Soviets in May 1945. After spending 10 years in Communist prisons, Audoersch was released and moved to Schleswig. He died in Ulm in 1991.

## NOTES AND SOURCES

The 87th Motorcycle was redesignated 91st Panzer Reconnaissance Battalion, and the 744th Army Motorized Engineer Battalion became the 87th Panzer Engineer Battalion, but the exact dates these events happened are unclear.

The 104th Panzer Brigade was formed on July 18, 1944, and spent three months on the Eastern Front, fighting at Narev and Ostenburg. Its home station was Bielefeld, Wehrkreis VI.

Bradley et al., Volume 1: 119–20; Volume 4: 432–33; Volume 5: 6–7; Chant 1979, Volume 17: 2277; Hartmann: 70–71; Keilig: 115, 120, 296; Kursietis: 107; Manstein: 488; Mehner, Volume 10: 520; Mellenthin 1977: 207–08; Scheibert: 378; Tessin, Volume 14: 193; Volume 5: 227; Volume 6: 194; RA: 100; OB 43: 208; OB 45: 301; Windrow: 11; Ziemke: 469.

# 26th Panzer Division

**COMPOSITION (1943):**   26th Panzer Regiment, 9th Panzer Grenadier Regiment, 67th Panzer Grenadier Regiment, 93rd Panzer Artillery Regiment, 26th Motorcycle Battalion, 93rd Tank Destroyer Battalion, 93rd Panzer Engineer Battalion, 93rd Panzer Signal Battalion, 304th Army Flak Artillery Battalion.

**HOME STATION:**   Potsdam, Wehrkreis III

A "first-wave" unit from the Brandenburg/Berlin area, the 26th Panzer Division originally bore the title 23rd Infantry Division and was formed by the expansion of cadres of the historic 9th Infantry (Potsdam) Regiment in 1934–35, adopting much of the tradition of the old Imperial Guards. It included the 67th Infantry Regiment (at Berlin-Spandau), the 68th Infantry Regiment (stationed at Brandenburg), and the elite 9th Infantry Regiment and 23rd Artillery Regiments, based at Potsdam. During World War II, it lived up to its ancestor unit's reputation as a fine combat unit. The 23rd Infantry was lightly engaged in Poland (mainly in the Polish Corridor), fought in Luxembourg, Belgium, and France in 1940, and invaded Russia in 1941. It crossed the Dnieper with the 2nd Panzer Army on the central sector and fought at Bialystok, Minsk, and Smolensk. It also took part in the Siege of Mogilev on the Dnieper from July 20–26, where it lost more than 1,000 men. The 23rd Infantry took part in heavy defensive fighting at Vyasma and pushed on to the gates of Moscow, suffering heavy casualties along the way. By January 1942 it had barely a thousand infantrymen left, and its nine infantry battalions were consolidated into three because of casualties. The divisional artillery was down to one 50mm anti-tank gun and three howitzers. It was surrounded south of Fedorovka by the Soviet winter offensive of 1941–42.

Rescued, the 23rd Infantry remained on the central sector until summer 1942, holding the line around Gshatsk, when it was finally relieved and sent to Brittany, France, and then Mons, Belgium, where it was reformed as the 26th Panzer Division. Activated on September 14, 1942, the new division consisted of the 26th Panzer Grenadier Brigade (9th and 67th Panzer Grenadier Regiments [two battalions each] plus the 26th Motorcycle [formerly 26th Reconnaissance] Battalion); the 93rd Panzer Artillery Regiment (the former 23rd Artillery Regiment); the 304th Army Flak Artillery Battalion; and the 93rd Panzer Engineer, 93rd Tank Destroyer, and 93rd Panzer Signal Battalions. The two-battalion 26th Panzer Regiment (the staff and II and III Battalions of the former 202nd Panzer Regiment) joined the division on January 1, 1943.

The new unit never lived up to the standards of its predecessor, although it was a fair combat division. It trained in France for about a year (mainly around Amiens) before being sent to Italy in July 1943. It remained on this front for the rest of the war, fighting in the Salerno and Anzio counterattacks, the battles of the Gustav Line, and in the retreat up the peninsula to the Gothic Line, including the battles of Orsogna, Frosinone, Rimini, Ravenna, and Bologna. Meanwhile, it gave up the 93rd Tank Destroyer Battalion on July 23, 1943 (it became part of the GHQ troops of the 14th Army), but added the 51st Tank Destroyer Battalion in October 1944. On June 11, 1944, it absorbed the 1027th Grenadier Regiment (reinforced) and in November took in the remnants of the 20th Luftwaffe Field Division. That same month the division was cited for distinguished action between the Apennines and the Adriatic. Reinforced with about a battalion of Panther tanks (from the 6th Panzer Regiment and the Brandenburg Panzer Grenadier Regiment), the 26th Panzer Division defended a sector of the Adriatic around Imola in early 1945. By this time it consisted of the 26th Panzer Regiment (two battalions), the 9th and 67th Panzer Grenadier Regiments (two battalions each), the Verstarktes Grenadier Regiment (two battalions of marching infantry), the 26th Panzer Reconnaissance Battalion, the 93rd Tank Destroyer Battalion, the 93rd Panzer Engineer Battalion, the 93rd Panzer Signal Battalion, and the 304th Army Flak Battalion.

The battered and depleted 26th Panzer Division fought its last battle south of the Po River in April. Stopped by one of Hitler's senseless orders, the 26th Panzer (and the bulk of the LXXVI Panzer Corps) were unable to retreat behind the Po River, as they could easily have done. Caught between the Po and the Apennines, it was destroyed by the Allied armies. Only a few men managed to swim across the Po and escape. The division lost all of its tanks and vehicles and virtually ceased to exist. The remnants that escaped this disaster surrendered at Imola a few days later.

Commanders of the 23rd Infantry/26th Panzer Division included Major General Count Walter von Brockdorff-Ahlefeld (March 1, 1938), Major General Heinz Hellmich (June 1, 1940), Colonel/Major General Kurt Badinski (January 17, 1942), Colonel/Major General/Lieutenant General Baron Smilo von Luettwitz (July 14, 1942), Colonel Hans Hecker (February 23, 1944), Luettwitz (returned to command, April 11, 1944), Colonel/Major General Eduard Crasemann (July 6, 1944), Major General Dr. Hans Boelsen (July 19, 1944), Crasemann (resumed command, August 26, 1944), Colonel Alfred Kuhnert (January 29, 1945), and Major General/Lieutenant General Viktor Linnarz (March 1, 1945).

## COMMANDERS

Count Walter von Brockdorff-Ahlefeldt (b. 1887) was promoted to lieutenant general on March 1, 1939, and to general of infantry the following year. He commanded II Corps from 1940 to 1942, and conducted a classic defense in the Demyansk Pocket on the northern sector of the Russian Front during the winter of 1941–42. He was in poor health in late 1942 and had to be relieved. An anti-Hitler conspirator as early as 1938, he died in Berlin on May 9, 1943. He had joined the 3rd Jaeger Battalion as a Fahnenjunker in 1908. Brockdorff, who was promoted to general of infantry on August 1, 1940, had also commanded the XXVIII Corps (June 1–21, 1940).

Heinz Hellmich (1890–1944) was born in Karlsruhe and joined the 136th Infantry Regiment as a Fahnenjunker in 1908. He served in World War I and the Reichswehr and was considered a rising star in the Wehrmacht, holding a number of important General Staff posts—including a tour of duty as a branch chief in the Air Ministry. Clearly earmarked for greater things, Hellmich was named commander of the elite Berlin-Brandenburg 23rd Infantry Division while only a colonel—a rare sign of official favor in 1940. (He was promoted to major general on September 1, 1941.) He led the division skillfully on the Eastern Front, but his health and his nerves collapsed during the Russian winter offensive and he had to be relieved of his command, ruining a most promising career. (Three of his regimental commanders also collapsed.) Hellmich returned to duty on April 1, 1942, as commander of Special Administrative Divisional Staff 141 (which later became the 141st Replacement Division)—a definite and serious demotion. Later he was inspector of *Osttruppen* (Eastern Troops), but he was not given another combat unit until early 1944, when he assumed command of the 243rd Infantry Division. This unit he led in Normandy, doing an excellent job with very limited resources against overwhelming forces, until June 16, when he was killed by a 20mm shell from an Allied fighter-bomber.

Kurt Badinski (b. 1890) joined the 9th Jaeger Battalion as a Fahnenjunker in 1910. After serving in World War I and in the Reichswehr, he was commander of the I/16th Infantry Regiment (1936–39) and commander of the 489th Infantry Regiment (1939–42). With six years' experience as a regimental commander, he was chosen to command the remnants of the 23rd Infantry Division after General Hellmich collapsed. He was promoted to major general on February 1, 1942, and to lieutenant general on March 1, 1943. Badinski later led the 269th Infantry Division on the Eastern Front and the 276th Infantry Division in France. He was captured trying to break out of the Falaise Pocket in August

1944. Released from the prisoner of war camps in mid-1947, he died in Oldenburg, Upper Bavaria, in 1966.

Baron Smilo von Luettwitz (1895–1975) was promoted to major general on September 1, 1942, and to lieutenant general on October 1, 1943. He became a general of panzer troops on September 1, 1944. During World War II, he served as adjutant, XV Motorized Corps (1938–40); commander, 12th Rifle Regiment (1940–42); commander, 4th Rifle Brigade (1942); commander, 26th Panzer Division (1942–44); and commander, XXXXVI Panzer Corps (1944). He commanded the 9th Army on the Eastern Front from September 1, 1944 to January 17, 1945, when he was relieved of his command by Field Marshal Schoerner for ordering the unauthorized evacuation of Warsaw. He was nevertheless given command of the LXXXV Corps on the Western Front on March 31, 1945, and led it until the end of the war. In the late 1950s, he was a lieutenant general and commander of the III Corps of the West German Army. Luettwitz began his military career as an infantry Fahnenjunker in 1914. Smilo von Luettwitz was one of the best panzer officers in World War II, yet he is virtually unknown today, because almost all of his service was in the East. His more famous cousin Heinrich commanded the 2nd Panzer Division and XXXXVII Panzer Corps during World War II.

For a sketch of Hans Hecker's career, see 4th Panzer Division.

Dr. Hans Boelsen (b. 1894) joined the army as a war volunteer in 1914 and was commissioned second lieutenant of infantry the following year. He was discharged from the service after the war but rejoined the army as a captain in 1934. During World War II, he served as IIa of the XXII Corps (1939–40), IIa of 1st Panzer Group (1940–41), commander of II/111th Rifle Regiment (1941), commander of the 160th Motorcycle Battalion (1941), battalion commander at the Infantry School (1942–43), acting commander of the 29th Panzer Grenadier Division (1944), acting commander of the 26th Panzer Division (1944), commander of the 18th Panzer Grenadier Division (1944–45), and commander of the 172nd Reserve Division (1945). He was promoted to major general in 1944 and to lieutenant general (by his own later declaration) in 1945. He died in Frankfurt am Main in 1960.

Eduard Crasemann (1891–1950) was born in Hamburg. He joined the 46th Artillery Regiment as a Fahnenjunker, fought in World War I, and was discharged in 1919. He rejoined the army as a captain in 1936, serving on the staff of OKH. During World War II he advanced rapidly, from a major commanding an artillery battery to a lieutenant general commanding a corps. Successively he led 5/73rd Artillery Regiment (1939–40), II/78th Artillery Regiment (1940–41), 33rd Panzer Artillery Regiment (1941–42), 15th Panzer Division (1942), 143rd Artillery Command (1943–44), 26th Panzer Division (1944), and XII SS Corps (1945). He was captured on April 16, 1945, and died in British captivity. He was promoted to major general on October 1, 1944, to lieutenant general on February 27, 1945, and to general of artillery on April 20, 1945. Crasemann held the Knight's Cross with Oak Leaves.

Alfred Kuhnert (b. 1898) was born in Upper Silesia. He joined the army at age 16 as a war volunteer and was discharged as a sergeant in 1919. He became a policeman in 1921, rising to the rank of lieutenant, and returned to active duty as a captain in 1935. He commanded 10/51st Infantry Regiment (1938–39), III/51st Infantry Regiment (1939–40), 38th Motorcycle Battalion (1940), and 51st Infantry Regiment (1942–43), and was chief of Special Staff II at OKH in 1944. He then served as acting commander of the 198th Infantry Division (August 1944), attended the divisional commanders' course in late 1944, and was then named acting commander of the 26th Panzer. He was soon transferred to Doeberitz near Berlin, where he helped organize new panzer divisions. Promoted to major general on April 20, 1945, he ended the war on assignment to Army Group North on the Eastern Front. He moved to Berlin after the war.

Viktor Linnarz (b. 1894) was a lieutenant in the 2nd Telegraph Battalion when World War I began. He served in the Reichswehr and was a major in the Army Personnel Office when the next war began. Promoted to a branch chief's job in 1940, he first saw field service as a commander of the 5th Panzer Brigade (June 3–August 31, 1941). Almost certainly wounded in action, he did not return to active duty for more than a year. In late 1942 he became an office group chief (P 1) at HPA and then deputy chief of HPA (1943–45). He was promoted to major general on January 1, 1943, and to lieutenant general on April 1, 1945. He resided in Hanover after the war.

## NOTES AND SOURCES

Angolia, *Field*, Volume 2: 350–51; Blumenson 1969: 289, 419; Bradley et al., Volume 1: 153–54, 474–75; Volume 2: 85–86; Volume 5: 221–22; Carell 1966: 80, 85–86, 181, 184; *D-Day Encyclopedia*: 289–90; Ernest F. Fisher Jr., *Cassino to the Alps* (Washington, D.C., 1977): 19, 82, 302, 498 (hereafter cited as "Fisher"); Albert N. Garland and Howard McG. Smyth, *Sicily and the Surrender of Italy* (Washington, D.C., 1965): 75 (hereafter cited as "Garland and Smyth"); Keilig: 52, 62, 193, 212; Kennedy: 74; Mehner, Volume 5: 330; Georg Staiger 26. *Panzer-Division: Ihr Werden und Einsatz, 1942–1945* (Nauheim, 1957); Tessin, Volume 4: 192–93, 240–41; RA: 46; OB 43: 208; OB 45: 147, 301. Also see Seaton: 232.

# 27th Panzer Division

**COMPOSITION:**   127th Panzer Regiment, 140th Panzer Grenadier Regiment, 127th Panzer Artillery Regiment, 27th Panzer Reconnaissance Battalion, 127th Tank Destroyer Battalion, 127th Motorized Engineer Battalion, 127th Panzer Signal Battalion.

**HOME STATION:**   Heidelberg, Wehrkreis XII

The 27th Panzer Division was formed in southern Russia from Group Michalek of the 22nd Panzer Division. It was organized in the Voronezh area under the general supervision of Headquarters, 2nd Army. Activated on October 1, 1942, it included the 127th Panzer Battalion (formerly III/204th Panzer Regiment) and 140th Panzer Grenadier Regiment (two battalions), both from the 22nd Panzer Division; Staff, I and II Battalions of the 127th Panzer Artillery Regiment, all from the 677th Artillery Regiment z.b.V. (part of 2nd Army's GHQ troops); 127th (formerly 560th) Tank Destroyer Battalion, another former GHQ unit; and 127th (formerly 260th) Engineer Battalion from the 260th Infantry Division. The division was also given the I/140th Panzer Artillery Regiment (from the 22nd Panzer Division); the I/51st Artillery Regiment (an army GHQ unit); and the 27th Panzer Reconnaissance and 127th Panzer Signal Battalions. Its total strength, however, was slightly less than 3,000 men.

The new division took part in the clearing of the Don region of Soviet forces and in the conquest of the Donets. During the retreat from Stalingrad, however, it was broken up and scattered over the whole southern sector of the Eastern Front; parts, for example, were attached to the Italian 8th Army; other elements fought at Voronezh and Voroshilovgrad under German command. The Kampf-

190

gruppe 27th Panzer Division took part in the retreat across the Donets and in the fighting south of Kharkov, suffering heavy casualties in the process. The division was disbanded after the Soviet winter offensive of 1942–43 had been stopped. At regimental strength or less to begin with, the 27th Panzer Division had lost half of its infantry by the end of 1942 and, as of January 1, 1943, had only 11 tanks under its direct command. (Twenty of its tanks were on detached duty with Headquarters, 2nd Army.)

It is difficult to assess the strengths of its other units, since the division had been broken up into seven battle groups by that time and was scattered all over the southern part of the Eastern Front. The 127th Panzer Engineer Battalion had only one officer and 35 men left, and the I/140th Panzer Grenadier Regiment had five officers and 165 men. By February 8, 1943, the division had an estimated strength of 1,590 men. Most of its equipment and survivors were absorbed by the 7th Panzer Division, although parts (including the 127th Panzer and 127th Panzer Signal Battalions) were sent to France, where they were absorbed by the 24th Panzer Division. The 127th Panzer Engineer Battalion became the 127th Army Motorized Engineer Battalion and was made a corps troop unit (General Headquarters or GHQ unit) under III Panzer Corps and later 4th Panzer Army.

Commanders of the 27th Panzer Division included Colonel Helmut Michalik (October 1, 1942), Colonel/Major General Hans Troeger (November 11, 1942) and Colonel Joachim von Kronhelm (late January 1943).

## COMMANDERS

Helmut Michalik (b. 1894) entered the service when World War I broke out as an officer cadet with the 1st Dragoons. After serving in the Reichsheer, he was commander of the 30th Antitank Battalion (1937–40); commander of the 140th Rifle Regiment (1940–late 1942); acting commander of the 27th Panzer Division (1942), and on the staff of 18th Army, then besieging Leningrad (1942–44). He was assigned to Army Group South Ukraine in 1944, and Keilig (p. 227) states that he was acting commander of a panzer division when he was mortally wounded in July 1944, but (contrary to his usual practice) does not state which division Michalik was commanding; nor do the relevent records shed any light on the matter. As of July 15, 1944, Army Group South Ukraine had six panzer divisions (3rd, 13th, 14th, 23rd, 24th, and Grossdeutschland) (Mehner, Volume 10: 504) and all of their commanders seem to be accounted for. It is possible, however, that Michalik served in this post without it appearing on the records, perhaps as an acting commander. In any case he was posthumously promoted to major general.

Hans Troeger left the 27th Panzer Division to take a brief leave before assuming command of the School for Panzer Troops in Germany. By then the decision to dissolve the division had probably already been made, so command devolved upon the senior regimental commander, Joachim von Kronhelm. Kronhelm was commander of III/78th Artillery Regiment (1941–42) and the 127th Panzer Artillery Regiment (1942–43). In March 1944, he was assigned to the staff of the General of Artillery at OKH and, later that year, was commander of Arko 313 and Arko 500.

## NOTES AND SOURCES

The 127th Panzer Battalion was initially attached to the III Panzer Corps before its men were sent back to Versailles, France. Naturally, they left their tanks in Russia.

KTB OKW, Volume II: 1387, 1394; Mehner, Volume 5: 330; Volume 6: 546; Scheibert: 209; Stoves, *Die 22. Panzer-Division*: 195–262, 301; Tessin, Volume 4: 253; Volume 6: 319; Volume 10: 93; OB 43: 209; OB 45: 302; Windrow: 12.

# 116th Panzer (Formerly 16th Panzer Grenadier) Division

**COMPOSITION:**  16th Panzer Regiment, 60th Panzer Grenadier Regiment, 156th Panzer Grenadier Regiment, 146th Panzer Artillery Regiment, 116th Panzer Reconnaissance Battalion, 228th Tank Destroyer Battalion, 675th Panzer Engineer Battalion, 228th Panzer Signal Battalion, 281st Army Flak Artillery Battalion.

**HOME STATION:**  Muenster, later Wuppertal, Wehkreis VI

The 16th Infantry Division—the forerunner of the 116th Panzer Division—was originally formed in Muenster, in the VI (Rhineland/Westphalia) Military District in October 1934. Its men were mainly Rhinelanders and Westphalians, but included a few Prussians. As Hitler had not yet renounced the Treaty of Versailles, it existed under the code name "Kommandant of Muenster" until October 15, 1935, when it received its formal designation. The original 16th Infantry consisted of the 60th Infantry Regiment at Luedenscheid, the 64th Infantry Regiment at Soest, the 79th Infantry Regiment at Muenster (with the divisional headquarters), and the 16th Artillery Regiment at Hamm. All regiments had three battalions, numbered I, II, and III. In addition, the I Battalion, 52nd Artillery Regiment was attached to the 16th Artillery Regiment. The divisional support units (reconnaissance, signal, engineer, field replacement, and antitank battalions, as well as hospital, supply, veterinary, and other units) bore the number 16.

The division was sent to the Lower Rhine on the Western Front during the mobilization of August 1939. It was transferred to the Eifel sector (the German Ardennes) in November and December 1939. During this "Phony War" phase of World War II, the division lost the 16th Field Replacement (Feldersatz) Bat-

talion, which was transferred to the 196th Infantry Division and became III
Battalion/362nd Infantry Regiment (III/362nd). This took place in January 1940.
The following month, the II/64th Infantry Regiment was transferred to the 290th
Infantry Division and became the I/503rd Infantry Regiment. The 16th Infantry
took part in the invasion of Luxembourg, Belgium, and France in May and June
1940. Considered one of the best divisions in the German Army, it took part in
the Battle of Sedan (the most important battle of the campaign), where General
Guderian and his panzers scored their decisive breakthrough. It then helped
protect the "Panzer Corridor" from Allied counterattacks as the tanks pushed to
the sea.

The following month, the fall of Dunkirk, the 16th was part of the 16th Army, and took part
in mopping up operations in western France. In July 1940 it was briefly posted
to western France on occupation duty. Sent back to Muenster in July, the original 16th Infantry Division was divided. Most of the division—including the
divisional headquarters—was used to form the 16th Panzer Division, which was
later destroyed at Stalingrad. Both the 64th and 79th Infantry Regiments and
the staff and II Battalion, 16th Artillery Regiment were assigned to the new
tank unit. Of the original units, only the 60th Infantry Regiment and I/16th
Artillery Regiment were sent to Wuppertal, where they formed the new 16th
Infantry Division (Motorized), which was activated on August 8, 1940.

The staff of the new division was originally from the East Prussian 228th
Infantry Division, which had fought in Poland in 1939. As the weeks passed,
new units were assigned to the division. Its 156th Motorized Infantry Regiment
was formed from the 1st Security Regiment and III/10th Infantry Regiment
(transferred from the 4th Infantry Division). It also received the 165th Motorcycle Battalion, which was formed from the now-defunct 3rd Machine Gun Battalion. The newly created 146th Artillery Regiment Headquarters was formed from
the staff of the 311th Artillery Regiment. Its I Battalion was the original I/16th,
II Battalion was formerly I/697th Artillery Regiment, and the III Battalion (the
division's heavy artillery battalion) was the former 621st Heavy Artillery Battalion, which was now absorbed into the 16th Motorized Division. (The division
thus had only three artillery battalions, instead of the usual four.) The division
also received the 341st Reconnaissance Battalion, the 228th Antitank Battalion,
the 228th Signal Battalion, and the 675th Engineer Battalion. Its supply and
support units bore the number 66.

The 16th Motorized Division was sent to western France in November 1940,
where it completed its divisional training. It was hurriedly transferred to Hungary in March 1941, fought in the Balkans in the spring of 1941, and took part
in the capture of Sarajevo. Sent back to Wehrkreis VI in May, it was on its way
east when the invasion of Russia began on June 22, 1941. It fought in the battles
in Ukraine in 1941, helping 1st Panzer Group (later Army) to break the Stalin
Line in July. It later took part in the Battle of Kiev—the largest battle of encirclement in World War II—where 667,000 Soviet soldiers were captured. It was
then assigned to the 2nd Panzer Army and took part in the opening push toward

Moscow in October 1941. By November, however, it was fighting in the Kursk sector, as part of 2nd Army, on the southern flank of Army Group Center. It remained here throughout the winter battles of 1941–42, during which it suffered heavy casualties. It was still in the Kursk area in June when the Stalingrad offensive began. During the lull following Stalin's failure to destroy Army Group Center, the 16th Motorized was reinforced with two new units: the 116th Panzer Battalion (formerly I Battalion/1st Panzer Regiment) and the 281st Army Flak Artillery Battalion, which was soon redesignated IV Battalion, 146th Motorized Artillery Regiment. The following year, however, this battalion again became the 281st Army Flak Battalion.

The 16th Division fought on the southern sector throughout 1942, taking part in the Battle of Voronezh before being transferred to the Caucasus, where it took part in the capture of Armavir and the Mailop oil fields. Then it was shifted north to cover the large gap between the 1st and 4th Panzer armies in the Kirgisen Steppe, the vast wilderness south of Stalingrad. The reconnaissance battalion penetrated to within 20 miles of Astrakhan, the furthest eastward advance of any German unit during the entire war. During this period, a small squad of men from the division captured a wild greyhound on the steppes and spontaneously decided to name the 16th the Greyhound Division. The name stuck and was soon given official sanction.

The 16th Motorized fought against the Russians in the critical Don sector during the winter of 1942–43, and took part in the battles around Rostov and the retreat to the Mius before being transferred to the newly reconstituted 6th Army in the spring of 1943. At this time it was redesignated 16th Panzer Grenadier Division. It did not take part in the Battle of Kursk but did fight in the retreat from the Mius, suffering heavy casualties in the fighting around Zaporozh'ye. It also fought in the battles of Taganrog, Saporoshe, Krivoy Rog, Novo, Nikolajewka, Uman, and others. In the winter of 1943–44 it suffered very heavy losses in the withdrawal from the lower Dnieper, and the remnants of the 16th Panzer Grenadier Division were then transported to Rheime, Wehrkreis VI, where they were reorganized as the 116th Panzer Grenadier Division, which was officially activated on March 28, 1944. Within a few months they were transported to Laval in western France, where they absorbed the much larger 179th Reserve Panzer Division (a Wehrkreis IX [Hessian-Thuringian] unit) in May.

The new division included the 16th Panzer Regiment (formed from the staff of the 69th Panzer Regiment), which included two battalions: I (formerly the 116th Panzer Battalion) and II (formerly the 1st Reserve Panzer Battalion of the 179th Panzer Division). The 60th and 156th Panzer Grenadier Regiments remained with the division, but now they had only two battalions each. The 116th Reconnaissance Battalion became a panzer reconnaissance unit and absorbed the 1st Reserve Panzer Reconnaissance Battalion. The other units (all of which had been seriously depleted) absorbed the reservists, but did not change their structure. The new division was on the north bank of the Seine (in the Pas de

Calais region) on D-Day but was not committed to action until late July. It fought in the defense of the bocage (hedgerow) territory in Normandy and in the counterattack at Mortain in August but was unable to halt the American breakout later that month. The 116th was encircled at Falaise and broke out with heavy losses.

The Greyhound Division was down to 600, 12 tanks, and no artillery by August 21, 1944. Pulled out of the line, it was sent to the Eifel, where it hurriedly absorbed the XII, XIII, and XIX Luftwaffe Fortress Battalions, as well as a number of new PzKw VI Panther tanks. By September 1, it had a strength of 3,400 men, 40 tanks, and a full regiment of artillery. (Many of its tanks were Tigers. As it retreated through Verdun, the division discovered a train load of PzKw VIs, which it promptly appropriated and thus saved from American capture.) Shortly thereafter, the Greyhounds were again sent back to the front, which was once more on the verge of collapse.

In mid-September it was in action at Aachen, when its divisional commander, Lieutenant General Count Gerhard von Schwerin-Krosigk, was relieved of his command by Hitler for ordering an unauthorized retreat from the city. Hitler's decision led to bloody street fighting in Aachen, but it was tactically correct, for it significantly delayed the American advance into western Germany. Meanwhile, the 116th Panzer was withdrawn to the Dusseldorf area to reform in September and October 1944. It absorbed the 108th Panzer Brigade on October 13 and was reinforced to a strength of 11,500 men, but still had a total of only 41 tanks. Sent back to the front, the 116th Panzer was unable to prevent the Americans from taking Aachen, which fell on October 21. Shortly thereafter the Greyhounds were committed to the Battle of the Huertgen Forest, where they spearheaded a major counterattack against the advancing Americans and captured Schmidt (with a loss of 15 tanks) on November 8. American losses were much heavier. Later that month, the division was sent to the Cologne sector, to rest and to prepare for the Battle of the Bulge.

On December 16, 1944, the 116th Panzer Division spearheaded the southern prong of Hitler's Ardennes offensive and suffered heavy casualties. Withdrawn to Kleve in January 1945, the 116th Panzer was in action in the Netherlands in February, trying unsuccessfully to halt the British and Canadian advance on Germany. The division was almost trapped in the Wesel Pocket (west of the Rhine), but managed to escape across the river on March 5 and blew up the bridge behind it. Shifting south in the spring, the mass of the division was encircled and destroyed in the Battle of the Ruhr Pocket. One small Kampfgruppe, however, had been detached and assigned to the 11th Army in central Germany. It fought on the Elbe and surrendered to the Americans at the end of the war.

Commanders of the 16th Infantry/16th Motorized/16th Panzer Grenadier/ 116th Panzer Division included Colonel/Major General/Lieutenant General Gerhard Glokke (April 1, 1934), Major General/Lieutenant General Gotthard Heinrici (assumed command October 1, 1937), Major General Heinrich Krampf

(February 6, 1940), Major General Hans Valentin Hube (May 17, 1940), Lieutenant General Friedrich-Wilhelm von Chappuis (August 8, 1940), Lieutenant General Sigfrid Henrici (March 16, 1941), Lieutenant General Johannes Streich (acting commander, August 13, 1941), Henrici (resumed command, November 12, 1941), Count Gerhard von Schwerin-Krosigk (November 13, 1942), Colonel Wilhelm Crisolli (acting commander, May 20, 1943), Schwerin (resumed command, June 27, 1943), Colonel Guenther von Manteuffel (acting commander, February 10, 1944), Colonel Heinrich Voigtsberger (acting commander, March 15, 1944), Colonel Dr. Ernst Pean (acting commander, March 20, 1944), Schwerin (returned, April 1944), Voigtsberger (acting commander again, September 1944), Colonel Gerhard Mueller (September 1944) and Colonel/Major General Siegfried von Waldenburg (September 14, 1944–end).

## COMMANDERS

For a sketch of the lives of Gerhard Glokke, Gotthard Heinrici, and Hans Valentin Hube, see 16th Panzer Division, Commanders.

Heinrich Krampf was born in Wuerzburg in 1888 and entered the army as a Fahnenjunker in the 3rd Bavarian Infantry Regiment in 1908. He commanded the 31st Infantry Regiment (1938–40) before assuming command of the 16th. Later he commanded the 304th Infantry Division (November 15, 1940–November 16, 1942), before being given a rear-area territorial command (Oberfeldkommandantur 579) (late 1942-December 1943). After heading a special staff at OKH in early 1944, Krampf apparently ran afoul of the Nazis and was unemployed from April to August. He was then placed in charge of the rear area of 4th Army in the East, a corps-level post he held to the end of the war, but without the usual promotion to full general. Krampf had been promoted to major general on December 1, 1939, and to lieutenant general on December 1, 1941. He retired to Munich.

Friedrich-Wilhelm von Chappuis (1886–1942) began his service as a Faehnrich (senior officer candidate) in the grenadier guards. He commanded the 5th Infantry Regiment (1937–38) and later served as chief of staff of the XIV Motorized (subsequently Panzer) Corps (1938–40), commander of the 15th Infantry Division (1940), the 16th Motorized Division (1940–41), and XXXVIII Corps (1941–42). He was relieved of his command on April 24, 1942. With his career ruined, Chappuis returned to Magdeburg, Germany in despair and shot himself on August 27, 1942. He had been promoted to general of infantry on April 1, 1941.

Sigfrid Henrici was born in Soest in 1889 and entered the army as a Fahnenjunker in the 11th Artillery Regiment in 1907. After World War I he was not selected for retention in the Reichsheer ("the 100,000-man army"), which was only allowed 4,000 officers. He joined the police in 1920 and, as a police colonel, rejoined the army in December 1935. The following year he was given command of the 29th Artillery Regiment, and in 1938 Henrici took charge of

XVI Artillery Command. He led the 30th Artillery Command the following year. After leading the 16th Motorized, he commanded the XXXX Panzer Corps on the Eastern Front from November 13, 1942, to September 30, 1943, when he fell seriously ill. He did not resume command of the XXXX for almost a year. Now a general of panzer troops, he led it from September 3, 1944, until the end of the war. After 10 years in Soviet prisons, General Henrici retired to Berlin in 1955. He died in Bad Nauheim in 1964.

For a sketch of Johannes Streich's career, see 21st Panzer Division, Commanders.

Count Gerhard von Schwerin-Krosigk was born in Hanover in 1899. He was educated at various cadet schools and entered the Imperial Army as a Faehnrich when World War I broke out in August 1914. Discharged in 1920, he returned to active duty two years later as a lieutenant in the 1st Infantry Regiment. He was a lieutenant colonel on the staff of OKH when World War II began. Schwerin commanded a battalion of the elite Grossdeutschland Regiment in France (1940). He later commanded the 200th Special Purposes Regiment (1941), the 76th Infantry Regiment (July 1941–November 1942) and was acting commander of the 8th Jaeger Division on the Eastern Front in July 1942, before taking command of the 16th. He was correctly labeled a defeatist by the Nazis in the fall of 1944, and they considered court-martialing him for his attempt to evacuate Aachen without permission. Possibly because he held the Knight's Cross with Oak Leaves and Swords, however, they decided not to do so. His friends at OKH even succeeded in smoothing over the incident and obtaining another command for Schwerin, who took over the 90th Panzer Grenadier Division in Italy in December 1944. On April 1, 1945, he assumed command of the LXXVI Panzer Corps in Italy and was promoted to general of panzer troops the same day—a most unusual and rapid promotion—again reflecting the fact that Schwerin was well-connected. On April 25 he surrendered his command to the Allies without permission, earning him the censure of Field Marshal Kesselring. He died in Bavaria in late 1980.

Guenther von Manteuffel was born at Weimar in 1891. He joined the service in 1911, was commissioned in the infantry, fought in World War I, and was discharged in 1920. He managed to rejoin the army in 1922 and served in the cavalry. He commanded the 3rd Motorcycle Battalion (1935–late 1939), the 3rd Rifle Regiment (1939–late 1941), the 83rd Rifle Replacement Regiment (early 1942–1943), and the 1st Ski Jaeger Brigade (1943). After serving as acting commander of the 16th Panzer Grenadier Division (1944), he was commandant of Aalborg, Denmark (1944), commander of the ad hoc Division North Jutland (1944–45), and commander of Higher Artillery Command H (April 1945). Manteuffel was promoted to major general on November 9, 1944. He is not to be confused with Baron Hasso von Manteuffel, who commanded the 5th Panzer Army in the Battle of the Bulge.

Heinrich Voigtsberger (b. 1903) joined the army as a Fahnenjunker in 1922 and was commander of a machine gun company when the war broke out. He took command of the 60th Panzer Grenadier Regiment in 1942 (as a major) and led it until he became acting commander of the Greyhounds. In October 1944, he was sent to a divisional commanders' course and in December 1944 assumed command of the 309th Infantry Division on the Eastern Front. He was promoted to major general on April 1, 1945. He died in Munich in 1959.

As a captain, Dr. Ernst Pean commanded I/146th Motorized Artillery Regiment.

Gerhard Mueller, a native of Breslau, was born in 1896 and was commissioned in the 154th Infantry Regiment in 1916. Like many officers not selected for the Reichsheer, he joined the police in 1920, and returned to the army as a captain in 1935. He commanded the 33rd Antitank Battalion (1938–41), during which time his division (the 33rd Infantry) was converted into the 21st Panzer and transferred to Africa, as part of the Afrika Korps. Mueller himself managed to obtain command of a panzer battalion, and later the 5th Panzer Regiment, which he led with some distinction in the Gazala Line–Tobruk battles. During the battles in Egypt, however, one of his arms was blown off. Transferred back to Berlin after he got out of the hospital, Mueller was a branch chief at OKH and acting commander of the 12th Panzer Division on the Eastern Front (June–July, 1944), before assuming temporary command of the 9th Panzer Division on September 2, 1944. (This division, however, had suffered so many casualties in the Normandy/Falaise battles that it had been temporarily merged with the 2nd Panzer Division for tactical purposes.) Mueller was named commander of the 116th Panzer Division a few days later. His performance as a divisional commander left much to be desired, and his staff's loyalty to General von Schwerin did not help. In an almost unprecedented move, the 116th's headquarters staff and senior commanders revolted against Mueller and refused to obey his orders. OKW had little choice but to court-martial the staff for mutiny or remove Mueller from command. They chose the latter course. Although he was nevertheless promoted to major general effective September 1, 1944, he was named deputy commander of the 9th Panzer Division (a definite demotion) and held no further important assignments. At the end of the war, he was deputy commandant of Pilsen. He died in Landau in 1977.

Siegfried von Waldenburg was born in 1898 and joined the Imperial Army as a Fahnenjunker in July 1916. Commissioned in the 1st Guards Grenadier Regiment in August 1917, he distinguished himself in World War I and was retained in the Reichsheer. He was a major on the General Staff and Ia (chief of operations) of the 6th Infantry Division when World War II broke out. Later he served as chief of staff of XII Corps (1940–41) and was named deputy military attaché to Rome in November 1941. He took command of the 26th Panzer Grenadier Regiment on April 17, 1944. Many people did not expect the young colonel to be successful in leading the depleted 116th, given the demoralized and fractious nature of its staff, and the depleted and battered condition of its combat regiments; however, despite his age and relative lack of command experience, Waldenburg proved more than equal to the task, and even earned the special praise of the Fuehrer himself—a rare distinction indeed for a General Staff officer in the fifth year of the war. Waldenburg was living in Hanover in 1955.

## NOTES AND SOURCES

Angolia, *Field*, Volume 2: 293–94; Blumenson 1960: 296, 505, 539–49, 577, 579; Bradley et al., Volume 2: 420–21; Volume 5: 327–29; Carell 1966: 119, 521, 550–56; Carell 1971: 134; Chant 1979, Volume 14: 1859–61; Volume 16: 2133; Cole 1965: 195; Harrison: Map VI; Hartmann: 71–72; Keilig: 133, 136, 216, 232, 335, 361; Kennedy: 74, Map 7; MacDonald 1963: 82, 282, 284; MacDonald 1973: 140, 357, 370; Mehner, Volume 3: 381; Volume 6: 543; Volume 7: 353; Schmitz et al., Volume 3: 207–15, 225–35; Speidel: 42; Theodor-Friedrich von Stauffenberg, Papers and personal communications; Tessin, Volume 4: 30–32; Volume 6: 264–65; RA: 100; OB 42: 64; OB 43: 191–92, 205; OB 45: 302.

# (130th) Panzer Lehr Division

**COMPOSITION:**   130th Panzer Lehr Regiment, 901st Panzer Lehr Grenadier Regiment, 902nd Panzer Lehr Grenadier Regiment, 130th Panzer Lehr Artillery Regiment, 130th Panzer Lehr Reconnaissance Battalion, 130th Tank Destroyer Battalion, 130th Panzer Lehr Engineer Battalion, 130th Panzer Lehr Signal Battalion, 311th Army Antiaircraft Battalion.

**HOME STATION:**   Wehrkreis III

The Panzer Lehr was formed from the Demonstration (Lehr) units of Panzer Training School II at Krampnitz and elements of the 137th Infantry Division, which provided part of the Staff and many of the divisional support troops. The division formed up in the Verdun-Nancy-Luneville area of France in late December 1943 and January 1944. On April 4, it was given the official designation "130th," but is usually referred to simply as the Panzer Lehr Division. It was especially designed to repel the Western Allies' invasion of 1944. The 130th Panzer and 902nd Panzer Grenadier Regiments, as well as the 130th Panzer Reconnaissance Battalion, were formed from previously existing Lehr units. The 901st Panzer Lehr Grenadier Regiment had been serving as an independent unit on the Eastern Front. The I/130th Panzer Regiment was a Tiger battalion. The antitank battalion was the former III/Panzer Lehr Regiment. The I/130th Panzer Lehr Artillery Regiment was formed from the Fahnenjunker Artillery School at Mourmelon; the II/130th Panzer Artillery was a newly formed unit; and III Battalion was the former 985th Motorized Artillery Battalion from Ulm. Sent to eastern France in early 1944, it was transferred to Budapest, Hungary, that spring, because the Russian Front seemed to be on the verge of collapse, and

201

the new Hungarian government seemed ready to defect. When this did not happen, the new division was soon sent back to the West and camped in the Orleans, France, area in May 1944 and in the Le Mans area in early June. When the Allied invasion came, the Panzer Lehr Division was one of the strongest divisions in the German Army, with 109 tanks, 40 assault guns, and 612 half-tracked vehicles—double the normal panzer division's component of half-tracks. At its maximum strength, the Panzer Lehr Division had 14,634 men. The division was rushed to Normandy and thrown into the Battle of Caen, where it helped check the British advance on Caen, but at a terrible cost. Ordered by 7th Army to travel to the front in broad daylight on June 6—a horrendous blunder—Panzer Lehr lost more than 130 trucks and fuel tankers, 84 self-propelled guns, half-tracks and prime movers, and five tanks on D-Day alone. The loss of the tankers in particular hamstrung the division throughout the Normandy campaign. It suffered further heavy losses in the unsuccessful counterattack against Bayeux and in the more successful defensive engagements around Villers-Bocage and Tilly. On June 25 it had only 66 tanks left, and by July 25 its combined tank/assault gun total stood at 50—or 22 percent of its original 230. Between June 6 and June 30, the division also lost 490 men killed, 1,809 wounded, 673 missing, and 435 on sick leave (mostly with combat fatigue)—a total of 3,407. Sent to oppose the American advance east of St.-Lô, it was struck by 1,600 U.S. heavy and medium bombers on July 25. General Bayerlein, the divisional commander, reported that the division lost 70 percent of its men killed, wounded, or dazed, and all of its frontline tanks were knocked out. It nevertheless tried to check the advance of the entire U.S. VII Corps with its last 15 tanks, most of which were hastily pulled out of the repair shops and rushed to the front. As a result, the Americans gained less than two miles on July 25. The next day, however, the U.S. 2nd Armored Division and other units broke through the shattered German lines and drove south, rupturing the entire German front. It was the beginning of the end for the Germans in France. The next day, Bayerlein reported that the Panzer Lehr Division was "finally annihilated." As the divisional historian notes, however, the division was still a fairly potent force and had not been annihilated—although it was badly damaged. On July 29, for example, it put up a sharp resistance at Percy, where 2nd Lieutenant von Knebel of the panzer regiment personally knocked out 13 Shermans. Lieutenant Colonel Willi Welsch, the commander of the 902nd Panzer Grenadier Regiment, was killed in this battle.

On August 2–3, the division was divided into three battle groups under the commanders and staffs of the Panzer Lehr, 901st Panzer Grenadier, and 902nd Panzer Grenadier Regiments, and fought in different sectors during the Battle of the Falaise Pocket. They broke out in three different thrusts—the grenadiers attaching themselves to the 116th Panzer and 12th SS Panzer Divisions. As of August 23, when the division at last reunited at Senlis, its strength by unit included the following:

130th Panzer Lehr Regiment: 180 men, 20 PzKw IV and V tanks

901st Panzer Grenadier Regiment: 800 men

902nd Panzer Grenadier Regiment: 300 men

130th Panzer Lehr Artillery Regiment: six 105mm and six 150mm self-propelled howitzers

130th Panzer Reconnaissance Battalion: 150 men, eight halftracks

130 Panzer Engineer Battalion: 150 men

Stragglers: 500 men

Wounded and personnel returning from leave: 750 men

On August 24, 22 new PzKw IVs arrived. Thus reinforced, the division was able to conduct a staged retreat into the West Wall, covering Bitburg, although casualties were again relatively heavy. On September 1, it had a strength of 11 tanks, no artillery, and less than 500 men. When it was assigned to the 1st Army as an independent formation later that month, the division's strength was one panzer grenadier battalion, six 105mm howitzers, one engineer company, five tanks, a reconnaissance platoon, and a 200-man special battalion formed from stragglers. It fought in the early Siegfried Line battles in Luxembourg with LXXXI Corps, before being rebuilt by the 6th Panzer Army at Paderborn, Wehrkreis VI. It received 72 new tanks, 21 assault guns, and hundreds of replacement soldiers, mostly of indifferent quality. It was quickly returned to the 1st Army, then fighting in the Saar sector, in November 1944 and helped prevent Army Group G from collapsing under Patton's heavy attacks—although the division itself was far from the elite force that had battled the Allies to a standstill in Normandy the previous June. General Balck, the commander in chief of Army Group G and a veteran armored commander, was so shocked by the low battle readiness of Panzer Lehr that he ordered the 25th Panzer Grenadier Division to send up a regiment to support it. Only its timely arrival prevented the U.S. 4th Armored and 4th Infantry Divisions from encircling it west of Domfessel on November 27.

Withdrawn from the line in early December, the Panzer Lehr Division was once again brought up to strength by an infusion of equipment and replacements—mostly of indifferent quality. Still, as of December 12, it had 30 PzKw IVs, 23 Panthers, 14 assault guns, and 14 howitzers (mostly heavies). It was soon committed to the Battle of the Bulge, where Panzer Lehr—badly led by General Bayerlein—besieged Bastogne as part of the XXXXVII Panzer Corps but failed to take the town. By January 1, 1945, the division had lost 2,465 men killed and another 1,475 wounded or ill. Some 75 percent of the division's rolling stock was out of action, although much of this loss was not permanent. The battle had so upset General Bayerlein that Friedrich von Stauffenberg described him as "drifting from embattled unit to embattled unit in a complete daze." He was already scheduled to be replaced by Colonel Horst Niemack, the incredibly brave commander of the elite Grossdeutschland Fusilier Regiment, but he was too busy dealing with massive Soviet assaults on East Prussia to leave his post; Bayerlein therefore handed command over to his Ia, Lieutenant Colonel Kurt Kauffmann, on January 25.

After the defeat of the Ardennes offensive, Panzer Lehr fought in the Battle of the Maas Line in the Netherlands (March 1945) but could not prevent the British and Canadians from breaking through the position. The division attempted to eradicate the American bridgehead at Remagen in early March but failed. In this battle the Lehr had only 600 men and 15 tanks left. The burned-out division retreated into the Ruhr Pocket in April 1945, and at the end of this battle surrendered to the U.S. 99th Infantry Division on April 15.

Commanders of the Panzer Lehr Division included Major General Oswin Grolig (assumed command December 27, 1943), Lieutenant General Fritz Bayerlein (February 10, 1944), Colonel Rudolph Gerhardt (acting commander effective August 23, 1944), Colonel Baron Paul von Hauser (acting commander, September 1944), Bayerlein again (returned to command, September 8, 1944), Lieutenant Colonel Kurt Kauffmann (January 5, 1945), Colonel/Major General Horst Niemack (January 15, 1945), and Colonel Baron von Hauser again (acting commander April 3–15, 1945).

## COMMANDERS

Oswin Grolig served as acting divisional commander from the time Colonel General Heinz Guderian, the chief of the Panzer Inspectorate, ordered the forming of the Panzer Lehr Division (December 27, 1943) until Bayerlein arrived from the Eastern Front. For a sketch of his career, see commanders, 25th Panzer Division.

Fritz Bayerlein (1899–1970), a native of Wuerzburg, joined the army as a Fahnenjunker in 1917. He left the service after World War I but soon rejoined the military as an enlisted man because he could not find employment in chaotic, postwar Germany. Commissioned in the infantry in 1922, Bayerlein was Ib (chief supply officer) of the 3rd Panzer Division (1938), Ia (chief of operations) of the 10th Panzer Division (1939–40), was Guderian's Ia in France and Russia (1940–41), chief of staff of the Afrika Korps (1941–42), chief of staff of Panzer Army Afrika (1942–43), and chief of staff of the 1st Italian-German Panzer Army. Wounded in the last days of the war in North Africa, he was evacuated to Europe. Upon recovery, he commanded the 3rd Panzer Division in Russia (1943) before being given command of Panzer Lehr, which he led on the Western Front from D-Day until almost the end of the war. He commanded the LIII Corps in the Battle of the Ruhr Pocket, where he surrendered to the Americans in April 1945. He was promoted to lieutenant general on May 1, 1944, and held the Knight's Cross with Oak Leaves and Swords. Despite his popularity with certain Western historians immediately after World War II, Bayerlein's handling of the Panzer Lehr Division in Normandy was mediocre and his conduct during the Battle of the Bulge was exceptionally poor. At one point, for example, he wasted valuable time trying to seduce a captured American nurse. At another point during the battle, in fact, Baron von Manteuffel, the commander of the 5th Panzer Army, was seriously considering relieving Baron von Luettwitz of the command of the XXXXVII Panzer Corps, which had bogged down outside Bastone. Apparently the only reason he did not do so was that Bayerlein was the senior divisional commander in the XXXXVII Panzer, and Manteuffel thought he was inferior to Luettwitz!

Rudolph Gerhardt was the commander of the Panzer Lehr Regiment (1944–January 1945). He had previously commanded the 7th Panzer Regiment (1943).

Baron Paul von Hauser was the commander of the 901st Panzer Grenadier Regiment (1944–45).

Kurt Kauffmann was Ia of Panzer Lehr from its inception in January 1944. He was promoted to lieutenant colonel later that year.

Horst Niemack was promoted to major general on April 1, 1945. Born in Hanover in 1909, young Niemack was educated in various cadet schools and joined the army as an officer cadet in the 18th Cavalry Regiment in 1927. When World War II broke out, he was a captain, commanding 3rd Company, 5th Reconnaissance Battalion (1939–40). Later he commanded the battalion itself (1940–41), served as a training group commander at Panzer Troop School II (1941–43), and led the 26th Panzer Grenadier Regiment (1943) and the Grossdeutschland Fusilier Regiment (1943–44). Wounded on August 22, 1944, he was hospitalized until the end of 1944. A holder of the Knight's Cross with Oak Leaves and Swords, Niemack was a much better divisional commander than Bayerlein. General Niemack was wounded again on April 2, 1945 (the day after he was promoted to major general), and was in a field hospital when he was captured. Horst Niemack joined the West German Army in 1957 as a brigadier general. After he retired, he became a member of the German Olympic Committee for equestrians. He died in an accident in 1992.

## NOTES AND SOURCES

The (130th) Panzer Lehr Reconnaissance Battalion (five companies) came from the Panzer Reconnaissance Demonstration Battalion of the Panzer Troops School, Berlin-Krampnitz.

Angolia, *Field*, Volume 1: 174–76; Blumenson 1960: 273, 422; Bradley et al., Volume 1: 241–42; Cole 1950: 464–65, 469; Cole 1965: 37, 473; D'Este, *Normandy*: 402–03; Harrison: 234, 334; Hartmann: 72–73; Keilig: 23, 243; MacDonald 1963: Map 11, 42; MacDonald 1973: 140, 221, 346, 370; Helmut Ritgen, *Die Geschichte der Panzer-Lehr-Division im Westen, 1944–1945* (Stuttgart: Motorbuch Verlag, 1979): 1 ff.; Scheibert: 174; Stauffenberg MS and personal communications; Tessin, Volume 14: 273–74; OB 45: 302–03. For the story of the destruction of Panzer Lehr in the Normandy campaign, see Paul Carell, *Invasion: They're Coming* (Boston, 1965; reprint ed., New York, 1966).

# 155th Reserve Panzer
# (Formerly Replacement) Division

**COMPOSITION:** 7th Reserve Panzer Battalion, 5th Reserve Panzer Grenadier Regiment, 25th Reserve Motorized Grenadier Regiment, 260th Reserve Artillery Battalion, 7th Reserve Tank Destroyer Battalion, 5th Reserve Panzer Reconnaissance Battalion, 19th Reserve Panzer Engineer Battalion.

**HOME STATION:** Ulm (later Stuttgart and Ludwigsburg), Wehrkreis V

This division was activated on August 26, 1939, as Replacement Division Staff 155 (Division Nr. 155). On November 9, it was transferred to Prague but returned to Wehrkreis V in September 1940. During its Czech period, it consisted of the 5th Infantry Regiment Regiment at Laun (14th, 56th, and 75th Battalions); 25th Infantry Replacement Regiment at Pisek (13th, 35th, and 119th Battalions); 35th Infantry Replacement Regiment at Budweis (34th, 109th, and 111th Battalions); 4th Machine Gun Battalion at Schlan; 25th Artillery Replacement Regiment at Pilsen (5th, 25th, 61st, and 77th Artillery Replacement Battalions and the 5th Observation Replacement Battalion); 18th Cavalry Replacement Regiment at Klattau; 5th Panzer Jaeger Replacement Battalion at Prague; 5th Signal Replacement Battalion at Kuttenberg; 5th Engineer Replacement Battalion at Pardubitz; and the 5th Supply (*Fahr*) Replacement Battalion at Prague.

By August 23, 1941, the divisional headquarters had moved to Stuttgart, and the division consisted of the 25th Infantry Replacement Regiment at Stuttgart; the 35th Infantry Replacement Battalion at Heilbronn; the 215th Infantry Replacement Regiment at Heilbronn (with the 460th and 470th Infantry Replacement Battalions and the 4th Machine Gun Replacement Battalion); the 25th Artillery Replacement Regiment at Karlsruhe (with the 25th, 61st, 77th, 215th, and 260th Battalions); the 18th Cavalry Replacement Battalion at Stuttgart-Bad Cannstatt; the 5th Panzer Jaeger Replacement Battalion at Karlsruhe; the 35th Engineer Replacement Battalion at Karlsruhe; and the 5th Supply Replacement Battalion at Rastatt. On May 12, 1942, the divisional staff was transferred again, this time to Ludwigsburg, and the 155th was reorganized. Now it consisted of the 7th Panzer Replacement Battalion at Boeblingen; the 5th Panzer Grenadier Replacement Regiment at Ludwigsburg (with the 86th and 215th Battalions); the 25th Motorized Infantry Replacement Regiment at Stuttgart (35th and 119th Battalions); 18th Cavalry Replacement Battalion at Bad Cannstatt; 5th Panzer Jaeger Battalion at Karlsruhe; 260th Motorized Artillery Replacement Battalion at Ludwigsburg; 5th Observation Replacement Battalion and 5th Panzer Engineer Replacement Battalion at Ulm; 5th Motorcycle Replacement Battalion at Villingen; and the 25th Motorcycle Replacement Battalion at Muellheim/Baden.

On April 5, 1943, the division was redesignated 155th Panzer Replacement Division, but with no change in its organizational structure; however, on August 1, 1943, it was redesignated 155th Reserve Panzer Division and was sent to Rennes in northwest France. Here it consisted of the 7th Panzer Reserve Battalion; 5th Reserve Panzer Grenadier Regiment (86th and 215th Battalions); 25th Reserve Motorized Grenadier Regiment (35th and 119th Battalions); 260th Reserve Motorized Artillery Battalion; 9th Reserve Motorized Reconnaissance Battalion; and 5th Reserve Panzer Jaeger Battalion. Later the division moved to Nîmes, France, and added the 1055th Panzer Signal Company. The division was used to train motorized and panzer troops, which were then often sent to other units. It was also used as a source of equipment for several understrength tank divisions. By March 1944 the division had only 60 tanks (PzKw IIIs and IVs). Admiral Ruge, Rommel's naval advisor, noted that the loss of trained personnel, which the 155th supplied to other armored units, had severely retarded the division's combat readiness.

In May 1944, this process was carried to its logical conclusion when the 155th Reserve Panzer was absorbed by the 9th Panzer Division. Its commanders included Major General Otto Tscherning (November 16, 1939), Major General/Lieutenant General Franz Landgraf (May 1, 1942), Major General Max Fremerey (August 1, 1942), Major General Kurt von Jesser (August 24, 1943), and Fremerey again (returned to command, September 6, 1943).

## COMMANDERS

Otto Tscherning (1891–1955), a Westphalian, joined the Imperial Army as a Fahnenjunker in 1899 and was commissioned in the 13th Field Artillery Regiment in 1900. He fought in World War I, was accepted into the Reichsheer, and was Artillery Fuehrer VII and deputy commander of the 7th Infantry Division in Munich in 1933. He retired as a lieutenant general in 1936 but was recalled to active duty when the war broke out. Initially he commanded Replacement Troops Command V, which was assigned to the 155th Replacement Division on November 9, 1939. Considered too old for active field service, Tscherning was nevertheless an excellent administrator and a good example of how the Wehrmacht used its older officers to great advantage. On May 10, 1942, when the 155th was moved to Ludwigsburg, General Tscherning remained in Stuttgart (his hometown) and took command of the 405th Replacement Division. He retired for a second and final time the following year.

Franz Landgraf (1888–1944) was born in Munich and joined the Bavarian 5th Infantry Regiment as a Faehnrich in 1909. After serving in World War I and in the Reichsheer, Landgraf commanded the 7th Panzer Regiment (1936–39), 4th Panzer Brigade (1939–41), and the 6th Panzer Division (1941–42). He oversaw the conversion of the 155th into a reserve panzer division and was promoted to lieutenant general on September 1, 1942, but fell ill and retired a month later. He died in Stuttgart in 1944.

Max Fremerey was born in Cologne in 1889 and joined the cavalry as an officer cadet in 1910. He served in World War I and in the Reichswehr, and was commander of the 17th Cavalry Regiment (1934–39) and the 3rd Higher Cavalry Command (1939). When World War II broke out Fremerey was given command of the 480th Infantry Regiment (1939–40)—somewhat of a demotion—but then led the 18th Rifle Brigade (1940–41) and the elite 29th Motorized Infantry Division on the Russian Front (1941–42). He returned to Germany—why is not clear—in late September 1942 while his division was engaged in the early stages of the Battle of Stalingrad. Fremerey was not reemployed until February 1943, when he became Commandant of Hanover. Fremerey seems to have either suffered a severe wound or his health failed; in any case, he received no further field commands, although his record as a divisional commander was good and he received his promotion to lieutenant general on June 1, 1943—more or less on schedule. Fremerey spent the rest of the war commanding the 155th Reserve Panzer Division (1943–44) and the 233rd Reserve Panzer Division in Jutland (1944–45). He was released from Allied captivity in 1947 and died in Kruen, Upper Bavaria, on September 20, 1968.

Kurt von Jesser (1890–1950), an Austrian, was born in Poland. He joined the Austro-Hungarian Army in 1910 as an officer cadet in the infantry. After fighting in World War I he was accepted into the new Austrian Army in 1919 and was commander of the 3rd Motorcycle Battalion in 1938, when Austria was annexed by the Third Reich. Jesser was immediately inducted into the Panzerwaffe, initially as a staff officer in the 2nd Panzer Regiment (1938–40). He later commanded the 36th Panzer Regiment in France and Russia (1940–42), commanded the XIII School for Mobile Troops (1942), and briefly led the mediocre 386th Motorized Infantry Division from December 1942 until it was absorbed by the 3rd Panzer Grenadier Division on March 1, 1943. The exact nature of his next assignment is unclear, although he reportedly commanded a security brigade in France. After briefly commanding the 155th, von Jesser was unemployed for more than a year, when he was given command of a fortified sector of Steiermark. Captured by the Russians but soon released, he died in

Vienna in 1950. General von Jesser was obviously not highly thought of as a panzer commander.

## NOTES AND SOURCES

Bradley et al., Volume 4: 71–72; Keilig: 95, 158, 350; Mehner, Volume 4: 384; Volume 5: 329; Volume 6: 544; Volume 7: 357; Friedrich Ruge, *Rommel in Normandy* (San Rafael, California, 1979): 96; Tessin, Volume 7: 92–94; RA: 6, 88; OB 43: 148; OB 45: 184.

# 178th Panzer Replacement Division

**COMPOSITION (1945):** 15th Panzer Replacement and Training Battalion, 85th Panzer Grenadier Replacement and Training Regiment, 128th Motorized Grenadier Training Regiment, 55th Panzer Reconnaissance Replacement and Training Battalion, 8th Panzer Jaeger Replacement Battalion.

**HOME STATION:** Liegnitz, Wehrkreis VIII

Created on December 15, 1940, from the motorized elements of the 148th and 158th Replacement Divisions in Lothringen and Alsace, the 178th Replacement Division (which was officially designated Division Nr. 178) was used to control motorized training and replacement units in Silesia. It initially consisted of the 15th Panzer Replacement Battalion at Sagan; the 85th Rifle Replacement Regiment at Liegnitz (controlling the 13th and 110th Rifle Replacement Battalions and the 55th Motorcycle Replacement Battalion); the 30th and 51st Motorized Infantry Replacement Battalions at Goerlitz; and the 116th Motorized Artillery Battalion at Liegnitz. (Later Staff, 128th Motorized Grenadier Training Regiment was formed to control the 30th and 51st Motorized Replacement Battalions, and the 116th Motorized Artillery was expanded into a regiment in November 1941.) The 178th Division never left Military District VIII. In autumn 1942 it retained both its training and replacement functions, despite the fact that almost all of the other replacement divisions in the Home Army had given up their training formations. The 178th was redesignated a motorized replacement division on April 20, 1942, and became a panzer replacement division on April 5, 1943, when it had the composition shown above. (The 116th Motorized Artillery Regiment was transferred to Oppeln and became part of the 432nd Replacement Division on March 31, 1943.)

210

The 178th Panzer Replacement Division (Panzer Division Nr. 178) was deactivated in December 1944 and January 1945, and most of the division's units were absorbed by Panzer (Field Training) Division Tatra in late 1944–early 1945. The 128th Regiment (now a replacement and training unit), however, remained in Silesia, directly under HQ, Wehrkreis VIII. It was destroyed when the Soviets overran Silesia in 1945.

Commanders of the 178th included Lieutenant General Curt Bernard (December 12, 1940), Lieutenant General Friedrich-Wilhelm von Loeper (May 1, 1942), Lieutenant General Karl-Friedrich von der Meden (October 1, 1944), Major General Hans-Ulrich Back (October 9, 1944), and Meden again (January 1, 1945).

## COMMANDERS

Curt Bernard was born in Berlin in 1886. He joined the 15th Dragoons as a Fahnenjunker in 1905. After fighting in World War I, he served in the Reichsheer and was a major general and chief of staff of Army Group 4 (1937–39). Shortly after the war broke out, he was promoted to lieutenant general and was given command of the 178th, a post he held until his retirement in 1942. Apparently his health was not robust enough for active campaigning. He died in Goettingen in 1954.

For the details of General Friedrich-Wilhelm von Loeper's career, see Panzer Division Tatra.

Karl-Friedrich von der Meden (b. 1896) was promoted to major general on October 1, 1943, and to lieutenant general on July 1, 1944. He served in jaeger (light infantry) regiments in World War I and in the cavalry between the wars, rising to major commanding I/5th Cavalry Regiment in 1939. During World War II, Meden commanded the 12th Reconnaissance Battalion (1939–41), the 48th Infantry Regiment (1941–42), the 1st Rifle Regiment (1942–43), the 17th Panzer Division (1943–44), and the 178th Reserve Panzer Division (1944–45). He settled in Hamburg after the war.

For a sketch of Hans-Ulrich Back's career, see 232nd Panzer Division.

## NOTES AND SOURCES

Bradley et al., Volume 1: 343–44; Keilig: 16, 30, 45, 208; Mehner, Volume 4: 384; Tessin, Volume 6: 265, 322; Volume 7: 194–95; RA: 132–33; OB 43: 152; OB 45: 194.

# 179th Reserve Panzer Division

**COMPOSITION:** 1st Reserve Panzer Battalion, 81st Reserve Panzer Grenadier Regiment, 29th Reserve Motorized Grenadier Regiment, 29th Reserve Panzer Artillery Battalion, 1st Reserve Panzer Reconnaissance Battalion, 9th Reserve Tank Destroyer Battalion, 29th Reserve Panzer Engineer Battalion, 81st Reserve Panzer Signal Battalion.

**HOME STATION:** Weimar, Wehrkreis IX

The 179th Reserve Panzer was originally created as a special purposes staff to control replacement and training units in the IX Military District. Formed in 1939, just after the outbreak of the war, it became the 179th Replacement Division (Division Nr. 179) on January 5, 1940. By March it consisted of the 72nd Motorized Infantry Replacement Regiment at Erfurt (71st, 86th, 187th, and 451st Battalions); the 52nd Infantry Replacement Regiment at Kassel (15th, 163rd, and 459th Battalions); the 81st Rifle Replacement Regiment at Meiningen (1st, 6th and 12th Battalions); the 205th Infantry Replacement Battalion at Frankfurt; the 1st Panzer Replacement Battalion at Erfurt; the 15th Artillery Replacement Regiment at Erfurt (29th, 65th, and 73rd Battalions); the 4th Motorized Reconnaissance Replacement Battalion at Sondershausen; the 29th Engineer Replacement Battalion at Hann Muenden; the 81st Motorized Signal Replacement Battalion at Weimar; the 15th Motorcycle Replacement Battalion at Rudolstadt; and the 9th Construction Engineer Replacement Battalion at Bad Langensalza. The 179th became a motorized replacement division staff on February 27, 1942, controlling all of the panzer and motorized units in Wehrkreis IX, and was reorganized as the 179th Panzer Replacement Division (also known as Panzer Replacement Division Staff 179) on April 5, 1943, when it became part of the Panzerwaffe.

On July 30, 1943, the division was again redesignated (to 179th Panzer Reserve Division) and was sent to the Laval area of western France. Here it controlled the units shown under "Composition," although it was quickly depleted by the regular panzer divisions, whose losses (and needs for trained replacements) were tremendous. By late January 1944, the division could only deploy one panzer company, one combat-ready foot battalion, and one coastal defense battalion. It lacked antitank weapons, communications equipment, and even transport for its artillery. On May 1, 1944, it was combined with the 16th Panzer Grenadier Division to form the 116th Panzer Division and ceased to exist on May 10.

Commanders of the 179th in its various incarnations included Major General Herbert Stimmel (January 10, 1940), Lieutenant General Max von Hartlieb gen. Walsporn (June 20, 1940), and Major General/Lieutenant General Walter Boltenstern (January 20, 1942–end).

## COMMANDERS

Herbert Stimmel (1886–1946) was a native of Darmstadt. He joined the army as a cadet in the 142nd Infantry Regiment in 1905, fought in World War I and served in the Reichswehr, and was commander of the 34th Infantry Regiment by 1934. Later he served as inspector of Recruiting Area Weimar (1938–40), and commander of the 179th Replacement Division (1940), the 98th Infantry Division (1940), and the 279th Infantry Division (1940–41). He was named an honorary lieutenant general on June 1, 1940, and was promoted to full rank a year later. He was inspector of Recruiting Area Eger (headquartered at Karlsbad) (1941–44) and commandant of Karlsbad (1944–45). He died in Russian captivity.

For a sketch of Max von Hartlieb gen. Walsporn's career, see 5th Panzer Division.

Walter Boltenstern (1889–1952) was a Silesian. Joining the army as a Fahnenjunker in the 5th Guards Grenadier Regiment, he fought in World War I and served in the Reichsheer. He commanded the 71st Motorized Infantry Regiment (1938–40) and the 29th Motorized Division (1940–41) on the Eastern Front before his health failed him in September. Upon recovery he was given command of the 179th, which he held for the rest of its existence. It was his last major assignment. Promoted to lieutenant general on August 1, 1942, Boltenstern retired after his division was absorbed, although he did occasionally sit on the Reich Military Court (1943–44). Arrested by the Russians at the end of the war, he died in a Soviet prison.

## NOTES AND SOURCES

Bradley et al., Volume 2: 131–32; Hartmann: 71; Keilig: 45, 335; Mehner, Volume 4: 384; Volume 7: 357; Friedrich Ruge, *Rommel in Normandy* (San Rafael, California, 1979): 62.

# 232nd Panzer Division

**COMPOSITION:**   101st Panzer Grenadier Regiment, 102nd Panzer Grenadier Regiment.

**HOME STATION:**   None

The 232nd Panzer Division was formed in Slovakia on February 21, 1945, from Panzer Field Training Division Tatra. The 101st Panzer Grenadier Regiment was the former 82nd Panzer Grenadier Replacement and Training Regiment, and the 102nd Panzer Grenadier Regiment was the former 85th Panzer Grenadier Replacement and Training Regiment. The divisional commander was Major General Hans-Ulrich Back, who had previously commanded the 178th Reserve Panzer Division and Panzer Field Training Division Tatra. Hurriedly sent to Army Group South on the Eastern Front, the 232nd fought in the Battle of the Raab Bridgehead, where it was smashed and overwhelmed at the end March, 1945. Only small remnants of the division escaped when the bridgehead collapsed. General Back only escaped the disaster because he had been severely wounded on March 29.

## COMMANDER

Major General Hans-Ulrich Back, was born in Saarbruecken in 1896 and joined the army as a Fahnenjunker when World War I broke out. He served as an infantry lieutenant for most of the war and was wounded four times. Not selected for the Reichsheer, he joined the Freikorps in 1920 and then the Hanover police. Returning to military duty as a captain in 1935, he commanded I/2nd

214

Rifle Regiment (1938–40), I/304th Rifle Regiment (1940), 304th Rifle Regiment (1940–42), 11th Panzer Grenadier Brigade (1942), Mobile Troops School XVII (1942–43), 16th Panzer Division (1943–44), 178th Panzer Replacement Division Staff (1944), Panzer Field Training Division Tatra (1945), and 232nd Reserve Panzer Division (1945). Despite a lengthy service commanding various divisions, Back was never promoted to lieutenant general. He was promoted to major general on February 1, 1944. He died in Hagen-Ernst in 1976.

## NOTES AND SOURCES

Bradley et al., Volume 1: 142–44; Keilig: 16; Mehner, Volume 12: 459; Tessin, Volume 8: 148; Windrow: 13.

# 233rd Reserve Panzer (Later Panzer) Division

**COMPOSITION:** 5th Reserve Panzer Battalion, 83rd Reserve Panzer Grenadier Regiment, 3rd Reserve Motorized Grenadier Regiment, 59th Reserve Artillery Battalion, 3rd Reserve Panzer Reconnaissance Battalion, 3rd Reserve Tank Destroyer Battalion, 208th Reserve Panzer Engineer Battalion, 1233rd Reserve Panzer Signal Company.

**HOME STATION:** Frankfurt an der Oder, Wehrkreis III

Established as the 233rd Motorized Replacement Division (Division 233 [mot.]) on May 15, 1942, the 233rd Reserve Panzer's initial task was to control motorized replacement and training units in the III Military District. It was reorganized as a panzer grenadier replacement division (July 7, 1942), a panzer replacement division (April 5, 1943), a reserve panzer division (August 10, 1943), and a panzer division (February 22, 1945). As of July 7, 1942, it included the 5th Panzer Replacement Battalion at Neuruppin; 83rd Panzer Grenadier Replacement Regiment at Eberswalde (3rd, 8th, 9th, and 50th Panzer Grenadier Replacement Battalions); 3rd Motorized Infantry Replacement Regiment at Frankfurt an der Oder (8th and 29th Motorized Infantry Replacement Battalions); 3rd Tank Destroyer Replacement Battalion at Potsdam (later Spremberg); 3rd Motorcycle Replacement Battalion at Freienwalde; 9th Cavalry (later Bicycle) Replacement Battalion at Fuerstenwalde; and the 208th Panzer Engineer Replacement Battalion at Rathenow.

On April 5, 1943, the 233rd was transferred from the Home Army to General Guderian's independent Panzer Inspectorate, and its bicycle battalion became a panzer reconnaissance unit. The division was posted to central Jutland (the pen-

216

insula of Denmark) in late 1943. It remained in Denmark, headquartered at Horsens, training panzer crews and motorized troops, until the end of the war. Except for an occasional Allied bombing or commando raid, it never saw combat.

In early February 1945, however, the divisional staff became Staff, Panzer Division Holstein. At the same time, the 5th Reserve Panzer Battalion was transferred to the Holstein Division as the 44th Panzer Battalion; the 83rd Reserve Panzer Grenadier Regiment and the 3rd Motorized Grenadier Regiment left the division to become the 139th and 142nd Panzer Grenadier Regiments of the Holstein unit, respectively; and the 3rd Reserve Panzer Reconnaissance Battalion became the 44th Panzer Reconnaissance Battalion in the new division. The other elements of the division now came under a variety of commands; however, Wehrmacht Command Denmark quickly formed a new divisional headquarters, the 233rd Panzer, which was fully activated by April. Organized for combat as a Kampfgruppe, it had only 34 tanks (including two command tanks). As of May 7, 1945—just before it surrendered—the 233rd Panzer Division consisted of the 42nd Panzer Grenadier Regiment (three battalions); 50th Panzer Grenadier Regiment (two battalions); 83rd Panzer Grenadier Regiment (two battalions); 233rd Panzer Reconnaissance Battalion; 1033rd Tank Destroyer Battalion (formerly the 3rd Reserve Tank Destroyer Battalion); 1233rd Artillery Regiment (which included only one battalion, the 1233rd [formerly 59th Reserve] Artillery Battalion); the 1233rd Panzer Engineer Battalion (formerly the 208th Reserve Engineer Battalion); and the 1233rd Panzer Signal Company.

Commanders of the 233rd Reserve Panzer included Lieutenant General Curt Jahn (assumed command, November 1, 1941), Lieutenant General Heinrich Wosch (March 1, 1943), Major General Kurt Cuno (August 8, 1943), and Lieutenant General Max Fremerey (June 7, 1944–end).

## COMMANDERS

Curt Jahn (b. 1892) was an officer cadet who was commissioned in the 30th Field Artillery Regiment in 1911. After fighting in World War I and serving in the Reichsheer, he commanded the 5th Artillery Regiment (1934–36), 35th Artillery Regiment (1936–37), 35th Artillery Command (1937–38), and the Artillery School (1938–40). In late 1940 he assumed command of the 121st Infantry Division (1940–41) and later commanded the 233rd Replacement (1942–43), the 709th Infantry Division (1943), Harko 308 (the 308th Higher Artillery Command) (1943–44), was acting commander of the 18th Panzer Grenadier Division and the 12th Infantry Division (1944), and commanded LXXXVII Corps (1944) and the German-Italian Corps Lombardi (1944–45). Jahn was promoted to lieutenant general in 1940 and to general of artillery in 1944.

A Silesian, Heinrich Wosch was born in Breslau in 1888. He entered the service as a cadet in the 19th Infantry Regiment in 1908, served in World War I and the Reichsheer, and was commander of the 8th Infantry Regiment (1938–

41) when World War II broke out. He later commanded the 14th Motorized Infantry Division (1941–42), the 233rd (1943), and the 408th Replacement Division (1944–45).

Kurt Cuno was born in Zweibruecken in 1896 and joined the 4th Bavarian Engineer Battalion as a Fahnenjunker in 1915. After serving in the Reichswehr, he was commander of the I/25th Panzer Regiment (1937–39), commander, 1st Panzer Regiment (1940), and headed a branch at OKH (1940). Later he commanded the 39th Panzer Regiment (late 1940–January 22, 1942). His health snapped under the rigors of the Eastern Front, and he did not return to active duty until late December 1942, as commander of mobile troops in Wehrkreis XIII. He took charge of the 233rd in 1943 and later served as general of motor pools at OKH (1944–end). He was promoted to lieutenant general in 1944. Released from Allied captivity in 1947, General Cuno died in Munich in 1961.

For a sketch of Max Fremerey's career, see 155th Reserve Panzer Division.

## NOTES AND SOURCES

The 233rd Reserve Panzer Division headquartered at Horsens, but its subordinate units were scattered throughout Jutland. The 5th Reserve Panzer Battalion was at Viborg, the 83rd Reserve Panzer Grenadier Regiment was headquartered in Aarhus, along with its 3rd Reserve Panzer Grenadier Battalion, but the 8th Reserve Panzer Grenadier Battalion was at Odder while the 9th Reserve Panzer Grenadier Battalion was located at Hommel. The 3rd Reserve Motorized Grenadier Regiment Staff was at Broedstrup, but the 8th Reserve Motorized Grenadier Battalion was at Give, the 29th was at Skanderborg, and the 50th billetted at Silkeborg. The 59th Reserve Artillery Battalion was located at Randers, the 3rd Reserve Panzer Reconnaissance Battalion was located at Hovndal, the 208th Reserve Panzer Engineer Battalion formed part of the Horsens garrison, while the 1233rd Panzer Signal Company was located at Hatting.

Bradley et al., Volume 2: 485–86; Keilig: 63, 95, 195, 377; Mehner, Volume 4: 384; Volume 7: 358; Stoves, *Die 22. Panzer-Division*: 263–71; Tessin, Volume 7: 151–54; RA: 6; OB 43: 26, 161; OB 45: 211.

# 273rd Reserve Panzer Division

**COMPOSITION:** 25th and 35th Reserve Panzer Battalions, 92nd Reserve Panzer Grenadier Regiment, 73rd Reserve Motorized Grenadier Regiment, 167th Reserve Panzer Artillery Battalion, 7th Reserve Panzer Reconnaissance Battalion, 7th and 10th Reserve Tank Destroyer Battalions, 19th Reserve Panzer Engineer Battalion.

**HOME STATION:** Wuerzburg, Wehrkreis XIII

The 273rd was formed on November 1, 1943, from the staff of the commander of Panzer Troops XIII, to control motorized and panzer training units and to train mobile troops from Wehrkreis XIII, VII, and others. It was the only German reserve division not derived from a replacement division staff. Sent to France shortly after it was formed, the 273rd was assigned to the 1st Army and held the zone between Bordeaux and the Spanish border, in addition to performing its training mission. It existed only about seven months, being absorbed by the 11th Panzer Division in May 1944. The headquarters staff joined the Staff, 11th Panzer Division; the 25th and 35th Reserve Panzer Battalions became II/ and I/15th Panzer Regiment; the 92nd Reserve Panzer Grenadier Regiment and the 73rd Reserve Motorized Grenadier Regiment now became the bulk of the 110th and 111th Panzer Grenadier Regiments, respectively; the 167th Reserve Panzer Artillery Battalion became III/119th Panzer Artillery Regiment; the 7th Reserve Panzer Reconnaissance Battalion was absorbed by the 11th Panzer Reconnaissance Battalion; and the 10th Reserve Tank Destroyer Battalion was absorbed by the 61st Tank Destroyer Battalion. Its commander was Lieutenant General Hellmut von der Chevallerie (November 11, 1943–May 9, 1944).

## COMMANDER

Hellmut von der Chevallerie was promoted to lieutenant general on May 1, 1943. A Berliner from a Hugenot family, he was born on November 9, 1896 and joined the army as a war volunteer when World War I broke out. Chevallerie was commissioned in the 5th Grenadier Guards Regiment in 1915 and remained in the Reichsheer after the armistice. During the World War II era, Chevallerie was adjutant of Wehrkreis XII and the XII Corps (1936–40), commander of the 86th Rifle Regiment (1940–42), commander of an important ad hoc battle group on the Eastern Front during the winter of 1941–42, commander of the 10th Rifle Brigade (1942), acting commander of the 22nd Panzer Division (1942), and commander of the 13th Panzer Division (1942–43). He either was wounded in action or experienced health problems in 1943, because he was off active duty for some time and never received another field command. Chevallerie later commanded the 273rd Reserve Panzer Division (1943–44) and Maneuver Area Bergen (1944–45). He was Military Commander in the Western Sudetenland in April 1945. He escaped the Soviets and settled in Wiesbaden after the war. He died there on June 1, 1965. His older brother, General of Infantry Kurt von der Chevallerie, the former commander of the 1st Army (1943–44), was arrested by the Soviets in 1945 and was never seen again.

## NOTES AND SOURCES

The commander of Panzer Troops XIII (which can also be translated as Panzer Commander XIII) directed armored units in Wehrkreis XIII.

Bradley et al., Volume 2: 422–24; Hartmann: 64; Tessin, Volume 8: 312–13; RA: 6, 118; OB 45: 223.

# Panzer Division Clausewitz

**COMPOSITION:**  Panzer Regiment Clausewitz, II/Panzer Regiment Feldherrn-halle 1, Panzer Grenadier Regiment Clausewitz 1, Panzer Grenadier Regiment Clausewitz 2, Tank Destroyer Battalion Clausewitz.

**HOME STATION:**  None

The ad hoc Panzer Division Clausewitz was formed on the orders of the Inspector General of Panzer Troops on April 6, 1945, near Lauenburg/Elbe, in the rear area of Army Group H. Its troops and subordinate units were drawn from several sources. The division staff came from Panzer Division Holstein. It also included the remnants of the 106th Panzer Brigade Feldherrnhalle, most of which had been destroyed in the Ruhr Pocket; II Battalion, 1st Feldherrnhalle Panzer Regiment from the Bergen Maneuver Area; the Feldherrnhalle Panzer Grenadier Replacement and Training Regiment from Magdeburg and Parchim; 42nd Panzer Grenadier Regiment, which came down from Denmark; the Grossdeutschland Assault Gun Battalion; and a few miscellaneous formations from the Panzer Gunnery School at Plutos. The units of the Clausewitz Division were fleshed out mainly from the boys of the Hitler Youth, which made up most of the strength of many of its units. Assigned to the 12th Army in the last days of the war, it attempted to rescue Berlin, which had been surrounded by the Soviets. It penetrated to within 20 miles of the Fuehrerbunker but was unable to relieve the city. Retreating to the west, it attacked the U.S. 1st Army and the British 2nd Army, in an attempt to prevent the encirclement of German forces in the Harz Mountains. It raised considerable havoc in the Allied rear but was ultimately encircled and finally destroyed by the U.S. 5th Armored Division near

Fallersleben, Braunschweig (Brunswick) on April 21, 1945. The remnants escaped to Primitz on the Elbe, near where they eventually surrendered. The young men and boys of this division still believed in Hitler and Nazism and had high morale despite their hopeless situation. They added the last touch of élan to the Nazi war effort. They were commanded by Lieutenant General Martin Unrein, a veteran panzer divisional commander.

## COMMANDER

Martin Unrein was promoted to major general on January 1, 1944, and to lieutenant general on July 1, 1944. He was given command of Panzer Division Clausewitz in early April 1945. Born in Weimar on New Year's Day, 1901, he joined the army as a senior officer cadet in early 1918 and was commissioned lieutenant in the 9th Cavalry Regiment in 1922. During World War II, he served as adjutant of XI Corps (1938–40), commander of the 268th Reconnaissance Battalion (1940), was on the staff of OKW (1940–41), and commanded the 6th Motorcycle Battalion (1941–42) and the 4th Panzer Grenadier Regiment (1942–43) before assuming command of the 14th Panzer Division after General Sieberg was mortally wounded. Initially he was an acting commander only, but he performed so well in his new post that his appointment was made permanent. Unrein took up residence in the town of Dachau after the war. He died in Munich on January 22, 1972.

## NOTES AND SOURCES

Chant, Volume 17: 2357–2361; Keilig: 352; Mehner, Volume 12: 459; Tessin, Volume 15: 45–46; Ziemke: 491.

# Panzer Division Feldherrnhalle 1

**COMPOSITION (Fall 1944):** Panzer Regiment Feldherrnhalle, Panzer Grenadier Regiment Feldherrnhalle, Panzer Artillery Regiment Feldherrnhalle; Panzer Reconnaissance Battalion Feldherrnhalle; Tank Destroyer Battalion Feldherrnhalle; Motorized Engineer Battalion Feldherrnhalle; Motorized Signal Battalion Feldherrnhalle.

**HOME STATION:** Danzig, Wehrkreis XX

This division was activated in southern France on June 20, 1943, largely from cadres of the 60th Motorized Division, most of which had been destroyed at Stalingrad. It was named Feldherrnhalle because of the high number of Brownshirt volunteers found in its ranks. Initially designated *Panzergrenadier-Division Feldherrnhalle* (Feldherrnhalle for short), the division consisted of the following: Grenadier Regiment Feldherrnhalle (I-III Battalion), formed from the 271st Grenadier Regiment Feldherrnhalle of the 93rd Infantry Regiment; Fusilier Regiment Feldherrnhalle (I-III Battalion), formed from the 120th Panzer Grenadier Regiment of the 60th Panzer Grenadier Division; Motorized Artillery Regiment Feldherrnhalle (I-III Battalion), formed from the 160th Motorized Artillery Regiment; Tank Destroyer Battalion Feldherrnhalle (Staff and one company), formed from the remnants of the 160th Panzer Battalion; Panzer Reconnaissance Battalion Feldherrnhalle, formed from the 160th Panzer Reconnaissance Battalion; and assorted divisional troops.

On July 17, 1943, the 282nd Army Flak Artillery Battalion (Motorized) joined the new division and was redesignated Army Flak Artillery Battalion Feldherrnhalle. A panzer battalion was added in December. It was designated

223

II/Panzer Regiment Feldherrnhalle, even though no I Battalion or regimental headquarters or staff yet existed. These were added in February 1944. Meanwhile, in August 1943, the division was sent to southeastern France during the period the post-Mussolini government in Italy was vacillating between Nazi Germany and the Allies, and the Italian 4th Army evacuated the Nice area and returned home. In late 1943, after German forces occupied Italy, the Feldherrnhalle Division was sent to the Eastern Front. As part of the 3rd Panzer Army, it fought in the successful defensive battles around Vitebsk in January 1944, before being sent to the Narva to help cover Army Group North's retreat from Leningrad. It performed well, despite its lack of training. The Feldherrnhalle was then rushed south in June to aid Army Group Center, which was under heavy Russian attack. The Feldherrnhalle Panzer Grenadier Division was unable to prevent the disaster and was itself overwhelmed by the Soviet outslaught and destroyed between Orscha and Mogilev.

What became the second Feldherrnhalle Panzer Grenadier Division began forming in the Estergom Maneuver Area in Hungary on July 19, 1944. Initially it consisted of the 109th Panzer Brigade, which controlled the 2109th Panzer Battalion, the 2109th Panzer Grenadier Regiment, and very little else. It was sent to Debreczen in the Warthegau, a district of Poland annexed by the Third Reich in 1939. Significantly reinforced (see "Composition") but still considerably understrength, it was redesignated Feldherrnhalle Panzer Grenadier Division on September 1, and the 109th Panzer Brigade and its subordinate units ceased to exist. By November 1944, it had a strength of 8,000 men, 25 PzKw IV and Vs, and a battalion of the superb Hummel 150mm self-propelled howitzers. It was sent to Hungary in November and was soon involved in the Siege of Budapest. Redesignated a panzer division on or about January 1, 1945, the Feldherrnhalle was surrounded—along with the IX SS Mountain Corps—in the Hungarian capital on December 26, 1944. After a particularly fierce struggle, the defenders of Budapest—including the Feldherrnhalle—broke out on February 12, 1945, and headed for German lines. Only about 800 of the 30,000-man garrison ever reached safety.

A third Feldherrnhalle division, which included the remnants of the original unit, was formed in Slovakia in March 1945. It was very much understrength until the remnants of the 182nd and 711th Infantry Divisions were attached to it. Both were Kampfgruppen, regiment-sized battle groups; but when combined with Feldherrnhalle, the three made a reasonable-sized division. Thus reinforced, Feldherrnhalle (which was redesignated Panzer Division Feldherrnhalle 1 in March) fought in Slovakia and Moravia in April 1945 and was surrounded in the huge Deutsch-Brod Pocket east of Prague at the end of the war. It surrendered to the Soviets in May 1945.

Commanders of the division included Major General/Lieutenant General Otto Kohlermann (assumed command February 17, 1943), Colonel Albert Henze (February 2, 1944), Colonel/Major General Friedrich-Carl von Steinkeller (April 3, 1944), and Colonel/Major General Guenther Pape (September 1, 1944).

## COMMANDERS

Otto Kohlermann was born in Magdeburg in 1896. An artilleryman, he was commander of the 5th Observation Battalion (1936–39). After briefly serving on the staff of the Artillery School at Jueterbog, Kohlermann commanded the 4th Artillery Regiment (1940–42), the 129th Artillery Command (early 1942), and the original 60th Motorized/Panzer Grenadier Division (May 15, 1942). He was flown out of the Stalingrad Pocket prior to the capitulation. Kohlermann, who was a holder of the Knight's Cross with Oak Leaves, was placed in charge of Higher Coastal Artillery Command West on May 6, 1944, and remained in this post until the end of the war. He was promoted to major general on July 1, 1942, and to lieutenant general exactly one year later.

Albert Henze (b. 1894) was a war volunteer of 1914 who rose to the rank of lieutenant of reserves during World War I. Discharged from the army at the end of the war, he returned as a captain in 1934. A major when World War II broke out, he was promoted to lieutenant colonel (1941), colonel (1942), major general (November 9, 1944), and lieutenant general (May 1, 1945). In the meantime, he commanded II/63rd Infantry Regiment (1939–42), 110th Infantry Regiment (1942–early 1944), the Feldherrnhalle Division (1944), the 19th Luftwaffe Field Division (1944–45), and the 30th Infantry Division (1945). A holder of the Knight's Cross with Oak Leaves, he was in Soviet prisons until 1955. General Henze died in Ingolstadt in 1979.

Friedrich-Carl von Steinkeller (b. 1896) was a cavalry officer in World War I. Discharged in 1919, he returned to active duty as a Rittmeister (captain of cavalry) in 1934. Steinkeller joined the panzer arm as adjutant of the XV Panzer Corps (1938–39). Later he commanded the 7th Motorcycle Battalion (1939–42), the 7th Panzer Grenadier Regiment (1942–44), and the Feldherrnhalle. He was captured by the Soviets on July 8, 1944, and spent the next 11 years in prisons. Steinkeller was promoted to major general on June 1, 1944.

Guenther Pape was born in Duesseldorf in 1907. He entered the army as a Fahnenjunker in 1927 and was commissioned lieutenant in the 15th Cavalry Regiment in 1932. He was a company commander in the 3rd Motorcycle Battalion when the war began. Later he commanded the battalion itself (which had been redesignated 3rd Panzer Reconnaissance) (1941–42) and the 394th Panzer Grenadier Regiment (1942–43). His inactivity between October 1943 and August 1944 (when he began a short course for prospective divisional commanders) was almost certainly the result of a serious wound. Pape was promoted to major general on December 1, 1944. A holder of the Knight's Cross with Oak Leaves, he became a brigadier general in the Bundeswehr (the West German Armed Forces) in 1957. He died in Duesseldorf in 1986.

## NOTES AND SOURCES

Bradley et al., Volume 5: 332–34; Keilig: 136, 179, 251; Mehner, Volume 12: 443, 458; Tessin, Volume 14: 75–76; Thomas, Volume 2: 142.

# Panzer Division Feldherrnhalle 2

**COMPOSITION:**   Panzer Regiment Feldherrnhalle 2, Panzer Grenadier Regiment Feldherrnhalle 3, Panzer Artillery Regiment Feldherrnhalle 2, 13th Panzer Reconnaissance Battalion, Tank Destroyer Battalion Feldherrnhalle 2, Motorized Engineer Battalion Feldherrnhalle 2, Motorized Signal Battalion Feldherrnhalle 2; Army Flak Artillery Battalion Feldherrnhalle 2.

**HOME STATION:**   Wehrkreis XX

Panzer Division Feldherrnhalle 2 was formed in March 1945 from the Replacement and Training Brigade Feldherrnhalle, which had recently been forced to abandon Danzig; the replacement units and other remnants of the 13th Panzer Division, which had been destroyed in Budapest; elements of the I Cavalry Corps; and the 110th Panzer Brigade (2110th Panzer Battalion and 2110th Panzer Grenadier Regiment). The new division (which was only at regimental strength) was sent to 8th Army in Slovakia in April and fought its only battles in Slovakia and on the upper Danube. At the end of the war, it tried to surrender to the Americans, but they insisted that it capitulate to the Russians. General Franz Baeke, the divisional commander, therefore disbanded the unit. It broke into small groups, some of which made it to the West. The rest went into Soviet captivity.

## COMMANDER

Dr. Franz Baeke (1898–1978), a Franconian, was a dentist by profession. He entered the service as a war volunteer in the 53rd Infantry Regiment in 1915 and was discharged as a sergeant in 1919. Returning to active duty as a second lieutenant of reserves in the 6th Reconnaissance Battalion (1937), he was promoted to lieutenant of reserves (1939), captain of reserves (1941), major of reserves (1942), lieutenant colonel of reserves (1943), colonel of reserves (1944), and major general of reserves (April 1945). His posts included commander, 1st Company, 6th Reconnaissance Battalion (1940–41); Ia, 11th Panzer Regiment (1941–42); commander, I/11th Panzer Regiment (1941–42); commander, II/11th Panzer Regiment (1942–43); commander, 11th Panzer Regiment (1943–44); and commander, 106th Panzer Brigade Feldherrnhalle (1944). Baeke did not formally assume command of the remnants of the 13th Panzer until March 9, 1945, when it was virtually certain that General Schmidhuber was dead. An incredibly brave officer, Baeke personally knocked out at least three Soviet tanks in close combat. He held the Knight's Cross with Oak Leaves and Swords. He was promoted to major general on April 1, 1945. Ironically, he died in Hagen, Westphalia, on December 12, 1978, as the result of injuries suffered in a traffic accident.

## NOTES AND SOURCES

Bradley et al., Volume 1: 158–59; Frank Kurowski, *Panzer Aces*, David Johnston, trans. (Winnipeg, Canada, 1992): 66; KTB OKW, Volume I: 1146; Mehner, Volume 12: 443; Tessin, Volume 14: 83.

# Fuehrer Begleit Division

**COMPOSITION (April 1945):** 1st Fuehrer Panzer Regiment, 1st Fuehrer Panzer Grenadier Regiment, 1st Fuehrer Panzer Artillery Regiment, 120th Panzer Reconnaissance Company, 673rd Tank Destroyer Battalion, 120th Panzer Signal Unit.

**HOME STATION:** Rastenburg, Wehrkreis I

The Fuehrer Begleit Division grew from *Wachregiment Berlin* (see Panzer Grenadier Division Grossdeutschland) and was initially organized on an ad hoc basis in 1938, to escort and guard Hitler when he made trips beyond the borders of Germany. It accompanied the Fuehrer in Sudetenland (1938), Czechoslovakia (1939), and Poland (1939), during which it was commanded by Colonel/Major General (later Field Marshal) Erwin Rommel. Formed from elements of the *Wach* (Guard) Regiment and the Grossdeutschland Motorized Infantry Regiment, it was christened Fuehrer Begleit Battalion and was established as a permanent unit in October 1939. In 1940, it accompanied the dictator to France.

In 1941, it was decided that a unit could not have guarding the Fuehrer as its primary task unless its men had combat experience. The men of the battalion were therefore sent to the front on a rotating basis. About half were stationed at Wolfsschanze (Fuehrer Headquarters near Rastenburg, East Prussia), while half formed a Kampfgruppe on the central sector of the Eastern Front. By the winter of 1941–42, the half at the front (dubbed the Fuehrer Begleit Battle Group or KG Fuehrer Begleit) included a tank company (equipped with completely obsolete PzKw Is!), a rifle company, and a heavy weapons company. Made up of first-class warriors, it was thrown into a number of crisis situations. By April 1942, it had lost all of its tanks.

The bulk of the battalion was sent back to the East when Stalin's spring offensive of 1942 caused a crisis near Kharkov. The battalion spent much of 1942–early 1943 attached to its mother unit, the Grossdeutschland Division.

In April 1943, the Begleit Battalion was divided into two battalions: the Fuehrer Grenadier and the Fuehrer Begleit Panzer Grenadier. One component of each served at the front while the other guarded Hitler at Rastenburg. Most of the Begleit Battalion, however, was sent to the front in January 1944, when the Red Army broke the Siege of Leningrad and Army Group North was on the verge of collapse. Kampfgruppe Fuehrer Begleit distinguished itself by preventing the Russians from cutting the 18th Army's Rollbann (main supply route) in heavy fighting. When it returned to East Prussia in mid-May, it was expanded into a regiment. The new men were supplied by Panzer Grenadier Replacement Battalion Grossdeutschland.

Fuehrer Begleit remained at Rastenburg until November, when it was expanded into a brigade, using troops provided by its sister unit, the Fuehrer Grenadier Brigade. It now included the Fuehrer Begleit Panzer Battalion (equipped with Panthers); the I and II Panzer Grenadier Battalions, Fuehrer Begleit Brigade; the 200th Assault Gun Brigade (supplied by OKH); a reconnaissance company; and a three-battery artillery battalion. With this composition, it was sent west and was in Army Group B's reserve when the Battle of the Bulge began on December 16, 1944. On December 18, it when into action against the Americans east of St. Vith, but failed to capture the town. Later, one American attack overran a grenadier battalion, but the U.S. advance was checked when the Panthers launched an immediate counterattack and quickly destroyed 20 Shermans. After the defenses of St. Vith were crushed, the Fuehrer Begleit was transferred to the Bastogne sector, where it engaged in futile attacks against the town from December 26 to 29. On December 30, the brigade lay a successful ambush against an American battle group attempting to break the siege. It destroyed 30 U.S. armored fighting vehicles (AFVs) against a loss of only four itself.

Seriously depleted, the Begleit Brigade took part in the retreat from the Ardennes and was withdrawn from the battle during the night of January 11–12, 1945. The rapidly pursuing Americans caused another crisis on January 14, however, and the Begleit was hurriedly sent back into action to hold them off. It was successful and continued to act as a rearguard until the campaign ended.

Back in Germany, both the Fuehrer Begleit and its sister brigade, the Fuehrer Grenadier, were withdrawn to Cottbus. They were officially upgraded to divisions on January 26, 1945, although they were never brought up to full strength.

The new Fuehrer Begleit Division consisted of the 102nd Panzer Regiment (Staff and II Battalion, which was the former II/Grossdeutschland Panzer Regiment); the 100th Panzer Grenadier Regiment (Staff, I and II Battalions from the old Fuehrer Begleit Brigade; III Battalion was the former 928th Bicycle Battalion); 102nd Panzer Reconnaissance Company; 673rd Tank Destroyer Battalion, equipped with assault guns; the 120th Panzer Artillery Regiment (Staff was the former 1036th Special Purposes Regimental Staff; I Battalion was the former

I/234th Artillery Regiment; II Battalion was the former II/5th Lehr [Demonstration] Artillery Regiment; and III Battalion was the former III/184th Artillery Regiment); and assorted service and support units, all bearing the number 120. None of the new units could be brought up to strength by February, however, when the new Fuehrer Begleit Division (FBD) was thrown into an offensive near Stettin, in an effort to push the Russians back across the Oder. The division did succeed in recapturing Lauban, which the Soviets retook in heavy fighting a few days later. The division was then sent south to Jagendorf, a critical position in the zone of the 1st Panzer Army. The FBD held the place in the face of repeated Soviet attacks. When the exhausted division was at last taken out of the line on April 3, it had destroyed 231 Soviet tanks, many with *Panzerfausten* (single shot, shoulder-fired, disposable antitank weapons). The division was reorganized again in April and received the designation shown above under "Composition."

The FBD had returned to the front by April 16, when the last Soviet offensive opened along the Lausitz/Neisse line in Saxony. Army Group Center was quickly smashed and, by April 20, the Fuehrer Begleit Division was encircled in the Spremberg pocket. It blew up its vehicles and most of its tanks (which were without fuel) and tried to break out, but was slaughtered in the fields and meadows around Neu Petershain by Soviet machine guns and artillery fire. Fewer than 400 men succeeded in reaching the Elbe, across which they swam. This remnant joined the Grossdeutschland Panzer Corps in Dresden and, as late as May 6, was still fighting the Soviets near that city. It surrendered to the Red Army near the Erzgebirge River on May 7.

The commander of the Fuehrer Begleit Division was Colonel/Major General Otto-Ernst Remer.

## COMMANDER

Otto-Ernst Remer was born in Brandenburg in 1912. He entered the service as a Fahnenjunker in 1933 and was a lieutenant commanding a company in an infantry regiment when World War II broke out. He became a battalion commander (I/10th Rifle) in 1942 and took over IV/Grossdeutschland Panzer Grenadier Regiment two months later, in April, 1942. Promoted to captain in 1941 and to major in 1943, he was transferred back to Germany as commander of the Grossdeutschland Wach Regiment at Doeberitz (near Berlin) on May 1, 1944, and played a prominent role in suppressing the coup of July 20. A grateful Fuehrer promoted him to colonel the next day (Remer bypassed the rank of lieutenant colonel altogether) and gave him command of the Fuehrer Begleit Brigade effective August 1, 1944. When the brigade was upgraded to a division, Remer was promoted to major general, effective January 31, 1945. An unreconstructed Nazi, he joined the neo-Nazi Socialist Reich Party in 1950, and in 1952 was sentenced to three months imprisonment for slandering the conspirators of July 20, whom he called traitors. The party was declared unconstitutional by the

West German courts and was dissolved later that year. Remer died in Marbella, Spain, in 1997.

## NOTES AND SOURCES

James Lucas, *Germany's Elite Panzer Force: Grossdeutschland* (London, 1978): 128–40 (hereafter cited as "Lucas, *Grossdeutschland*"); Keilig: 273; Louis L. Snyder, *Encyclopedia of the Third Reich* (New York, 1976): 293; Tessin, Volume 14: 77–78; Thomas, Volume 2: 195.

# Fuehrer Grenadier Division

**COMPOSITION (April 1945):** 2nd Fuehrer Panzer Regiment, 3rd Fuehrer Panzer Grenadier Regiment, 4th Fuehrer Panzer Grenadier Regiment, 2nd Fuehrer Panzer Artillery Regiment, Fuehrer Flak Battalion, 101st Panzer Reconnaissance Company, 124th Tank Destroyer Battalion, 124th Panzer Engineer Unit, 124th Panzer Signal Unit.

**HOME STATION:** Rastenburg, Wehrkreis I; later Berlin, Wehrkreis III

This division was activated as the Fuehrer Grenadier Battalion in April 1943, from elements of the Fuehrer Begleit Battalion (see Fuehrer Begleit Division for its early history). Its men rotated between guard and security duty at Fuehrer Headquarters near Rastenburg, East Prussia, and combat duty on the Eastern Front, mostly with the Fuehrer Begleit Battle Group. Eventually, it reached a strength of seven companies. In late June 1944, however, it was decided to expand it into a small panzer brigade. Its I and II Grenadier Battalions were drawn from the original battalion; the III Battalion was formed at Wandern and the IV Battalion at Rastenburg. The 17th (infantry howitzer) Company, 18th (light antiaircraft or flak) Company and the 19th (panzer engineer) Company came directly under the control of the brigade headquarters, as did the Fuehrer Panzer Battalion, which was equipped with Panther tanks. A V Grenadier Battalion was established later.

The new brigade was a "Fuehrer fire brigade," directly and immediately at the disposal of the dictator. This might have been a significant fact in the summer of 1944, as the Soviets pushed to within 60 miles of Rastenburg.

In September 1944, the brigade was reorganized and the I and V Grenadier

Battalions were transferred to the Fuehrer Begleit Regiment, and the Fuehrer Grenadier Brigade was transferred to the Fallingbostel Maneuver Area and reorganized. It now included three battalions: I (formerly III) was equipped with SPW halftracks; II (formerly IV) was grenadier; and III was the former Fuehrer Panzer Battalion and was still equipped with Panthers. It also had signal, infantry gun, fla and panzer engineer companies. In addition, a tank destroyer and a three-battery artillery battalion were added.

The elite brigade was sent into action almost immediately, as the Red Army pushed into East Prussia near Gumbinnen on October 17. The Fuehrer Grenadier Brigade clashed with their spearheads on October 21 and, in fierce hand-to-hand fighting the next day, hurled them back. The Soviets left behind 30 T-34 tanks. They came again the next day, using heavy close air support and virtual human wave tactics. The Fuehrer Grenadier Brigade was finally forced to retreat on October 27 to avoid being surrounded, but was back in action on November 2. Attached to 5th Panzer Division, it took part in the counterattack which recaptured Goldap later that day. The Fuehrer Grenadier and 5th Panzer found a sizable number of raped and/or murdered Germans. Taken out of the line on November 30, the FGB was hurriedly sent West, for Hitler planned to use them in a major offensive in the Ardennes the next month. It began on December 16, and it was his last gasp on the Western Front. The brigade was committed to action on December 19, with the task of holding a part of the southern side of the bulge against the counterattacks of Patton's U.S. 3rd Army. After the American spearheads broke the encirclement of Bastogne on December 26, the Fuehrer Grenadier was pulled off of the southern sector and sent to join the forces still besieging the town, leaving behind the I Battalion, which was unable to disengage. By this time, the brigade's average grenadier company had only 30 men left, and the brigade had only 25 operational tanks and assault guns. It was nevertheless committed to the battle and suffered particularly heavy losses in the Battle of Dahl, a small village near Bastogne. The Americans had taken the place, but the Fuehrer Grenadier Brigade was ordered to recapture it by counterattack. They succeeded in retaking part of the village, but were thrown out again in heavy fighting. By the time this battle was over, the brigade had fewer than 80 grenadiers left. It was taken out of the line on January 16, 1945, and officially upgraded to division status 10 days later.

The new division formed at Cottbus, largely from Grossdeutschland replacement units. It consisted of the 101st Panzer Regiment (Staff Company, I and III Battalions); the 99th Panzer Grenadier Regiment (I and II Battalions from the old Fuehrer Grenadier Brigade; III Battalion was the former 929th Grenadier Battalion); the 911th Army Assault Gun Brigade (three companies); the 124th Panzer Artillery Regiment (I Battalion was the former brigade artillery; II Battalion was the 423rd Army Artillery Battalion; and III Battalion was the former II/500th Panzer Artillery Regiment); and the division support units, all bearing the number 124. The FGD (as it was abbreviated) was well below strength, however. At this stage of the war, the Third Reich lacked the manpower to bring even the elite Fuehrer units up to strength.

Hurriedly formed, the new FGD was rushed to Stettin in February, where it took part in the abortive attempts to push the Russians back across the Oder. It also took part in the recapture of Lauban, where it suffered heavy casualties.

In April, the Fuehrer Grenadier was reorganized for the last time. The 101st Panzer Regiment became the 2nd Fuehrer Panzer Regiment, the 99th Panzer Grenadier Regiment became the 3rd Fuehrer Panzer Grenadier Regiment, and a new unit, the 4th Fuehrer Panzer Grenadier Regiment, was formed. Only two battalions strong, its men came from Bicycle Regiment Sommer, the 124th Field Replacement Battalion, and III/Grossdeutschland Replacement and Training Regiment. At the same time, the I/99th Panzer Grenadier Regiment became part of the division's panzer regiment, the 124th Panzer Artillery Regiment became the 2nd Fuehrer Panzer Artillery Regiment, and a flak battalion was added from the Luftwaffe. The other divisional units remained the same and retained the number 124.

The division fought in Pomerania until late March, when it was hurriedly sent to Vienna. It was cut off in the city on April 7, but broke the encirclement the next day. By April 12, Vienna was lost and the FGD took part in the retreat through Austria, which temporarily halted on April 26. The division formed the rearguard of Army Group South in the last days of the war (May 1–8) and surrendered to the Americans at Trahwein on May 9. The survivors of the FGD were turned over to the Soviets a few days later. Most of them never saw home again.

The Fuehrer Grenadier Division was commanded by Major General Hellmuth Maeder.

## COMMANDER

Hellmuth Maeder (b. 1908) was a police officer from 1928 until 1935, when he joined the army as a lieutenant. He was promoted to major general on January 30, 1945—less than 10 years later—earning the Knight's Cross with Oak Leaves and Swords in the process. He commanded III/522nd Infantry Regiment (1940–42), 522nd Infantry Regiment (1942–44), and the Weapons School and Training Brigade of Army Group North (1944) before assuming temporary command of the 7th Panzer. Later he attended a brief divisional commanders' course and led the Grossdeutschland Grenadier Brigade (1944–45) and the Fuehrer Grenadier Division (1945). Not released from Soviet prisons until 1955, he was a brigadier general in the Bundeswehr in 1958. He died in Kolbenz in 1984.

## NOTES AND SOURCES

The 101st Panzer Reconnaissance Company may have been redesignated 124th Reconnaissance in April 1945, but this is not certain.

Keilig: 214; Lucas, *Grossdeutschland*: 128; Tessin, Volume 14: 76–77; Thomas, Volume 2: 51.

# Panzer Division Holstein

**COMPOSITION:**   44th Panzer Battalion, 139th Panzer Grenadier Regiment, 142nd Panzer Grenadier Regiment, 144th Panzer Artillery Regiment, 44th Panzer Reconnaissance Battalion, 144th Tank Destroyer Battalion, 144th Panzer Engineer Battalion, 144th Panzer Signal Company.

**HOME STATION:**   Frankfurt an der Oder, Wehrkreis III

Panzer Division Holstein was formed in the Aarhus-Horsens-Give area of Denmark (on the Jutland peninsula) on February 10, 1945, mainly using elements of the 233rd Reserve Panzer Division and Alarm (emergency) units from Wehrkreis II. It was initially designated Kampfgruppe Panzer Division Holstein and was commanded by Lieutenant General Max Fremerey, who simultaneously commanded the 233rd Reserve Panzer Division. The divisional staff consisted of a motorcycle platoon, a light antiaircraft platoon, a troop of field police, a rations section, and virtually nothing else. The 44th Panzer Battalion was the former 5th Reserve Panzer Battalion, which consisted of five companies (three PzKw IV companies, a Stu IV assault gun company, and a staff company); the 139th Panzer Grenadier Regiment (two battalions) was created from the former 83rd Reserve Grenadier Panzer Regiment (8th and 9th Reserve Panzer Grenadier Battalions); the 142nd Panzer Grenadier Regiment (two battalions) was the former 3rd Reserve Panzer Grenadier Regiment (93rd Reserve Panzer Grenadier Battalion and 8th and 50th Motorized Grenadier Battalions); the 144th Motorized Artillery Battalion was previously the former 59th Reserve Panzer Artillery Battalion (three batteries of light artillery); 144th Panzer Engineer was the former 208th Reserve Panzer Engineer Battalion; and the 144th Panzer Signal Company was the former 1233rd Panzer Signal Company.

Despite its impressive-sounding order of battle, the Holstein had only 45 tanks and was well below divisional strength in manpower. The division was hurriedly sent to the 11th Army of Army Group Vistula on the Eastern Front, where it fought in Hitler's hastily launched and ill-fated Stargard offensive in February. Later it fought in the defense of Kolberg (also in Pomerania), escaping encirclement only at the last moment. It then defended the west bank of the Oder north of Stettin, as part of the 3rd Panzer Army. It had only 18 tanks left and 20 to 25 of its original 80 APCs. A few days later, it was absorbed by the 18th Panzer Grenadier Division on April 6, 1945. The divisional staff was sent to Lauenburg and used to organize Panzer Division Clausewitz; small elements of the division, however, returned to Denmark and rejoined the 233rd Reserve Panzer Division.

Colonel Ernst Wellmann, the senior regimental commander, led a Kampfgruppe of the Holstein Division, which was incorporated into the 18th Panzer Grenadier Division. The permanent commander of the Holstein Division was Lieutenant General Martin Unrein. Colonel Ernst Wellmann was acting divisional commander when the division was absorbed by the 18th Panzer Grenadier.

## COMMANDERS

For a sketch of Max Fremerey's career, see 155th Reserve Panzer Division, Commanders. For the career of General Unrein, see Panzer Division Clausewitz, Commanders.

Ernst Wellmann, (1904–1970), a native of Wartheland, held the Knight's Cross with Oak Leaves. He had previously commanded I/3rd Panzer Grenadier Regiment of the 3rd Panzer Division (1942) and then the regiment itself (1943–44).

## NOTES AND SOURCES

KTB OKW, Volume IV: 1898; Mehner, Volume 12: 458; Seemen: 268; Stoves, *Gepanzerten*: 263; Tessin, Volume 14: 113–14; Thomas, Volume 2: 433.

# Panzer Division Jueterbog

**COMPOSITION:** Panzer Battalion Jueterbog, Panzer Grenadier Regiment Jueterbog, Panzer Artillery Regiment Jueterbog, Panzer Reconnaissance Company Jueterbog, Panzer Engineer Company Jueterbog, Panzer Signal Company Jueterbog, Panzer Flak Artillery Battalion Jueterbog (?).

**HOME STATION:** Jueterbog, Wehrkreis III

This "division" barely reached regimental strength and only existed for a short period of time. It was formed on February 20, 1945, largely from units stationed in the Jueterbog Maneuver Area (the main German artillery training facility, not far from Berlin). The divisional staff was the former Staff, 10th Panzer Brigade. The panzer battalion was formed from the staff and three companies of the Panzer Lehr Battalion Kummersdorf at Jueterbog. Panzer Grenadier Regiment Jueterbog (I and II Battalions, plus engineer and flak companies) came from Alarm units in Berlin. The division had several flak artillery pieces from the army and the Luftwaffe, but it is not clear if the division's flak battalion was ever formed. The I Battalion of Panzer Grenadier Regiment Jueterbog 2 arrived from Munich and joined the division on March 3, but the plans to create a second grenadier regiment never materialized beyond that point. On February 26, the division (which was dubbed a Kampfgruppe—a regiment-sized combat force) was attached to the 16th Panzer Division, which was part of the 4th Panzer Army in Silesia. Shortly thereafter, in March 1945, the Jueterbog Division was absorbed by the 16th Panzer Division in lower Silesia.

## NOTES AND SOURCES

The Jueterbog Panzer Artillery Regiment consisted only of the regimental staff and I Battalion (three batteries), both from the 510th Artillery Battalion. Panzer Grenadier Regiment Jueterbog 1 had only two understrength battalions.

Stoves, *Gepanzerten*: 263–64; Tessin, Volume 14: 126–27.

# Panzer Division Kurmark

**COMPOSITION:** (151) Panzer Regiment Kurmark, (152) Panzer Grenadier Regiment Kurmark, Panzer Fusilier Regiment Kurmark, (151) Panzer Artillery Regiment Kurmark, (151) Panzer Reconnaissance Battalion Kurmark, (151) Tank Destroyer Battalion Kurmark, (151) Panzer Engineer Battalion Kurmark, (151) Panzer Signal Company Kurmark, Army Flak Artillery Battery Kurmark.

**HOME STATION:** Frankfurt an der Oder, Wehrkreis III

The history of Panzer Division Kurmark, as author James Lucas pointed out, was "short, hard and disastrous." It was formed at Frankfurt an der Oder from Kampfgruppe Langkeit, an emergency unit hastily thrown together in mid-January 1945, and the understrength Grossdeutschland Motorized Replacement and Training Brigade. Its panzer artillery had only the Staff plus I and III Battalions; its panzer grenadier regiment had only two battalions, and they were mounted on bicycles; and all of its battalions were below authorized strength. Its tank destroyer unit consisted of four companies equipped with *Panzerschreck* rocket launchers and single-shot, disposible Panzerfausten. A motorcycle company was added later. Its fusilier regiment was the former 1235th Grenadier Regiment and had been formed from the officer cadets of Fahnenjunker School I in Dresden, so some of the division's human material at least was very good. On the other hand, not only the division but also its individual components lacked unit training and some of its men had been pulled off leave trains. The elite Grossdeutschland NCOs, however, quickly instilled spirit into their units and Kurmark's morale was remarkably high. The panzer regiment (Major Helmut Hudel) included I Battalion, a Panther unit which was the former I/26th Panzer Regiment (of the

26th Panzer Division). Its II Battalion was the former 1551st Tank Destroyer Battalion, which consisted of a Staff, one company of PzKw IVs, and three companies of Jagdpanzer 38 Hetzers, which were excellent self-propelled anti-tank vehicles. Some of the tanks, however, had turrets but no guns. The division commander, Colonel Willi Langkeit, a Stalingrad veteran, acted with great energy and boldness in outfitting his unit, to the point of seizing vehicles from factories and incorporating equipment, weapons, and even entire units from training establishments without authorization.

Kurmark was hurriedly sent to the 9th Army on the Eastern Front (then on the Oder) and fought in the Battle of Sternberg, where it broke through encircling forces and rescued the garrison. Kurmark itself was then encircled by Red Army units, some of which were equipped with the latest Joseph Stalin tanks. The division fought its way out, but lost all of its soft-skinned vehicles and heavy weapons in the process.

Kurmark was rebuilt in February and March. On April 16, 1945, the Russians launched their last offensive—aimed at Berlin—and the 9th Army was directly in its path. The Soviet attack included more than a million men, backed by 22,000 guns. The divisions on either side of Kurmark collapsed and the ad hoc panzer division was encircled on April 17. Elements of the division managed to break out and rejoin the main force, but the 9th Army was itself encircled on April 21 and destroyed in the Halbe Pocket by the Soviets. The Kurmark Division, however, managed to break out and escape to the Colpin woods southwest of Frankfurt an der Oder, where it was struck by huge Soviet forces. Most of the division was overwhelmed, but elements of Kurmark nevertheless managed to escape to the west, crossing the Elbe and joining the 12th Army on May 5. It surrendered to the Americans on May 8, 1945. Willi Langkeit (who was promoted to major general on April 20, 1945) was the division's only commander.

## COMMANDER

Willi Langkeit (1907–69) was a young East Prussian officer who had entered the service as a Fahnenjunker in the infantry in 1924. Commissioned second lieutenant in the 1st Motorcycle Battalion in 1934, he was a company commander (8/36th Panzer Regiment) when the war broke out. Later he commanded II/36th Panzer Regiment of the 14th Panzer Division (1941–42) and the 36th Panzer Regiment (1943–44). He was seriously wounded in Stalingrad and was flown out of the pocket on January 19, 1943—one of the last men to be evacuated. Considered a brilliant young leader, he commanded 36th Panzer Regiment (1943–44) in the rebuilt 14th Panzer Division, and the Grossdeutschland Panzer Regiment (1944). He was named commander of the Grossdeutschland Replacement and Training Brigade on November 1, 1944, and was a natural choice to command the new division. A holder of the Knight's Cross with Oak Leaves, he was an officer in the West German Border Guards after the war.

## NOTES AND SOURCES

Major Hudel had been a company and battalion commander in the 7th Panzer Regiment. He held the Knight's Cross with Oak Leaves.

The artillery regiment initially included only three batteries: two heavy and one light from a Feldherrnhalle unit. Later a II Battalion (consisting of three assault gun batteries) was added, as was a III Battalion (the former III/SS Artillery Lehr Regiment).

Angolia, *Field*, Volume 2: 291; Keilig: 197; Seemen: 34, 174; Tessin, Volume 14: 132–33, 138. For a detailed account of General Langkeit's career, see James Lucas, *Hitler's Enforcers* (London, 1996): 54–70.

# Panzer Division Muencheberg

**COMPOSITION:** Panzer Battalion Kummersdorf, Panzer Grenadier Regiment Muencheberg 1, Panzer Grenadier Regiment Muencheberg 2, Panzer Artillery Regiment Muencheberg, Panzer Reconnaissance Company Muencheberg, 682nd Tank Destroyer Battalion, Tank Destroyer Company Muencheberg, Engineer Company Muencheberg, Signal Company Muencheberg, 301st Army Flak Artillery Battalion.

**HOME STATION:** Muencheberg, Wehrkreis III

Activated on March 8, 1945, in the Muencheberg sector (between Berlin and Frankfurt an der Oder-Kuestrin), Panzer Division Muencheberg never reached divisional strength and was a panzer unit in name only; it had just a handful of tanks and barely enough vehicles to transport its wounded. Most of its original formations were Alarm units, formed from the Replacement Army battalions and school troops from the Berlin area. Its staff was the former Staff, 103rd Panzer Brigade. On March 14, 1945, Panzer Battalion Kummersdorf was redesignated I/29th Panzer Regiment, even though no regimental headquarters existed. It had four tank companies (Panthers and Tigers) and was the only fully armored or motorized unit in the division. Its panzer grenadier regiment had only two battalions and its artillery regiment had only one battalion of four or five light batteries. It nevertheless fought very well, largely because of the personal example of its commander, Major General Werner Mummert, who was both tough and incredibly brave. (He held the Knight's Cross with Oak Leaves and Swords.)

Panzer Division Muencheburg was hastily sent to the Eastern Front in mid-

March. As part of the 9th Army, it fought against Soviet forces attempting to push across the Oder River near Kuestrin and checked their advance in the hills to the west. Later it took part in the Battle of Seelow Heights, where the Russians finally broke through. It retreated to Muencheberg, where it was involved in street fighting; then to the "Hardenberg position," and finally into Berlin itself. Here it defended the southeastern suburbs before being summoned into the city itself on April 26. It fought in the Zoobunker area and in the Tiergarden, and lost its last tank near the Brandenburg Gate. General Mummert was wounded on May 1 but continued in command until the end. Hitler committed suicide on the afternoon of April 30, but the trapped panzer division continued to fight for another five days. It finally broke up on May 4. Its survivors tried to make their way to Anglo-Saxon lines, but very few made it; most of the men ended up in Soviet captivity.

## COMMANDER

Werner Mummert (1897–1950), a Saxon, entered the Imperial Army as a war volunteer in August 1914 and earned a commission as a reserve lieutenant in 1916. Discharged at the end of World War I (in December 1918), he reentered the service as a reserve lieutenant in the 11th Infantry Regiment in 1936. He became a reserve Rittmeister (captain of cavalry) in 1938, as a member of the 10th Cavalry Regiment. He later commanded a reconnaissance battalion for an infantry division and the 14th Panzer Reconnaissance Battalion (1939–44). He was given command of the 103rd Panzer Grenadier Regiment in January 1944 and took charge of the Muencheberg Panzer Division in January 1945, when its cadres were just beginning to form. He was promoted to major general of reserves on February 1, 1945. Mummert was captured on May 4 and died in a Soviet prison.

## NOTES AND SOURCES

Chant 1979, Volume 17: 2376; Keilig: 235; Cornelius Ryan, *The Last Battle* (New York, 1966); Tessin, Volume 14: 161–62; Juergen Thorwald, *Defeat in the East* (New York, 1951; reprint ed., New York, 1980): 206–43.

# Panzer Division Norway

**COMPOSITION:**   Panzer Battalion Norway, Panzer Grenadier Regiment Norway, Panzer Artillery Battalion Norway, Tank Destroyer Battalion Norway, Panzer Engineer Battalion Norway.

**HOME STATION:**   Oslo, Norway

Panzer Division Norway was formed in Norway on October 1, 1943, to deter Swedish allegiance to the Allies. (For a time, Hitler considered using it to spearhead a possible invasion of Sweden.) It was about regimental strength and lacked combat and support units of every kind, including reconnaissance troops (even those were equipped with bicycles), signal troops, and assault guns. Its tank battalion (three companies) had 47 PzKw III tanks, which had been left behind when the 25th Panzer Division was transferred to Russia. All its tanks had unsatisfactory transmissions. The division, which was part of the Army of Norway's reserve, never saw combat. On July 1, 1944, it was cannibalized and many of its units were sent to the 25th Panzer Division. It lost its panzer battalion (which was absorbed into the 103rd Panzer Brigade as the 2103rd Panzer Battalion); its III/Panzer Grenadier Regiment Norway, which became the II/146th Panzer Grenadier Regiment of the 25th Panzer Division; its antitank battalion, which became the 87th Tank Destroyer Battalion (25th Panzer Division); and Panzer Artillery Battalion Norway, which became III/91st Panzer Artillery Regiment (also part of the 25th Panzer Division). In addition, its I and II Grenadier Battalions had apparently been consolidated into a single battalion (I/Panzer Grenadier Regiment Norway) sometime earlier, leaving the unit with a headquarters staff and a single battalion. The division was downgraded to

Panzer Brigade Norway on July 13, 1944. A new (small) panzer battalion was assigned to it and its panzer grenadier battalion was renamed Panzer Grenadier Battalion Norway (and was later renamed Assault Battalion Norway). This two-battalion brigade was sent to the Narvik sector in northern Norway in January 1945, when it appeared that the Soviets might invade that region, but they never did. Now a part of XXXVI Corps, 20th Mountain Army, the brigade surrendered to the Western Allies in May 1945, having never fought a battle. Its commanders included Lieutenant Colonel Prince Max zu Waldeck (1942–43), Colonel/ Major General Reinhold Gothsche (1943), and Colonel Max Roth (December 10, 1943–end).

## COMMANDERS

Prince Max zu Waldeck later commanded the 611th Tank Destroyer Battalion, a General Headquarters unit in the East.

Reinhold Gothsche (b. 1893) entered the service as an infantry officer-cadet in 1914. After serving in World War I, where he was severely wounded twice, he joined the Reichsheer and, in 1935, was commander of a cavalry battalion. Later he was commander of the I/3rd Panzer Regiment (1935–37), was on the staff of the War Ministry (1937), and was a branch chief in the Army Personnel Office (1937–43). After commanding Panzer Brigade/Panzer Division Norway, he was briefly Rear Area Commander, 7th Army (1944), commander of the 520th Field Administrative Command at Antwerp (1944), was Rear Area Commander, 1st Parachute Army (Korueck 534) (1944–45), and was commander of the 591st Field Administrative Command in what was formerly Czechoslovakia. He was summarily executed in Pressnitz, Bohemia, on April 22, 1945, allegedly for dissipating his strength. Apparently his main crime was running afoul of the Nazis. His conviction was overturned by the Berlin Provincial Court in 1952. Reinhold Gothsche was promoted to major general on October 1, 1943.

Max Roth led the 15th Panzer Regiment as a lieutenant colonel in 1942.

## NOTES AND SOURCES

The 103rd Panzer Brigade was later absorbed by Panzer Division Muencheberg.

Bradley et al., Volume 4: 368–70; Keilig: 111; KTB OKW, Volume IV: 1878; Scheibert: 307; Tessin, Volume 14: 176–77; Earl F. Ziemke, "The German Northern Theater of Operations, 1940–1945." United States Department of the Army *Pamphlet 20-271*, Office of the Chief of Military History (Washington, D.C., 1959): 267.

# Panzer Division Silesia

**COMPOSITION:** Panzer Battalion Silesia, Panzer Grenadier Regiment Silesia, Panzer Artillery Regiment Silesia, Panzer Reconnaissance Company Silesia, Tank Destroyer Company Silesia, Panzer Engineer Company Silesia, Panzer Signal Company Silesia.

**HOME STATION:** Doeberitz, Wehrkreis III

Panzer Division Silesia, which was sometimes referred to as Panzer Division Doeberitz, was a regiment-sized Kampfgruppe. It was organized from Alarm Kampfgruppen from Wehrkreise VIII, IV, and III, and from residual elements of the Silesian 178th Reserve Panzer Division. Its staff was formed from elements of Headquarters, Wehrkreis IV. Its tank battalion was the former 303rd Panzer Battalion (three companies, formerly of the 15th Panzer Replacement and Training Battalion and elements of the former 3rd Panzer Reconnaissance Replacement Battalion); its panzer grenadier regiment (the former 128th Panzer Grenadier Replacement Regiment) had only two understrength battalions; and its artillery regiment controlled only two battalions. Its I Battalion was the former I/106th Artillery Regiment. In March, the division was reinforced with the 303rd Panzer Battalion, which was equipped with assault guns. A second infantry regiment (Panzer Grenadier Regiment Silesia 2) and a panzer flak artillery battalion were in the process of forming when, in March 1945, the division was absorbed by Panzer Division Holstein, which was in turn absorbed by the 18th Panzer Grenadier Division on March 26, 1945. Its men ended up on the Eastern Front, fighting on the Oder. Most of them were forced to surrender to the Soviets at the end of the war. The Silesia Division's commander was apparently Colonel Ernst Wellmann.

246

## NOTES AND SOURCES

Stoves (*Gepanzerten*: 274) lists Lieutenant General Friedrich von der Meden as the divisional commander, although Keilig (p. 220) states that he was commanding a special staff under 4th Panzer Army at the time. Mehner lists Colonel Scheuenemann as the divisional commander. Presumably he is referring to Walter Scheuenemann, but this is not certain. Scheuenemann, however, was only a captain in 1943. Kursietis (p. 237) states that Colonel Wellmann was the division's commander, which seems more likely to this author. Wellmann had commanded the I/3rd Panzer Grenadier Regiment (1942) and the 3rd Panzer Grenadier Regiment (1943), and was certainly the more logical choice, based on seniority and experience.

Keilig: 220; Kursietis: 237; Mehner, Volume 12: 456; Scheibert: 398; Seemen: 39, 354; Stoves, *Gepanzerten*: 274; Tessin, Volume 14: 228–29.

# Panzer (Later Panzer Field Training) Division Tatra

**COMPOSITION:** Panzer Battalion Tatra; 1 company, 4th Panzer Replacement and Training Battalion; 82nd Panzer Grenadier Replacement and Training Regiment; 85th Panzer Grenadier Replacement and Training Regiment; 1 company, 8th Tank Destroyer Replacement and Training Battalion; Artillery Battalion Tatra; 1 company, 89th Panzer Engineer Lehr Replacement and Training Battalion; 1 and 2 Companies, 482nd Grenadier Training Battalion; Field Replacement Battalion Tatra.

**HOME STATION:** Slovakia

Panzer Division Tatra was formed from Home Army units in Slovakia in August 1944, when it looked as if that country might try to defect from the Axis. Its staff included cadres from the veteran 1st Panzer Division. The 82nd Panzer Grenadier Replacement and Training Regiment came from Mahr Weisskirchen, Austria (Wehrkreis XVII), as did I/82nd. Its II Battalion (the former 10th Panzer Grenadier Replacement and Training Battalion) came from Friedburg, Prussia. The 85th Panzer Grenadier Replacement and Training Regiment was from Gleiwitz in Wehrkreis VIII; I/85th was the former 13th Panzer Grenadier Replacement and Training Battalion from Neisse (Wehrkreis VIII) and II/85th Panzer Grenadier Replacement and Training Regiment was the former 30/51st Motorized Grenadier Battalion from Goerlitz. Its panzer battalion (three companies) included 28 obsolete PzKw IIIs and IVs and three Tigers. Despite the improvised and ad hoc nature of its organization, the Tatra Panzer Division played a major role in suppressing the Slovak Military Mutiny of 1944 and recapturing Bratislava (Pressburg) from the rebels and their Soviet advisors. Following this action, the division resumed its training mission, was redesignated Panzer Field Training Division Tatra, and was placed under Headquarters, Army Group South. In December 1944 it absorbed the XVII Panzer Command (including its panzer grenadiers) and the panzer troops of Wehrkreis VIII, as well as Panzer KG von Ohlen (a panzer grenadier battalion, a tank company, and a battery of 150mm guns) from the 178th Panzer Replacement Division. In March 1945, however, the Tatra Division was itself absorbed by the 232nd Reserve Panzer Division. Its commanders were Lieutenant General Friedrich-Wilhelm von Loeper (August 1944) and Major General Hans-Ulrich Back (January 1, 1945).

## COMMANDERS

Lieutenant General Friedrich-Wilhelm von Loeper (b. 1888) started his military career as a lieutenant in the 1st Guards Infantry Regiment in 1908. He led the 64th Infantry Regiment (1935–37), the 4th Rifle Regiment (1937–38), the 1st Light Division (1938–39), the 81st Infantry Division (late 1939–40), and the 10th Motorized Infantry Division (1940–42). He took command of Panzer Division Tatra in August 1944 and Division Ludwig in January 1945.

For more details about Hans-Ulrich Back's career, see 232nd Panzer Division.

## NOTES AND SOURCES

Keilig: 16, 208; Stoves, *Gepanzerten*: 275; Tessin, Volume 6: 265, 322; Volume 14: 239.

# Panzer Grenadier Division Grossdeutschland

**COMPOSITION (late 1944):**  Grossdeutschland Panzer Regiment, Grossdeutschland Panzer Grenadier Regiment, Grossdeutschland Fusilier Regiment, Grossdeutschland Artillery Regiment, Grossdeutschland Panzer Reconnaissance Battalion, Grossdeutschland Tank Destroyer Battalion, Grossdeutschland Panzer Engineer Battalion, Grossdeutschland Panzer Signal Battalion, Grossdeutschland Army Flak Artillery Battalion, Grossdeutschland Assault Gun Battalion.

**HOME STATION:**  Berlin, Wehrkreis III

Contrary to the misconceptions of many, the Grossdeutschland Division was neither an SS nor a panzer division. It was, at various stages in its development, an army motorized infantry regiment, a motorized infantry division, and a panzer grenadier division. Its composition, however, *was* that of a panzer division, which is why so many people believe it was a panzer division and why it is covered here; however, it never officially received the designation "panzer division." Why it was not officially made a panzer division is a mystery to this author.

The division could trace its ancestry back to June 21, 1921, when the Berlin Guard Regiment (*Wachregiment Berlin*) was created. Every day at noon, one of its companies, accompanied by military musicians, would march through the Brandenburg Gate and down the Unter den Linden. In June 1922, however, it was downgraded to *Wachtruppe Berlin*—in effect, to a battalion. It did not receive the designation "Grossdeutschland," however, until June 1939, when it was expanded into a full regiment of four motorized battalions.

Grossdeutschland (literally "Greater Germany" or larger Germany) was sent

250

to the Grafenwoehr Maneuver Area and trained as a motorized infantry unit. It first saw action as part of Guderian's XIX Corps in the invasion of France, taking part in the attack over the Maas, in the decisive Battle of Sedan, and in the drive to the English Channel. Later it took part in the breaking of the Weygand Line, in the Seine River crossings, and in the subsequent pursuit of the disintegrating French Army. It occupied Lyon on June 19.

In July 1940, the 17th Motorcycle Battalion was assigned to the regiment, and it was sent to Alsace, where it trained for the invasion of the United Kingdom. Subsequently reinforced with artillery and flak units, Grossdeutschland (or GD) took part in the invasion of Yugoslavia, where it captured the Belgrade radio transmitter. Hurriedly sent north, the regiment took part in the initial invasion of the Soviet Union, attacking across the Bug River with the 7th Panzer Division. It fought in the Battles of Bialystok and Minsk (June 24–July 6), in the pursuit to the Dnieper River (July 7–10), and in the breakthrough of the Soviet defenses on the Dnieper, where the fighting was particularly bitter and sometimes hand-to-hand (July 11–14). GD also took part in the capture of Smolensk (July 14–20) and the overunning of the Desna positions (July 18–23). It was involved in the defensive fighting near Jelnja (July 24–August 22) and Desna (August 18–30), before taking part in the Battle of Kiev and the subsequent pursuit (September 1941). The Grossdeutschland Regiment then took part in the fighting east of Romny (September 26–October 3), in the double battle of encirclement of Vyasma-Bryansk (October 10–20), and in the subsequent efforts to capture Moscow. It was heavily engaged in the fighting around Tula from October 21 to December 5. When Stalin launched his winter offensive on December 6, the elite regiment suffered heavy casualties and the motorcycle battalion was practically wiped out at Kolodesnaja, near Tula. As of January 6, 1942, Grossdeutschland's casualties in the East totalled 900 killed, 3,056 wounded, and 114 missing—well over half its strength. It continued in the line, however, and suffered such heavy casualties in the fighting around Orel that its II Battalion had to be disbanded.

Meanwhile, several new GD battalions had been recruited and the decision had been made to upgrade Panzer Grenadier Regiment Grossdeutschland to a full motorized infantry division. The new unit was formed on March 3, 1942, in the Wandern Maneuver Area (*Truppenuebungsplatz Wandern*) near Berlin. Its men had to be in perfect health (they were not allowed to wear or need glasses, for example), had to be in excellent physical condition, could not have a criminal record, and had to be politically reliable. Like its predecessor, its soldiers were specially selected volunteers from all over Germany. Its unofficial title was, in fact, "The Bodyguard of the German People." The Grossdeutschland Division fought exceptionally well throughout the rest of the war. It would be redesignated a panzer grenadier unit on May 19, 1943. Meanwhile, in April 1942, the old GD Regiment was withdrawn from the line and joined the rest of the division at Rjetschiza on the Dnieper.

As of May 21, 1942, it included the 1st Grossdeutschland Infantry Regiment (three battalions from the old Grossdeutschland Motorized Infantry Regiment); the newly created 2nd Grossdeutschland Infantry (later Fusilier) Regiment (three battalions); the Grossdeutschland Panzer Battalion (formerly I/100th Panzer Regiment), the newly formed Grossdeutschland Motorcycle Battalion, the Grossdeutschland Tank Destroyer Battalion (formerly 643rd Tank Destroyer Battalion), the Grossdeutschland Panzer Artillery Regiment (three battalions), the Grossdeutschland Army Flak Artillery Battalion (formerly the 285th Army Flak Artillery Battalion), the Grossdeutschland Assault Gun Battalion (formerly the 192nd Assault Gun Battalion), the Grossdeutschland Panzer Engineer Battalion (formerly the 43rd Engineer Battalion), and the Grossdeutschland Panzer Signal Battalion (formerly 309th Signal Battalion).

Initially sent to the 4th Panzer Army on the southern sector of the Eastern Front in June 1942, it was soon sent north, into the zone of Army Group Center, where it fought several defensive actions around Rzhev (September 10–January 10, 1943). In late November, it was practically encircled in the Lutschessa Valley, east of Rzhev, by several Soviet armored units, and suffered more than 10,000 casualties before it could extricate itself. It nevertheless remained in the line until January. Hurriedly sent south, it fought around Kharkov (January 19–March 31, 1943) and helped recapture the city, before being placed in reserve at Smolensk. Here it hastily rebuilt and, among other things, received Staff, Grossdeutschland Panzer Regiment (formerly Staff, 203rd Panzer Regiment) and II/GD Panzer Regiment (formerly II/203rd Panzer Regiment of the 23rd Panzer Division). Its motorcycle battalion was reorganized into a panzer reconnaissance unit, it added a IV artillery battalion, and the Grossdeutschland Panzer Battalion became I/Grossdeutschland Panzer Regiment. On July 1, 1943, a Tiger battalion joined the division and became III/Grossdeutschland Panzer Regiment, and the Grossdeutschland Division became a panzer unit in everything but name; in fact, with about 300 tanks, it was considerably stronger than the average panzer division in 1943.

After resting and refitting from late March to July 5, 1943, the GD Division was thrown into Operation Citadel as part of the 4th Panzer Army. Grossdeutschland fought in the Battle of Kursk (July 5–12), in the defense of Kharkov, in the defense of Orel and Bryansk (July 18–August 5), in the defensive actions west of Kharkov (August 6–September 14), and in the retreat behind the Dnieper (September 15–28). So heavy was the fighting that, by September 29, the division had only one operational tank remaining. It spent most of the rest of 1943 defending a sector of the river near Kremenchug.

The year 1944 brought no rest for the elite but battered division. It fought at Kirovograd (January 5–18), on the lower Dnieper (January 19–March 6), north of Nikolayev, and in the retreat to the Bug (March 7–27). In the meantime, the division was reinforced with an entire new panzer regiment—the 26th—which was equipped with entirely new PzKw V Panther tanks. The majority of them did not survive very long, however, because the regiment was decimated in the fighting around Cherkassy in February. The 26th Panzer Regiment was sent back to France to rebuild, was caught up in the Normandy fighting, and did not rejoin the division until October. Fortunately for Grossdeutschland, its own organic tank regiment was also reinforced. It now consisted of I Battalion (five companies of Panthers), II Battalion (five companies of PzKw IVs) and III Battalion (four companies of Tigers). The division's main reinforcement, however, was the 1029th Grossdeutschland Grenadier Regiment (Reinforced), formed from the division's reserves. It included two battalions of motorized infantry, an artillery battalion, and two antitank companies.

By the end of March, GD had been pushed out of Russia and into Romania. It fought in northern Bessarabia and in the Carpathian foothills (March 27–April 25), in the defensive battles on the upper Moldau (April 26–end of May), and in the counterattacks north of Jassy (June 2–6).

During a lull in the fighting in May, the GD Fusilier Regiment was taken out of the line and briefly returned to Germany, where it was reequipped entirely with half-tracks. It and the GD Panzer Grenadier Regiment were both so reduced by casualties, however, that both their IV Battalions were disbanded. The Fusilier Regiment was back at the front in time to take part in the Jassy counterattacks, where it lost so many men that its I Battalion had to be disbanded. The 1029th Grossdeutschland Regiment was disbanded shortly thereafter, and its survivors were used to reconstitute the I/Fusilier Regiment. After Jassy, the GD Panzer Engineer Battalion was reinforced to almost regimental strength.

In August, the division was again sent to the most critical section of the Eastern Front—Gumbinnen, East Prussia. Army Group North had been isolated in the Baltic states and GD was among those units responsible for reestablishing a corridor to it. This the division was able to do by August 25. Then a lull descended on the East Prussian-Lithuania-Latvia sector for more than a month. Hitler, however, did not take advantage of this last opportunity to pull back the 16th and 18th Armies. On October 5, the Red Army launched a massive offensive that again isolated Army Group North in Courland. Grossdeutschland was pushed back into the Memel bridgehead, fighting there until being evacuated to East Prussia by the German Navy at the end of 1944.

The remnants of the once-proud Grossdeutschland Panzer Grenadier Division reformed in the Willenberg, East Prussia, area in January 1945. They were back in action on the 15th, as two Soviet fronts (army groups) drove on Koenigsberg (now Kaliningrad, Russia). After heavy defensive fighting in February, Grossdeutschland launched a sharp counterattack in early March and reestablished contact between the East Prussian capital and Ermland. The enemy by now was just too strong, however, and Grossdeutschland was forced to retreat through Ermland and over the Frisches Haff, into Samland. After a two-week lull, it was back in action during the retreat through Samland (including the Battle of Pillau) and in the defense of the Frische Nehrung (April 12–30, 1945). It was still holding out when Hitler committed suicide. Between January 15 and April 22,

254    THE PANZER LEGIONS

1945, the division suffered 16,988 casualties. A mere 4,000 men survived. This remnant was evacuated by the German Navy and deposited in Schleswig-Holstein, where they were able to surrender to the British.

Commanders of the Grossdeutschland Regiment/Division included Colonel/ Major General Wilhelm-Hunold von Stockhausen (assumed command June 1, 1939), Colonel/Major General/Lieutenant General Walter Hoernlein (April 1, 1941), Lieutenant General Baron Hasso von Manteuffel (February 1, 1944), and Colonel/Major General Karl Lorenz (September 1, 1944). Acting commanders included Lieutenant General Hermann Balck (April 3–June 30, 1943).

## COMMANDERS

Wilhelm-Hunold von Stockhausen (b. 1891), a Westphalian, joined the 80th Fusilier Regiment as a Faehnrich in 1911. He commanded the Potsdam NCO School (1936–39) before assuming command of the Grossdeutschland Motorized Infantry Regiment in 1939. Thereafter, he commanded the 1st Rifle Brigade (1941–42) and the 281st Security Division (1942–July 1944). He was then unemployed for five months, suggesting a wound. Meanwhile, he had been promoted to major general (April 1, 1942) and lieutenant general (1944). He assumed command of a Kampfgruppe in East Prussia at the end of 1944 and led it until the capitulation. The Soviets extradited him to Yugoslavia, where he remained in prison until 1952. Following his release, he settled in Koblenz.

Walter Hoernlein (b. 1893) is the officer most commonly associated with the Grossdeutschland formation. He joined the Imperial Army in 1912 and progressively commanded I/69th Infantry Regiment (1936–39), 80th Infantry Regiment (1939–41), Grossdeutschland Motorized Infantry Regiment (1941–42), the Grossdeutschland Division (1942–44), LXXXII Corps (1944–45), Wehrkreis II (1945), and XXVII Corps (1945). He was promoted to major general (April 1, 1942), lieutenant general (January 1, 1943), and general of infantry (November 1, 1944). A holder of the Knight's Cross with Oak Leaves, he settled in Cologne, where he died in 1961.

For a sketch of Hasso von Manteuffel's career, see 7th Panzer Division. For Balck's career, see 11th Panzer Division.

Karl Lorenz (b. 1904) was only a company commander (1/18th Engineer Battalion) when World War II broke out. He rose quickly, mainly within the Grossdeutschland Division, commanding the 290th Engineer Battalion (1940–42), the Grossdeutschland Engineer Battalion (1942), the Grossdeutschland Panzer Grenadier Regiment (1942–44), and finally the division itself. He was promoted to major general on September 1, 1944. He died in 1964.

## NOTES AND SOURCES

During the French campaign, the 43rd Engineer Battalion and the 640th Assault Gun Battalion (six Sturmgeschuetz StuG IIIs) were attached to the division.

When it was created in the spring of 1942, the Headquarters Staff of the Grossdeutschland Panzer Artillery Regiment was formed from Staff, 622nd Artillery Regiment. Its three battalions came from the 400th Artillery Battalion, I/109th Artillery Regiment, and the 646th Artillery Regiment.

The Grossdeutschland Division underwent its final major reorganization in December 1944. Its panzer and Panzer Grenadier Regiments were reduced to two battalions each, the artillery regiment was reduced to three battalions, and the assault gun battalion was transferred to the Brandenburg Division as II/Brandenburg Panzer Regiment. The III/Grossdeutschland Panzer Regiment became the Grossdeutschland Heavy Panzer Battalion, was taken from the division, and became part of the corps troops of the Grossdeutschland Panzer Corps. The same thing happened to the other battalions the division lost that month, except for the assault gun unit.

Keilig: 146, 210, 335; Lucas, *Grossdeutschland*: 1 ff.; Bruce Quarrie, *Panzer-Grenadier-Division "Grossdeutschland"* (London, 1977): 3 ff.; Helmuth Spaeter, *Panzerkorps Grossdeutschland Bilddokumentation* (Friedberg, 1984): 1 ff.; Tessin, Volume 14: 94–101; Thomas, Volume 2: 38.

# Appendix 1

# Table of Equivalent Ranks

| U.S. Army | German Army |
|---|---|
| General of the Army | Field Marshal *(Generalfeldmarschall)* |
| General | Colonel General *(Generaloberst)* |
| Lieutenant General | General *(General)* |
| Major General | Lieutenant General *(Generalleutnant)* |
| Brigadier General | Major General *(Generalmajor)* |
| Colonel | Colonel *(Oberst)* |
| Lieutenant Colonel | Lieutenant Colonel *(Oberstleutnant)* |
| Major | Major *(Major)* |
| Captain | Captain *(Hauptmann)* |
| First Lieutenant | Lieutenant *(Oberleutnant)* |
| Second Lieutenant | Lieutenant *(Leutnant)* |

| SS Rank | German Army Equivalent |
|---|---|
| *Reichsführer SS* (Himmler) | Commander in Chief of the Army* |
| None | Field Marshal |
| *Oberstgruppenführer* | Colonel General |
| *Obergruppenführer* | General |
| *Gruppenführer* | Lieutenant General |
| *Brigadeführer* | Major General |
| *Oberführer* | None |
| *Standartenführer* | Colonel |
| *Obersturmbannführer* | Lieutenant Colonel |
| *Sturmbannführer* | Major |
| *Hauptsturmführer* | Captain |
| *Obersturmführer* | First Lieutenant |
| *Untersturmführer* | Second Lieutenant |

*Held by Field Marshal Werner von Blomberg (1933–38), Field Marshal Walter von Brauchitsch (1938–December 1941), and Hitler (December 1941–April 1945).

# Appendix II

# The Higher Panzer Headquarters

## 1ST PANZER ARMY

Formed as the XXII Corps in August 1939, this headquarters was redesignated Panzer Group von Kleist and, as such, directed the decisive attack in the French campaign of 1940. Officially upgraded to 1st Panzer Group on November 11, 1940, it played the major role in the conquest of Yugoslavia in April 1941. Subsequently, the panzer group directed the armor for Army Group South in southern Russia (1941) and was upgraded to 1st Panzer Army on October 25, 1941. It fought on the southern sector of the Eastern Front until January 1945, when it was transferred to the central sector. At the end of the war, it was in Czechoslovakia.

Commanders of the 1st Panzer Group/Army included Colonel General Ewald von Kleist (assumed command, November 16, 1940), General of Cavalry/Colonel General Eberhard von Mackensen (assumed command, November 22, 1942), General of Panzer Troops Hans Valentin Hube (October 29, 1943), General of Panzer Troops Erhard Raus (May 1, 1944), Colonel General Gotthard Heinrici (August 15, 1944), and General of Panzer Troops Walther Nehring (March 20, 1945).

## 2ND PANZER ARMY

Formed as the XIX Motorized Corps on February 4, 1938, this headquarters was under the command of Heinz Guderian when the war broke out. It was upgraded to Panzer Group Guderian on June 1, 1940, and was redesignated 2nd Panzer Group on November 16, 1940. It became 2nd Panzer Army on October 5, 1941. The 2nd Panzer fought on the Eastern Front from June 1941 to September 1943, when it was sent to the Balkans to disarm the Italian forces in the region (Italy had defected), to suppress rebellions, and to guard against an Allied invasion. It was back in action in January 1945, when the Eastern Front arrived in the Balkans. It fell into Soviet hands at the end of the war.

Commanders of the 2nd Panzer Group/Army included Colonel General Heinz Guderian (assumed command, November 16, 1940), Colonel General Rudolf Schmidt

258

(December 25, 1941), General of Infantry Heinrich Cloessner, acting commanding general (July 10, 1943), Colonel General Walter Model (simultaneously commanding general, 9th Army) (July 15, 1943), General of Infantry/Colonel General Dr. Lothar Rendulic (August 15, 1943), General of Mountain Troops Franz Boehme (June 25, 1944), and General of Artillery Maximilian de Angelis (July 18, 1944–end).

## 3RD PANZER ARMY

Formed as the XV Motorized Corps, this staff was upgraded to 3rd Panzer Group on November 16, 1940, and to 3rd Panzer Army on January 1, 1942. It fought on the Eastern Front for four years, and surrendered to the British at the end of the war.

Its commanders included Colonel General Hermann Hoth (assumed command, November 16, 1940), General of Panzer Troops/Colonel General Georg-Hans Reinhardt (October 8, 1941), General of Panzer Troops Erhard Raus (August 16, 1944), and General of Panzer Troops Hasso von Manteuffel (March 10, 1945).

## 4TH PANZER ARMY

Formed at 4th Panzer Group when Headquarters, XVI Motorized Corps was upgraded, this HQ directed units on the Eastern Front from 1941 to 1945. It was upgraded to 4th Panzer Army on January 1, 1942. The 4th Panzer was trapped in eastern Germany and Czechoslovakia at the end of the war, and most of its men ended up in Soviet captivity.

Commanders of the 4th Panzer Group/Army included Colonel General Erich Hoepner (assumed command, February 17, 1941), General of Infantry/Colonel General Richard Ruoff (January 1, 1942), Colonel General Hermann Hoth (May 31, 1942), General of Panzer Troops/Colonel General Erhard Raus (November 15, 1943), Colonel General Josef Harpe (May 1, 1944), General of Panzer Troops Hermann Balck (June 28, 1944), and General of Panzer Troops Fritz Hubert Graeser (September 30, 1944–end).

## 5TH PANZER ARMY (1942–43)

Formed from the ad hoc LXXXX Corps in Tunis on December 8, 1942, the 5th Panzer Army spent its entire career fighting Anglo-Saxons in Tunisia. After its supply lines collapsed, it surrendered to the British and Americans on May 12, 1943. Commanders of the 5th Panzer Army included Colonel General Hans-Juergen von Arnim (assumed command, December 8, 1942) and General of Panzer Troops Gustav von Vaerst (March 9, 1943).

## 5TH PANZER ARMY (1944–45)

Panzer Group West was formed from the staff of the General of Panzer Troops at OB West on January 24, 1944, and was upgraded to 5th Panzer Army on August 5, 1944. The second 5th Panzer Army spent its entire career on the Western Front, fighting in Normandy, the Siegfried Line, and the Battle of the Bulge, among other campaigns. It was trapped in the Ruhr Pocket at the end of the war and surrendered there on April 17, 1945.

Commanders of Panzer Group West/5th Panzer Army included General of Panzer

Troops Baron Leo Geyr von Schweppenburg (assumed command, January 24, 1944), General of Panzer Troops Heinrich Eberbach (July 5, 1944), SS Colonel General Josef "Sepp" Dietrich (August 28, 1944), General of Panzer Troops Baron Hasso von Manteuffel (September 12, 1944), and Colonel General Josef Harpe (March 9, 1945).

## 6TH PANZER (LATER SS PANZER) ARMY

On September 24, 1944, the 6th Panzer Army was activated in Wehrkreis VI from part of the Staff, Wehrmacht Commander Belgium-Northern France and the remnants of the army's XII Corps Headquarters, which had been mauled on the Eastern Front. It was rounded out with Waffen-SS men. Its purpose from the beginning was to direct Hitler's Ardennes offensive (December 1944–January 1945). It did so, but with little success. Sent East after this failure, it fought in Austria and surrendered to the Americans at the end of the war. It was redesignated an SS panzer army in February 1945. Its commander throughout its existence was SS Colonel General Josef "Sepp" Dietrich.

## 11TH SS PANZER ARMY

This staff was formed in Pomerania from the staff of Himmler's defunct *OB Oberrhein* (Supreme Command, Upper Rhine) on January 26, 1945. It was initially commanded by SS General of Waffen-SS Felix Steiner (assumed command, January 28, 1945), who was succeeded by the army's General of Artillery Walther Lucht (March 1945). Although initially formed as an SS panzer staff, the army merely referred to it as "11th Army," and in the last, confusing days of the war, it may have been officially downgraded, but this is doubtful. In any case, the 11th fought in Pomerania under Army Group Vistula (February–March, 1945), but was transferred to OB West in April, after Army Group B (5th Panzer and 15th Armies) was surrounded in the Ruhr Pocket. It tried to halt the American advance through central Germany and cover the rear of the 12th Army, but was quickly overrun by the Allies. Its headquarters was captured on April 21, 1945, and it ceased to exist. General Lucht was absent from his HQ at the time and General of Infantry Otto Hitzfeld was reportedly acting as army commander at the end.

## PANZER ARMY AFRIKA

Panzer Army Afrika was formed as Panzer Group Afrika on September 1, 1941, from elements of the Afrika Korps and German officers attached to the Italian High Command, Africa. It was upgraded to panzer army status on January 30, 1942, and became the (1st) Italian-German Panzer Army on February 22, 1943. It was destroyed when Tunisia fell in May 1943.

Commanders of the panzer group/army included Colonel General/Field Marshal Erwin Rommel (assumed command, September 1, 1941), General of Panzer Troops Georg Stumme (September 25, 1942), Lieutenant General Ritter Wilhelm von Thoma (October 24, 1942), Field Marshal Rommel (October 25, 1942), General of Panzer Troops Gustav Fehn (acting commander, January 1943), and Italian General Messe (March 9, 1943).

## I SS PANZER CORPS

Formed in Berlin-Lichterfelde on July 27, 1943, this corps was used by Hitler as a "fire brigade"—i.e., it was sent to critical places, often to deal with crises. It was sent to upper

Italy in November 1943. When the situation in Italy was stabilized, it was sent to France (January–August 1944), where it fought in the Normandy campaign. So badly was it depleted at Falaise and in the retreat across the Seine that it had to be sent back to Germany to rebuild. It fought in the Ardennes campaign (December 1944–January 1945), in eastern Germany (January–March 1945), in Hungary (March), and in the defense of Austria (April 1945). It was in lower Austria when the war ended and surrendered to the Anglo-Americans.

Commanders of the I SS Panzer Corps included General of Waffen-SS Josef "Sepp" Dietrich (assumed command, July 27, 1943), SS Lieutenant General Georg Keppler (acting commander, September 1944), and SS Lieutenant General Hermann Priess (October 24, 1944–end).

## II SS PANZER CORPS

The II SS Panzer Corps was formed in July 1942, as the SS Panzer Corps. It was sent to northern France in August and took part in the occupation of Vichy France in November. It captured Toulon in December and remained there until January 1943, when it was sent to the Eastern Front. It fought in the battles of Kharkov and Kursk, among others. It was redesignated II SS Panzer Corps in June 1943. Sent to northern Italy in August 1943, it was transferred to the Alençon area of France in January 1944, and remained there until April, when it was hurriedly rushed to the Eastern Front. After fighting in eastern Galicia, it returned to France and fought in the Normandy campaign (July–August 1944). After retreating through France and Belgium, it was sent to the Netherlands to rebuild. Here it fought in the Battle of Arnhem (September 1944), where it virtually destroyed the British 1st Airborne Division and the Polish Parachute Brigade. Later it fought in the Ardennes (December 1944–January 1945), in eastern Germany (February 1945), Hungary (March 1945), and Austria (April 1945). It surrendered to the Americans.

Commanders of the II SS included General of Waffen-SS Paul Hausser (assumed command, June 1, 1942) and SS Lieutenant General Wilhelm Bittrich (June 28, 1944), who was promoted to general of Waffen-SS on August 1, 1944.

## III PANZER CORPS

Formed as Wehrkreis III in 1920, the III was both a corps headquarters and a territorial command until Germany mobilized in August 1939. The field components became Headquarters, III Corps, and invaded Poland on September 1. It also fought in Belgium and France (1940). It was upgraded to III Motorized Corps on March 21, 1941, and to III Panzer Corps on June 21, 1942. It spent the entire 1941–45 period on the Eastern Front.

Commanders of the III Corps included General of Artillery Curt Haase (assumed command, September 1, 1939), General of Cavalry Eberhard von Mackensen (November 1, 1941), and Lieutenant General/General of Panzer Troops Hermann Breith (January 3, 1943–end). Lieutenant General Friedrich Schulz was acting commander of the corps in December 1943.

## III (GERMANISCHEN) SS PANZER CORPS

The III SS Panzer Corps was formed at Grafenwoehr on March 15, 1943. It was made up of Germanic volunteers from all over Europe. The III SS was posted to the Balkans later that year and, in December 1943, was sent to the northern sector of the Eastern Front, where it distinguished itself in the retreat from Leningrad and especially in the Narva battles. It remained on the Eastern Front until the end of the war, fighting in Courland, Pomerania, and on the Oder. It surrendered to the British at the end of the conflict.

Its commanders included SS Lieutenant General/General of Waffen-SS Felix Steiner (assumed command, March 15, 1943), General of Waffen-SS Georg Keppler (October 30, 1944), and SS Major General Joachim Ziegler (March 1945–end). Apparently, Lieutenant General Martin Unrein was acting corps commander in January–February, 1945.

## IV PANZER CORPS

This corps headquarters was formed in the rear area of Army Group South on October 10, 1944, from the remnants of the IV Corps (which had been destroyed in Romania). Its staff and corps units came from Operations Staff East Hungary, Assault Division Rhodes, and the 17th Panzer Grenadier Brigade. It fought on the southern sector of the Eastern Front from October 1944 until the end of the war. It was redesignated Panzer Corps Feldherrnhalle on November 27, 1944. It surrendered to the Americans, who turned most of its men over to the Soviets. The corps was commanded by General of Panzer Troops Ulrich Kleemann throughout its existence.

## IV SS PANZER CORPS (1943)

The original Headquarters, IV SS Panzer Corps was activated in the Poitiers area of France on August 5, 1943, but was never fully formed. It was absorbed by Staff, VI SS Corps in November 1943.

## IV SS PANZER CORPS (1944–45)

The second IV SS Panzer Corps was formed in the zone of OB West on June 30, 1944, from the former Staff, VII SS Panzer Corps. It was sent to Warsaw in August and remained there until December, when it was sent to Hungary. After fighting in the Lake Balaton area, it retreated into Austria in April 1945, and surrendered to the Americans at Enns at the end of the war.

Its commanders included General of Waffen-SS Albert Wuennenberg (assumed command, June 1944) and SS Lieutenant General/General of Waffen-SS Herbert Otto Gille (August 6, 1944).

## V (LATER XI SS PANZER) CORPS

Formed as Wehrkreis V in 1920, the field elements of V Corps went to war in 1939. It fought in the Western campaign of 1940 and on the Eastern Front (1941–44). Virtually destroyed in the Crimea (April 1944), it was taken over by SS and redesignated XI SS Panzer Corps on July 24, 1944 (see XI SS Panzer Corps). Its acting commander at the time was General of Infantry Dr. Franz Beyer.

## VII SS PANZER CORPS

Authorized for formation on October 3, 1943, it was not organized until April 1944. It never left Germany. On June 30, 1944, it was absorbed by the IV SS Panzer Corps. Its commander was SS Lieutenant General Matthias Kleinheisterkamp.

## XI SS PANZER CORPS

This headquarters was formed on July 24, 1944, in Ottmachau bei Neisse, Wehrkreis VIII, just three days after Heinrich Himmler assumed command of the Replacement Army. It was formed around the remnants of the army's V Corps, which had been smashed on the Eastern Front. All of its support and service support units were transferred from the army to the SS. The XI SS first saw action in western Galicia (August 1944–January 1945), but was transferred north, where it defended the fortress of Kuestrin on the Oder River. It was part of 9th Army during the Battle of Berlin and was destroyed by the Soviets. Its commander throughout its existence was General of Waffen-SS Matthias Kleinheisterkamp.

## XIV MOTORIZED (LATER PANZER) CORPS (1938–43)

This unit was formed in Magdeburg on April 1, 1938, as the XIV Motorized Corps. It controlled Germany's motorized divisions until the army was mobilized in August 1939. The XIV did not become a panzer corps until June 21, 1942. Meanwhile, it distinguished itself, serving in Poland (1939), Belgium (1940), France (1940), the Balkans (1941), and southern Russia (1941–43). The original XIV was surrounded in Stalingrad in November 1942 and was destroyed there on January 29, 1943.

Commanders of the first XIV Motorized/Panzer included General of Infantry Gustav von Wietersheim (assumed command, April 1, 1938), Lieutenant General/General of Panzer Troops Hans Valentin Hube (September 15, 1942), and Lieutenant General Helmuth Schloemer, who surrendered it to the Russians.

## XIV PANZER CORPS (1943–45)

A second XIV Panzer Corps was created in southern Russia on March 5, 1943, from the survivors of the Stalingrad disaster. (General Hube had been flown out of the pocket on Hitler's personal orders on January 15, 1943.) Soon transferred to France, it directed all German forces in the Battle of Sicily (July–August 1943), and spent the rest of the war on the Italian Front.

Its commanders included General Hube (assumed command, March 5, 1943), Lieutenant General Hermann Balck (October 1943), Hube again (acting commander, October 1943, after Balck was injured in an airplane crash), and Lieutenant General/General of Panzer Troops Fridolin von Senger und Etterlin (October 23, 1943–end). He surrendered it to the Americans on May 2, 1945.

## XV MOTORIZED CORPS

See 3rd Panzer Army.

## XXIV PANZER CORPS

Formed in 1938 as Frontier Command Saarpfalz, this headquarters was mobilized as XXX Corps on August 26, 1939. It served on the Saar Front (1939–40) before taking part in the French campaign, where it played a strictly secondary role. Sent back to Germany in November, it was reorganized and redesignated a motorized corps on November 16, 1940. It became a panzer corps on November 27, 1942. It spent four years on the Eastern Front, mostly on the southern sector. It ended the war in Budweis, Moravia, where it surrendered to the Soviets.

Commanders of the XXIV included General of Engineers Walter Kuntze (assumed command, September 1, 1939), General of Cavalry Baron Leo Geyr von Schweppenburg (February 15, 1940), Major General Dietrich von Saucken (acting commander, December 27, 1941), Major General/Lieutenant General/General of Panzer Troops Baron Willibald von Langermann und Erlenkamp (assumed command, January 8, 1942, and killed in action at Storoshewoje on October 3, 1942), General of Panzer Troops Otto von Knobelsdorff (October 10, 1942), Lieutenant General/General of Artillery Martin Wandel (assumed command, December 1, 1942; missing in action at Chilino, January 14, 1943), Lieutenant General Arno Jahr (assumed command on January 14, 1943, and killed in action at Podgornoje, January 20, 1943), Lieutenant General Karl Eibl (assumed command, January 20, 1943, and killed in action near the Don River the next day), Colonel Otto Heidkaemper (acting commander, January 21, 1943), General of Panzer Troops Walther Nehring (February 10, 1943), Lieutenant General Fritz-Hubert Graeser (acting commander, July 1, 1944), Nehring (August 1944), Lieutenant General Hans Kaellner (assumed command March 22, 1945, and killed in action at Sokolnica, April 1945), and General of Artillery Walter Hartmann (April 1945–end).

## XXXIX PANZER CORPS

This unit was formed in Gotha, Wehrkreis IX, on January 27, 1940, as the XXXIX Motorized Corps. It was redesignated XXXIX Panzer Corps on July 9, 1942. It fought in France (1940) and on the Eastern Front (1941–44), mostly on the northern and central sectors. It was largely destroyed when Army Group Center was crushed in June 1944, but was hastily rebuilt in Lithuania and Courland. It defended East Prussia in November 1944; then it was sent west, where it fought in the Ardennes offensive. Sent to the East again in February 1945, it fought in Silesia and Pomerania. In April 1945, it was assigned to 12th Army on the Elbe and surrendered to the Western Allies at the end of the war.

Commanders of the XXXIX Motorized/Panzer Corps included Lieutenant General/General of Panzer Troops Rudolf Schmidt (assumed command, February 1, 1940), General of Panzer Troops Hans-Juergen von Arnim (November 11, 1941), Lieutenant General/General of Artillery Robert Martinek (assumed command December 1, 1942; killed in action at Beresinow on June 28, 1944), Lieutenant General Otto Schuenemann (assumed command on June 28, 1944, and killed in action the next day), Lieutenant General/General of Panzer Troops Dietrich von Saucken (July, 1944), Lieutenant General/General of Panzer Troops Karl Decker (assumed command, October 15, 1944; committed suicide, April 21, 1945), and Lieutenant General Karl Arndt (April 1945–end).

## XXXX PANZER CORPS

Formed in Luebeck, Wehrkreis X, as the XXXX Corps on January 26, 1940, this unit fought as an infantry corps in France (1940). Redesignated a motorized corps on September 15, 1940, it took part in the invasion of Greece (1941) and in the Russian campaign (1941–45). It was redesignated XXXX Panzer Corps on July 9, 1942. The XXXX fought at Kharkov (1942), in the Caucasus campaign (1942–43), in the Donets and Dnieper battles (1943), and in the subsequent retreats across Ukraine and Romania (1943–44). Transferred to East Prussia in August 1944, it was sent south again in January 1945, and fought in western Galicia. It ended the war in Silesia and surrendered to the Russians.

Its commanders included Lieutenant General/General of Cavalry/General of Panzer Troops Georg Stumme (assumed command, Feburary 15, 1940), Lieutenant General Hans Zorn (acting commander January 15, 1942), Stumme (resumed command, February 16, 1942), General of Panzer Troops Baron Leo Geyr von Schweppenburg (June 26, 1942), Lieutenant General/General of Panzer Troops Gustav Fehn (October 1, 1942), General of Panzer Troops Hermann Balck (acting commander, November 12, 1942), Lieutenant General/General of Panzer Troops Sigfrid Henrici (November 13, 1942), General of Mountain Troops Ferdinand Schoerner (October 10, 1943), General of Panzer Troops Otto von Knobelsdorff (February 1, 1944), and Henrici again (August 3, 1944–end).

## XXXXI PANZER CORPS

This unit was formed in Brieg, Wehrkreis VIII, on February 24, 1940, as the XXXXI Motorized Corps. In late 1940, its home station was moved to Breslau and later to Oels. The corps fought in Belgium and France in 1940 (and was at the decisive Battle of Sedan). After serving as an occupation force in the Netherlands and in Paris, it was sent east, and fought on the Russian Front until 1945. It was virtually destroyed at Bobruisk in June 1944, when Army Group Center was smashed. Hastily rebuilt, it fought in East Prussia until March 1945, when it was sent to the 12th Army on the Havel. It surrendered to the Western Allies at the end of the war.

Commanders of the XXXXI Motorized/Panzer Corps included Lieutenant General/General of Panzer Troops Georg-Hans Reinhard (assumed command, February 15, 1940), Lieutenant General Otto Ottenbacher (October 6, 1941), General of Panzer Troops Walter Model (November 1, 1941), Lieutenant General/General of Panzer Troops Josef Harpe (January 15, 1942), Lieutenant General/General of Artillery Helmuth Weidling (October 20, 1943), Lieutenant General Ehrenfried Boege (February 1, 1944), Lieutenant General Edmund Hoffmeister (acting commander, June 20, 1944, captured on July 1, 1944), and Major General/Lieutenant General Rudolf Holste (April 20, 1945).

## XXXXVI PANZER CORPS

The XXXXVI was formed in Goerlitz, Wehrkreis VIII, on October 25, 1940, as a motorized corps. It was redesignated a panzer corps on June 14, 1942. It fought in Yugoslavia (1941) and on the Eastern Front (1941–45), mostly on the central sector. It ended the war fighting in Pomerania with the 3rd Panzer Army and managed to surrender to the British.

Commanders of the XXXXVI included General of Panzer Troops Heinrich von Scheel gen. von Vietinghoff (assumed command, November 1, 1940), General of Infantry Hans Zorn (assumed command, October 1, 1942; killed at Krassnaja-Roschtscha on August 2, 1943), Lieutenant General/General of Infantry Hans Gollnick (August 2, 1943), Lieutenant General/General of Infantry Friedrich Schulz (March 22, 1944), Lieutenant General Baron Smilo von Luettwitz (July 27, 1944), Lieutenant General Maximilian Felzmann (acting commander, August 29, 1944), Lieutenant General/General of Panzer Troops Walter Fries (September 21, 1944), and Lieutenant General/General of Infantry Martin Gareis (January 1, 1945). Lieutenant General Baron Hans-Karl von Esebeck was acting commander of the corps from November 22, 1942, until about the end of the year.

## XXXXVII PANZER CORPS

This staff was formed in Hanover, Wehrkreis XI as a motorized corps. It was upgraded to a panzer corps on June 21, 1942. It fought on the Russian Front (1941–44) before being transferred to France in April 1944. It fought in Normandy, Metz, the Siegfried Line campaign, the Ardennes, and the Battle of the Ruhr Pocket, where it was destroyed. Its survivors surrendered to the Americans.

Commanders of the XXXXVII Motorized/Panzer Corps included General of Artillery/ General of Panzer Troops Joachim Lemelsen (assumed command, November 25, 1940), General of Panzer Troops Erhard Raus (October 1943), Lieutenant General Rudolf von Buenau (acting commander, November 1, 1943), Lieutenant General Nikolaus von Vormann (December 26, 1943), General of Panzer Troops Baron Hans von Funck (March 5, 1944), and General of Panzer Troops Heinrich von Luettwitz (September 5, 1944–end).

## XXXXVIII PANZER CORPS

The XXXXVIII Motorized Corps was formed in Koblenz, Wehrkreis XII, on December 14, 1940. Later its home base was Nancy, France. It became a panzer corps on June 21, 1942. The corps fought on the Eastern Front (1941–45), and spent almost all of its time on the southern sector. After fighting in Silesia, it was assigned to the 12th Army in April 1945, and thus managed to surrender to the Western Allies.

Commanders of the XXXXVIII included Lieutenant General/General of Panzer Troops Werner Kempf (assumed command, January 6, 1941), Lieutenant General/General of Panzer Troops Rudolf Veiel (February 19, 1942), Kempf again (May 5, 1942), Lieutenant General Ferdinand Heim (November 1, 1942), Major General Dietrich von Choltitz (acting commander, November 16–20, 1942), Major General Hans Cramer (acting commander, November 20–26, 1942), Major General Heinrich Eberbach (November 26, 1942), Cramer again (acting commander, December 1942), General of Panzer Troops Otto von Knobelsdorff (December 10, 1942), von Choltitz (acting commander, May 7, 1943), von Knobelsdorff (August 30, 1943), General of Panzer Troops Eberbach (October 1, 1943), von Knobelsdorff (November, 1943), General of Panzer Troops Hermann Balck (November 15, 1943), Lieutenant General/General of Panzer Troops Fritz-Hubert Graeser (August 5, 1944), Lieutenant General/General of Panzer Troops Baron Maximilian von Edelsheim (September 21, 1944), and Lieutenant General Wolf Hagemann (April 1945–end).

## LVI PANZER CORPS

The LVI was formed in Bad Salzuflen, Wehrkreis VI, as a motorized corps. It became a panzer corps on March 1, 1942. It crossed into the Soviet Union on June 22, 1941, and served primarily on the central sector. It escaped the disaster at Bobruisk (June–July 1944), but was smashed when the Russians broke out of the Baranov bridgehead on the Vistula in January 1945. It was chosen to defend Berlin in the last weeks of the war, which it valiantly attempted to do, but without success. Hitler committed suicide on April 30, 1945, and the LVI Panzer surrendered on May 2. Many of its men, including its last commander, died in Soviet prison camps.

Commanders of the LVI Motorized/Panzer Corps included General of Panzer Troops Erich von Manstein (assumed command, February 15, 1941), General of Panzer Troops Ferdinand Schaal (September 13, 1941), Lieutenant General/General of Infantry Friedrich Hossbach, Lieutenant General Anton Grasser (acting commander, November 15, 1941), Hossbach (1942–44), General of Infantry Johannes Block (killed in action near Baranov), General of Cavalry Rudolf Koch-Erpach (February 16, 1945), and General of Artillery Helmuth Weidling (April 12, 1945).

## LVII PANZER CORPS

The LVII was formed as a motorized corps in Augsburg, Wehrkreis VII, on February 15, 1941. It was upgraded to a panzer corps on June 21, 1942. It spent four years on the Eastern Front, taking part in the drive on Moscow, the Caucasus campaign, the retreat to the Dnieper, and the Hungarian and Silesian campaigns. It ended the war with the 4th Panzer Army on the Eastern Front.

Commanders of the LVII included Lieutenant General/General of Panzer Troops Adolf Kuntzen (assumed command, March 15, 1941), and Lieutenant General/General of Panzer Troops Friedrich Kirchner (November 15, 1941–end). Acting commanders at various times included Lieutenant General/General of Panzer Troops Baron Hans-Karl von Esebeck (December 1, 1943–February 19, 1944), Lieutenant General Dr. Franz Beyer (May 25–June 2, 1944), and Lieutenant General Carl Puchler (July 1944).

## LVIII PANZER CORPS

The LVIII Panzer Corps was formed in Ludwigsburg, Wehrkreis V, on July 28, 1943, as the LVIII Reserve Panzer Corps. Its initial mission was to control the 155th and 177th Reserve Panzer Divisions in France. It was redesignated LVIII Panzer Corps on July 6, 1944, and was sent to the Western Front. It fought in Normandy, the Siegfried Line, the Lunéville offensive, and the Battle of the Bulge. It was trapped in the Ruhr Pocket and destroyed there in April 1945. Its commanders included General of Panzer Troops Baron Leo Geyr von Schweppenburg (July 28, 1943), Lieutenant General/General of Panzer Troops Walter Krueger (January 1, 1944), and Lieutenant General Walter Botsch (March 25, 1945).

## LXXVI PANZER CORPS

The LXXVI was formed on June 29, 1943, as an infantry corps from elements of the LXVI Reserve Corps in France. On July 22, 1943, it was redesignated LXXVI Panzer and was sent to Italy a few days later. It served on the Italian Front for the rest of the war, fighting in the defense of Rome, in the Gustav Line battles, and in the battles for

Anzio and Florence, among others. It surrendered to the Anglo-Americans near Bologna in April 1945.

Commanders of the corps included General of Panzer Troops Traugott Herr (assumed command, June 25, 1943) and Lieutenant General/General of Panzer Troops Count Gerhard von Schwerin (April 1, 1945).

## AFRIKA KORPS

The Afrika Korps was officially created on February 21, 1941, from the Staff, Commander of German Troops in Libya. It was actually formed five days earlier. It registered an incredible record of military success and heroism before it was destroyed when Tunisia fell. The Afrika Korps surrendered on May 12, 1943. Its commanders included Lieutenant General/General of Panzer Troops Erwin Rommel (assumed command, February 14, 1941), Lieutenant General/General of Panzer Troops Ludwig Cruewell (September 1, 1941), Lieutenant General/General of Panzer Troops Walther Nehring (May 29, 1942), Lieutenant General/General of Panzer Troops Ritter Wilhelm von Thoma (September 1, 1942), General of Panzer Troops Gustav Fehn (November 13, 1942), Lieutenant General Heinz Ziegler (acting commander, February 20, 1943), and Lieutenant General/General of Panzer Troops Hans Cramer (March 1, 1943). Of these commanders, Cruewell was captured, Nehring was wounded, von Thoma was captured, Fehn was wounded, and Cramer was captured, all while commanding the Afrika Korps. Later, Fehn was murdered by partisans in Yugoslavia in 1945 and Rommel was forced to commit suicide in 1944.

## PANZER CORPS FELDHERRNHALLE

See IV Panzer Corps.

## PANZER CORPS GROSSDEUTSCHLAND

The formation of the Headquarters, Panzer Corps Grossdeutschland began on September 28, 1944, but it proceeded slowly and no commander was appointed until November. The Staff and GHQ troops came from the disbanded 18th Artillery Division and the remnants of the XIII Corps, which had been smashed on the Eastern Front. It was initially planned that the corps would control the Grossdeutschland and Brandenburg Panzer Grenadier Divisions, but, when it reached the field, it directed other units as well. It fought on the Eastern Front from February to May 1945, fighting on the Oder and Neisse, and surrendered to the Soviets at the end of the war. Its commanders were General of Panzer Troops Dietrich von Saucken (assumed command, November 10, 1944) and Lieutenant General/General of Panzer Troops Georg Jauer (March 12, 1945).

## PANZER CORPS HERMANN GOERING

Parachute Panzer Corps Hermann Goering was formed on October 1, 1944, from elements of the 1st Hermann Goering Parachute Panzer Division. It was on the Vistula

River between Warsaw and Modlin at the time, but it was soon transferred to Lithuania. It fought in Lithuania (October 1944), Courland (October 1944), and East Prussia (November 1944–March 1945), before being evacuated by sea and sent to the 4th Panzer Army in Czechoslovakia. It was here when the war ended. Most of its men were forced to surrender to the Soviets. Lieutenant General Wilhelm Schmalz commanded it throughout its existence.

# Appendix III

# Chronology of the Second World War

## 1939

*September 1:*   Germany invades Poland; World War II begins.

*September 27:*   Warsaw falls.

*October 6:*   Last Polish resistance ends. A total of 800,000 Poles killed or captured by the Germans. German losses: 13,111 killed or missing, 27,278 wounded.

## 1940

*April 9:*   Germany invades Denmark and Norway; Denmark capitulates.

*May 10:*   Western campaign begins as Germany invades Luxembourg, Belgium, the Netherlands, and France.

*May 14:*   The Dutch surrender.

*May 18:*   Antwerp falls.

*May 20:*   The panzers reach the English Channel near Abbeville.

*May 21:*   Anglo-French counterattack at Arras.

*May 24:*   Hitler issues halt order to panzer forces advancing on Dunkirk.

*June 4:*   Dunkirk evacuation ends. Some 224,585 British and 112,546 French and Belgian soldiers escape. British leave behind 1,200 guns, 1,250 antiaircraft and antitank guns, and 75,000 vehicles. Dunkirk occupied the next day.

*June 5:*   German attack on France proper and the Weygand Line begins.

*June 9:*   Anglo-French forces complete the evacuation of Narvik. End of Norwegian campaign.

*June 10:*    Italy declares war on France and the United Kingdom.

*June 14:*    Fall of Paris.

*June 14–16:*    Russia invades and occupies the Baltic states of Lithuania, Latvia, and Estonia.

*June 21:*    French sign armistice. France surrenders.

*June 25:*    French surrender takes effect. Germany lost 27,074 killed, 111,034 wounded, and 18,383 missing. Allies lost 90,000 killed, 200,000 wounded, and 1,900,000 captured or missing.

*July 2:*    Hitler orders the preparation of Operation Sealion, the invasion of Great Britain.

*July 9:*    Romania placed under the military protection of Germany.

*July 21:*    Hitler announces to OKH that he intends to invade Russia in 1941.

*December 9:*    British launch offensive in North Africa.

## 1941

*February 7:*    British complete the conquest of Cyrenaica. Italian 10th Army destroyed; 130,000 men lost.

*February 12:*    First German forces, the vanguard of the Afrika Korps, land in Tripoli, Libya.

*March 26–27:*    Pro-Axis government of Yugoslavia overthrown.

*March 31:*    Rommel and Afrika Korps begin first Cyrenaican campaign.

*April 4:*    Afrika Korps captures Benghazi.

*April 6:*    Germany invades Yugoslavia and Greece.

*April 11:*    Rommel isolates Tobruk, beginning a 242-day siege.

*April 12:*    Belgrade falls.

*April 13:*    Rommel encircles Tobruk.

*April 23:*    Greece surrenders.

*April 27:*    Athens occupied.

*May 20:*    Crete invaded.

*June 15–17:*    Operation Battleaxe, a British attempt to relieve Tobruk, is defeated.

*June 22:*    Operation Barbarossa begins.

*June 23–24:*    Battle of Raseiniai (Rossieny); 300 Soviet tanks and 100 guns destroyed by 3rd Panzer Group. Appearance of Klim Voroshilov (KV-1) heavy tanks surprise the Germans.

*June 24:*    Vilna and Kaunas, Lithuania, fall to Germans.

*June 26:*    Manstein's LVI Panzer Corps seizes the Daugavpils crossings over the Dvina.

*June 27:*   2nd and 3rd Panzer Groups begin encirclement of Minsk Pocket.

*June 28:*   Minsk, the capital of Belorussia, 200 miles from the border, falls.

*June 30:*   Lvov and Brest-Litovsk captured. Guderian's panzers cross the Berezina River.

*July 3:*   Resistance ends in Minsk Pocket. Soviets lose 324,000 men, 3,332 tanks, and 1,809 guns.

*July 4:*   Ostrov captured.

*July 6:*   1st Panzer Group breaks Stalin Line.

*July 8:*   Pskov (on Lake Peipus) captured.

*July 9:*   Vitebsk captured.

*July 10:*   Panzer division spearheads cross the Dnieper.

*July 16:*   Smolensk falls.

*July 17:*   More than 300,000 Reds trapped east of Smolensk.

*August 5:*   End of the Battle of the Smolensk Pocket. Soviets lose 310,000 captured, 3,205 tanks, and 3,120 guns.

*August 3–8:*   Uman Pocket cleared. A total of 103,000 Russians captured, 317 tanks, and 1,100 guns captured or destroyed.

*August 8:*   Guderian encircles several Soviet divisions at Roslavl, southeast of Smolensk and 110 miles south of Moscow; 38,000 Reds captured, 250 tanks and 359 guns captured or destroyed.

*August 12:*   Hitler sends 2nd Panzer Group toward Kiev and 3rd Panzer Group toward Leningrad—both away from Moscow.

*August 17:*   Novgorod (in zone of Army Group North) and Kiev and Dnepropetrovsk (in Ukraine) captured.

*August 24:*   Soviet pocket at Gomel collapses. Russians lose 84,000 captured, 144 tanks and 848 guns captured or destroyed.

*September 8:*   Schluesselburg (Petrokrepost) captured, Leningrad isolated. Heavy fighting at Vyasma and Bryansk.

*September 15:*   Kiev encircled.

*September 19:*   Kiev falls.

*September 21:*   Germans reach the Sea of Azov, cutting off the Crimea.

*September 22:*   German forces reach the southern shore of Lake Ladoga, cutting off Leningrad.

*September 26:*   End of the Battle of the Kiev Pocket. Soviets lose 667,000 captured, 3,718 guns, 884 armored vehicles captured or destroyed.

*September 30:*   2nd Panzer Group begins offensive against Orel and Bryansk; 1st Panzer Group reaches the Dnieper River in Ukraine. Two days later, 3rd and 4th Panzer Groups launch offensive toward Vyasma.

*September 30–October 17:*  Double Battle of Vyasma-Bryansk. Soviets lose 663,000 men, 1,242 tanks, and 5,412 guns.

*October 5–10:*  Battle of the Chernigovka Pocket on the Sea of Azov. More than 100,000 Soviet soldiers captured; 212 tanks and 672 guns captured or destroyed by 1st Panzer Group.

*October 7:*  First snow falls in Russia.

*October 8:*  Orel falls.

*October 14:*  Vyasma Pocket collapses.

*October 20:*  Rostov and Stalino (Donetsk) captured.

*October 24:*  Kharkov, the main industrial city of Ukraine, captured.

*October 30:*  Siege of Sevastopol begins.

*November 16:*  Army Group Center launches its last drive on Moscow.

*November 17:*  Soviet Rostov counteroffensive begins.

*November 18:*  British 8th Army begins Operation Crusader, an attempt to relieve Tobruk. After an extremely fluid battle, the siege is broken on December 5.

*November 25:*  Final push toward Moscow begins.

*November 27:*  3rd Panzer Group reaches Volga Canal, 19 miles from Moscow.

*November 28:*  Soviets recapture Rostov.

*December 6:*  Stalin's winter offensive begins on central sector with 100-division attack.

*December 10:*  British forces break the Siege of Tobruk after 242 days.

*December 11:*  Germany declares war on the United States.

*December 15:*  Russians recapture Klin and Istra.

*December 16:*  Russians recapture Kalinin.

*December 19:*  Hitler sacks Field Marshal von Brauchitsch and names himself commander in chief of the army; also issues his first "stand or die" order.

*December 26:*  Red Army launches amphibious assault on Kerch peninsula on the eastern Crimea.

## 1942

*January 21:*  Rommel begins 2nd Cyrenaican campaign.

*January 23:*  Russians launch major offensive along a 250-mile front between Smolensk and Lake Ilmen.

*January 26:*  Rommel recaptures Benghazi.

*February 8:*  German II Corps isolated in the Demyansk Pocket with 103,000 men.

*February 23:*   Russians recapture Dorogobuzh on the Dnieper.

*April 9:*   Russians recapture Orel.

*May 12:*   Russians launch major spring offensive aimed at Kharkov and Kursk.

*May 15:*   Colonel General von Manstein's 11th Army recaptures Kerch and inflicts 176,000 casualties on Stalin's armies.

*May 17:*   Russians suspend Kharkov offensive due to counterattack by 1st Panzer Army.

*May 20:*   Kerch peninsula overrun by German 11th Army. One hundred thousand Soviets surrender.

*May 24:*   Russian Kharkov forces trapped in huge pocket at Izyum, west of the Donets River.

*May 26:*   In North Africa, Panzer Army Afrika begins an offensive against the Gazala Line and Tobruk.

*May 29:*   End of the Battle of Izyum (Kharkov). Russians lose 239,000 men, 1,250 tanks, and 2,026 guns. Germany loses 20,000 men.

*June 7:*   Manstein's 11th Army begins offensive against Sevastopol.

*June 13–14:*   British evacuate the Gazala Line.

*June 21:*   Tobruk captured by Panzer Army Afrika.

*June 23:*   Rommel invades Egypt.

*June 28:*   German summer offensive begins.

*July 1:*   First Battle of El Alamein begins; Panzer Army Afrika checked 60 miles west of Alexandria, Egypt.

*July 2:*   Sevastopol falls. Russians lose 90,000 men, 460 guns.

*July 4:*   Germans advance along a broad front toward the Don River.

*July 6:*   Germans capture Voronezh.

*July 23:*   Rostov recaptured. Germans take 240,000 prisoners.

*July 29:*   Caucasus offensive begins.

*August 9:*   Maikop oil fields captured.

*August 11:*   Germans smash Soviet 4th Tank Army near Kalach, in the bend of the Don River.

*August 20:*   Panzers reach the Volga north of Stalingrad.

*August 23:*   Germans capture the town of Elbrus on the east coast of the Black Sea.

*August 31:*   1st Panzer Army crosses Terek River.

*September 6:*   Heavy fighting in the Black Sea port of Novorossiysk.

*September 7:*   6th Army attacks city center in Stalingrad.

*September 24:*   Hitler fires Franz Halder as chief of the General Staff.

*October 23:*   The Battle of El Alamein begins.

*November 1:*   In the Caucasus sector, German efforts to take the Grozny oil fields are repulsed.

*November 4:*   Panzer Army Afrika crushed, begins withdrawal from El Alamein and Egypt.

*November 8:*   Allied forces land in Algeria and Morocco, recapture French North Africa.

*November 9:*   Germans land in Tunisia, begin forming 5th Panzer Army.

*November 11:*   Hitler occupies Vichy France.

*November 13:*   Tobruk falls to British.

*November 19:*   Soviet winter offensive begins north and south of Stalingrad.

*November 23:*   Red Army forces link up at Kalach, 50 miles west of Stalingrad, encircling the 6th Army in Stalingrad Pocket.

*December 10:*   General Kurt Zeitzler named chief of the General Staff of the German Army.

*December 12:*   Manstein launches Operation Winter Storm, the attempt to relieve Stalingrad.

*December 16:*   Reds attack and rout Italian 8th Army on the Don.

*December 19:*   6th Panzer Division reaches a point within 30 miles of Stalingrad.


## 1943

*January 3:*   Caucasus withdrawal begins.

*January 23:*   British capture Tripoli.

*January 31:*   Field Marshal Paulus and 6th Army staff captured in Stalingrad.

*February 2:*   Northern pocket surrenders; end of resistance in Stalingrad; 90,000 Germans surrender. Total German losses: 240,000 men.

*February 5:*   Soviet forces reach the Donets.

*February 11:*   Battle of Kharkov begins.

*February 14:*   Reds recapture Rostov. Rommel launches Kasserine Pass offensive in Tunisia.

*February 16:*   Soviets recapture Kharkov.

*February 19:*   Manstein counterattacks toward Kharkov and Belgorod.

*February 28:*   Kasserine counteroffensive ends.

*March 2:*   Rzhev evacuated by German 9th Army.

*March 12:*   Heavy street fighting inside Kharkov.

*March 14:*   Kharkov falls to Manstein's panzer troops. Soviets lose 615 tanks and 354 guns.

*March 18:*   Grossdeutschland Division retakes Belgorod.

*May 6:*   Allies launch final offensive in Tunisia.

*May 7:*   Tunis and Bizerte fall.

*May 12:*   Last German forces in Tunisia surrender. Army Group Afrika, including the 5th Panzer Army and 1st Italian-German Panzer Army (formerly Panzer Army Afrika), surrenders. More than 230,000 Axis troops captured.

*July 5:*   Operation Citadel, the Battle of Kursk and the largest tank battle in history, begins.

*July 11:*   Allies land in Sicily.

*July 12:*   Russians counterattack in rear of Model's 9th Army; largest tank clash in history takes place near the village of Prochorovka.

*July 13:*   Hitler ends the Kursk offensive.

*July 25:*   Mussolini overthrown; Hitler vows to restore Fascism, occupy Italy.

*August 3:*   Red Army launches offensive toward Kharkov.

*August 4:*   Soviets recapture Belgorod and Orel.

*August 17:*   Last German troops evacuate Sicily.

*August 23:*   Reds recapture Kharkov.

*August 30:*   Reds smash Army Group A, capture Taganrog.

*September 3:*   Russians cross the Desna.

*September 7:*   Stalino (on the Black Sea) falls.

*September 8:*   Italian surrender to the Western Allies made public; Germans disarm Italian Army.

*September 9:*   Hitler finally approves a withdrawal from Ukraine to the Dneiper. Allied forces land in Italy at Salerno.

*September 10:*   German troops seize Rome.

*September 21:*   Russians reach the Dnieper along a 300-mile front.

*September 22:*   Reds establish a bridgehead on the west bank of the Dnieper.

*September 24:*   Germans abandon Smolensk and Roslavl.

*October 1:*   Allies capture Naples.

*October 9:*   Kuban evacuated.

*October 28:*   Manstein's counteroffensive in the Krivoy Rog sector ends. Soviets lose 15,000 men, 350 tanks, and 350 guns.

*November 1:*   Last German land link to the Crimea cut by Soviets.

*November 6:*   Kiev falls to the Russians.

*November 12:*   Zhitomir falls.

*November 14–19:*   Germans launch counteroffensive, recapture Zhitomir.

*December 29:*   Manstein orders the withdrawal of all his forces to the Dnieper.

*December 31:*   Reds retake Zhitomir.

## 1944

*January 8:*   Kirovograd falls to Soviets.

*January 22:*   Allies land at Anzio, 35 miles south of Rome.

*January 28:*   Siege of Leningrad broken after 900 days.

*February 3:*   60,000 Germans encircled at Korsun (Cherkassy).

*February 12:*   German relief forces halted 10 miles from Korsun.

*February 16–17:*   Encircled German forces break out of the Cherkassy Pocket, losing about 30,000 men.

*February 22:*   Reds recapture Krivoy Rog in heavy fighting.

*March 1:*   Red forces drive across the Narva River.

*March 6:*   Stalin launches offensive in Ukraine along a 100-mile front.

*March 10:*   Uman falls.

*March 15:*   Russians break through German defenses on the Bug River.

*March 18:*   Reds reach Romanian border, capture Yampol on the eastern bank of the Dniester (Dnestr).

*March 20:*   Wehrmacht completes the occupation of Hungary.

*March 23:*   Reds encircle Tarnopol.

*March 26:*   Red Army reaches the Prut River in the Ukraine along a 50-mile front.

*March 28:*   1st Panzer Army encircled in "Hube Pocket."

*April 5:*   Tarnopol falls.

*April 8:*   Russian offensive begins in the Crimea.

*April 9:*   1st Panzer Army escapes.

*April 10:*   Black Sea port of Odessa falls to Russians.

*May 11:*   Allied armies in Italy launch major offensive against the Gustav Line.

*May 12:*   Remnants of 17th Army in the Crimea destroyed at Sevastopol.

*May 18:*   In Italy, Monte Cassino falls to Allies.

*June 4:*   American forces enter Rome.

*June 6:*   D-Day; Allies land in Normandy.

*June 22:*   Russian summer offensive begins against Army Group Center, beginning the Battle of Vitebsk-Minsk. By early July, Army Group Center will lose 28 divisions, 300,000 men, 215 tanks, and 1,500 guns.

*June 24:* Soviets reach the Dvina River in the Baltic sector.

*June 25:* LIII Corps breaks out of Vitebsk but is destroyed two days later; 80,000 Germans captured.

*June 27:* Last German resistance in Cherbourg ends.

*July 1:* Reds cross the Berezina.

*July 3:* Minsk falls.

*July 13:* After five days of street fighting, the Russians capture Vilna.

*July 14:* Germans abandon Pinsk; Red offensive extended into northern Ukraine.

*July 17:* Russians cross Bug River and swing into Poland.

*July 18:* Americans capture St.-Lô in Normandy.

*July 19:* German XIII Corps (five divisions) surrounded at Brody in Ukraine; only remnants escape. Russians cross into Latvia near Dvinsk (Daugavpils).

*July 20:* Anti-Nazi conspirators, led by Colonel Count Claus von Stauffenberg, attempt to kill Hitler and overthrow the Nazi government. They narrowly miss.

*July 22:* End of the fighting in the Brody Pocket.

*July 24:* Lublin falls to Stalin's forces.

*July 25:* American heavy bombers blast Panzer Lehr Division in Normandy. Russians reach the Vistula.

*July 26:* U.S. armored forces launch major offensive, which breaks the deadlock in Normandy.

*July 27:* Reds take Lwow (Lvov).

*July 28:* Brest-Litovsk falls.

*August 1:* Russians reach the Gulf of Riga, isolating Army Group North in the Baltic States. The non-Communist Polish Home Army revolts, seizes most of Warsaw.

*August 6:* Germans launch disastrous Avranches counteroffensive in Normandy.

*August 7:* Russian summer offensive finally checked after an advance of more than 400 miles; German panzer divisions smash Soviet III Tank Corps at Wolomin, northeast of Warsaw.

*August 17:* British capture Falaise. Russians reach the East Prussian border.

*August 20:* Romania defects to Allies, trapping most of 6th and much of 8th German armies (16 divisions).

*August 22:* Russians capture Jassy (Iasi).

*August 24:* Bordeaux and Cannes occupied by Allies.

*August 25:*   Paris liberated.

*August 26:*   Bulgaria declares its neutrality, begins disarming German forces in the country. Hitler orders the evacuation of Greece.

*August 28:*   Russian troops enter Transylvania. In southern France, Marseilles and Toulon fall to Franco-American forces.

*August 29:*   Two pockets cleared on the Prut River in Romania; 180,000 Germans captured. Soviet forces occupy Constanta on the Romanian Black Sea coast, cross into Bulgaria.

*August 30:*   Ploesti falls. Slovakian military revolts against the Germans.

*August 31:*   Bucharest falls.

*September 1:*   Nice falls.

*September 2:*   Finland accepts Stalin's armistice terms, leaves the Axis. Lyon falls.

*September 3:*   Brussels liberated by British.

*September 4:*   British capture Antwerp.

*September 5:*   U.S. forces halted by still resistance on Moselle River.

*September 11:*   First American forces cross into Germany near Stalzenburg; Americans liberate the city of Luxembourg.

*September 15:*   Americans capture Nancy, attack Siegfried Line.

*September 16:*   Sofia, the capital of Bulgaria, captured by Russians.

*September 17:*   Allies launch Operation Market-Garden, aimed at capturing Arnhem and outflanking the Siegfried Line.

*September 18:*   5th Panzer Army launches a series of unsuccessful counterattacks aimed at eliminating American bridgeheads over the Moselle.

*September 24:*   Guderian orders Army Group South Ukraine to withdraw to the Danube.

*September 25:*   British survivors begin withdrawing from Arnhem, their offensive defeated.

*October 2:*   Polish Home Army surrenders to Germans in Warsaw.

*October 10:*   Tank battle near Debrecen, Poland; three Soviet corps destroyed. Russian forces reach the Baltic Sea near Memel, cutting off Army Group North in Courland for the last time.

*October 13:*   Americans capture Aachen after a fierce battle; British enter Athens; Russians capture Riga, the capital of Latvia.

*October 14:*   Russians and Yugoslav partisans surround Belgrade, the capital of Yugoslavia.

*October 20:*   Belgrade falls.

*November 7:*   Reds cross the Danube.

*November 19:*   Americans capture Metz.

*November 26:*   Soviets reach the outskirts of Budapest.

*December 3:*   Americans capture an intact bridge over the Saar near Saarlautern, compromising the Siegfried Line.

*December 5:*   Saarlautern falls.

*December 16:*   The Battle of the Bulge begins.

*December 21:*   Bastogne surrounded.

*December 26:*   Bastogne encirclement broken, but siege continues.


## 1945

*January 10:*   Germans begin counteroffensive toward Strasbourg.

*January 12:*   Soviets break out of Baranov Bridgehead on the Vistula; 1,300,000 Reds attack in Poland and East Prussia, smashing Army Group Center.

*January 13:*   Kielce falls.

*January 16:*   Ardennes Salient eliminated. Radom, Poland, falls to Soviets. Hitler abandons Rastenburg headquarters and moves to the bunker under the Reichschancellery in Berlin.

*January 17:*   Reds capture Warsaw.

*January 19:*   Soviets capture Krakow and Lodz.

*January 22:*   German evacuation of Memel begins.

*January 26:*   Russians reach the Gulf of Danzig northeast of Elbing (Elblag), cutting off East Prussia from the Reich; 3rd Panzer and 4th Armies cut off in East Prussia.

*January 29:*   Reds enter Pomerania.

*February 5:*   Heavy fighting in Kuestrin (Kostrzyn), about 50 miles northeast of Berlin.

*February 8:*   Battle of the Reichswald begins as British begin offensive to clear the area between the Meuse and the Rhine.

*February 9:*   Colmar Pocket crushed. German forces west of the Rhine from Strasbourg to the Swiss border are eliminated. Elbing falls.

*February 11:*   Budapest garrison breaks out; of 30,000 men, 800 escape.

*February 13:*   Budapest falls. Pruem is captured; organized resistance ends in the Reichswald.

*February 15:*   German Stargard offensive begins in Pomerania; fails.

*February 20:*   Allies break through Siegfried Line at several points.

*February 22:*    Americans cross the Saar River.

*February 23:*    Russians capture Poznan.

*February 28:*    Soviets capture Neustettin.

*March 6:*    Americans capture the west bank section of Cologne (i.e., most of the city). Germans counterattack around Lake Balaton in Hungary.

*March 7:*    Americans cross the Rhine at Remagen.

*March 8:*    Americans capture Bonn.

*March 12:*    Kuestrin falls.

*March 13:*    Russians attack Koenigsberg, the capital of East Prussia.

*March 18:*    Kolberg (Kolobrzeg), East Prussia, falls to Soviets.

*March 20:*    Saarbruecken captured by U.S. forces.

*March 28:*    Heinz Guderian replaced as chief of the General Staff; succeeded by General of Infantry Hans Krebs.

*March 29:*    Frankfurt am Main falls, Mannheim abandoned.

*March 30:*    Danzig captured by Russians.

*April 1:*    Army Group B encircled in the Ruhr.

*April 4:*    Bratislava falls. French capture Karlsruhe.

*April 9:*    Koenigsberg falls.

*April 10:*    Hanover (Hannover), Lower Saxony, captured by Americans.

*April 12:*    American tanks reach the Elbe. U.S. President Franklin D. Roosevelt dies.

*April 13:*    Vienna falls.

*April 16:*    Russians begin their last offensive.

*April 18:*    End of the Battle of the Ruhr Pocket; 325,000 Germans surrender.

*April 19:*    Leipzig captured by Americans; British attack Bremen.

*April 20:*    Americans capture Nuremberg.

*April 21:*    French forces take Stuttgart; Poles and Americans capture Bologna in Italy.

*April 24:*    Berlin encircled; Reds capture Potsdam; Americans take Ulm.

*April 25:*    U.S. and Soviet forces link up, cutting Germany in half.

*April 26:*    British take Bremen; Russians capture Stettin and Brno, Czechoslovakia.

*April 28:*    Mussolini shot; Americans reach Venice, capture Augsburg.

*April 30:*    Hitler commits suicide. Munich and Turin occupied by U.S. forces.

*May 2:*    German resistance in Berlin ends. All fighting in Italy ends. British reach the Baltic, sealing off Schleswig-Holstein and Denmark.

*May 3:*   Hamburg surrenders to the British; Americans take Innsbruck, Brenner Pass.

*May 7:*   Breslau surrenders to Soviets.

*May 8:*   Germany surrenders. V-E Day.

*May 9:*   Soviets capture Prague. Fighting officially ends at 11:01 p.m.

## Appendix IV

# Profiles of the Non-Army Panzer Divisions

### (1st) PARACHUTE PANZER DIVISION HERMANN GOERING

*1943:*  Formed in southern France as part of the Luftwaffe.

Fought in North Africa, Sicily, Italy (1943–44), and on the Eastern Front (1944–45). Surrendered to the Russians at the end of the war.

### 1st SS PANZER DIVISION LEIBSTANDARTE ADOLF HITLER

*March 1933:*  Raised as a bodyguard battalion for Adolf Hitler.

*1938:*  Expanded into a motorized infantry regiment.

*1941:*  Expanded into a motorized infantry division.

*Late 1942:*  Reorganized and redesignated as a panzer grenadier division.

*October 1943:*  Reorganized as a panzer division.

The LAH fought in Poland (1939), Holland, Belgium, and France (1940), the Balkans (1941), and Russia (1941–42). Rebuilt in France, 1942. Took part in the occupation of Vichy France (1942). Fought at Kursk (1943) and was then sent to northern Italy (1943). Sent back to southern Russia (late 1943–44). Normandy (1944). Rebuilt, September 1944. Later fought in the Ardennes (1944–45), Hungary (1944–45), and Austria (1945). Surrendered to the Americans at the end of the war.

### 2ND SS PANZER DIVISION DAS REICH

*October 1939:*  Formed as SS Motorized Division Verfuegungstruppe (SS-VT).

*December 1940:*  Renamed SS Motorized Division Das Reich.

*October 1943:*   Reorganized as a panzer division.

*May 1945:*   Surrendered to U.S. forces at Pilsen.

Das Reich fought in Holland, Belgium, and France (1940), the Balkans (1941), and Russia (1941–42). Rebuilt in France (1942). Back to Russia (1943–44). Normandy campaign (1944). Rebuilt, September 1944. Ardennes (December 1944–January 1945), eastern Germany, Hungary, and Austria (1945).

### 3RD SS PANZER DIVISION TOTENKOPF

*November 1939:*   Formed as SS Motorized Division Totenkopf, mainly from concentration camp guards.

*October 1943:*   Reorganized as a panzer division.

*May 1945:*   Surrendered to U.S. forces; handed over to Soviets.

The "Death's Head" division fought in Belgium (1940), France (1940), Russia (1941–44), Hungary (1944–45), and Austria (1945).

### 5TH SS PANZER DIVISION VIKING

*December 1940:*   Raised as SS Motorized Division Viking; included Germanic troops from several countries, including Denmark, Norway, the Netherlands, and others.

*October 1943:*   Reorganized as a panzer division.

*May 1945:*   Surrendered to the British at Furstenfeld.

The Viking Division fought on the Eastern Front for four years (1941–45).

### 9TH SS PANZER DIVISION HOHENSTAUFFEN

*March 1943:*   Formed in France as a panzer grenadier division.

*October 1943:*   Reorganized as a panzer division.

*May 1945:*   Surrendered to the Americans at Linz.

The Hohenstauffen Division served in Russia (1944), Normandy (1944), Arnhem (1944), the Ardennes (1944–45), Hungary, and Austria (1944–45).

### 10TH SS PANZER DIVISION FRUNDSBERG

*February 1943:*   Formed in France as a panzer grenadier division.

*October 1943:*   Reorganized as a panzer division.

*April 1945:*   Virtually destroyed by the Russians at Spremberg.

*May 1945:*   Remnants surrendered to the Soviets at Shonau.

The Hohenstauffen Division served in Russia (1944), Normandy (1944), Arnhem (1944), the Ardennes (1944–45), and the Eastern Front, mainly in eastern Germany (1944–45).

## 12TH SS PANZER DIVISION HITLER JUGEND

*July 1943:*   Raised in Belgium as a panzer grenadier division.

*October 1943:*   Reorganized as a panzer division.

*May 1945:*   Surrendered to the U.S. Army at Enns.

The Hitler Youth Division fought in Normandy (1944), the retreat through France (1944), the Ardennes (1944–45), Hungary, and Austria (1945). It was probably the best German division to fight in Normandy.

## 26TH SS PANZER DIVISION

Formed as an emergency battle group in 1944, this unit was redesignated 49th SS Panzer Grenadier Brigade on June 18, 1944. Shortly thereafter, it was upgraded to panzer division status in August 1944, for no apparent reason. It had only three grenadier battalions. It fought only one battle, against Patton's 3rd Army at Troyes. It fought well, but was virtually destroyed by the end of August. Its remnants were absorbed by the 17th SS Panzer Grenadier Division. The appropriate records do not even mention that this unit had any tanks, and it seems quite possible that it had none. For a brief history of this division and the Battle of Troyes, see Samuel W. Mitcham Jr., *Retreat to the Reich* (Greenwood Press, 2000).

## 27TH SS PANZER DIVISION

Formed as an emergency battle group in 1944, this unit was redesignated 51st SS Panzer Grenadier Brigade on June 18, 1944. Shortly thereafter, it was upgraded to panzer division status in August, 1944, for no apparent reason. It had only two grenadier battalions and fewer than 3,000 men. It fought only one battle, against Patton's 3rd Army in the Troyes sector. It fought well, but was seriously depleted by the end of August. Its remnants were absorbed by the 17th SS Panzer Grenadier Division.

# Appendix V

# German Staff Positions

## Chief of Staff (normally present only in corps-level or higher headquarters)

| | |
|---|---|
| Ia | Chief of Operations (de facto chief of staff in divisions or lower units) |
| Ib | Chief Supply Officer (Quartermaster) |
| Ic | Chief Intelligence Officer |
| IIa | Chief Personnel Officer or Adjutant |
| IIb | Second Personnel Officer |
| III | Judge Advocate |
| IVa | Chief Administrative Officer |
| IVb | Chief Medical Officer |
| IVc | Chief Veterinary Officer (normally absent in panzer divisions) |
| IVd | Chaplain |
| V | Motor Transport Officer |

Normally, the divisional staff was broken into three operational groupings:

1. the *Fuehrungsabteilung* or tactical detachment was headed by the Ia and included the Ic and various attached, combat-oriented subordinates, including air liaison officers and the Ia of attached artillery units. The Ia's tactical headquarters was also known as the division's command post (CP).

2. the *Quartermeister* or supply group was headed by the Ib. It included the IVa, IVb, IVc, and V.

3. the *Adjutantur* or personnel group was headed by the IIa, who was responsible for officer records, personnel actions, etc. The Adjutantur included the IIb (responsible for enlisted personnel), the III, the IVd, and various other sections necessary for the functioning of a staff headquarters, such as motor pools, security detachments, and the like. The staff company (called the Headquarters Company in the U.S. Army) was responsible to the IIa.

Most of the staff officers in a division were not General Staff officers; however, to hold an I-type position (Ia, Ib, or Ic), an officer (with very few exceptions) had to be a member of the General Staff.

In addition to the three major groups, divisions had special staffs assigned to them on a temporary or permanent basis. These staffs or sections might be headed by a senior military police officer, a gas protection officer, or a senior artillery commander (the Arko). After July 20, 1944, each division had a political indoctrination section, headed by a National Socialist Guidance Officer.

# Bibliography

Adair, Paul. *Hitler's Great Defeat*. London: 1994.

Angolia, John C. *On the Field of Honor*. San Jose, Calif.: 1979–1980. 2 Volumes.

Barrett, Correlli, ed. *Hitler's Generals*. London: 1989.

Bartov, Omar. *The Eastern Front, 1941–1945: German Troops and the Barbarisation of Warfare*. New York: 1986.

Benoist-Mechin, Jacques. *Sixty Days That Shook the West: The Fall of France*. New York: 1963.

Blumenson, Martin. *Breakout and Pursuit*. Washington, D.C.: 1960.

———. *Salerno to Cassino*. Washington, D.C.: 1969.

Brehm, Werner. *Mein Kriegstagebuch, 1939–1945: Mit der 7. Panzer-Division 5 Jahre in West und Ost*. Kassel: 1953.

Brett-Smith, Richard. *Hitler's Generals*. San Rafael, Calif.: 1976.

Brownlow, Donald G. *Panzer Baron: The Military Exploits of General Hasso von Manteuffel*. North Quincy, Mass.: 1975.

Carell, Paul. *Foxes of the Desert*. New York: 1960.

———. *Hitler Moves East, 1941–1943*. Boston: 1965. Reprint ed., New York: 1966.

———. *Invasion: They're Coming*. New York: 1963. Reprint ed., New York: 1973.

———. *Scorched Earth*. Boston: 1971.

Chandler, David G., and James Lawton Collins, Jr., eds. *The D-Day Encyclopedia*. New York: 1997.

Chant, Christopher, et al. *The Marshall Cavendish Illustrated History of World War II*. New York: 1979. 25 Volumes.

——— et al. *Hitler's Generals*. New York: 1979.

Chapman, Guy. *Why France Fell: The Defeat of the French Army in 1940*. New York: 1968.

Clark, Alan. *Barbarossa: The Russian-German Conflict, 1941–45*. New York: 1965.

Cole, Hugh M. *The Ardennes: The Battle of the Bulge*. Washington, D.C.: 1965.

———. *The Lorraine Campaign*. Washington, D.C.: 1950.

Cooper, Matthew, and James Lucas. *Panzer: The Armored Force of the Third Reich*. New York: 1976.

Corum, James S. *The Roots of the Blitzkrieg: Hans von Seeckt and German Military Reform*. Lawrence, Kans.: 1992.

Desch, John. "The 1941 German Army/The 1944–45 U.S. Army: A Comparative Analysis of Two Forces in Their Primes," in Editors of Command Magazine, *Hitler's Army: The Evolution and Structure of the German Forces*. Conshohocken, Pa.: 1995.

D'Este, Carlo. *Decision in Normandy*. New York: 1983.

Dupuy, T. N. *A Genius For War: The German Army and General Staff, 1807–1945*. Fairfax, Va.: 1987.

Edwards, Roger. *Panzer: A Revolution in Warfare, 1939–1945*. London: 1989.

Eisenhower, John S. D. *The Bitter Woods*. New York: 1969.

Fisher, Ernest F., Jr. *Cassino to the Alps*. Washington, D.C.: 1977.

Fraser, David. *Knight's Cross: A Life of Field Marshal Erwin Rommel*. New York: 1994.

Garland, Albert N., and Howard McG. Smyth. *Sicily and the Surrender of Italy*. Washington, D.C.: 1965.

Geyr von Schweppenburg. "Panzer Group West (Mid 43–July 1944)." United States Army Military History Institute *MS # B-258*. Unpublished manuscript on file at the United States Army Military History Institute, Carlilse Barracks, Pennsylvania.

———. "Panzer Group West (Mid 43–July 1944)." United States Army Military History Institute *MS # B-466*. Unpublished manuscript on file at the United States Army Military History Institute, Carlilse Barracks, Pennsylvania.

Goebbels, Paul Joseph. *The Goebbels Diaries*. Louis P. Lochner, ed. and trans. New York: 1948. Reprint ed., New York: 1971.

Grams, Rolf. *Die 14. Panzer-Division, 1940–1945*. Bauhein: 1957.

Guderian, Heinz. *Panzer Leader*. Constantine Fitzgibbon, trans. New York: 1957. Reprint ed., New York: 1972.

Harrison, Gordon A. *Cross-Channel Attack*. Washington, D.C.: 1951.

Hartmann, Theodor. *Wehrmacht Divisional Signs, 1938–1945*. London: 1970.

Haupt, Werner. *A History of the Panzer Troops*. Edward Force, trans. West Chester, Pa.: 1990.

Hermann, Carl Hans. *68 Kriegsmonate: Der Weg der 9. Panzerdivision durch zweiten Weltkrieg*. Vienna: 1975.

———. *Die 9. Panzerdivision, 1939–1945*. Friedberg: n.d.

Irving, David. *Trail of the Fox*. New York: 1977.

Jackson, W. G. F. *The Battle for North Africa, 1940–43*. New York: 1975.

Kameradschaftsbund 16. Panzer- und Infanterie-Division. *Bildband der 16. Panzer-Division*. Bad Nauheim: 1956.

Keilig, Wolf. *Die Generale des Heeres*. Friedberg: 1983.

Kennedy, Robert M. *The German Campaign in Poland (1939)*. United States Department of the Army *Pamphlet 20-255*. Washington, D.C.: 1956.

Knobelsdorf, Otto von. *Geschichte der niedersaechsischen 19. Panzer-Division*. Bad Nauheim: 1958.

*Kriegstagebuch des Oberkommando der Wehrmacht (Wehrmachtfuehungsstab)*. Frankfurt-am-Main: 1961.

Kurowski, Frank. *Panzer Aces*. David Johnston, trans. Winnipeg, Canada: 1992.

Lucas, James. *Germany's Elite Panzer Force: Grossdeutschland*. London: 1978.

_____. *Hitler's Enforcers*. London: 1996.

MacDonald, Charles B. *The Last Offensive*. Washington, D.C.: 1973.

_____. *The Siegfried Line Campaign*. Washington, D.C.: 1963.

Manstein, Erich von. *Lost Victories*. Chicago: 1958.

Manteuffel, Hasso von. *Die 7. Panzer-Division im Zweiten Weltkrieg*. Friedburg: 1986.

Mellenthin, F. W. von. *German Generals of World War II*. Norman, Okla.: 1977.

_____. *Panzer Battles*. Norman, Okla.: 1956. Reprint ed., New York: 1971.

Mehner, Kurt, ed. *Die Geheimen Tagesberichte der deutschen Wehrmachtfuehrung im Zweiten Weltkrieg, 1939–1945*. Osnabrueck: 1984–1995. 12 Volumes.

Military Intelligence Division, U.S. War Department. "The German Replacement Army (Ersatzheer)." Washington, D.C.: 1945. On file at the U.S. Army War College, Carlisle Barracks, Pennsylvania.

Mitcham, Samuel W., Jr. "Arnim," in Corelli Barrett, ed., *Hitler's Generals*. London: 1989, pp. 335–60.

_____ and Gene Mueller. *Hitler's Commanders*. Lanham, Md.: 1992.

_____ and Friedrich von Stauffenberg. *The Battle of Sicily*. New York: 1991.

Moll, Otto E. *Die deutschen Generalfeldmarshaelle, 1939–1945*. Rastatt/Baden: 1961.

Munzel, Oskar. *Die deutschen Panzer Truppen bis 1945*. Herford and Bonn: 1965.

Paul, Wolfgang. *Geschichte der 18. Panzer-Division, 1940–1943*. Freiburg: n.d.

Plocher, Hermann. "The German Air Force Versus Russia, 1941." United States Air Force Historical Studies *Number 153*. United States Air Force Historical Division, Aerospace Studies Institute, Maxwell Air Force Base, Alabama: 1965. On file in the Air University archives.

Preradovich, Nikolaus von. *Die Generale der Waffen-SS*. Berg-am-See: 1985.

Quarrie, Bruce. *Panzer-Grenadier-Division "Grossdeutschland."* London: 1977.

Rebentisch, Ernst. *Zum Kaukasus und zu den Tauern: Die Geschichte der 23. Panzer-Division, 1941–1945*. Esslingen: 1963.

Riebenstahl, Horst. *The 1st Panzer Division*. Edward Force, trans. West Chester, Pa.: 1990.

Ritgen, Helmut. *Die Geschichte der Panzer-Lehr-Division im Westen, 1944–1945*. Stuttgart: 1979.

———. *The 6th Panzer Division, 1937–45*. London: 1982. Reprint ed., London: 1985.

Rommel, Erwin. *The Rommel Papers*. B. H. Liddell Hart, ed. New York: 1953.

Ruge, Friedrich. *Rommel in Normandy*. San Rafael, Calif.: 1979.

Ryan, Cornelius. *The Last Battle*. New York: 1966.

Salisbury, Harrison E. *The 900 Days: The Siege of Leningrad*. New York: 1969.

Scheibert, Horst. *Bildband der 6. Panzer-Division, 1939–1945*. Bad Nauheim: 1958.

———. *Die Traeger des deutschen Kreuzes in Gold*. Friedberg: n.d.

Schmitz, Peter, Klaus-Juergen Thies, Guenter Wegmann and Christian Zweng. *Die deutschen Divisionen, 1939–1945*. Osnabrueck: 1993–1997. 3 Volumes.

Seaton, Albert. *The Russo-German War, 1941–45*. New York: 1970.

Seemen, Gerhard von. *Die Ritterkreuztraeger, 1938–1945*. Freidberg: 1976.

Senger und Etterlin. *Die 24. Panzer-Division, vormals 1. Kavallerie-Division, 1939–1945*. Vohwinckel-Neckargemuend: 1962.

Senger und Etterlin, Frido von. *Neither Fear Nor Hope*. George Malcolm, trans. New York: 1963. Reprint ed., Novato, Calif.: 1989.

Snyder, Louis L. *Encyclopedia of the Third Reich*. New York: 1976.

Spaeter, Helmuth. *Panzerkorps Grossdeutschland Bilddokumentation*. Friedberg: 1984.

Speidel, Hans. *Invasion, 1944*. New York: 1968.

Staiger, Georg. *26. Panzer-Division: Ihr Werden und Einsatz, 1942–1945*. Nauheim: 1957.

Stauffenberg, Friedrich von. "Panzer Commanders of the Western Front." Unpublished manuscript in the possession of the author.

———. "Papers." Unpublished papers in the possession of the author.

Stoves, Rolf O. G. *Die Gepanzerten und Motorisierten deutschen Grossverbaende (Divisionen und selbstaendige Brigaden 1935–1945)*. Friedberg: 1986.

———. *Die 1. Panzerdivision, 1935–1945: Die deutschen Panzerdivision in Bild*. Friedberg: n.d.

———. *Die 22. Panzer-Division, 25. Panzer-Division, 27. Panzer-Division und 233. Reserve-Panzer-Division*. Friedberg: 1985.

Tessin, Georg. *Verbaende und Truppen der deutschen Wehrmacht und Waffen-SS im Zweiten Weltkrieg, 1939–1945*. Osnabrueck: 1973–81. 16 Volumes.

Thomas, Franz. *Die Eichenlaubtraeger: 1940–1945*. Osnabrueck: 1997–1998. 2 Volumes.

Thorwald, Juergen. *Defeat in the East*. New York: 1980.

United States Department of the Army. *Pamphlet 20-260*. "The German Campaign in the Balkans" (Spring, 1941). Washington, D.C.: 1953.

United States Military Intelligence Service. "Order of Battle of the German Army, 1942." Washington, D.C.: 1942.

_____. "Order of Battle of the German Army, 1943." Washington, D.C.: 1943.

_____. "Order of Battle of the German Army, 1944." Washington, D.C.: 1944.

_____."Order of Battle of the German Army, 1945." Washington, D.C.: 1945.

United States War Department. Technical Manual *TM-E 30–451*, "Handbook on German Military Forces." Washington, D.C.: 1945.

Werthen, Wolfgang. *Geschichte der 16. Panzer-Division, 1939–1945*. Bad Nauheim: 1958.

Windrow, Martin. *The Panzer Divisions*. London, 1985.

Young, Desmond. *Rommel: The Desert Fox*. New York: 1965.

Ziemke, Earl F. "The German Northern Theater of Operations, 1940–1945." United States Department of the Army *Pamphlet 20-271*. Office of the Chief of Military History. Washington, D.C.: 1959.

_____. *Stalingrad to Berlin: The German Defeat in the East*. Washington, D.C.: 1966.

# Index

# Individuals

The rank shown is the highest the individual attained during World War II (excluding posthumous promotions).

Adam, General of Mountain Troops Wilhelm, 8, 27

Altrock, Lieutenant General Konstantin von, 5, 26

Angelis, General of Artillery Maximilian de, 259

Angern, Major General Guenther, 102, 105, 133, 134

Apell, Lieutenant General Wilhelm von, 166

Arnim, Colonel General Hans-Juergen von, 139–40, 259, 264

Arndt, Lieutenant General Karl, 264

Aschoff, Colonel Dr. Albrecht, 133, 135

Audoersch, Major General Oskar, 182, 183–84

Back, Major General Hans-Ulrich, 133, 211, 214–15

Bader, General of Artillery Paul, 110, 111

Badinski, Lieutenant General Kurt, 186, 187–88

Baeke, Major General Dr. Franz, 226–27

Baessler, Major General Johannes, 97, 98, 120

Balck, General of Panzer Troops Hermann, 91, 105, 106–07, 203, 254, 259, 263, 265, 266

Bayerlein, Lieutenant General Fritz, 51, 55, 202, 203, 204–205

Beck, Colonel General Ludwig, 8, 10, 12, 13

Bergmann, Lieutenant General Friedrich, 139

Bernard, Lieutenant General Curt, 211

Betzel, Lieutenant General Clemens, 61, 63

Beyer, General of Infantry Dr. Franz, 262, 267

Bismarck, Major General Georg von, 155, 160, 162

Bittrich, General of Waffen-SS Wilhelm, 261

Block, General of Infantry Johannes, 267

Blomberg, Field Marshal Werner von, 4, 6, 7, 8, 12, 27, 257

Bodenhausen, Lieutenant General Baron Erpo von, 110, 111

Boege, Lieutenant General Ehrenfried, 265

Boehme, General of Mountain Troops Franz, 259

Boelsen, Lieutenant General Dr. Hans, 187, 188

Boemers, Colonel Walter, 97, 99

Boettcher, Lieutenant General Karl, 160, 161

Boineburg-Lengsfeld, Lieutenant General Baron Hans von, 60, 170, 171

Boltenstern, Lieutenant General Walter, 213

Borowietz, Lieutenant General Willibald, 125, 127–128

Botsch, Lieutenant General Walter, 267

Brandenberger, General of Panzer Troops Erich, 88, 89, 90

Brandt, General of Cavalry Georg, 177–178

Brandt, SS Lieutenant Colonel Wilhelm, 6, 26

Brauchitsch, Field Marshal Walter von, 12, 257, 273

Brelow, Major General Kurt von, 7

Breith, General of Panzer Troops Hermann, 8, 55, 57, 261

Brockdorff-Ahlefeld, General of Infantry Count Walter von, 186, 187

Broich, Lieutenant General Baron Friedrich von, 102, 103

Bronsart von Schellendorff, Colonel Heinrich von, 66, 69

Brueckner, Colonel Erich, 170, 172

Bruer, Colonel Albert, 160, 161–162

Brux, Colonel Albert, 139, 141

Buch, Major General Fritz von, 170, 171–172

Buenau, Lieutenant General Rudolf von, 266

Burgsthaler, Major Hugo, 166, 167

Chales de Beaulieu, Walter, 7

Chappuis, General of Infantry Friedrich-Wilhelm von, 197

Chevallerie, Lieutenant General Helmuth von der, 114, 166, 219, 220

Chevallerie, General of Infantry Kurt von der, 220

Christern, Colonel Hans, 61, 83, 85

Choltitz, General of Infantry Dietrich von, 106, 107, 266

Clausewitz, Major General Karl von, 5, 26

Cloessner, General of Infantry Heinrich, 259

Conze, Major General Wilhelm, 8

Cramer, General of Panzer Troops Hans, 266, 268

Crasemann, General of Artillery Eduard, 125, 127, 187, 188

Crisolli, Major General Wilhelm, 76, 77–78, 114, 197

Cruewell, General of Panzer Troops Ludwig, 66, 105, 106, 268

Cuno, Lieutenant General Kurt, 217, 218

Decker, General of Panzer Troops Karl, 66, 69, 264

Deckert, Major General Hans-Joachim, 150, 152

Demme, Major General Rudolf, 139, 141

Denkert, Lieutenant General Walter, 150, 151–152

Dietrich, SS Colonel General Josef, 260, 261

Duevert, Lieutenant General Walter, 114, 115, 154

Eberbach, General of Panzer Troops Heinrich, 60, 61, 62, 260, 266

Edelsheim, General of Panzer Troops Reichsbaron Maximillian von, 176, 177, 266

Eibl, Lieutenant General Karl, 264

Elster, Major General Wolfgang, 168

Elverfeldt, Major General Baron Harald Gustav von, 97, 99

Esebeck, General of Panzer Troops Baron Hans-Karl von, 48, 49–50, 105–106, 125, 126, 127, 266, 267

Faber du Faur, Lieutenant General Moritz von, 114–115

Fabiunke, Major General Karl, 48, 50

Faeckenstedt, Lieutenant General Felix, 66, 69

Falkenstein, Lieutenant General Hans
von, 120, 122
Fehn, Gustav, 66, 68, 260, 265, 268
Feldt, Lieutenant General Kurt, 176, 266
Fellgiebel, General of Signal Troops
Erich, 28, 147
Fessmann, General of Panzer Troops
Ernst, 8, 54, 55
Feuchtinger, Lieutenant General Edgo,
160, 163
Fischer, Lieutenant General Wolfgang,
102, 103
Franz, Major General Gerhard, 171
Fremerey, Lieutenant General Max, 207,
208, 217, 235
Friebe, Lieutenant General Helmut, 88,
91
Friebe, Major General Werner, 88, 91
Fries, General of Panzer Troops Walter,
266
Fritsch, Colonel General Baron Werner
von, 6, 8, 9, 12, 26
Froelich, Major General Gottfried, 88,
90–91
Fromm, Colonel General Friedrich
"Fritz," 30, 32
Fuller, British Major General J. F. C., 6
Funck, General of Panzer Troops Baron
Hans von, 82, 83–84, 160, 266

Garies, General of Infantry Martin, 266
Gawantka, Major General Georg, 102
Gerhardt, Colonel Rudolph, 204, 205
Geyr von Schweppenburg, General of Pan-
zer Troops Baron Leo, 54, 55–56, 260,
264, 265, 267
Gille, General of Waffen-SS Herbert, 262
Glaesemer, Colonel Wolfgang, 82, 84
Glokke, General of Infantry Gerhard, 133,
196
Gneisenau, General Count August Wil-
helm, 4, 25, 26
Goebbels, Minister of Propaganda Dr.
Paul Joseph, 146
Goering, Reichsmarschall Hermann, 14
Gollnick, General of Infantry Hans, 265
Gothsche, Major General Reinhold, 245
Graessel, Colonel Max, 120, 121, 122

Graeser, General of Panzer Troops Fritz-
Hubert, 259, 264, 266
Grasser, General of Infantry Anton, 267
Grolig, Major General Oswin, 43, 160,
182, 183, 204
Guderian, Colonel General Heinz, 4, 6, 7,
8, 10, 12, 13, 14, 16, 19, 20, 24, 28,
33, 46, 48–49, 100, 102, 135, 146,
160, 279, 281

Haarde, Lieutenant General Johann,
182–183
Hagemann, Lieutenant General Wolf, 266
Halder, Colonel General Franz, 13, 27,
28, 88, 90, 135, 161, 274
Hake, Colonel Friedrich von, 106, 114,
116
Halle, Major, 97
Hammerstein, Colonel General Kurt von,
8, 21
Hansen, General of Artillery Christian,
121
Harpe, Colonel General Josef, 4, 8, 110,
111, 259, 265
Hartlieb gennant Walsporn, Lieutenant
General Max von, 66, 67, 213
Hartmann, General of Artillery Walter,
264
Hasse, Colonel General Curt, 3
Hauenschild, Lieutenant General Ritter
Bruno von, 176–177
Hauser, Major General Eduard, 114, 116
Hauser, Colonel Baron Paul von, 204,
205
Hausser, SS Colonel General Paul, 261
Hax, Major General Heinrich Georg, 89,
91–92
Hecker, Major General Hans, 61, 64,
186
Heidkaemper, Lieutenant General Otto,
60, 62, 264
Heigl, Fritz, 6
Heim, Major General Friedrich, 120,
121–22, 266
Heinrici, Colonel General Gotthard, 133,
196, 258
Hellmich, Lieutenant General Heinz, 186,
187

Henrici, General of Panzer Troops Sigfrid, 197–198, 265
Henze, Lieutenant General Albert, 224, 225
Herff, Colonel (later General of SS) Maximilian von, 125, 126–127
Herr, General of Panzer Troops Traugott, 114, 115–116, 268
Herzog, Colonel of Reserves Hans, 67, 70
Heydrich, Reinhardt, 12
Hielscher, Colonel Edgar, 60, 61
Hildebrandt, Lieutenant General Hans-Georg, 160, 162
Himmler, Reichsfuehrer-SS Heinrich, 12, 127
Hitler, Adolf, 7, 8, 12, 13, 17, 18, 19, 20, 21, 24, 25, 27, 28, 29, 32, 42, 48, 89, 90, 92, 110, 121, 130, 146, 147, 151, 163, 177, 186, 196, 200, 228, 232, 233, 236, 257, 272, 273, 274, 275, 276, 277, 281, 283
Hitzfeld, General of Infantry Otto, 260
Hoepner, General of Panzer Troops Erich, 14, 259
Hoernlein, General of Infantry Walter, 254
Hoffmann, Colonel Ernst Wilhelm, 61, 63
Hoffmann-Schoenborn, Guenther, 67, 69–70
Hoffmeister, Lieutenant General Edmund, 265
Holste, Lieutenant General Rudolf, 265
Hossbach, General of Infantry Friedrich, 267
Hoth, Colonel General Hermann, 16, 28, 259
Hube, Colonel General Hans Valentin, 22, 133, 134, 197, 258, 263
Hubicki, Lieutenant General Dr. Ritter Alfred von, 97
Hudel, Major Helmut, 240, 241
Huebner, Major General Werner, 88, 89
Huelsen, Major General Heinrich-Hermann von, 97, 98, 160, 162–163
Huenersdorff, Major General Walter von, 7
Huppert, Colonel Helmut, 42, 44

Jahn, General of Artillery Curt, 217
Jahr, Lieutenant General Arno, 264
Jauer, General of Panzer Troops Georg, 182, 183, 268
Jesser, Major General Kurt von, 207, 208–209
Jolasse, Lieutenant General Erwin, 97, 98–99
Junck, Hans, 61, 63
Juergen, Colonel Friedrich-Wilhelm, 121

Kaellner, Lieutenant General Hans, 150, 151, 264
Kahler, Colonel Hans-Joachim, 110, 111
Kaltenbrunner, Ernst, 147
Kauffmann, Colonel Kurt, 204, 205
Keitel, Field Marshal Wilhelm, 12, 27
Kempf, General of Panzer Troops Werner, 7, 266
Keppler, SS Lieutenant General Georg, 261, 262
Kessel, General of Panzer Troops Mortimer von, 154, 155–156
Kesselring, Luftwaffe Field Marshal Albert, 105, 198
Kirchheim, Lieutenant General Heinrich, 160–161
Kirchner, General of Panzer Troops Friedrich, 42, 43, 267
Kleeman, General of Panzer Troops Ulrich, 262
Kleinheisterkamp, SS Lieutenant General Matthais, 263
Kleinschmidt, Lieutenant Colonel Albert, 88, 90
Kleist, Field Marshal Ewald von, 16, 19, 27–28, 113, 258
Knabe, Colonel Gustav-Georg, 160, 161
Knebel-Doeberitz, Colonel Rudolf von, 176, 177
Knobelsdorff, General of Panzer Troops Otto von, 150–151, 264, 265, 266
Koch-Erpach, General of Cavalry Rudolf, 267
Koetz, MG Karl, 67, 70
Kohlermann, Lieutenant General Otto, 224, 225

Koll, Lieutenant General Richard, 42, 43–44

Kraeber, Major General Ewald, 171, 172

Krampf, Lieutenant General Heinrich, 133–134, 196, 197

Krebs, General of Infantry Hans, 281

Kretschmer, Major General Theodor, 133, 139, 141

Kronhelm, Colonel Joachim von, 191–192

Krueger, General of Panzer Troops Walter, 43, 43, 267

Kuehn, General of Panzer Troops Friedrich, 8, 14, 54, 55, 120, 121

Kuehn, Colonel Dr. Walter, 114, 116

Kuett, Major General Rudolf, 166

Kuhnert, Major General Alfred, 187, 189

Kuntze, General of Engineers Walter, 264

Kuntzen, General of Panzer Troops Adolf, 88, 89, 267

Landgraf, Lieutenant General Franz, 207, 208

Lang, Rudolf, 55

Langermann-Erlenkamp, General of Panzer Troops Baron Willibald von, 60, 62, 264

Langkeit, Major General Willi, 240

Lattmann, Major General Martin, 120, 122

Lauchert, Major General Meinrad von, 48, 51

Lemelsen, General of Panzer Troops Joachim, 66, 67–68, 266

Lemke, Max, 83, 85

Lenski, Lieutenant General Arno von, 48

Lewinski, Major von, 11

Licht, Major General Rudolf-Eduard, 139, 140

Liebenstein, Major General Baron Kurt von, 55, 160, 162

Linnarz, Lieutenant General Viktor, 187, 189

Lippert, Major General Rolf, 66, 69

Loeper, Lieutenant General Friedrich-Wilhelm, 211, 249

Lorenz, Major General Karl, 254

Lucht, General of Artillery Walter, 260

Ludwig, Colonel Guenther, 120, 122

Luebbe, Vollrath, 48, 49

Luettwitz, General of Panzer Troops Baron Heinrich von, 47, 48, 50, 155, 266

Luettwitz, General of Panzer Troops Baron Smilo von, 51, 186, 187, 188, 266

Lutz, General of Panzer Troops Oswald, 4, 7, 9, 10, 12, 26, 27

Mack, Major General Erwin, 170, 171

Mackensen, Colonel General Eberhard von, 258, 261

Maeder, Hellmuth, 83, 234

Manstein, Field Marshal Erich von, 21, 165, 267, 274, 275, 276, 277

Manteuffel, General of Panzer Troops Baron Hasso von, 50, 82, 84, 197, 198, 254, 259, 260

Marcks, Lieutenant General Werner, 42, 44, 160, 163

Martinek, General of Artillery Robert, 264

Mauss, Lieutenant General Dr. Karl, 82, 85, 88, 90

Meden, Lieutenant General Karl-Friedrich von der, 139, 211, 247

Mellenthin, Major General Friedrich-Wilhelm, 88, 91, 99–100

Menny, Lieutenant General Erwin, 125, 145, 147

Messe, Italian General, 260

Metz, Lieutenant General Eduard, 66, 68

Michalik, Colonel Helmut, 191

Mickl, Major General Johann, 106, 107

Mikosch, Major General Hans, 114, 116, 169

Model, Field Marshal Walter, 4, 21, 54, 55, 56–57, 259, 265

Moltke, General Helmuth Karl Bernard ("Moltke the Elder"), 5, 26

Mueller, Dietrich von, 133, 135

Mueller, Major General Gerhard, 97, 99, 110, 197, 199

Mueller-Hildebrandt, Major General Burkhart, 133, 134–135

Mummert, Major General of Reserves Werner, 121, 242, 243

Munzel, Major General Oskar, 48, 51–52,
    120, 121
Mussolini, Benito, 17

Natzmer, Major General Oldwig von, 4
Nedtwig, Johannes, 66, 68–69
Nehring, General of Panzer Troops Wal-
    ther, 10, 145, 146, 258, 264, 268
Neumann-Silkow, Major General Walter,
    88, 125, 127
Niemack, Major General Horst, 203–204,
    205
Nostitz, Count Eberhard von, 48, 51
Mostitz-Wallwitz, Major General Gustav-
    Adolf von, 176, 177

Olbrich, Colonel Herbert, 113
Oppeln-Bronikowski, Major General Her-
    mann von, 155, 156
Ottenbacher, Lieutenant General Otto,
    265
Otto, General of Infantry Paul, 114

Palm, Colonel Walter, 121
Pape, Major General Guenther, 224, 225
Paulus, Field Marshal Friedrich, 10, 24,
    275
Pean, Colonel Dr. Ernst, 197, 199
Philipps, Lieutenant General Wilhelm, 55,
    57
Praun, General of Signal Troops Albert,
    145, 147
Priess, SS Lieutenant General Hermann,
    261
Prittwitz und Gaffron, Major General
    Heinrich von, 120, 125, 126
Puchler, Lieutenant General Carl, 267

Radlmaier, Lieutenant General Ritter Lud-
    wig, 3–4, 6, 8, 60, 61
Radowitz, Lieutenant General Josef von,
    171, 172–173
Randow, Major General Heinz von, 125,
    160, 162
Raus, General of Panzer Troops Erhard,
    258, 259, 266
Ravenstein, Lieutenant General Johann
    von, 160, 161

Reichenau, Field Marshal Walter von, 7,
    27, 42
Reinhardt, Colonel General Georg-Hans,
    16, 27, 60, 61, 259, 265
Remer, Major General Otto-Ernst,
    230–231
Rendulic, Colonel General Dr. Lothar,
    259
Rodt, Lieutenant General Eberhard,
    166–167
Rommel, Field Marshal Erwin, 17, 23,
    80, 83, 125, 139, 159, 160, 161, 162,
    228, 260, 268, 273, 274
Rossmann, Major General Josef, 170,
    172
Roth, Colonel Max, 245
Rothkirch und Panthen, Lieutenant Gen-
    eral Friedrich-Wilhelm von, 114, 115
Rothenburg, Colonel Karl, 86
Ruoff, Colonel General Richard, 259

Saucken, General of Panzer Troops
    Dietrich von, 60, 63, 264, 268
Sauvant, Major Bernhard, 136
Schaal, General of Panzer Troops Ferdi-
    nand, 102–103, 264, 266, 268
Schaefer, Sergeant Georg, 40, 44
Scharnhorst, General Count Wilhelm von,
    4, 25, 26
Schell, Lieutenant General Adolf von,
    182, 183
Scheller, Lieutenant General Walter, 97,
    98, 105
Scheuenemann, Colonel Walter, 247
Schilling, Lieutenant General Walter, 139,
    140–141
Schleiben, Lieutenant General Wilhelm
    von, 145, 147
Schleicher, Lieutenant General Kurt von,
    3, 7, 8, 27
Schlieffen, General Count Alfred von, 5,
    26
Schloemer, Lieutenant General Helmuth,
    263
Schmalz, Luftwaffe Lieutenant General
    Wilhelm, 269
Schmidhuber, Major General Gerhard, 82,
    114, 117

Schmidt, Lieutenant General Gustav, 150, 151

Schmidt, Rudolf Colonel General, 42, 43, 258–259, 264

Schneider, Lieutenant General Dr. Edgar, 61, 62–63

Schoene, Colonel Volkmar, 55

Schoenfeld, Major General Henning, 48, 51

Schoening, Colonel of Reserves Wilhelm, 114, 117

Schoerner, Field Marshal Ferdinand, 265

Schuenemann, Lieutenant General Otto, 264

Schulz, General of Infantry Friedrich, 261, 266

Schwantes, Major General Guenther, 150

Schwerin-Krosigk, Lieutenant General Count Gerhard von, 196, 198, 199, 268

Scotti, Lieutenant General Friedrich von, 88, 90

Schroetter, Major General Joseph, 88, 89–90

Schulz, Major General Adalbert, 82, 84–85

Schulz, Colonel Dr. Johannes, 97, 98, 99

Seeckt, Gen Hans von, 3, 26, 30

Seitz, Lieutenant Colonel Hermann, 138

Senger und Etterlin, General of Panzer Troops Fridolin von, 139, 140, 263

Sickenius, Major General Rudolf, 131, 135, 136

Sieberg, Major General Friedrich, 120, 122

Sintzenich, Lieutenant General Rudolf, 125, 126

Skorzeny, SS Colonel Otto, 78

Soeth, Major General Walter, 42, 55, 57–58

Speck, Lieutenant General Ritter Hermann von, 125, 126

Stauffenberg, Colonel Count Claus von, 90, 275

Steiner, General of Waffen-SS Felix, 260, 261

Steinkeller, Lieutenant General Friedrich-Carl von, 224, 225

Stever, Lieutenant General Joachim, 60, 61–62

Stimmel, Lieutenant General Herbert, 213

Stockhausen, Lieutenant General Wilhelm-Hunold von, 254

Strachwitz, Lieutenant Colonel of Reserves Count Hyazinth, 136

Streich, Lieutenant General Johannes, 160, 197

Stumme, General of Panzer Troops Georg, 82, 83, 171, 260, 265

Stumpff, General of Panzer Troops Horst, 154, 155

Stollbrock, Colonel Heinrich-Wilhelm, 48, 52

Stuelpnagel, General of Infantry Otto von, 6–7, 26

Teege, Colonel Wilhelm "Willi," 125

Tempelhoff, Colonel Hans-Georg von, 167

Thoma, General of Panzer Troops Ritter Wilhelm von, 4, 8, 11, 139, 140, 154, 155, 260, 268

Thomale, Wolfgang, 8

Thuengen-Rossbach, Lieutenant General Baron Karl von, 145, 146

Thunert, Lieutenant General Eberhard, 42, 44

Treuhaupt, Colonel Kurt, 133, 136, 182, 183

Treusch von Buttlar-Brandenfels, 106, 108

Troeger, Lieutenant General Hans, 114, 116–117, 182, 191

Tschischwitz, General of Infantry Erich von, 4, 207–8

Unrein, Lieutenant General Martin, 120, 121, 222, 236, 262

Usedom, Colonel Horst von, 110, 111

Vaerst, General of Panzer Troops Gustav von, 125, 127, 259

Veiel, General of Panzer Troops Rudolf, 48, 49, 266

Vietinghoff gennant Scheel, Colonel General Heinrich von, 66, 67, 265

Voigtsberger, Major General Heinrich, 197, 198–199

Volckheim, Ernst, 5, 6, 15, 26

Vollard-Bockelberg, General of Artillery Alfred von, 4, 25

Vormann, General of Panzer Troops Nikolaus von, 102, 171, 172, 266

Wagner, Colonel Herbert von, 88, 90

Waldeck, Colonel Prince Max zu, 245

Waldenburg, Major General Siegfried von, 197, 199–200

Wandel, General of Artillery Martin, 264

Weber, Major General Ritter Karl von, 139, 140

Weichs, Field Marshal Baron Maximilian von, 42, 43

Weidling, General of Artillery Helmuth, 265, 267

Wellmann, Colonel Ernst, 236, 246, 247

Werner-Ehrenfeucht, Major General Heinz-Joachim, 171, 172

Wessel, Lieutenant General Walter, 110, 111

Westhoven, Lieutenant General Franz, 55, 57, 160

Wietersheim, General of Infantry Gustav von, 109, 263

Wietersheim, Lieutenant General Wend von, 106, 107–108

Woermann, Lieutenant Colonel Dr., 133, 134

Wosch, Lieutenant General Heinrich, 217–218

Wuennenberg, General of Waffen-SS Albert, 262

Zeitzler, Colonel General Kurt, 20, 28, 275

Ziegler, General of Artillery Heinz, 268

Ziegler, SS Major General Joachim, 262

Zollenkopf, Colonel Helmuth, 97, 100, 160, 163

Zorn, General of Infantry Hans, 265

# Unit Index

# German Panzer and Related Units

## HIGHER HEADQUARTERS

### Armies

1st Panzer: 16, 18, 22, 28, 130, 132, 258, 272, 277
2nd Panzer: 18, 20, 258–259, 272
3rd Panzer: 18, 19, 23, 28, 259, 272
4th Panzer: 18, 21, 28, 259
5th Panzer: 24, 259–260, 275, 276, 279
6th Panzer (later SS Panzer): 24, 260
11th SS (also known as 11th SS Panzer): 260
Panzer Army Afrika: 17, 260, 274, 275, 276
Panzer Group von Kleist: see 1st Panzer Army

### Panzer Corps

I SS: 260–261
II SS: 74, 261
III: 261
III (germanischen) SS: 261–262
IV: 138, 262
IV SS: 262
VII SS: 263
XI SS: 262, 263
XIV: 30, 263

XV: 16, 30. Also see 3rd Panzer Army
XVI: 13, 14, 30. Also see 4th Panzer Army
XIX: 14, 16, 30. Also see 2nd Panzer Army
XXIV: 132, 264
XXXIX: 264
XXXX: 264–265
XXXXI: 16, 265
XXXXVI: 265–266
XXXXVII: 205, 266
XXXXVIII: 266
LVI: 266–267, 271
LVII: 267
LVIII: 267
LXXVI: 267–268
Afrika Korps: 17, 124, 157, 159, 268, 271
Feldherrnhalle: 182. Also see IV Panzer Corps
Grossdeutschland: 145, 230, 255, 268
Hermann Goering: 268–269

## DIVISIONS

### Panzer

1st: 9, 16, 22, 37–45, 129, 176, 248
2nd: 9, 10, 13, 14, 16, 17, 18, 30, 40, 46–52, 164

303

3rd: 9, 13, 14, 16, 18, 22, 53–58, 60, 65, 143, 157
4th: 13, 14, 16, 17, 22, 59–64, 105, 112, 119
5th: 13, 14, 16, 17, 18, 22, 23, 28, 40, 65–70, 104, 233
6th: 16, 18, 22, 71–78, 165, 275
7th: 14, 18, 25, 79–86, 191, 251
8th: 14, 16, 17, 18, 78, 87–92, 101
9th: 13, 16, 17, 30, 93–100, 207
10th: 13, 16, 18, 20, 101–113, 123
11th: 16, 17, 18, 22, 65, 104–108, 182, 219
12th: 16, 17, 18, 22, 25, 109–111
13th: 16, 17, 24, 25, 47, 111, 112–118, 226
14th: 16, 17, 18, 20, 22, 25, 28, 60, 119–123, 180
15th: 16, 17, 20, 124–28, 157, 158
16th: 16, 17, 18, 19, 20, 22, 39, 129–136, 194, 213, 237
17th: 16, 17, 18, 22, 25, 132, 137–142
18th: 16, 17, 18, 39, 119, 143–148
19th: 16, 17, 18, 22, 149–152, 182
20th: 16, 17, 18, 149, 153–156
21st: 16, 17, 20, 54, 125, 128, 157–163
22nd: 19, 73, 164–167, 190
23rd: 19, 20, 165, 168–173
24th: 19, 20, 47, 174–178, 191
25th: 20, 144, 179–184, 244
26th: 20, 185–189, 239, 240
27th: 25, 165, 175, 190–192
116th: 193–200, 202, 123
(130th) Panzer Lehr: 23, 201–205, 278
155th Reserve: 21, 95, 100, 206–209
178th Panzer Replacement: 15, 210–211, 246, 249
179th Reserve: 15, 195, 212–213
232nd: 214–215, 249
233rd Reserve Panzer (later Panzer): 21, 33, 180, 216–218, 235
273rd Reserve: 105, 108, 219–220
Clausewitz: 25, 221–222
Doeberitz: see Panzer Division Silesia
Feldherrnhalle 1: 24, 25, 223–225
Feldherrnhalle 2: 114, 226–227
Fuehrer Begleit: 28, 228–231
Fuehrer Grenadier: 182, 229, 232–234

Grossdeutschland: 228, 229, 250–256, 276
Holstein: 25, 217, 221, 235–236, 246
Jueterbog: 25, 237–238
Kempf: 103
Kurmark: 239–241
Lehr: see (130th) Panzer Lehr Division
Muencheberg: 25, 242–243, 245
Norway: 154, 180, 181, 244–245
Silesia: 25, 246–247
Tatra: 24, 44, 211, 248–249

## Other Army, Luftwaffe and SS Divisions

1st Light: see 6th Panzer Division
(1st) Parachute Panzer "Hermann Goering": 283
1st SS Panzer "Leibstandarte Adolf Hitler": 104, 283
2nd Light: see 7th Panzer Division
2nd SS Panzer "Das Reich": 18, 283–284
3rd Light: see 8th Panzer Division
3rd Panzer Grenadier: 144
3rd SS Panzer "Totenkopf": 81, 182, 284
4th Light: see 9th Panzer Division
5th Light: see 21st Panzer Division
5th SS Panzer "Viking": 284
9th SS Panzer "Hohenstauffen": 284
10th SS Panzer "Frundsberg": 284–285
12th SS Panzer "Hitler Jugend": 202, 285
13th Motorized: 59
14th Panzer Grenadier: 145
15th Panzer Grenadier: 20, 96, 125
16th Panzer Grenadier: 40, 129, 194
17th SS Panzer Grenadier: 285
18th Artillery: 145
18th Panzer Grenadier: 236, 246
25th Panzer Grenadier: 203
26th SS Panzer: 285
27th SS Panzer: 285
29th Panzer Grenadier: 101
60th Panzer Grenadier: 109, 143, 223
90th Light: 158
164th Light Afrika: 158

## BRIGADES

### Panzer

1st: 9, 15, 37, 39

2nd: 15, 46
3rd: 15, 17, 53, 157
4th: 10, 13, 15, 101, 102
5th: 13, 15, 59, 60
6th: 13, 15
8th, 13, 15, 65
10th: 237
16th: 130, 131
21st: 154
100th: 164
101st: 23, 168
102nd: 23
103rd: 23, 180–181, 244, 255
104th: 23, 181, 184
105th: 23, 96
106th "Feldherrnhalle": 23, 221
107th: 23
108th: 23, 138, 196
109th: 23, 24, 224
110th: 23, 24, 114, 117, 224, 226
111th: 23, 181
112th: 23, 159
113th: 23, 105
150th: 78

## Rifle

1st: 37
2nd: 46
3rd: 53
4th: 59, 60
5th: 65
6th: 72, 73
7th: 80, 81
8th: 87, 92
9th: 93, 100
10th: 101, 102
11th Motorized: 104
11th Rifle: 105
12th: 109, 110
14th: 119, 123
15th: 124
17th: 137, 138
18th: 143
19th: 149, 152
20th: 153
22nd: 164

23rd: 168, 169
26th, 186

## Other Brigades

20th Schnelle (Mobile), later Bicycle: 156
200th Assault Gun: 229
911th Army Assault Gun: 233
931st Mobile: 158
Feldherrnhalle Replacement and Training:
   117, 226
Fuehrer Begleit: see Fuehrer Begleit Division
Grossdeutschland Motorized Replacement
   and Training: 239
Panzer Brigade Norway: 245

# REGIMENTS

## Panzer

1st: 9, 15, 37, 40, 41, 44, 195
2nd: 9, 15, 17, 37, 38, 129, 131, 136, 182
3rd: 9, 10, 12, 15, 46, 47, 94
4th: 9, 11, 15, 17, 28, 46, 47, 111, 112,
   117
4th Replacement: 137
5th: 9, 10, 15, 17, 53, 54, 94, 157, 158
6th: 9, 10, 11, 12, 15, 53, 58, 186
7th: 10, 12, 15, 38, 101, 102, 123
8th: 10, 11, 13, 15, 17, 38, 101, 102, 124,
   125
9th: 144, 179, 180, 181
10th: 11, 12, 87, 92
11th: 11, 12, 14, 15, 71, 72, 73, 74, 78
15th: 11, 15, 17, 38, 65, 104, 105, 108,
   219
16th: 193, 195
18th: 17, 143, 144
21st (later Panzer Battalion): 17, 153, 154
22nd: 159
23rd: 74, 173
24th: 174, 175, 176
25th: 11, 15, 79, 80, 81, 86
26th: 185, 186, 253

27th: 17, 149, 150, 152
28th: 111, 143
29th: 17, 109, 110, 111, 117, 242
31st: 13, 15, 67
33rd "Prinz Eugen": 93, 94, 96, 100
33rd Replacement: 137
35th: 13, 15, 38, 59, 60, 105
36th: 13, 15, 28, 38, 59, 60, 119, 120, 123
39th: 17, 137, 138, 139
69th: 195
83rd Reserve: 235
100th: 158, 252
101st: 233, 234
102nd: 229
109th: 139
127th: 190
130th Panzer Lehr: 201, 202, 203
(151st) Panzer Regiment Kurmark: 24, 239
201st: 168, 169, 173
202nd: 186
203rd Beute: 168, 252
204th: 164, 165, 190
204th Beute: 168
Clausewitz: 221
Feldherrnhalle 1: 221, 223, 224
Feldherrnhalle 2: 226
Fuehrer 1: 24, 228 (also called Panzer Regiment, Fuehrer Begleit Division)
Fuehrer 2: 232
Grossdeutschland: 24, 78, 229, 252, 255

### Panzer Grenadier

1st: 37, 40
2nd: 46, 47
3rd: 53
3rd Reserve: 216, 217, 218, 235
4th: 71, 72
5th: 109, 110
5th Reserve: 100, 207
6th: 79, 81
7th: 79, 81, 82
8th: 87, 92
9th: 185, 186
10th: 93, 96, 100

11th: 93, 96, 100
12th: 59, 60
13th: 65, 112
14th: 65
21st: 174, 175, 176
25th: 109, 110
25th Reserve Motorized Grenadier: 100, 206, 207
26th: 174, 175
28th: 87, 92
29th Reserve Motorized Grenadier: 212
33rd: 59, 60, 112
40th: 137, 139
42nd: 217
47th: 158
50th: 217
52nd: 119, 143
59th: 153
60th: 193, 194, 195
60th Motorized: 129, 136
63rd: 132, 137, 138, 139
64th: 129, 131, 132, 136
66th: 112, 117
67th: 185, 186
69th: 39, 101, 102
72nd Motorized Infantry Replacement: 212
73rd: 149, 152
73rd Reserve Motorized: 108, 219
74th: 149, 152
79th (later Fusilier Regiment [Corps]): 129, 131, 132, 136
81st Reserve: 212
83rd Reserve: 216, 217, 218
85th Panzer Grenadier Replacement and Training, 210, 214
86th: 101, 102
92nd Motorized Infantry: 109
92nd Reserve: 108, 219
92nd Panzer Grenadier Replacement and Training: 214
93rd: 112, 117
98th: 92
99th: 233, 234
100th: 229
101st: 143, 145, 214
102nd: 214
103rd: 119, 120

104th: 124, 125, 128, 157, 158
108th: 119, 120
110th: 104, 108, 219
111th: 104, 108, 219
112th: 153, 154, 156
113th: 37, 39
114th: 71, 72, 75
115th: 124, 125, 128
120th: 223
125th: 158, 159
126th: 168
128th: 168, 246
129th: 164, 165
139th: 217, 235
140th: 164, 165, 190, 191
142nd: 217, 235
146th: 179, 180, 181, 192, 244
147th: 179, 180, 181
(152nd) Panzer Grenadier Regiment
    Kurmark: 239
156th: 193, 194, 195
192nd: 158, 159
200th: 157, 158
304th: 46, 47
394th: 53, 54
890th Motorized Grenadier: 156
891st: 175
901st Panzer Lehr Grenadier: 201, 202, 203
902nd Panzer Lehr Grenadier: 201, 202,
    203
1030th "Feldherrnhalle": 117
1031st Motorized Grenadier: 173
2109th: 224
2110th: 226
2112th: 159
Clausewitz 1: 221
Clausewitz 2: 221
Feldherrnhalle (1): 223
Fuehrer 1: 228
Feldherrnhalle 2: 226
Feldherrnhalle 3: 226
Fuehrer 3: 232, 234
Fuehrer 4: 232, 234
Grossdeutschland Fusilier Regiment: 204,
    205, 253
Grossdeutschland Motorized Infantry: see
    Grossdeutschland Panzer Grenadier
    Regiment

Grossdeutschland: 204, 205, 252, 253
Jueterbog (1): 237, 238
Panzer Fusilier Regiment Kurmark: 239
Muencheberg 1: 242
Muencheberg 2: 242
Norway: 181, 244
Silesia: 246

## Panzer Artillery Regiments

2nd: 109, 110
4th: 119, 120, 123
13th: 112, 117
16th: 129, 131, 136
19th: 149, 152
27th (later Battalion): 137, 139
33rd: 124, 125, 128
56th Motorized: 39
73rd: 37, 40, 41
74th: 46, 47
75th: 53, 157
76th: 71, 73
78th: 79, 81
80th: 87, 92
88th: 143
89th: 174, 175
90th: 101, 102
91st: 179, 180, 181, 182
92nd: 153
93rd: 185, 186
102nd: 93, 94, 95, 96
103rd: 59, 60
116th: 65
119th: 104, 108, 219
120th: 229
124th: 234
127th: 190
128th: 168
130th Panzer Lehr: 201, 203
140th: 164, 165
146th: 193, 194, 195
(151st) Kurmark: 239, 241
155th: 157, 158
160th Motorized: 223
167th Reserve: 108, 219
500th: 233
1233rd: 217

Fuehrer 1: 228
Feldherrnhalle 1: 223
Feldherrnhalle 2: 226
Muencheberg: 242
Fuehrer 2: 232, 234
Grossdeutschland: 250, 252, 255
Silesia: 246

## BATTALIONS

### Army Flak Artillery

228th: 70
272nd: 150
273rd: 46, 52
274th: 130, 131
275th: 117
276th: 119, 120, 123
277th: 105
278th: 168
279th: 180
281st: 193, 195
282nd: 223
283rd: 174, 175
285th: 252
286th: 92
287th: 95, 96
289th: 164
290th: 60
292nd: 144
296th: 86
297th: 138, 141
298th: 73
299th: 37, 40
301st: 242
303rd: 110, 111
304th: 185, 186
305th: 158, 159
311th: 201
314th: 53, 58
606th Light: 157
609th Light: 158
Fuehrer: 232
Feldherrnhalle 1: 223
Feldherrnhalle 2: 226
Grossdeutschland: 250, 252

### Artillery (Panzer or Motorized)

29th Reserve: 212
59th Reserve: 216, 217, 218, 235
91st Panzer: 179
116th Motorized Replacement: 210
260th Panzer: 206, 207
1233rd: 217
Motorized Artillery Lehr Battalion
    Ohrdruf: 38. Also see 73rd Panzer Artil-
    lery Regiment
Panzer Artillery Battalion Norway: 244
(Panzer) Artillery Battalion Tatra: 248

### Motor Transport Battalions (*Kraftfahrabteilungen*)

2nd: 53
3rd: 8, 53
(4th) Leipzig: 38
5th: 38
6th: 53
7th: 4

### Motor Vehicle Training Commands (*Kraftfahrlehr-kommando*)

Ohrdruf: 8, 9, 37, 38. Also see 2nd Pan-
    zer Regiment
Zossen

### Motorcycle

1st: 37, 40
2nd: 46, 47. Also see 2nd Panzer Recon-
    naissance Battalion
3rd: 53, 58
3rd Replacement: 216
4th: 179
5th: 207
6th: 71, 72, 73
7th: 79, 80, 81, 86
8th: 87, 92, 179
10th: 101

15th: 124, 125, 157, 158
16th: 129, 130, 131
17th: 137, 138, 251
18th: 143, 144
19th: 149, 150
20th: 153, 154
22nd: 109, 111
23rd: 168
24th: 47, 167
25th: 207
26th: 185, 186
34th: 59
43rd: 112, 117
55th: 65
55th Replacement: 210
59th: 94
61st: 104, 105
64th: 119, 120, 123
87th: 179, 180
128th: 168
165th: 194
Grossdeutschland: 252

## Panzer

1st Reserve: 195, 212
5th Reserve: 216, 217, 218, 235
7th Replacement: 153
7th Reserve: 206, 207
10th Replacement: 149
11th Replacement: 149
15th Replacement and Training: 210, 246
18th: 144, 145
25th: 11, 12
25th Reserve: 108, 219
25th Replacement: 149
33rd: 13, 15, 93, 94, 95
35th Replacement: 153
35th Reserve: 108, 219
40th: 15, 178–79
44th: 217, 235
51st: 95
65th: 11, 12, 13, 14, 15, 16, 71, 72, 73
66th: 13, 14, 16, 79, 80
67th: 13, 14, 15, 16, 87, 92
88th: 10, 11, 53
103rd: 144

116th: 195
127th: 191, 192
138th: 150
160th: 144, 223
190th: 158
214th: 179
223rd: 159
303rd: 246
500th Heavy: 21, 28
501st Heavy: 21, 28
502nd Heavy: 21, 28
503rd Heavy: 21, 28, 74
504th: 165
504th Heavy: 21, 28, 125, 145
505th Heavy: 21, 28
506th Heavy: 21, 28, 96
507th Heavy: 21, 28, 47
508h Heavy: 21, 28
509th Heavy: 21, 28
510th Heavy: 21, 28
2103rd: 181, 244
2104th: 181
2109th: 224
2110th: 114
2111th: 181
2112th: 159
Grossdeutschland Heavy: 255
Jueterbog: 237, 238
Kummersdorf: 242
Norway: 180–81, 244
Silesia: 246

## Panzer Engineer

13th: 112
16th: 129, 131
19th: 149
19th Reserve: 206, 219
27th (later Company): 137, 139
29th Reserve: 212
32nd: 109, 110
33rd: 124
37th: 37, 38, 41
38th: 46
39th: 53
40th: 174, 176
50th: 164

51st: 168, 169
57th: 71
58th: 79
59th: 87
79th: 59
86th: 93, 94, 96
87th: 179, 181
89th: 65
89th Lehr Replacement and Training: 248
90th: 101
92nd: 153
93rd: 185, 186
98th: 143
124th: 232
127th: 190, 191
128th: 168
130th Lehr: 201, 203
144th: 235
(151st) Kurmark: 239
200th: 157
208th Reserve: 216, 217, 218, 235
220th: 158
231st: 104
675th: 193, 194
Motorized Engineer Battalion Feldherrnhalle (1): 223
Motorized Engineer Battalion Feldherrnhalle 2: 226
Grossdeutschland: 250, 252, 253
Norway: 244

## Panzer Grenadier (called Rifle prior to 1942) and Motorized

1st Replacement: 212
3rd Replacement (later Reserve): 216,
   218
6th Replacement: 212
8th Replacement (later Reserve): 216,
   218, 235
9th Replacement (later Reserve): 216,
   218, 235
10th Replacement and Training: 248
12th Reserve: 108, 212
13th Replacement: 210, 248
20th Reserve Motorized: 108
29th Motorized Replacement: 216, 218

30th Motorized Replacement: 210
35th Reserve: 100, 206, 207
40th Reserve: 108
41st Reserve Motorized: 108
50th Motorized: 235
50th Replacement: 216, 218
51st Motorized Replacement: 210
71st Motorized Replacement: 212
86th Motorized Replacement: 212
86th Reserve: 100, 207
93rd Reserve: 235
110th Rifle Replacement: 210
119th Reserve Motorized: 100, 207
128th Motorized Training: 210, 211
187th Motorized Replacement: 212
215th Reserve Motorized: 100, 207
451st Motorized Replacement: 212
482nd Grenadier Training: 248
1009th Replacement Grenadier: 44
2104th: 181
2110th: 114, 226
Grossdeutschland Replacement: 229
Norway: 245

## Panzer/Motorized Reconnaissance

1st Reserve: 195, 212
2nd: 47, 109, 111. Also see 2nd Motorcycle Battalion
3rd: 53, 58, 157, 158
3rd Reserve: 216, 217, 218, 246
4th Motorized: 212
4th: 37, 38, 41
5th: 46, 47, 206. Also see 24th Motorcycle Battalion
6th: 73
7th: 59, 80, 86
7th Reserve: 108, 219
8th: 65, 92
9th: 93, 94, 96
9th Reserve Motorized: 207
11th: 104, 108, 219
13th: 112, 117, 226
14th: 119, 123
16th: 129, 131
17th: 138

19th: 149, 150
20th: 153
24th: 174, 175, 176
25th: 179, 180, 181
26th: 186
27th (later Company): 137, 139, 190
33rd: 127
37th: 79, 81
40th: 119, 123
44th: 217, 235
55th Replacement and Training: 210
57th: 71, 73
59th: 87
88th: 143, 144, 145
90th: 101
116th: 193, 195
128th: 168, 173
130th Lehr: 201, 203, 205
(151st) Kurmark: 239
160th: 223
231st: 104, 105
233rd: 217
341st Motorized: 194, 195
580th: 158
Feldherrnhalle: 223
Grossdeutschland: 250
Panzer Lehr: 159

## Panzer Signal

2nd: 109, 110
13th: 112
16th: 129
19th: 144
27th (later Company): 137, 139
33rd: 124
37th: 37, 38
38th: 46, 47
39th: 53
59th: 87
79th: 59
81st Reserve: 212
82nd: 71
83rd: 79
85th: 65, 93, 94, 96
86th: 174, 176
87th: 179

88th: 143
90th: 101
92nd: 153
93rd: 185, 186
120th: 223
124th: 232
127th: 175, 179, 180
128th: 168
130th Panzer Lehr: 201
140th: 164
200th: 157, 158
228th: 193, 194
341st: 104
Feldherrnhalle 1: 223
Feldherrnhalle 2: 226
Grossdeutschland: 250, 252

## Tank Destroyer

3rd Reserve: 216, 217
4th: 119, 120
7th Reserve: 206, 207, 219
8th Replacement: 210
8th Replacement and Training: 248
9th Reserve: 212
10th Reserve: 219
13th: 112, 117
16th: 129, 131
19th: 149
27th (Flak): 137, 141
33rd: 124
37th: 37, 38, 39, 40, 44
38th: 46, 47
39th: 54, 157, 158
40th: 174, 176, 178
41st: 71, 73
42nd: 79
43rd: 87
49th: 59
50th: 93, 94, 96
51st: 186
53rd: 65
61st: 104, 219
87th: 179, 180, 244
88th: 143
90th: 101
92nd: 153

93rd: 185, 186
124th: 232
127th: 190
128th: 168, 169
130th: 201
140th: 164
144th: 235
(151st) Kurmark: 239
200th: 158
228th: 193, 194
231st: 104
471st: 178
508th: 109, 111
543rd: 53, 54
560th: 190
605th: 157
643rd: 252
673rd: 228, 229
682nd: 242
1033rd: 217
1551st: 240
Clausewitz: 221
Feldherrnhalle 1: 223
Feldherrnhalle 2: 226
Grossdeutschland: 252
Norway: 244

## COMPANIES

Panzer Company, LXXXI Corps
91st Motorized Artillery Battery: 179, 180
101st Reconnaissance: 232
102nd Reconnaissance: 229
120th Panzer Reconnaissance: 228
124th Reconnaissance: 234
144th Panzer Signal: 235
(151st) Panzer Signal Kurmark: 239
514th Tank Destroyer: 179
702nd Motorized Heavy Infantry Howitzer: 39
1055th Panzer Signal: 207
1233rd Panzer Signal: 235
1233rd Reserve Panzer Signal: 216, 217, 218, 235

2110th Panzer Engineer: 114
Panzer Engineer Company Jueterbog: 237
Panzer Reconnaissance Company Jueterbog: 237
Panzer Signal Company Jueterbog: 237
Army Flak Artillery Battery Kurmark: 239
Engineer Company Muencheberg: 242
Panzer Reconnaissance Company Muencheberg: 242
Tank Destroyer Company Muencheberg: 242
Signal Company Muencheberg: 242
Panzer Company Paris: 159
Panzer Engineer Company Silesia: 246
Panzer Reconnaissance Company Silesia: 246
Panzer Signal Company Silesia: 246
Tank Destroyer Company Silesia: 246

## MISCELLANEOUS UNITS

1st Machine Gun Battalion: 130
2nd Machine Gun Battalion: 157, 158
3rd Machine Gun Battalion: 194
5th Observation Replacement Battalion: 207
7th Machine Gun Battalion: 119
7th Reconnaissance Regiment: 80
8th Machine Gun Battalion: 157
8th Reconnaissance Regiment: 87, 101
9th Reconnaissance Regiment: 93, 94
12th Cavalry Regiment (Motorized): 9
83rd Light Motorized Flak Battalion (Luftwaffe): 44
89th Field Replacement Battalion: 176
192nd Assault Gun Battalion: 252
Grossdeutschland Assault Gun Battalion: 221, 250
Grossdeutschland Replacement and Training Regiment: 234
Field Replacement Battalion Tatra: 248

## About the Author

SAMUEL W. MITCHAM, JR. is a Professor of Geography at the University of Louisiana at Monroe. An internationally recognized authority on Nazi Germany and the Second World War, he is the author of more than a dozen books on the subject, including *Why Hitler?* (Praeger, 1996), *The Desert Fox in Normandy* (Praeger, 1997), and *Retreat to the Reich* (Praeger, 2000), as well as several dozen articles.

# Stackpole Military History Series

# *Real battles. Real soldiers. Real stories.*